Restoring the Chain of Friendship

Restoring the Chain of Friendship

*British Policy and the
Indians of the Great Lakes, 1783–1815*

TIMOTHY D. WILLIG

University of Nebraska Press
Lincoln *&* London

Library of Congress Cataloging-in-Publication Data
Willig, Timothy D.
  Restoring the chain of friendship: British policy
and the Indians of the Great Lakes, 1783–1815 /
Timothy D. Willig.
    p. cm.
Includes bibliographical references and index.
  ISBN 978-0-8032-4817-5 (cloth: alk. paper)
  ISBN 978-0-8032-9893-4 (paper: alk. paper)
  1. Indians of North America—Great Lakes
Region (North America)—Treaties. 2. Indians
of North America—Great Lakes Region (North
America)—Government relations. 3. Great
Britain—Foreign relations—Treaties. 4. Great
Britain—Foreign relations—United States.
5. United States—Foreign relations—Great
Britain. 6. United States—History—1783–1815.
I. Title.
  E78.G7W55 2008   323.1197077—dc22
2007039049

For my parents,
Dave and Claudette Willig,
and to the memory of my uncle,
Bob Willig (1918–2004),
whose love of
American Indian history
lives on in me

Contents

Illustrations

Maps

Acknowledgments

When I reflect on the past several years, I am humbled to consider the dozens of individuals who have either assisted me or provided valuable advice along the way. As this book is deeply rooted in my graduate school experience, I owe most all of its ultimate success to Gerald McFarland, my PhD adviser and principal mentor at the University of Massachusetts Amherst. His valuable thoughts, insights, and many hours of patient work proved to be the determining factors in helping to bring about a quality dissertation, laying the foundation for the present study. Moreover, his steadfast friendship and consistent helpfulness have been crucial in my scholarly endeavors both during and after my years at the University of Massachusetts, and his wisdom continues to influence my career. In addition, his wife, Dorothy, contributed her thoughts and spent time editing the later dissertation drafts. I am much indebted to them both.

I am also grateful to my other dissertation committee members—Neal Shipley, Leonard Richards, and Lewis Mainzer—for their constructive reading of the manuscript; in particular, I have profited greatly from my close friendship and years of study with Professor Shipley, who mentored my PhD field on eighteenth- and nineteenth-century Britain. I would also like to thank Neal Salisbury of Smith College for his careful reading and valuable insights on much of the dissertation's first draft. Finally, I want to express my appreciation to Joseph Ellis of Mount Holyoke College for permitting me to research and write the core of the dissertation's first chapter as my semester project in his graduate readings course on the Revolutionary generation in the autumn of 1997. He graciously welcomed this idea, despite the fact that frontier diplomacy was not a central theme to that course.

More recently, I am indebted to three scholars who provided detailed critiques of the manuscript after its acceptance for publication by the University of Nebraska Press: Helen Hornbeck Tanner of the Newberry Library, John Sugden, and a third scholar who remains anonymous. Their insights proved invaluable. I also appreciate Gregory Dowd (University of Michigan) who commented on the fourth chapter—on Joseph Brant and the Grand River lands—when I presented an excerpt of this at the annual meeting of the Organization of American Historians in Boston in March 2004.

A few other individuals provided me with advice that has over time influenced this project. More than a dozen years ago, my Master's mentor at Western Michigan University, Donald Fixico (now at Arizona State University), first began challenging me to consider Tecumseh and those allied to him in fresh and alternative ways; I have sought to do so ever since. Professor Fixico's advice and friendship have proven pivotal in my career. I also appreciate the encouragement, research suggestions, and writing tips that prolific scholar Alan Taylor (University of California–Davis) gave me when he visited the University of Massachusetts in February 2001 and again when we crossed paths at Canada's National Archives in Ottawa in October 2002. In addition, I am thankful to my close friend and fellow Loyalist Grif Cook of Sumnerville, Michigan, for his expertise on border warfare and on arms and armor of early Euro-America.

I must express my appreciation to His Grace, the twelfth Duke of Northumberland, for permitting me to view the microfilm copy of the original journal of Major John Norton during my visit to the British Library in London, January 2000. Though available in published form since 1970, Norton's original journal has been in the possession of the Northumberland line since Norton personally dedicated it to his friend Hugh Percy, second Duke of Northumberland, in 1816. The journal remains in the present duke's principal home and library at Alnwick Castle. I want to also thank His Grace for permitting me to reproduce John Norton's portrait (by artist Thomas Phillips, circa 1816) within this study. Visitors to the duke's London home, the Syon House in Brentford, Middlesex, will find this painting displayed there. I also appreciate the staffs at Northumberland Estates and the Courtauld Institute for facilitating my requests, and particularly the staff at the Syon House, who patiently answered my many questions during my visit there in the summer of 2006.

I am very thankful for a number of funding and fellowship opportunities, beginning with those during my years in graduate school. I want to acknowledge my late friend and benefactor, Elizabeth Rieth of Goshen, Indiana, for providing me with years of funding, without which I could never have begun graduate school. During my PhD studies, two student grants from the history department at the University of Massachusetts, in addition to the Phillips Fund for Native American Research through the American Philosophical Society, Philadelphia, helped bring the dissertation to a successful finish. Later, short postdoctoral fellowships at the David Library of the American Revolution in Washington Crossing, Pennsylvania, and at the Newberry Library in Chicago proved helpful with the project's expansion and polishing. Specifically, I would like to thank the David Library's directors, Dick Ryerson and Meg McSweeney; staff member Marcia Scull; and former library president Francine Stone. At the Newberry Library, John Aubrey, reference librarian of the Ayer Collection; Helen Hornbeck Tanner, senior researcher; Jim Grossman, director of education; and Brian Hosmer, director of the D'Arcy McNickle Center for American Indian History, helped to make my stay there a successful one.

Regarding my years of research both during and after graduate school, I am indebted to numerous archival and library staff for their hard work, patience, and in some cases suggestions in helping me to glean the most pertinent research information. Most recently, I am particularly grateful to Nigel Butterwick, associate director of the Hesburgh Library at the University of Notre Dame, and Sue Dietl and Judy Kendall, both in Hesburgh's Access Services. The special borrowing privileges they granted me in 2005 and 2006 enabled me to bring this study to completion. Several others I want to thank include: Patricia Kennedy and Tim Dube at the Library and Archives of Canada, Ottawa; Bob Garcia, Parks Canada, Cornwall, Ontario, and Fort Malden Archives, Amherstburg, Ontario; Dennis Carter-Edwards, Parks Canada, Cornwall; Carl Benn, City of Toronto's Museums and Heritage Services; Larry Nelson, Fort Meigs Historical Park, Perrysburg, Ohio; John Gibson and Janet Nelson, Burton Historical Collection, Detroit Public Library; Peg Hart, Arts and Literature, Detroit Public Library; John Carrigan and Brian Dunnigan, William L. Clements Library, Ann Arbor, Michigan; Suzanne Morin and Nicole Vallieres, McCord Museum, Montreal; Julie Thomas, Chicago Historical Society; Christopher Peebles and Steve Ball, Glenn A. Black Laboratory of Archaeology, Bloomington, Indiana; Daniela Ford, British Library, London; Lori Mestre, W. E. B. DuBois Library, University of Massachusetts Amherst; Sharon Carlson and her staff at the Archives and Regional History Collection, Western Michigan University, Kalamazoo; and Linda Neff and Ann Kauffman, Goshen Public Library, Goshen, Indiana. I am also appreciative of the helpfulness of the general staffs at the National Archives of the United Kingdom (formerly the Public Record Office), Kew Gardens, United Kingdom; the National Army Museum, Chelsea District, London; the Indiana Historical Society, Indianapolis; the Baldwin Reading Room, Toronto Public Library; the Ontario Historical Society, Toronto; the Bentley Historical Library, Ann Arbor, Michigan; and the Talman Reading Room, Weldon Library, University of Western Ontario, London.

I also appreciate the words of encouragement and support I have received from my friends and colleagues here at Onondaga Community College. Specifically, the school's Teaching Center provided me with an Onondaga President's Incentive Grant that covered all copyright costs and reproduction fees in gaining permissions for the book's illustrations. The Teaching Center's director, Debbie Irwin; her assistant, Fran Whitmore; and Barbara Risser, former vice president of academic affairs at Onondaga (now president of Finger Lakes Community College, Canandaigua, New York) are the individuals who brought this about. Finally, I am grateful for the many prayers of my parents, family, and friends, and particularly to the Lord, for sustaining me during these years and for leading me to each of these esteemed persons.

Sections of chapters 1, 3, and 4 have been previously presented as conference papers: a portion of chapter 1 at the Annual Meeting on Iroquois Studies, Rensselaerville, New York (October 1, 2005); part of chapter 3 at the New England Historical Association's Spring Meeting, Buzzards Bay, Massachusetts (April 20, 2002); and a section of chapter 4 at the Annual Meeting of the Organization of American Historians, Boston, Massachusetts (March 28, 2004).

Restoring the Chain of Friendship

Introduction

The Chain of Friendship in the Colonial Past

The latter years of the eighteenth century marked a period of change and uncertainty in both Europe and North America. Events previously thought impossible had occurred. In 1783 the British Empire was compelled to acknowledge the loss of the majority of its North American colonies, and within a decade the mainland of the European continent would undergo a series of revolutionary conflicts. In their struggle for independence, the American colonists and their allies, most notably Britain's imperial rival France, had dealt the British nation a very rare defeat in modern history.[1] Indeed, when Lord Cornwallis surrendered his army at Yorktown to the allied French and American forces in October 1781, British fifers and drummers unwittingly foreshadowed the future by prophetically playing "The World Turned Upside Down." Louis XVI's ancient regime in France had little time to enjoy this lone victory against Britain, since France's involvement in the American Revolution led directly to the demise of the old order in French government and society, brought Louis's execution in 1793, and sank his nation into more than two decades of warfare, finally ending in 1815. In this new age of revolution and rampant republicanism, the British government would take whatever measures necessary to preserve its age-old constitution and way of life, defined by the common law, habeas corpus, Protestantism, and the sanctity of private property.[2] To ensure these ends, Crown and

Parliament strove to secure the nation's remaining imperial interests in Canada, the Caribbean, South America, the Mediterranean, and India, while protecting its overseas trade.

In the forty-year period between the outset of the American Revolution in 1775 and the defeat of Napoleon in 1815, Britain had few military allies, and the Crown's allies in Europe were all characterized by temporary ententes, crafted for immediate convenience. In some cases, such as Spain in 1795, former allies even defected, becoming Britain's enemies during the long years of bitter struggle against revolutionary France. Thus, in the era spanning 1775 to 1815, nowhere did Great Britain find allies more faithful and persevering than among the indigenous peoples of North America. Indian nations from along the Gulf of Mexico to the frozen lakes and tundra of Canada fought for the Crown, and many would have continued to do so after 1815 had Britain further prosecuted an American war. The purpose of this study is to examine the changing relationship between Britain and its Native allies in the vast region of the Great Lakes, from the dark days ending the American Revolution until the War of 1812. In 1783 many questions loomed. What would become of the Crown's Indian allies? Would the newly formed United States respect the territorial integrity of these nations? How would this affect the "Chain of Friendship," the historical alliance between the Indians and their "British Father," and what diplomatic changes would this entail? Would the Crown be faithful to its wartime Indian allies, and would it defend the Indians' territorial rights against the expanding United States? In an era of peace, would Britain consciously alter its Indian policies, perhaps to the detriment of the Indians? Just as important, how would the Natives adapt and respond to any forthcoming policy changes? Would they want to continue an alliance with their British Father? If not, would they pursue a neutral course, or would they seek closer ties with the Americans?

The Chain of Friendship between Britain and its Native allies bears a rich history, traced to a time when colonial New York, under successive Dutch and English governments in the mid-seventeenth century, entered into multiple agreements with the Indians of the Hudson Valley and, most important, the Iroquois League. The latter, including the Mohawks, Oneidas, Onondagas, Cayugas, and Senecas, had subjugated many of their surrounding tribes, ultimately adding links to the so-called chain.[3] Originally known as the "Covenant Chain," this general entente subsequently included other English colonies, and in 1677 the expanded Covenant Chain became the formal basis upon which the English colonies crafted their future Indian policy and diplomacy. Thus in the North the Iroquois served as the diplomatic liaison through which the English colonial governments had dealings with other tribes that were considered inferior members of the chain. The metaphor of the Covenant Chain would continue to describe British-Indian relations for more than a century and a half, beyond the close of the era of frontier wars.

By 1760, in the midst of the global conflict commonly remembered as the Seven Years' War, the fortunes of war had placed Great Britain in possession of much of the interior of North America. In the Great Lakes region, British troops occupied key posts relinquished by defeated French garrisons. At Detroit in December 1760, British agent George Croghan lost no time in extending the "Ancient Chain of Friendship" to the western tribes, ushering in a period of diplomacy between Britain and the Natives of the Great Lakes.[4] In the summer of 1761, Croghan's superior, Sir William Johnson, superintendent of British Indian affairs, met with an even larger group of western leaders—including Wyandots, Ottawas, Ojibwas, Potawatomis, Kickapoos, Miamis, Delawares, and Shawnees—who declared their "intentions to keep the Covenant Chain bright and lasting and so to hand it down to posterity."[5]

Yet it seemed that the Chain of Friendship with the nations of the Great Lakes was fully severed in 1763 and 1764 when more than a dozen Indian tribes attempted to rid themselves of the British and very nearly succeeded. Far from viewing the occupying British troops as conquerors, the Indians of the interior, with their interpretation of the Chain of Friendship, had perceived them as guests. In the conflict traditionally known as Pontiac's Conspiracy, the Native confederacy in the Great Lakes revolted against Major General Sir Jeffrey Amherst's British policy of limiting trade with the Indians and eliminating the ceremonial distribution of gifts to the tribes.[6] With the exception of Forts Detroit, Niagara, and Pitt, every major British post in the West either succumbed to Native military pressure or was abandoned. In the end, neither side fully mastered the other in Pontiac's war, and perhaps the most crucial result of the conflict was that it demonstrated to each side its need to cooperate with the other. By the end of the war the Indians saw more clearly their growing reliance on European goods and weaponry, and they now realized that the French most likely were never going to return. As for the British, the war demonstrated that they did not possess the level of hegemony in Indian country that they had once imagined, and that their continued imperial presence in the Great Lakes would require a substantial degree of Native consent.

Though one might assume that Pontiac's war would have permanently damaged British-Indian relations, just the opposite occurred. Once the two sides developed a mutual respect for the other, the foundation was laid for the type of relationship with the tribes that Croghan and Johnson had originally envisioned. One scholar has described this fresh understanding resulting from Pontiac's war as the restoration of a diplomatic "middle ground," while another regards it as "[a]n unprecedented balance of power," both implying mutual obligations.[7] Now the Chain of Friendship could truly flourish, better than it had prior to Pontiac's war when suspicions abounded. Consequently, when Sir William Johnson negotiated the end to hostilities with the western tribes in the summer of 1764, he capped off the ceremonies by giving the tribal delegations a "great Belt" consisting of twenty-three rows of beads with the year etched on it, representing "the great Covenant Chain." An unnamed Ojibwa chief present suggested keeping "the Belt of the Covenant Chain at Michillimackinac ... where all our people may see it." This Ojibwa leader then reminded Johnson "to hold fast by it [the Covenant Chain], to remember what has been said, and to abide by your Engagements [promises]."[8] There-after, the Chain of Friendship continued to subsist, albeit tenuously at times, between Britain and the nations of the Great Lakes, remaining a symbol of friendship and strength for the next nineteen years before encountering its greatest test, the end of the American Revolution in 1783.

With 1783 as its starting point, the present study canvasses numerous changes in British-Indian relations between the Revolution and the War of 1812. This crucial twenty-nine-year period had three distinct phases. The first, 1783–95, saw Britain enjoy its greatest influence over the allied tribes of the Ohio Valley, as this alliance inflicted two significant defeats on American forces before suffering its own demise against Anthony Wayne's victorious "Legion" in 1794, followed by the Treaty of Greenville in 1795. Then, between 1796 and 1807 British-Indian policy was wholly transformed, and British officials, both in Canada and at Whitehall in London, implemented a policy of retrenchment in an effort to vastly reduce the government's financial obligations and diplomatic ties to its former allies, particularly those Natives dwelling in U.S. territory. During this decade of relative calm, Anglo-American relations appeared stable, and the former British-Indian wartime coalition tended to fade. Finally, from 1807 to 1812 close British-Indian relations were in part revived as the U.S. expansionist policy continued to alarm and provoke the Natives and as Britain's relations with the Americans continued to deteriorate as a by-product of British maritime policies primarily aimed at crippling Napoleonic France. In other words, when Great Britain and the Natives of the Old Northwest again became military allies, this restored relationship was formed more in the context of sharing a common enemy than out of a sense of devotion and respect for traditional allegiances. Thus after 1807, when British agents attempted to restore their government's former Chain of Friendship, the Native responses were often varied and lukewarm. The British-Indian alliance that was re-formed on the immediate eve of the War of 1812 was a matter of necessity for both Britishers and Natives alike.

The principal thesis of this study argues that Britain, in its efforts to unite the Indians prior to the War of 1812, could not fully restore the Chain of Friendship, but instead ultimately had to settle for multiple chains of friendship. The argument also emphasizes the fact that Whitehall for the most part did not achieve a long-term Indian policy, and that Britain's diplomatic initiatives did not have a uniform effect when implemented in different regions of the Empire's North American borderlands. In practice, British Indian agents were compelled to tailor Whitehall's directives to conform to the unique circumstances and conditions of each of the separate geographical areas in which Britain conducted its affairs with indigenous peoples. This study specifically compares British relations with Indians living in both the United States and Canada who were generally served by the Crown's three principal Indian agencies in Upper Canada at Forts Amherstburg (Malden) near Detroit, Fort St. Joseph near Mackinac, and Fort George in the vicinity of Niagara, between 1783 and 1812.[9] The argument here is that the Native peoples in each of these vast regions, with their diverse histories and varied political and military goals, often played key roles in shaping local variations in British policies. Factors affecting these bonds included: the fur trade, geographical position, Indian relations and warfare with the United States, the influence of British Indian agents, intertribal relations between various Native groups, religious concerns and prophetic movements, degree of Indian acculturation, and the constitutional issues of Native sovereignty and legal status.

The last of these issues, namely the questions of Native sovereignty and legal status, were added dimensions that Crown officials in Canada had to consider when dealing with Indians in Canada, as opposed to those dwelling in the United States. Wanting to provide a refuge for their defeated wartime allies, British officials established three Native reserves in Upper Canada by 1796, including the Bay of Quinte (1784), the Grand River (1784), and Chenail Ecarte (1796).[10] The first two were comprised mainly of Iroquois and other eastern peoples who had lost their lands and homes during the American Revolution, while Chenail Ecarte was intended to accommodate refugee allies who were defeated by Anthony Wayne's U.S. Legion a decade later. At the Bay of Quinte and at Chenail Ecarte, British-Indian relations remained static during this period, but the Grand River inhabitants, the most numerous of the three groups, attempted to redefine their traditional relationship with their British allies by asserting their sovereignty. Therefore chapters 4 and 5, covering Upper Canada, focus principally on the Grand River controversy.

Previously, two seminal works have provided insights into British-Indian relations in the Great Lakes region during the period covered by this study. In *Crown and Calumet: British-Indian Relations, 1783–1815* (1987), Colin Calloway offers an important analysis using an ethnohistorical approach to understand both British and Native perspectives of this relationship as these cultures interacted in the contexts of trade, war, and diplomacy. Calloway de-emphasizes policy history, concentrating more on issues of intercultural contact and racial conceptions and misunderstandings of Native social and economic structures. Robert S. Allen's *His Majesty's Indian Allies: British Indian Policy in the Defence of Canada, 1774–1815* (1993) provides a policy history that lucidly demonstrates how Britain's Indian policy effectively slowed American expansion and saved Upper Canada, but failed to preserve Native lands and cultures. Until the time of his death, Allen had worked in the Canadian government's Department of Indian and Northern Affairs, giving him a unique perspective on the evolution of British and Canadian Indian policy from the period of the fur trade and frontier wars until modern times.

More recently, Pulitzer Prize–winning author Alan Taylor has completed a fine study detailing the political outcomes of the American Revolution in New York and Upper Canada, entitled *The Divided Ground: Indians, Settlers, and the Northern Borderland of the American Revolution* (2006).[11] Taylor's work cuts through the many complexities of postwar New York and its Canadian border region by examining the rival careers of former friends Joseph Brant, illustrious Mohawk leader, and missionary Samuel Kirkland. With its heavy focus on affairs in New York and on the schemes of American officials, both at the national and regional levels, Taylor's *Divided Ground* differs from the present study. While not intended as a full analysis of British-Indian policy in the Great Lakes, or as a study on the British Indian Department, Taylor's *Divided Ground* nevertheless better illuminates the postwar career of Joseph Brant and his struggles at the Grand River reserve in Upper Canada than any scholarly work heretofore. By illustrating this struggle for power and sovereignty in response to British policy at the time, Taylor has nicely anticipated the history presented in the chapters that follow.

The present study is also a policy history, but the reader will find that it incorporates more Native perspectives than previous monographs on Euro-American frontier policy, whether British or American. Moreover, this book takes into account the fact that British policy, as it made its way down from Whitehall to the actual setting in which it was applied, became elastic and even protean in virtually every respect save one, the issue of Native sovereignty. In other respects, the rational coherence and long-term stability seemingly implicit in the term "policy" were frequently lacking in Britain's relations with its Native allies on both sides of the Canadian-U.S. border. At the center of policy making in Whitehall, relations with indigenous peoples on the Empire's North American periphery were at best tertiary concerns compared to the imperial bureaucracy's primary focus on Britain's powerful European rivals, especially revolutionary France, and to a secondary focus on whether the United States would take an antagonistic or a neutral posture toward British interests. Whitehall officials, distracted by these more pressing crises, often issued directives to their North American subordinates without devoting the necessary time and energy needed to construct a cohesive long-term plan for imperial relations with Britain's Native allies in Canada and the United States. Consequently, the lack of a dominant policy gave Native leaders and British agents in the field more latitude for improvisation and a far greater impact in defining the British-Indian relations that resulted. Moreover, the lack of a definitive British policy in this period not only has meant that a much richer history exists in which Natives interacted with British and Canadian leaders in diverse ways but also that these First Peoples were prominent in shaping that history. By acknowledging and illustrating these protean aspects of British-Native diplomacy and the various nuances of intercultural relations that resulted, the present study makes a unique contribution to understanding how British-Indian relations evolved in North America between 1783 and 1815.

I

The Quest for a Just Peace, 1783–95

The twelve years immediately after the United States and Great Britain signed the Treaty of Paris in 1783 were marked by great volatility in British relations with the Crown's wartime Native allies in North America. British officials in western territories, Quebec, and London struggled to find a balance between competing and often contradictory aims: restoring the Indians' faith in British friendship and maintaining strong trade ties with them, while avoiding a general conflict between the United States and western tribes that might draw Britain into another unwanted war with its former colonies. Meanwhile, Indians who lived in parts of western New York, the upper Ohio River valley, and the Great Lakes region that Britain had ceded to the United States labored to construct military, cultural, and political alliances that would enable them to retain their lands and their sovereignty in the face of expansionist pressure from the newly established United States.

This chapter traces how these themes played out in three brief periods between the Treaty of Paris and the Treaty of Greenville (1795), the latter negotiated between the United States and tribes in the Ohio Valley and Great Lakes. The first period, 1783–89, saw Britain retain possession of its forts in the trans-Appalachian West and witnessed Native efforts to build an intertribal coalition capable of resisting U.S. expansion. The second period, 1789–92, produced a number of successes for the Natives as they developed, with encouragement from the British, intertribal village communities along the Maumee River and dealt defeats to two major American military expeditions. The third and final section covers the years 1793 to 1795, during which British diplomatic and military leaders largely stood aside as their Native allies went down to defeat at the hands of the United States.

Growth of the Intertribal Confederacy, 1783–89

After having ceded most of the territory south of the Great Lakes to the United States in the Treaty of Paris of 1783, Britain continued to maintain a presence within the northern borders of the new republic by garrisoning eight posts on land ceded to the Americans. Moreover, the Indian inhabitants continued to defy the exaggerated American claims of conquest over their homelands. Nevertheless, many long-term policy choices remained unsettled. Evacuation of the upper country was still a possibility, but if that step was taken, how would it affect the British fur trade and the future of the British-Indian alliance? Furthermore, Whitehall also pondered the security of its possessions north of the Great Lakes, the region soon to be partitioned off as the province of Upper Canada.[1] Eventually, Britain would have to demonstrate the extent of its resolve to defend these interests.

These issues arose due to the terms of the Treaty of Paris. The British government had been so eager to extricate itself from its problems in North America that it signed an agreement that neither restored British honor nor protected the sovereign territory of its Indian allies. When the French commissioner Count de Vergennes realized the full extent of the proposed British territorial cession, he remarked, "You will notice that the English buy the peace more than they make it. Their concessions . . . exceed all that I should have thought possible."[2] Realistically, Britain merely needed to grant political independence to its thirteen rebelling colonies, without making further territorial concessions. By retaining possession of the upper country and Great Lakes, the British government could have better protected the rights of its Native allies and its Canadian possessions north of the Great Lakes. A majority in Parliament also thought the treaty far more generous than anything they had imagined. When news of the terms reached them, the government of Lord Shelburne and his liberal ministry collapsed under a storm of protest.[3]

As a result of this diplomatic blunder, British leaders in Canada and officers in the British Indian Department faced the difficult assignment of simultaneously withdrawing from the war while somehow convincing their Native allies that the peace was honorable rather than disastrous. The unenviable task of actually addressing Britain's Iroquois allies fell upon Sir John Johnson, the superintendent general of Indian Affairs, while Alexander McKee, the department's second-highest ranking officer, was to acquaint the western nations with the news. In May 1783 Sir Frederick Haldimand, governor-general of Quebec, ordered Johnson, the son of the late Sir William Johnson (d. 1774), former superintendent, to "repair immediately to [Fort] Niagara" to address the Six Nations (Iroquois) and other tribes of the Covenant Chain regarding the peace.[4] Johnson and McKee would need to strike a fine balance between truth and grace in their crucial addresses. They must convince their late allies that the king had not abandoned them, that the treaty was just, that the Americans would recognize their rights, and that the king in the future would continue in his role as their protector.

Johnson, known as Owassighsishon (He Who Makes the Roof to Tremble) among the Iroquois, delivered his long-awaited speech on July 23. He reassured the Six Nations' leaders that nothing had changed in their relationship to the king, who still regarded them "as his children" and "faithful allies," and "should the Americans molest, or claim any part of our country, we shall then ask assistance of the King our father." But Johnson "could not harbor the idea that the United States [would ever] act so unjustly or unpolitically as to endeavour to deprive [them] of any part of [their] country under the pretense of having conquered it." Finally, the superintendent affirmed "the boundary line agreed upon . . . to be just."[5] Johnson's reassurances were generally well received.[6] Similarly, McKee, an adopted Shawnee known as White Elk, reiterated these sentiments when he later addressed the nations farther west. In an effort to preserve British interests in the upper country, McKee gathered representatives from the western nations and tribes from the northern lakes and addressed them at a council held at Lower Sandusky in August and September 1783. The tribal delegations included Wyandot, Mingo, Delaware, Shawnee, Ottawa, Potawatomi, Ojibwa, and even a few Creek and Cherokee representatives. A deputation of Iroquois representatives was also present, participating in a leadership role and supporting McKee. Like Johnson, McKee argued that the Americans would recognize Indian sovereignty north of the Ohio River, and promised that the king "will continue to promote your happiness by his protection."[7]

Although leery of the proposed peace settlement and its ramifications, the Indians appeared less shaken after Johnson's and McKee's calming reassurances. Uncertain about future relations with whites, the Indians certainly had no reason to suspect that the United States would attempt to extend its sovereignty over their lands, particularly after their intertribal alliances had achieved a string of victories against American armies in the war's final four years alone: Wyoming Valley (July 1778), Cherry Valley (November 1778), Minisink (Delaware Valley, July 1779), Mohawk Valley (May 1780 and October 1781), Schoharie Valley (October 1780), La Balme's Defeat (Wabash Valley, November 1780), Lochry's Defeat (Ohio River, August 1781), Sandusky (June 1782), and Blue Licks (Kentucky, August 1782).[8] Thus, based on their wartime feats and an apparent continuation in their relationship with their "British Father," the Natives initially had no reason to interpret the war's end as anything more than a truce, and certainly did not believe themselves bound by a treaty they had not signed to relinquish territories that they had defended so successfully.[9]

Shortly after Johnson and McKee delivered their respective speeches, Governor-General Haldimand made two crucial decisions to help bolster Native confidence in British fidelity toward them. First, he defied the terms of the peace by refusing to evacuate the northern posts within American territory.[10] The governor-general made this determination on his own, before knowing that the Americans would renege on their part of the treaty.[11] Haldimand's decision aimed at achieving multiple goals: to placate the Indians, protect British fur trade interests, reduce the threat of a general Indian war against the Americans, and hamper American expansion into lands west of the Appalachians. To the degree that Haldimand simply sought to maintain a status quo in the western country, his actions were consistent with Britain's wartime Indian policies, but he also initiated policy changes in response to postwar conditions. At the request of Sir John Johnson and Mohawk leader Joseph Brant, the governor-general moved to set aside lands in Canada along the Grand River, specifically for the British-allied Six Nations and their dependencies who had lost their homelands during the war.[12] Haldimand's actions temporarily brought about the desired continuity he sought, bolstering the confidence of both the Iroquois and western tribes that had fought for the Crown.

The governor-general's pivotal decision to resettle the loyal Iroquois in Canada indicated that the British leaders there would attempt to act in good faith toward their indigenous allies, regardless of the home government's betrayal at Paris the year before.[13] Moreover, by receiving Crown lands, the refugee Iroquois would be encouraged to believe that their British Father cared for them as much as he did for his white children, the American Loyalists who also received new tracts of land in Canada, Nova Scotia, and the Bahamas. The motivations underlying both the Haldimand Grant and the retention of Britain's western posts seemed parallel. The two measures sought to protect the rights and preserve the sovereignty of both the western Indians and Britain's Iroquois allies, while simultaneously securing the interests of pro-British traders and their Native clients in the upper country.[14]

British postwar Indian policy, a basis for continuity and unity among the allied tribes, contained another traditional feature. As primary architect of that policy, Haldimand made his decisions compatible with past British policy, which attempted to utilize the Iroquois

League's alleged supremacy over the western tribes as the key to controlling the nations throughout the Great Lakes.[15] This rationale was in keeping with the frontier diplomacy originally practiced by English colonial leaders in 1677, when the colonial government of New York first established its Covenant Chain alliance with the Iroquois League.[16] In 1761, after the British conquest of Canada and eviction of French civil authority, Sir William Johnson continued to recognize Iroquois leadership over the western tribes in an extended "Chain of Friendship," which included the nations of the Great Lakes and upper country.

Despite the tumultuous changes brought by the American Revolution, Haldimand saw no need to abandon the Covenant Chain approach, and the governor-general continued to envision a general Indian policy carried out under the auspices of the Iroquois, particularly the Mohawks, who most ardently favored British interests. Late in 1783, he reassured Indian agent Daniel Claus, son-in-law of the late Sir William Johnson, "I have always considered the Mohawks as the first Nation deserving of the attention of Government and I have been particularly interested for their Welfare and reestablishment."[17] The governor also saw little need for a separate Indian policy tailored specifically to the interests of the Great Lakes nations. Haldimand predicted, "The conduct of the Western Indians (tho' infinitely a more numerous people) will always be governed by that of the Six Nations, so nice a management of them may not, therefore, be necessary—some presents and marks of friendship are nevertheless due to them for their past services, and should from time to time be dispersed among them."[18] By naming the late Sir William Johnson's son, John, as superintendent general of Indian Affairs in 1782, followed by the declaration of the Haldimand Grant two years later, the governor-general hoped to re-create the prewar British Indian policy that would assure a continuation of British imperial interests among the nations of the interior.

Haldimand's continuation of the former Indian policy had little chance of succeeding in the confused geopolitical setting of the post-

Revolution years. After losing most of their homeland during the war, and witnessing the extinguishing of the League's council fire at Onondaga in 1777, the Iroquois were in no position to wield the sort of influence that Haldimand and Sir William Johnson had once imagined. Two of the League's six nations, the Tuscaroras and Oneidas, had sided with the Americans in the war, and before the League could recover and reunite at the war's conclusion, American commissioners quickly negotiated a new treaty with the Iroquois in 1784 at Fort Stanwix. The commissioners demanded Iroquois compliance based on a claim of conquest. All Six Nations were present, and all grudgingly acquiesced in the American demands for cession of virtually all Iroquois territory on American soil (acknowledged by the Treaty of Paris) outside of the state of New York.[19] In contrast to the British strategy, the U.S. government attempted to reduce Iroquois prestige, hoping to terminate whatever vestige of Iroquois suzerainty remained over the western tribes.

In spite of the Six Nations' decline after the Revolution, Mohawk leader Joseph Brant attempted to assume a position of intertribal leadership over the confederated tribes in the Great Lakes that continued to resist American expansion.[20] Without any hereditary authority among his own people, Brant's claim to authority rested on his record as a war leader. Warriors in the West recalled Brant's participation in key frontier actions during their recent struggle against the Americans. The Mohawk sachem had led them to a brilliant victory over a sizable portion of George Roger Clark's army on the Ohio River in the summer of 1781 (Lochry's Defeat), and his presence in the Ohio country late in the war marked Brant as a leader who always fought for the Western Confederacy's best interests.[21] In addition to these feats, the Mohawk warrior also held additional influence by virtue of his status as the late Sir William Johnson's brother-in-law and his rank as a captain in the British Indian Department.

Although Brant, Haldimand, Sir John Johnson, and others shared the expectation of future Iroquois leadership among the Great Lakes tribes, several developments worked against this policy. Guy Carleton (recently titled Lord Dorchester), who replaced Haldimand as governor-general of Quebec late in 1786, did not attempt to sustain Haldimand's outdated theory of Iroquois leadership over the western nations. Moreover, when Dorchester arrived in 1786, only a year after Haldimand predicted permanent Iroquois hegemony, occurrences in the West foreshadowed a new era and a separate path for the western nations. Brant, hoping to reestablish the old wartime alliance, traveled to the principal Shawnee villages of Mackachack and Wapatomica in southwestern Ohio late in 1786. Shortly after his arrival there, a Kentucky militia under the command of Benjamin Logan invaded the region, destroying both villages.[22] Although Brant and numerous others were absent hunting when the Kentuckians attacked, the raid prompted all of the tribal delegations to seek a new site for a general council fire. They agreed to hold a council at the Wyandot village known as Brownstown, situated along the Huron River at the west end of Lake Erie, roughly sixteen miles south of Detroit.

The move to Brownstown marked a key turning point in Indian affairs in the Old Northwest. On Christmas Eve, 1786, the leaders of the newly established confederacy at Brownstown formally met with the British at Detroit and requested direct intervention and continuing support.[23] From their location close to Detroit, the intertribal councils would now come more heavily under the influence of the British army and Indian Department, and especially Alexander McKee. American Indian agent Thomas Forsyth later asserted that the British led the confederacy at Brownstown, which drew its Native members from among the "Shawanoes, Delawars, Mingoes, Wyandots, Miamies, Chipeways, Ottawas and Pottawatimies."[24] According to Forsyth, there existed an official belt of wampum that symbolized all of the nations in the confederacy and placed the British at the head. At Brownstown, Forsyth continued, "The British government is always represented by their Indian Agent, and most generally accompanied by a military officer."[25] Forsyth's information was based on his contact with numerous Indians during his long career in the Great Lakes. He compared the new Western Confederacy's meeting place at Brownstown to the old Iroquois League's gathering place "on the Mohawk River at Sir William Johnston's [Johnson's] place of residence."[26] The geographical shift paralleled a shift in leadership, since the Brownstown confederacy's resistance to U.S. hegemony depended on British assistance rather than on military cooperation with the Six Nations. The host Wyandots at Brownstown, nominally the confederacy's Native leaders, were in fact largely under British influence.[27]

The growing importance of the British in the confederacy's reconfiguration was also attributable to other factors. The Wyandots were led by a pro-British chief, Adam Brown, whose life and origins remain largely a mystery. Some sources suggest that he was probably not even a full-blooded Wyandot, but either a mixed-blood or "an English boy" from Virginia captured in 1755.[28] His very obscurity partially hints at why the British would so soon wield so much influence among the confederacy at his council fire. Lacking the stature of Brant, or of other contemporary war leaders such as Blue Jacket, Little Turtle, or Buckongahelas in the North, or Alexander McGillivray or Dragging Canoe in the South, Adam Brown was merely a village chief who gained what influence he did have by consistently supporting British interests in the West. The appeal to the British of working with a relatively weak leader like Brown was that they were ensured a key position in the confederacy.

Consequently, Brownstown provided the British with an intertribal forum in which British personnel, ostensibly neutral, could continue to influence belligerent Indian groups as they had done during wartime. Such an arrangement meant that the confederacy could be aligned in a manner that would suit Britain's frontier needs. For example, in spite of the Wyandots' favored status as host of the council fire, British agents looked to the Shawnees to head the intertribal alliance. The Shawnees and their neighbors held a strategic geographic position in defending Brownstown and Detroit, and British agents developed particularly close ties with them in these years of uncertainty.

Britain's new relationship with the Brownstown confederacy had

FIG. 1. Ensign John Caldwell, King's Eighth Regiment, circa 1776–85 (painting, circa 1785, artist unknown). Ensign John Caldwell of His Majesty's Eighth Regiment of Foot served on the Detroit frontier during the American Revolution. Caldwell is pictured in attire that he wore while on a diplomatic mission to the Shawnees in Ohio country in 1780. © National Museums Liverpool, *Museum of Liverpool*.

FIG. 2. *General Sir Guy Carleton, Lord Dorchester, Governor-General of Canada* (artist and date unknown). Though traditionally remembered for his successful defense of Canada during the American Revolution and for his reforms that favored French Canadians, Lord Dorchester was also Canada's first governor-general to recognize that wartime British Indian policies were outdated and that autonomous Indians in the Great Lakes would require more direct and separate attention under British policy. © Library and Archives Canada. Reproduced with the permission of the Minister of Public Works and Government Services Canada (2006). Source: Library and Archives Canada/c-002833.

its risks. First, it might involve the British government in a renewed conflict with the Americans. Also, closer diplomatic ties to the Indians always meant greater expenditures for the Crown, money Whitehall was loath to expend.[29] Further complicating matters, British personnel who lived nearer to the Indians in the upper country did not entirely share the views of their superiors in Quebec and London. Writing at a time when Haldimand, Dorchester, and Lord Sydney (secretary of state of the Home Department) all wanted to reduce expenses and obligations to the western Indians, Alexander McKee informed his superior in the Indian Department, Sir John Johnson, that the British were obligated to demonstrate "some favourable support toward their [the Indians'] right of the country: this is the object that secures their reliance on and attachment to us, which must continue while this is their expectation."[30] McKee and several of his cohorts in the Indian Department, particularly Matthew Elliott, Jacques Baby, William Caldwell, George Ironside, and Simon Girty, spoke from the viewpoint of men who lived among the Indians in the Ohio region and had Native wives. Elliott and Caldwell had formed a partnership in the fur trade among the Ohio Indians after the Revolution, but Logan's raid dealt a lethal blow to this enterprise along the Great Miami River. Logan's men also destroyed Alexander McKee's home in the nearby Shawnee village of Kishpoko on the same expedition.[31] Clearly, the Indian Department's officers who served on the frontier held vested interests in their desire for the British government to intervene on behalf of the nations that resisted American expansion. The conflicting interests of the British government and their Indian agents in the field frequently affected how policy was carried out in the upper country in the decades from 1785 to 1815. Policies formulated at Whitehall often sounded very different when agents described them in council to the Indians.[32]

Finding it unsafe to remain in the region of the Great Miami River after Logan's raid, Shawnee refugees began migrating to new homes along the Maumee River, situated in the far northwestern portion of present-day Ohio, a region where the Miami, Wyandot, Ottawa, and Delaware nations already had villages. The move to the Maumee River valley made it convenient for the Indian Department from Detroit to maintain contact with these villagers; several departmental officers and fur traders once again made their homes among their clientele and adopted families, further contributing to the formation of diverse intertribal enclaves along the Maumee. These sites included Kekionga at the headwaters of the Maumee; the Glaize (present-day Defiance, Ohio), located at the confluence of the Auglaize and Maumee rivers; Roche de Bout; and the Foot of the Rapids.[33]

In the latter 1780s the principal Miami village of Kekionga and its surrounding cluster of Indian towns became the most important of these intertribal communities. Miami, Delaware, and Shawnee villages thronged the banks of the Maumee, St. Joseph's, and St. Mary's rivers at what was probably the most important confluence and portage in the Old Northwest. Little Turtle, one of the Miami leaders who lived near this site, once referred to Kekionga as "that glorious gate . . . through which all the good words of our chiefs had to pass from the north to the south, and from the east to the west."[34] At no time was Kekionga more important to the confederacy's interests than those years (1786–90) during which it existed as an intertribal society. In addition to Little Turtle, other prominent Miami and Shawnee leaders—Le Gris, Pacanne, Blue Jacket, Snake, and Captain Johnny—lived in Kekionga's proximity at the time.[35] The Miami village of Le Gris, also known as Miamitown, sat within the angle formed by the confluence of the St. Joseph and Maumee rivers, opposite to Kekionga, which was situated on the western edge of the rivers' confluence.[36] Little Turtle's village was located a few miles northwest of Kekionga, near the headwaters of the Eel River, a tributary to the Wabash. This intertribal collection of villages, along with others scattered along the Wabash and Maumee rivers, formed the heart of the resistance to American attempts to expand north of the Ohio River, and it represented the geographic nexus of the more important member tribes of the Brownstown confederacy. Thus the alliance that was formally created under British auspices at Adam Brown's Wyandot village in December 1786 quickly began to crystallize on the Maumee, and as the military activities of these villages escalated, Kekionga and its surrounding multitribal community collectively served as the center of operations. In one six-month period during 1786, no fewer than twenty-six war parties embarked from this cluster of villages.[37]

The tribes that gathered near Kekionga did not need to alter their customs and beliefs when they consolidated their communities. During the 1820s, C. C. Trowbridge, secretary to Michigan territorial governor Lewis Cass, carried out ethnographic field studies among the Miamis, Delawares, and Shawnees, conducting interviews with some of the former militants who had resided in the Maumee Valley during the 1780s and 1790s, including Le Gros (a Miami leader, not to be confused with Le Gris), Black Hoof (Shawnee), and the younger Captain Pipe (Delaware).[38] Trowbridge found that these tribes spoke similar Algonquin languages.[39] Furthermore, all three groups generally observed some form of patrilineal, hereditary succession when determining chiefs, and, according to Trowbridge, the Miamis established both war and village chiefs by patrilineal descent.[40] In the case of the Shawnees, Trowbridge indicated that the village chiefs also descended patrilineally, and in matters of war, Shawnees based leadership qualifications on merit, requiring a prospective war chief to "have led at least 4 war parties into the enemies country successively, that he should at each time take one or more scalps & that he should return his followers unhurt to their villages."[41] The Delawares practiced a tradition closely paralleling that of the Shawnees, choosing leaders who possessed valuable experience and leadership skills.[42]

Trowbridge's findings and more modern studies indicate that these three tribal groups also shared similar clan and kinship systems. Shawnee and Miami children always belonged to their father's clan, but in spite of patriclan identification, Miami children developed stronger ties to their mother's family, indicating a matrilocal community.[43] Later in the nineteenth century, the Shawnees also developed matrilocal kinship systems, but possibly not until after their final defeat and removal. However, the Delaware nation consisted of clans, or phratries, that were both matrilineal and matrilocal.[44] Consequently, the women of all three societies occupied key positions in the social organizations of their respective tribes, notwithstanding patriclan structures in two of them and patrilineal leadership in all three. Furthermore, Trowbridge acknowledged occasions on which the Shawnees and Miamis appointed women leaders.[45]

Perhaps most important, the Shawnees, Miamis, and Delawares adhered to similar spiritual convictions and cosmological beliefs. The three nations along the Maumee considered sacred power to be of paramount importance, and they strove to attain this through similar methods of ritual and ceremony. A pantheon of deities, or manitous, loomed as either a potential source of power or a labyrinth of destruction. In 1824 and 1825 Tenskwatawa (Tecumseh's brother, the Shawnee Prophet) and Captain Pipe, respectively, both explained to Trowbridge "that we live upon an island," under which lies "a vast body of water, and that the earth [the "island"] is supported by a great Turtle, swimming in it, and placed there for that purpose by the Great Spirit." If anyone questioned a Delaware, asking "What supports this Turtle?" Captain Pipe explained that "they shrewdly answer, 'The Turtle is a Monaatwau [manitou] and requires no resting place.'" The aging Delaware leader also ascribed "earthquakes to the moving of this supporter, and ... suppose[d] that he [the Turtle] will one day dive so deeply as to sink the earth and destroy its inhabitants."[46]

In the depths of this watery underworld there existed a number of powerful manitous and evil spirits that were believed to frequently ascend to the earth's surface by way of rivers, lakes, and springs. The most powerful of these evil manitous took the form of great horned serpents, and tribal shamans constantly attempted to harness the sacred power of these beings.[47] The most potent medicine bags were thought to contain small fragments taken from the body of one of these serpents; such concentrated power could guarantee victory over one's enemies and unlimited success in the hunt.[48] The Shawnee Prophet informed Trowbridge, "On the eve of a battle which is expected to be severely contested," Shawnee warriors "address their prayers to Motshee Monitoo [the supreme evil spirit]" and "[w]ar parties sometimes leave a small quantity of tobacco by the side of a Spring ... praying at the same time to the deity inhabiting it." Le Gros noted a similar practice among the Miamis.[49] Thus the militant nations that gathered in the Maumee Valley in order to resist American encroachments enjoyed similar patterns in language, government, and kinship, and they practiced like methods of gaining sacred power.

These common traits fostered a large degree of cooperation among the Ohio nations of the Western Confederacy. By 1790 the collection of various tribal villages situated along the Maumee, when supported by groups from Brownstown, could muster more than two thousand warriors. This concourse of nations cohabiting the same region began to alter Native conceptions of tribal possession and sovereignty. The various nations consciously attempted to speak with one voice and were not tolerant of an individual nation seeking to cede territory that all of the confederacy's members now deemed common property. The last known instance (prior to 1795) in which a member of the confederacy attempted to assert its territorial sovereignty to the exclusion of another member came at the end of 1789, when a land dispute occurred between some Miamis and Delawares, during which the Delaware faction threatened to defect from the confederacy and join the Spanish in the Mississippi Valley.[50] No records indicate that this group of Delawares carried out its threat to defect. In fact, just the opposite occurred, as additional factions of Shawnees and Delawares continued to settle at the multitribal community.[51] In the winter of 1789–90, the confederacy's leaders met in council and affirmed pan-tribal unity, declaring their plight "a public grievance, in which all were concerned—that therefore every able bodied man, ought and should turn out, to assist in repelling the enemy, who had come into their country, to take their land from them."[52] Keenly aware of the threat they faced from the United States, the confederacy recognized the need for mutual tribal support and joint land possession as essential if the tribes were to avoid future debacles such as those on the Mad River in 1786, when Logan's raiders easily destroyed the principal Shawnee villages of Mackachack and Wapatomica.

After Logan's raid, the Shawnee refugees found new homes among the Miamis near Kekionga, embracing their new intertribal status. The continued development of intertribal unity at this site was facilitated by the pro-British sentiments shared by these villages' inhabitants. The presence of white traders and Indian agents, namely George Ironside, Alexander McKee, the Girty brothers, John Kinzie, and a number of loyal French traders, all helped to cultivate these ties.[53] As a result, the British sphere of influence from Detroit and Brownstown remained strong along the Maumee from 1786 to 1794, and most of the inhabitants near Kekionga were British partisans. When Henry Hay, a British trader from Detroit, wintered at Kekionga in 1789–90, he noted that one of the leading French traders, Antoine Lasselle, "is a good loyalist and is always for supporting his King."[54]

The group of traders with whom Hay lodged dealt constantly with the more prominent war leaders, including Le Gris, Little Turtle, Blue Jacket, Captain Johnny, and Snake. When the Shawnee leader "the Wolfe" sought to move his people to a site near Kekionga, Snake solicited the opinion of "the Principal Traders & Inhabitants of the place" to aid in determining whether to invite the Shawnee newcomers.[55] Furthermore, when the disaffected Delawares threatened to move to Spanish territory in 1789, it was most likely Alexander McKee who prevented their defection. George Girty had informed Hay that if "Capt. McKee would Immediately send in a String of wampum to hinder them from taking such a step it would no doubt immediately stop them."[56] Girty's brief statement speaks volumes, for it suggests that in the minds of the Natives living at Kekionga and its proximity, the British agents, especially McKee, had become influential in the reconstructed confederacy as early as 1789.

As the British influence rose to new heights within the villages of the multitribal community along the headwaters of the Maumee, Hay and his cohorts showed little concern over the possible consequences of their growing involvement in the escalating war between the confederacy and the Americans. War parties went out regularly, often returning with prisoners and scalps; of one such occasion Hay wrote: "I was shown this morning the heart of the white Prisoner I mentioned the Indians had killed some time ago . . . it was quite drye, like a piece of dryed venison, with a small stick run from one end of it to the other & fastened behind the fellows bundle that killed him, with also his scalp."[57] The British and the French living near Kekionga often hosted these Indian guests and even "billetted" members of war parties "like soldiers." When "another party came in from war" the same day, they "danced with a stick in . . . hand & scalp flying," before "some of the warriors came over in the evening, to our [Hay's] House."[58]

The position of the British traders and agents near Kekionga in the period following the American Revolution reflects the ambiguity of British-Indian relations in general at the time. The intertribal residents in Kekionga's vicinity considered the British as brethren and a leading member of the confederacy, particularly after 1786. Yet Governor-General Frederick Haldimand and his successor, Lord Dorchester, never intended to increase the British presence among the tribes within the territorial boundaries of the newly formed United States, whether at Brownstown or on the Maumee. For example, in 1787 Dorchester issued a set of orders to the Indian Department, hoping "to diminish the enormous expense" of the government's Indian budget, while simultaneously demonstrating "the King's paternal care and regard" for Britain's former allies. Dorchester's instructions included a restrictive clause, stating, "No persons belonging to, or employed in the Indian Department, is [sic] to be permitted to trade, directly or indirectly, or to have any share, profit, or concern therein."[59] Apparently the injunction did not faze such trader/agents along the Maumee as Ironside and the Girty brothers, all of whom continued to participate in the British fur trade during this period.[60] Lord Dorchester had recognized the potential dangers of unmonitored trade, authorizing post commandants to intervene: "In all matters of trade where the

Indians are concerned . . . at any time the interference of the Officer commanding may be necessary." Lord Dorchester sought "the utmost Justice" for the Indians, but he also worried that anything less could undermine "the safety of the Post, and the security of the Trade."[61]

Although Dorchester's fears regarding his agents' role in Indian trade were not unfounded, Britain was compelled to rely on the fur trade activities of non-Indian agents in order to maintain strong ties with the Indians. After withdrawing from the American war and ceding much Indian land, the British had to rely on the continuing fur trade as the only means available to soothe Native discontent.[62] Moreover, the North West Company was organized immediately after the close of the American Revolution (1783–84) and represented British efforts to bring greater structure and stability to both the fur trade and the Crown's frontier Indian relations. The company enhanced the careers of the McGillivray family and the famed Alexander Mackenzie. More important, such a pooling of resources among the traders and merchants brought about greater cooperation among men who had once been bitter rivals. The company's sales escalated dramatically in the first two years of operation, and the reported overall revenues remained high throughout the 1780s.[63]

The expansion of the British fur trade and the activities of the North West Company throughout this period brought about vast changes in Indian communities. The expanding fur trade not only bolstered the traders' influence, but it also accelerated the process of limited acculturation for the Indians and a growing interdependence between traders and Indians. When the trade grew, Natives became ever more reliant on manufactured goods, which in turn compelled them to continue to engage in a market economy and augment their bounties still further.[64] Moreover, the fur trade fostered liquor abuse among the Indians and probably hastened the spread of disease. Such a destabilization of tribal social infrastructures, coupled with a rapid depletion of game, eventually led to a greater economic, political, and military reliance on Britain.[65] Yet Whitehall and leaders in Canada certainly did not want the close attachment to the Indians that the fur trade would bring, particularly at a time when Indians were preparing for war with the Americans.

Considering this inherent contradiction, Britain could not indefinitely employ the fur trade as a means of cultivating good relations with the Crown's former Indian allies while simultaneously trying to keep them at arm's length.[66] As long as these conditions persisted, Whitehall could never develop a sound and consistent Indian policy that would fully satisfy the tribes in the Great Lakes and upper country, and also maintain amiable Anglo-American relations and peace on the frontier. Dorchester's orders to the Indian Department reflected this ambiguity. In striving to reduce expenses and decrease the Indian budget, the governor-general regarded the Indians as "free and Independent people," but he simultaneously instructed the agents to inform the Indians that they would continue to "merit" the king's friendship only "by acting as good and obedient Children ought to do."[67] In seeking to pacify the Indians, cut costs, and prevent the potential threats to the upper province, Dorchester's policy reflected the sentiments of his superiors at Whitehall; in theory, the measure encouraged greater Indian autonomy, while in actuality it fostered heavier Native reliance on British support. British leaders could not vacillate indefinitely, and with the confederacy already in a state of intermittent war with the United States, the British government would be forced to determine the extent of its resolve to support its former allies with both material and military assistance.

The Confederacy's Zenith, 1789–92

The Native and British residents of Kekionga and the nearby villages thought little of the long-term repercussions of British-Indian trade relations as the continued British presence made the community's infrastructure even more complex. In some cases, Indians chose to handle matters internally, but on other occasions tribal leaders sought the advice and direct intervention of British traders and agents. For example, in the previously-noted instance in which the Shawnee leader, "the Wolfe," wanted to move his entire village near to Kekionga in

1790, "Capt. Snake" called a meeting "of the Principal Traders & Inhabitants of the place," seeking their advice and support in order to determine whether to welcome the potential newcomers to Kekionga; the Shawnee leader addressed the traders and other village inhabitants as "Fathers & Brothers."[68]

Snake's courtesy on this occasion did not entitle the traders to the privilege of permanent participation in Kekionga's councils, nor was it an indication of Native deference to British authority. In asking the advice of "Fathers & Brothers," Snake considered the whites at Kekionga as his own relations, but an acknowledgment of familial ties did not concede authority to the white residents. In stark contrast to the courtesy shown white traders in 1790, captive Thomas Ridout's harrowing experience in 1788 demonstrated the traders' limited influence at Kekionga. During his brief captivity, Ridout sat before an Indian tribunal that excluded all traders, and with the exception of the interpreter Simon Girty, probably barred all whites. Ridout recalled, "The Indian traders who lived on the other side of a river . . . had long expected me, but dared not intercede for me whilst my life was at issue."[69] Ridout, a British subject and an avowed Loyalist, narrowly avoided torture and execution as a suspected American spy. The traders' exclusion in Ridout's case, after having sat in council on previous occasions, indicates much about how the tribes at Kekionga and along the Maumee understood their relationship to Britain. They viewed their British friends as brothers in commerce and allies in war, but certainly not as anyone possessing sovereign authority in Native councils. Thus the confederacy's leaders of the upper Maumee never relinquished the authority of making critical decisions pertaining to war and diplomacy.

The Natives' belief in their own sovereignty at Kekionga would not go unchallenged for long. Existing in a local community that lacked complete unanimity and in an alliance that had no clear leader, the tribes in Kekionga's vicinity were vulnerable to attack. When a poorly trained and ill-equipped American army commanded by Josiah Harmar marched to Kekionga in the autumn of 1790, the leaders there could not even muster enough warriors to defend their homes or protect their crops from the invaders' torch, despite knowing of Harmar's advance from the outset. The inadequate number of warriors was due partly to the timing of the autumn hunt, but the lack of coordination among the confederacy's leaders posed the bigger threat to the alliance.[70] Some, such as the Wyandot leaders, who did not live near Kekionga, may have yet held out hope for a general peace.[71] Without an adequate defense, the inhabitants of Kekionga themselves burned their principal Miami village and evacuated shortly before the American army's vanguard arrived on the same day, October 15. In the ensuing days, the regular army and militia proceeded to burn and destroy any of the remaining Indian towns and all of the crops they could find. Despite suffering the loss of their homes and crops, the warriors of Kekionga dealt Harmar a serious drubbing, as Miami war chief Little Turtle successfully orchestrated multiple ambushes against Harmar's ill-prepared army.[72]

Little Turtle's successes notwithstanding, Harmar's raid was a psychological blow to Kekionga's inhabitants. Unable to defend their homes and crops against a poorly disciplined army, the confederacy's warriors pondered the future, realizing they would face more capable adversaries. Moreover, tribal differences and disagreements among Native leaders caused them to squander an opportunity to crush Harmar's battered army. While Blue Jacket and the Shawnees wanted to deliver the coup de grâce against the retreating Americans, a total lunar eclipse of a full moon caused much consternation among some of the allied warriors preparing to pursue Harmar's men. Several interpreted the phenomenon as an ominous warning of certain disaster if they attempted to pursue the Americans. The Ottawas, who had belatedly been rushed to the scene by British agents positioned lower on the Maumee, simply packed up and left, and to Blue Jacket's chagrin, other groups soon followed.[73] When considering their close ties to the Ojibwas, it would seem that the Ottawas interpreted eclipses as ominous signs. According to C. C. Trowbridge, nineteenth-century ethnologist, the Ojibwas understood eclipses as calamitous, whereas

Blue Jacket and the Shawnees had viewed ecliptical phenomena as "precursors of war."[74] Until they overcame such divisions, the confederacy would not become a united force and could not hope to win a war against the Americans.

Still smarting from the lost opportunity to destroy Harmar's army, Blue Jacket understood all too well that he needed British aid if the Indians were to achieve the unity he sought. Losing no time, the Shawnee leader journeyed to Detroit to plead for direct support, arriving there even before the remnants of Harmar's army had completed their march back to Cincinnati. On November 4, with McKee as translator, Blue Jacket addressed Major John Smith, commandant at Detroit, arguing that Britain and the confederated tribes held a common cause against the Americans, and that the "Great Father" was indebted to the Shawnee people, who had faithfully served their father, the king. Blue Jacket also appealed to Britain's vested interest in protecting trade with its former allies, asserting that that trade was the common bond, as he put it, "which links us together in amity and interest."[75]

Though not wanting another American war, the British officers at Detroit also did not want to completely spurn Blue Jacket's pleas for support. The Shawnee war leader was one of the most influential chiefs among the intertribal coalition developing along the Maumee, and, as son-in-law to Jacques Baby, a Detroit-based British Indian agent, Blue Jacket was also a British partisan. The British authorities had previously honored the Shawnee leader with an officer's commission, which, according to white captive Oliver M. Spencer, entailed "the half pay of a brigadier general from the British crown." Spencer also recalled an occasion when Snake and Simon Girty visited the illustrious Shawnee, whom the captive youth described as "dressed in a scarlet frock coat, richly laced with gold and confined around his waist with a party-colored sash, and in red leggings and moccasins ornamented in the highest style of Indian fashion. On his shoulders he wore a pair of gold epaulets, and on his arms broad silver bracelets; while from his neck hung a massive silver gorget and a large medallion of His Majesty, George III."[76] The British influence on Blue Jacket and, conversely, the latter's reliance on Britain's aid reached their zeniths about the time the Shawnee war chief had gained his maximum influence within the coalition's leadership ranks.

In council at Detroit, British commandant Major Smith listened attentively to Blue Jacket's pleas, and responded with assurances of friendship and words of compassion, but he promised nothing other than to seek his superiors' counsel on the matter. He immediately wrote to Lord Dorchester, and in the meantime he did his best to supply the Shawnee delegation with gifts and food. Smith's gifts helped temporarily sustain the homeless inhabitants of Kekionga, and his promises to place the Natives' appeals before Lord Dorchester gave Blue Jacket, Little Turtle, and Kekionga's other refugees a glimmer of hope. But in truth, neither Smith nor Dorchester could do much to offer further protection to the Indians, and all that McKee could later suggest was that the displaced villagers who lost their homes in Harmar's raid move farther down the Maumee, which would place them nearer to Detroit and shorten the supply line of the Indian Department.[77] Early in 1791, therefore, many refugees from the region of Kekionga and Miamitown began doing just that, relocating at the Glaize. By the summer of 1791, the community at the Glaize included almost all of the prominent figures of whom Hay had written about during his stay at Kekionga a little more than a year earlier. Blue Jacket, Captain Johnny, Snake, Little Turtle, Buckongahelas, and those in their villages all built new homes at or near the Glaize. Nearly two thousand people resided at the Glaize by 1792.[78]

Oliver M. Spencer's memoir of his captivity at the Glaize during the early 1790s offers a glimpse into life in this intertribal community, especially into the role that spirituality played in Native resistance to U.S. expansion at the time. Upon his arrival at the Glaize, Spencer was placed in the household of his captor's mother, Coocoochee, a Mohawk prophetess. Though she was not a member of any of the tribes—Shawnee, Miami, and Delaware—that predominated numerically at the Glaize, Coocoochee nevertheless was treated as a revered member of the intertribal village community. Her respected position was based on her reputation as a medicine woman who conversed with numerous spirits and accurately forecast the results of raids.[79] For example, when more than fifty Shawnee warriors from Blue Jacket's and Snake's villages sought her out in 1792, she prophesied the success of their raid, and after they subsequently won a significant victory, they returned to the Glaize with much plunder and honored Coocoochee by giving her a share of their spoils.[80]

Coocoochee's shared refugee status with those at the Glaize gave her greater influence and credibility among them, as she dwelled among those who, like herself, were uprooted from distant homes and were now unsettled as a result of war. Among the spirits with whom Coocoochee conversed was that of her husband, Cokundiawsaw, a Mohawk war chief who had migrated into the Ohio region to join the Shawnees and Mingoes already living there, only to lose his life against Harmar's army at Kekionga.[81] On the occasion of the Feast of the Dead in the spring of 1792, a little more than a year after Cokundiawsaw's death, his widow removed his remains to the site of her new dwelling at the Glaize. Buried in a sitting position with his weapons, blanket, and moccasins, Cokundiawsaw's body faced the West, his spirit's final destination. Yet Coocoochee's ongoing conversations with her husband's spirit and the manner in which his friends tended his grave suggest that they believed that Cokundiawsaw's spirit still lingered and was not prepared for its final journey.

The general belief in the lingering presence of Cokundiawsaw's spirit and the confidence the warriors placed in Coocoochee indicate that the intertribal community at the Glaize, though experiencing displacement and adversity, continued to rely on means of gaining sacred power with which to overcome hardship. After sustaining considerable losses in the fight against Harmar, the warriors from Kekionga, though victorious, sought a new home at the Glaize. Without food after Harmar's destructive raid, much of the surviving remnant of Kekionga's populace relied heavily on the British at Detroit to supply their needs in the upcoming winter, and this caused a sudden evacuation of their former villages. Under ordinary circumstances, Cokundiaw-saw, a distinguished war chief of the Mohawks, would have received a ceremonial burial to assuage his mourning relatives, to prevent calamities from evil spirits, and to assist his spirit on its journey. As it was, due to Coocoochee's move to the Glaize, Cokundiawsaw's grave remained unattended for more than a year, until his widow reinterred his remains. Thus Cokundiawsaw's spirit remained restless.

Because Cokundiawsaw and his family had lived among the Shawnees for several years before his death, the family could no longer have practiced the formal Condolence Ceremony of their Iroquois heritage, but Cokundiawsaw did not even receive the Shawnee variation of the Condolence Ceremony.[82] The death feast that Coocoochee finally observed for her fallen husband was held much later than it should have been by both Iroquois and Shawnee standards;[83] both groups believed that a spirit kept restless for so long was dangerous.[84] Yet by conferring with the dead and prophesying to departing war parties at the Glaize, Coocoochee, if not directly assuaging the passions of the lingering ghosts, could perhaps at least foretell of calamities they might cause. Though war and displacement interrupted the observance of sacred rituals, Coocoochee's experiences illustrate how various customs merged and how distinct peoples united to act as one. The Mohawk medicine woman was in effect fulfilling a role that Shawnee and Miami shamans would have performed for their own peoples in more ordinary times.

As Coocoochee's presence became more vital to those living at the Glaize, she also developed closer ties with the British traders and agents living there. In her household, she raised a mixed-blood grandson, thought to be Simon Girty's son, and Coocoochee's daughter married George Ironside, one of the traders who had migrated to the Glaize from Kekionga after Harmar's raid. This couple lived directly across the Maumee River from Coocoochee.

The marriage between Ironside and Coocoochee's daughter suggests an increasing interdependence between the British and the Indians living at the Glaize. Ironside had married into a prominent family; his mother-in-law's power and his brothers-in-laws' status as warriors ensured him a position of respect. Ironside's new dwelling at the Glaize was situated in the center of the combined villages. Instead of living on the periphery as he and the other traders had done at Kekionga, he and his fellow traders and agents were now situated at the hub of interaction at the Glaize. Moreover, like Ironside, the Indian agents at the Glaize, namely Matthew Elliott, Alexander McKee, and the Girty brothers, also had Native wives and families. These men had become integrated members of this intertribal community.[85] Near Ironside's house and the Auglaize River stood a small palisaded perimeter surrounding two British Indian Department buildings, one of them a permanent residence for James Girty, an interpreter in the Indian Department who had once lived near Kekionga, the other a supply depot and part-time residence for Elliott and McKee.[86] This storehouse enabled the Indian Department's branch at Detroit to more quickly feed and arm the warriors at the Glaize, giving the department a more active role in dealing with the intertribal groups there than the British had previously undertaken at Kekionga.[87]

Direct British involvement along the Maumee became more apparent late in 1791, when the Indian Department assisted the allied warriors in planning and carrying out the attack that destroyed Arthur St. Clair's American army on November 4 more than fifty miles from either the Glaize or Kekionga.[88] In addition to providing arms and intelligence, a number of the Indian Department's officers took part in the action. Simon Girty led a group of Wyandots in the battle, and Matthew Elliott was also present;[89] many other department officers also probably fought against St. Clair that day, but they did so using extreme discretion, since the act was a violation of Britain's official neutral status in the ongoing war between the United States and the Indians of the Northwest. In all, the American army suffered more than one thousand casualties, over six hundred of them fatalities.[90] Only several scores of army personnel and civilians returned to Fort Washington (Cincinnati) completely unscathed.

Although certainly one of the greatest victories ever for Native

Americans over Euro-Americans, St. Clair's defeat ironically exposed the confederacy's weakness, showing a heightened dependence on the British.[91] While the Indian victory marked the high tide of the fortunes of the northwestern confederacy in its struggles to thwart American expansion, it also tended to weave Indian and British interests together more tightly in the Ohio Valley and upper country. Furthermore, since the U.S. government remained steadfast in refusing to acknowledge Native sovereignty in the Old Northwest, the war would continue. Confidence soared at the Glaize; the confederacy and its leaders saw no reason why their overwhelming success against American arms should not continue, particularly with support from their supposedly neutral British confederates. Consequently, in the years immediately following St. Clair's defeat, the British Indian Department enjoyed its strongest influence ever among the intertribal communities at the Glaize and along the Maumee.

In the wake of the momentous Indian victory over St. Clair, events at the Glaize tended to define genuine British-Indian relations. Despite the British government's proclamations of neutrality and its urging the leaders in Canada to reduce Indian expenditures, actual ties and relations with the Indians in the upper country were primarily shaped and carried out by those Indian agents on site, Alexander McKee and his staff.[92] Within this nebulous situation, McKee's position became particularly delicate. As the war wore on, Blue Jacket, Little Turtle, Buckongahelas, Captain Johnny, Snake, and other leaders near the Glaize trusted the British more heavily, and they viewed McKee as their lifeline to this support.

John Graves Simcoe, the lieutenant governor of Upper Canada, also relied heavily on McKee, expecting him to maintain British interests within the confederacy, both in matters of trade and war. Simcoe and other British leaders had grown increasingly concerned about the activity of the traders in the Ohio Valley and its potential to undermine government policy. If the British fur trade became the sole element in developing ties between the British and Indians, Whitehall could find itself bound to the traders' diplomacy, conducted by profit-seeking individuals on the frontier. Simcoe wrote to McKee, complaining that the "self-interested & Venal Traders" would lead the Indians to believe "that G. Britain will sooner or later engage in a War with the States in the defence of the Western Indians [those Indians within the borders of the United States]," and that if the traders should find it in their own interest, they would not hesitate to "counteract the general Instructions & Conduct of his Majesty's Servants, & buoy up the Indians by that false hope."[93] A year later Simcoe defended the practice of distributing gifts to Indians at a distance farther from the posts, partly to "rescue the Savage from . . . the rapacity of Our Traders."[94] Thus British leaders depended on the handful of agents who did not have personal vested interests in the trade, such as McKee, to maintain the status quo in British-Indian diplomacy, particularly at a time when the traders' influence was significant throughout Indian country.

When it came to war and diplomacy, Simcoe also relied on McKee to influence the confederacy's leaders in Britain's favor, but again without making any permanent commitments on the government's part. Late in the summer of 1792, Simcoe sent careful instructions to McKee, detailing the specific goals and policy he wanted carried out in the confederacy's general council to be held at the Glaize that fall. McKee was told to work toward a peace settlement that would encourage the continued development of "so numerous a Confederacy" among the Natives, and to preserve the Indians' territory by creating Simcoe's proposed "extensive . . . Barrier" lying between American territory and British possessions.[95] In addition to preserving the integrity of Indian possessions, Simcoe also hoped that such a buffer occupied by a militant confederacy would permanently protect Upper Canada's sparsely settled Loyalist communities from American expansion.

In order to best carry out Simcoe's instructions without alienating the Indians, damaging the unity of the confederacy, or igniting a war between Britain and the United States, McKee remained purposefully vague in his communications with the primary Native leaders along the Maumee. Although he obeyed Simcoe by not promising the king's intervention, no record exists that McKee expressly told the

Indians that this would never happen. In fact, the subsequent words and actions of the confederacy's leaders indicate that they continued to harbor hopes that their British Father would defend their interests. After lengthy deliberations in the October council at the Glaize, a deputation, primarily under militant Shawnee influence, addressed McKee as Simcoe's representative. Painted Pole, a Shawnee civil chief who dwelled at the Foot of the Rapids near McKee's residence, served as spokesperson, and the chief made it clear that he and the rest of the confederacy's delegation expected the British to protect Indian interests: "Father; At this Council fire which is in the center of our Country, is placed the Heart of the Indian Confederacy to which we have always considered our father to be joined, therefore we hope on this great occasion, that he will exert himself to see justice done to us, as it must be through his power & mediation that we can expect an end to our troubles."[96]

Knowing that Native hopes hung on every word he spoke, McKee remained evasive; he merely passed the speech on to Simcoe, allowing the latter to draft a response. Simcoe, in his answer, adopted a well-established practice in Euro-Indian diplomacy, seizing upon the Indians' own rhetoric as he implied the king's goodwill toward them:

Children & Brothers,
You say "at this Council fire, which is in the centre of your country, is placed the heart of all the Indian Confederacy, to which you have always considered your Father to be joined." The King your Father from the earliest moment of his reign, has believed this union to be necessary for your welfare, & no less so to that of the neighbouring countries; and ... your late superintendant [sic] general, Sir William Johnson, in all his Councils inculcated its propriety.[97]

Simcoe's diplomatic endeavors mirrored those of the confederacy's leaders, who viewed themselves as using the British to compel the Americans to agree to a just peace, a peace that would preserve their intertribal territorial claims. Similarly, Simcoe hoped to use the strength of a united confederacy to bring about a peace that would protect Upper Canada against the United States by threatening the use of continued Native warfare to compel the Americans to seek terms favorable to Britain. Although Simcoe and the Indian leaders may have acted in self-interest and tried to manipulate each other, both probably believed that their interests were intertwined. In Simcoe's case, this took the form of urging Britain's Native allies to strengthen the confederacy, arguing to the leaders at the Glaize that it was "necessary for your welfare."[98]

The council at the Glaize addressed three principal issues, namely the confederacy's territorial goals, their reactions to further revelations concerning the intentions of the U.S. government, and the extent to which the confederacy should rely on British support.[99] While the tribal leaders in attendance at the council advocated the notion of unity and strength within the confederacy, these issues exposed the fact that the confederacy lacked clear leadership and that its members were divided on the objectives for which they were fighting. Moreover, the council also indicated the loss of Iroquois influence among the western nations.

Tensions over the confederacy's goals were immediately evident when the Shawnee leaders, whose influence within the coalition was rising, challenged the influence and position of the Six Nations.[100] Since the Iroquois had been divided, defeated, and driven from their homes in New York during the Revolution, they were in no position to offer further military support to anti-American resistance movements. Instead, Six Nations' leaders now served as diplomats and liaisons between the U.S. government and the Western Confederacy's leaders, attempting to aid the resistance efforts by brokering a permanent peace. Painted Pole opened the sessions by upbraiding the delegates of the Six Nations for arriving late, and by revealing his suspicion that the Iroquois lacked genuine loyalty to the confederacy. He sarcastically concluded, "We suppose you have been constantly trying to do us some good, and that was the reason of your not coming sooner to join us."[101] Buckongahelas, the most important Delaware leader, agreed, exclaiming,

Don't think because the Shawanoes only have spoke to you, that it was their sentiments alone, they have spoke the sentiments of all the Nations.

All of us are animated by one Mind, one Head and one Heart and we are resolved to stick close by each other & defend ourselves to the last.[102]

The militant leaders directed these statements at the Iroquois faction led by the Seneca chief Red Jacket, who arrived at the Glaize with a peace proposal from the U.S. government. The Six Nations' lack of fidelity to the confederacy's goals seemed confirmed when Red Jacket encouraged a negotiated peace with the Americans, stating, "Brothers, we know that the Americans have held out their hands to offer you peace. Don't be too proud Spirited and reject it."[103] The next day Painted Pole heatedly responded to Red Jacket, accusing him of selling out to the Americans:

I can see what you are about from this place. Brother of the 6 Nations, you are still talking to the Americans your head is now towards them, and you are now talking to them. When you left your village to come here, you had a bundle of American Speeches under your Arm. . . . Brothers of the 6 Nations, all the different Nations here now desire you to speak from your Heart and not from your Mouth & tell them what that bundle was which you had under your Arm when you came here. We know what you are about—we see you plainly.[104]

Stunned by Painted Pole's indictment, Red Jacket defended himself and his fellow representatives from the Six Nations, exclaiming, "You have talked to us a little too roughly, you have thrown us on our backs."[105]

A key difference that divided the opposing factions in the council at the Glaize was whether to trust British efforts or negotiate with the Americans as the best means of protecting Indian territorial claims.

Given their perspective, the Six Nations had little choice but to nego-tiate with the Americans. Shortly after the Revolution, the Iroquois were compelled to relinquish all land claims in Ohio and Pennsylva-nia, and the state of New York began to lay claims to Iroquois posses-sions within its boundaries.[106] Though the postwar Iroquois League grew weak and divided, the U.S. government sought to utilize the re-maining influence of some of its leaders in an effort to control the na-tions farther west. Such a position for Iroquois headmen could only draw the suspicion of the allied tribes on the Maumee. Later, Painted Pole again addressed the Six Nations pointedly, making it clear that no true member of the confederacy could continue to have such deal-ings with the Americans: "All the Americans wanted was to divide us, that we might not act as one Man. . . . Now Brothers of the 6 Na-tions; This is the way they served you, and you have listened to them. We know they want to break you off from the Nations here. But the Great Spirit, has now put it in your hearts, not to be broken off by them, from the general Indian Confederacy."[107] In his final speech at the council, Painted Pole indicated upon whom the confederacy ac-tually did depend, asserting, "We have a reliance on our Father [the king] seeing justice done to us, as we have always found we may con-fidently depend upon him."[108] The Six Nations delegation, led by Red Jacket, unwilling to be deemed an enemy to the hopes of their western allies, accepted the Shawnee hard-line position against concessions to the Americans and left the council promising to show unity with the rest of the confederacy at the anticipated Sandusky conference with U.S. commissioners in 1793.[109] In the meantime, the Shawnees and Delawares continued to ignore the speeches that the Americans sent to them, and they merely passed them on to the officers in the British Indian Department, arguing, "They [the Americans] mean to dupe us as usual, but we mean to be ready to receive [fight] them."[110]

Soon after Red Jacket's departure, Joseph Brant belatedly made his way to the Glaize. As a youth, Brant had become the protégé and brother-in-law of the late Sir William Johnson, who had taken Brant's older sister, Molly, as his mistress and eventual common-law wife. As a result of his close connections with the Johnsons, Brant learned English, received some formal education, joined the Anglican faith, and received a captain's commission in the British Indian Department. By 1786, he had twice traveled to England, where he met several key figures, including Hugh Percy (later the second Duke of Northumberland), Home Secretary Lord Sydney, Charles James Fox, King George III, and the archbishop of Canterbury. Like Red Jacket, Brant came with peace proposals from the U.S. government, having just come from the U.S. capital at Philadelphia. By the time Brant reached the mouth of the Maumee River, several of the western Indians met him, informing him that the council at the Glaize had ended, but they briefly held a smaller council with the Mohawk sachem. Learning the determinations made at the prior council, Brant did not even bother to present the American proposals. Instead, the Mohawk representative sat and listened to the words of the Shawnee leader Snake, who reiterated the Native position, exclaiming, "General Washington has always been sending to us for peace. Now if he is true and wants peace, the Ohio [River] must be the boundary line, as we long ago agreed upon, and we will meet him at Sandusky."[111] Hence Brant had no chance to present the American overtures for peace even if he had wanted to, and he probably knew how roughly Painted Pole and the other leaders had handled Red Jacket, so the Mohawk leader said little. Instead, Brant merely encouraged the westerners to remain united and not trust President Washington. In doing so, Brant managed temporarily to maintain some standing in the confederacy.

To the Shawnees and other militant nativists at the Glaize, the Six Nations' efforts at peace appeared to be more collusion than compromise. Of the points of diplomacy that the U.S. secretary of war Henry Knox issued to Brant, one read "that the United States will make arrangements to teach the Indians, if agreeable to them, to raise their own bread and Cattle as the white people do."[112] By this time, much of the former Iroquois homeland in New York had been thoroughly canvassed by settlers, missionaries, and reformers, and the Six Nations' delegations at the Glaize, whether from Canada or New York, were already under extreme pressure to begin adapting to white ways. But few proposals could have been more alarming to the western Indians. Specifically, Painted Pole reminded the Six Nations of the documents recovered from St. Clair's baggage in the wake of the battle, claiming that the contents of these documents authorized St. Clair "to put them [the Indians] at his back & give them Hoes in their hands to plant corn for him & his people & make them labour like their beasts, their oxen & their Packhorses."[113] Thus the Natives believed that peace with the Americans, unlike with the British or the French, would entail much more than sharing land; it also would mean the imposition of a new lifestyle, one that would undermine traditional gender roles, consequently angering the deities and causing calamities.

The proceedings at the Glaize clearly demonstrated that the Six Nations no longer held the influence over the western nations that they had once enjoyed. The very fact that an intertribal council as important as the one held at the Glaize could occur without Brant indicates the loss of the Mohawk chief's status. With the possible exception of McKee, British leaders had not foreseen this growing rift in the confederacy. Only seven years earlier, Haldimand had predicted perpetual Iroquois hegemony over the western Indians, and as late as summer's end 1792 John Graves Simcoe, unaware of the growing anti-Iroquois sentiment within the confederacy, continued to envision such a role for the Six Nations.[114] Less than a year later, by the time of the general council at the Foot of the Rapids along the lower Maumee (1793), Simcoe better understood Brant's declining status and threw British support behind the confederacy's more militant faction.

Division and Defeat, 1793–95

The gulf between the Six Nations and the Western Confederacy widened during the summer of 1793, when the confederacy's leaders met in a council held at the Miami Rapids.[115] Brant's reception there in late May 1793 confirmed his plummeting status and the Six Nations'

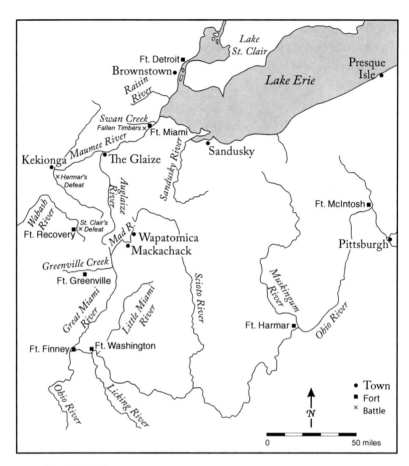

MAP 1. The Ohio Valley, 1784–94

declining position among the western tribes. In his journal, the Mohawk leader recalled that the Shawnees accused him of being "a Traitor, & that I only came there to receive Money and that they would have nothing to do with me."[116] Brant strove for unity within the confederacy, but he advocated a renegotiated boundary line with the American commissioners, one that would produce a lasting peace. He envisioned a compromise based on the Muskingum River, which would have given the United States some territory northwest of the Ohio River, but it would also have required the U.S. government to relinquish some of the lands it had acquired in the Fort Harmar Treaty—thus a true compromise. Though Brant and his supporters did not realize it, this proposal was doomed from the start because the American commissioners were not authorized to make any concessions remotely resembling Brant's plan.[117]

In spite of Brant's declining influence among the Maumee tribes, he managed to temporarily gain some support at the council from other factions present. The Ottawas, Ojibwas, and Potawatomis began to follow a course more independent of the confederacy.[118] Their future interests would lie more in the North, and with closer ties geographically to the Lakes region and economically to the British fur trade there than to the tribes of the Maumee and Wabash valleys. Moreover, this triumvirate, like the Six Nations, had little to lose by endorsing the Muskingum boundary and relinquishing part of southeastern Ohio, territory distant from their own country. While loyal to the Brownstown confederacy since its inception in 1786, the Potawatomis, Ottawas, and Ojibwas had little to gain in fighting a protracted war to defend the southern boundary of the Shawnees, whereas the possibility of a reasonable compromise with the Americans grew ever more appealing. Thus in the midst of the proceedings at the Miami Rapids, these three nations supported Brant's proposal, opting for a peacefully negotiated boundary. On behalf of all three, the Ottawa chief Egushwa graciously acknowledged Brant's past services and placed his trust in any settlement that the Mohawk leader thought most proper. The Ottawa leader stated, "You were the Promoter of this Confederacy and from your knowledge of the English, of the Americans, & the Indians, you are able to judge of our true Interest, we therefore place full Confidence in You."[119] The dispute over this boundary widened the division in the confederacy; henceforth the British could never again fully unite the tribes of the Old Northwest and Upper Canada.

At one point during the council, it appeared that Brant might have garnered general support for his Muskingum compromise, but Alexander McKee took matters into his own hands and privately met with the leaders of the militant faction at midnight on August 9. After this meeting, these leaders, with the Shawnee war chief Captain Johnny as their spokesperson, issued without further discussion their "final Resolution" in favor of a boundary set at the Ohio River. When Brant protested this maneuver, Delaware leader Buckongahelas responded by "pointing at Col. McKee, [saying] that is the Person who advises us to insist on the Ohio River for the line."[120] Moravian missionary John Heckewelder later recalled that the message sent from the Foot of the Rapids to the American commissioners "was both Impertinent & Insolent" and used "Language . . . that no Person having knowledge of Indians, would believe it an Indian Speech." Heckewelder added, "We saw quite plainly that the Indians were not allowed to act freely and independently, but under the influence of evil advisers."[121]

McKee probably believed that he had merely followed orders by asserting his influence in the general council, since Simcoe reminded him during the proceedings "to exert your ascendency [*sic*] over the Indians in inclining them to accede to those [American] offers, if they be consistent with their safety, and benefit, or to reject them if they seem likely to prove injurious to their real Interests."[122] Furthermore, the British Indian Department had its closest ties to the Indians of the Maumee Valley, most of whom belonged to the militant nativistic faction, and beginning with Harmar's defeat, the backbone of the resistance came from that quarter. Consequently, it made sense to build a confederacy around this core of resistance. Therefore British leaders probably believed, albeit mistakenly, that the optimum degree of unity in the confederacy would have to come through those nations that had most heartily participated in the recent victories over the Americans. Simcoe knew that any American army sent against Detroit would have to traverse this region of entrenched Native resistance. Finally, McKee was linked by marriage and kinship to the Shawnees, and he tended to favor their interests.

Simcoe approved of McKee's actions because he, like the western Native leaders, questioned Brant's loyalty and no longer trusted him. The lieutenant governor suspected that Brant "was pledged to [the U.S.] Congress to give it as his opinion to the Council, that the Indian Nations should give up part of the territory, on the northern side of the Ohio."[123] Simcoe also believed that the United States sought "an alliance with the Six Nations," hoping to turn "them against the Western Indians."[124] Finally, the lieutenant governor realized that Brant probably possessed goals that would not always coincide with British interests; he therefore wanted to reduce the Mohawk's influence. Simcoe wrote,

> He [Brant] is labouring to effect a pacification upon such terms and principles as He shall think proper and which will eventually make him that mediator which the United States have [*sic*] declined to request from His Majesty's Government. . . . He considers the Indian Interests as the first Object—that as a second, tho' very inferior one, He prefers the British . . . to the people of the States, yet I . . . consider the use He has made of his Power to be the subject of just alarm and that it is necessary by degrees and on just principles that it should be diminished.[125]

Simcoe understood that Brant, already in the midst of a sovereignty dispute with the British government regarding the Grand River lands in Upper Canada, would do whatever was necessary to protect the Iroquois in Canada and in the United States. Consequently, the desire of both Simcoe and McKee for peace and unity was merely conditional. It was better to risk a continued war with a fractured Indian confederacy than to place a stronger confederacy in the hands of a principal chief whose loyalties to Britain had become dubious.

Although Brant complained of McKee's interference, his protests went unheeded, and by late October 1793 he was virtually isolated. Prior to Brant's complaints, McKee had written to Simcoe, blaming the Six Nations for the prevailing divisions within the confederacy and actually claiming that he himself had favored a compromise regarding the boundary. McKee predicted, "However conscious I may be of having used no improper influence in the Councils of the Confederacy . . . I nevertheless expect from the malevolent, disappointed and ill disposed to be blamed for the opinions which the Indians have adopted and for their Resolution which put an end to the negotiations."[126] Simcoe swallowed it whole and assured McKee that his conduct was "perfectly proper in all respects."[127] At the same time, Simcoe was inclined to accept McKee's view that Brant was to blame for the fractured state of the confederacy, declaring, "I suspect that the principle of disunion arose from this Chieftain."[128]

Simcoe's anti-Brant explanation of the confederacy's troubles failed to acknowledge the schism's deeper and more complicated sources, which included old tribal rivalries, the competing political and territorial needs of the confederacy's various members, and the degree of McKee's manipulative influence among tribal leaders. But the existence of factional divisions after the council at the Foot of the Rapids was undeniable. Moreover, the emergence of three broad subgroups—the Six Nations, the Maumee Valley tribes, and the triumvirate faction that consisted of the Potawatomis, Ojibwas, and Ottawas—was a major development that threatened to undermine the position of relative strength the confederacy had previously enjoyed through its victories over Harmar and St. Clair.

After the council at the Foot of the Rapids, the confederacy continued to rely heavily on the British. At the conclusion of the proceedings, the western nations sent a speech to Lieutenant Governor Simcoe, with the Shawnee war leader Captain Johnny serving as spokesman:

Father,

Always considering that your Heart is placed in the center of the Indian Confederacy, we must expect, that our great dependance [*sic*] is still on you.... We need not we hope, again repeat, the great reliance we have on you for your advice & assistance; and altho' many have united themselves with us at this Council fire, yet we can depend on nothing, so certainly as your protection & friendship ... at no former period have we stood in so much need of both.[129]

In his petition to Simcoe, Captain Johnny also added that he and the other Native leaders "look up to the Great God who is a Witness to all that passes here, for his pity & his help," demonstrating that the nativist faction appealed not only to their British Father but also to the Great Spirit for deliverance and for the restoration of their country.[130]

Indeed, Captain Johnny's concerns were well-founded. Since a peace between the Western Confederacy and the United States never materialized, the Indians of the Maumee Valley knew that renewed American invasions were imminent. Furthermore, after St. Clair's debacle, President Washington appointed Anthony Wayne, one of the ablest American officers of the early Republic, to lead a much larger, reorganized army back into Indian country. Known as "the Legion," Wayne's force numbered more than five thousand men, and the aggressive commander had already begun constructing a chain of forts in southwestern Ohio prior to the confederacy's council at the Foot of the Miami Rapids in the summer of 1793. While the debates in council over whether to seek a compromise peace or to issue ultimatums to the U.S. government had continued to weaken and divide the Indian coalition, Wayne's army grew stronger, ultimately gaining the initiative. Native efforts to form a consensus with which to negotiate a peaceful resolution had strategically benefited the Americans. Wayne immediately followed up the failed negotiations by sending his Legion deeper into Indian country to construct Fort Greenville (the site of today's Greenville, Ohio) in the early autumn of 1793, and in December the army moved still farther north, stopping at the site of St. Clair's defeat, where they constructed Fort Recovery.[131]

By early 1794 Wayne's U.S. Legion was now virtually in a position in which it could not lose an Indian war. The confederacy's leaders understood this, but they continued to harbor the expectation of direct British intervention. British leaders themselves wondered whether another Anglo-American war was inevitable, and on February 10, 1794, Lord Dorchester addressed an Indian audience, publicly predicting that Britain would again be at war with America in less than a year.[132] The governor-general reasoned that the Americans had violated the Treaty of Paris, and that the Republic's subsequent purchases of Native lands would be deemed invalid once Britain rectified the upstart nation's "infringement on the King's rights."[133] Consequently, in the West, Native confidence soared once the confederacy's leaders learned of Dorchester's speech and Simcoe's decision to act on McKee's advice to fortify the country to the south of Detroit.[134] For Simcoe, the need to defend the upper province against an anticipated invasion had temporarily superseded Whitehall's policy of fiscal retrenchment for the defense and Indian budgets of the Canadian provinces. Therefore in the spring, Simcoe's redeployment consisted of constructing blockhouses along western Lake Erie at the mouth of the River Raisin and on Turtle Island at the mouth of the Maumee. Most important, the British built Fort Miami, a full-size fortress at the Foot of the Miami Rapids, containing cannons larger than the artillery of Wayne's U.S. Legion.

These activities and troop movements had an electrifying effect among the Indians; Native confidence in the British soared. Throughout the spring, remnants of the confederacy began to respond favorably to calls requesting them to regather at the Glaize. Even the Ojibwas, Ottawas, and Potawatomis, despite harboring resentment against the Maumee Valley tribes and the tribes' insistence upon pushing the Ohio River–boundary ultimatum the previous year, accepted the invitation. Simcoe wrote to Lord Dorchester, "It appears that the Chippewas [Ojibwas], in consequence of some superstitious circumstances have unanimously determined upon War."[135] In truth, the Ojibwas' renewed enthusiasm was probably due more to Simcoe's decision to fortify the lower Maumee with British troops and cannons; it did not necessarily portend a restoration of the confederacy's waning unity. In any case, by June 1794 the alliance numbered approximately 1,500 warriors, consisting of Wyandots, Shawnees, Miamis, Delawares, Potawatomis, Ottawas, and Ojibwas.[136] Even Brant and the Six Nations, though not yet themselves prepared to fight, saw the necessity for the western nations and the Indians of the Great Lakes to continue to resist, particularly after Brant's talks with the American authorities ended when the Americans informed him that they could never agree to his proposed Muskingum boundary.[137] This seeming restoration of the confederacy's unity, while more apparent than real, led Simcoe to believe that "there is every appearance of the most general union of the Indians, against the United States, that has yet been known."[138] Simcoe's confidence aside, the factious confederacy would soon be put to the test.

For their part, the Natives continued to look to Britain for military assistance and seemed to think they had good reason to expect it. On June 26, 1794, Wayne and his staff questioned two Shawnee prisoners, who informed the general: "[T]hey [the British] told the Indians the[y] were now come to help them to fight, & if they the Indians wou'd generally turn out & join them they wou'd advance & fight the American Army."[139]

Three weeks earlier, the Americans questioned two Potawatomis, who informed them that "the British say they will have 1500 militia," and that "Governor Simcoe had been sending [the] Pota.[watomis] messages all previous winter."[140] Whatever basis the Natives had for believing the British would send troops, they knew from mid-June onward that the British traders and Indian agents who shared their country, whose destinies were therefore intertwined with their own, would fight in the confederacy's campaign. This at any rate was the conclusion of a council of war held near the Glaize on June 16, 1794; a British officer recorded in his diary: "Resolved, therefore, that we shall join the [Indian] army now in readiness to march."[141] To seal this determination, the council leaders handed Matthew Elliott a belt of black wampum, binding him and the other whites to assist in the upcoming battle. All white personnel dwelling in the Maumee Valley, whether traders, agents, or officers, were compelled to fight.

The apparent restoration of unity within the confederacy proved to be a mirage. After waiting at the Glaize for last-minute reinforcements on June 18, Shawnee chief Blue Jacket learned that a group of 127 Ottawas and Ojibwas from the Straits of Mackinac and Saginaw Bay had raped women and pillaged the villages along the lower Maumee while the men of those villages were absent, preparing to fight the Americans.[142] Much of the lingering antagonism between these groups stemmed from the disagreements between the northern-oriented Lake Indians and those of the Maumee Valley in council the previous year. The northern tribes believed, perhaps justifiably, that the Shawnee-led militant faction had unnecessarily prolonged the war when, at McKee's urging, it issued the Ohio River–boundary ultimatum to the Americans.[143] The intraconfederacy conflict remained unresolved twelve days later, when the Natives launched a poorly conceived attack on U.S. forces at Fort Recovery. Not only did the attackers have to lift their siege when their ammunition ran low, but during the course of the battle some of the Shawnee and Delaware warriors, still angry about the Ottawa-Ojibwa raid on their villages, fired on a contingent of northern Lake Indians.[144]

As a result, the Ottawas and Ojibwas withdrew, returning to their homes in the North, even though McKee and Elliott tried in vain to prevent their departure. McKee feared that this defection would spread, predicting that "the Indians in this part of the country will feel a sensible diminution of their strength by the example they [the Ottawas and Ojibwas] shew all the other Lakes Indians as well as those who are here as those who are expected and whom they must meet on their way home."[145] McKee's concerns were well founded, as the confederacy's fighting strength was nearly cut in half with the northerners' departure, leaving the militant faction of Maumee tribes alone to defend themselves against Wayne's advancing Legion later in the summer.[146]

After the failed attack on Fort Recovery, Little Turtle sensed that adequate British support would never be forthcoming. Realizing that the problem lay less with the officers in the Indian Department and more the with British government's refusal to go to war, Little Turtle bypassed McKee and went straight to the highest-ranking British army officer in the West, Colonel Richard England at Detroit. Little Turtle requested soldiers and artillery, and he informed the colonel that if the Native alliance remained unassisted by the English, "they would be obliged to desist in their plan of attempting to stop the progress of the American Army."[147] Colonel England gave no satisfaction, and Little Turtle, as a consequence, recommended the start of peace negotiations with the United States. Furthermore, in a council held in August the Miami chief informed the other key intertribal leaders that he would no longer serve as a coalition war leader in the ongoing campaign to stop Wayne's U.S. Legion, but Little Turtle promised his continued services as a warrior once the others overruled his suggestion to make peace.[148]

Though moved by Little Turtle's pleas, Colonel England was compelled to obey orders. Unlike McKee, Elliott, the Girtys, and other British who lived with Natives along the Maumee River and who worked to keep the intertribal coalition together, Colonel England and his superiors in Quebec and London pursued a policy of nonintervention and withdrawal that would soon result in the signing of the so-called Jay's Treaty. In June 1794 Britain had opened negotiations with U.S. diplomat John Jay, hoping to resolve several issues left over from the American Revolution, one of which was the withdrawal of all British posts from American soil.[149] Among others, these included Detroit, Michilimackinac, Miami, and Niagara, all lifelines to Indians who lived within the borders of the United States but who looked to the British for aid and sustenance. Britain, at war with revolutionary France since January 1793, could not afford to go to war to protect the Indians, especially for a part of the empire that administrators and policy makers at home regarded to be of secondary importance.

Knowledge of these ongoing peace efforts made leaders in Canada and army personnel even more hesitant to support their former allies, and this became painfully clear to the Indians on August 20, 1794, at Fallen Timbers, when Wayne's U.S. Legion routed the remnants of the confederated tribes and chased them for miles. The American dragoons pursued the fleeing warriors virtually to the gates of the British Fort Miami, located near the Foot of the Rapids, where just a year earlier the divided confederacy had bickered about what kind of boundary ultimatum they should present to the American peace commissioners. Major William Campbell ordered the gates closed, denying any refuge to the routed warriors. Stunned by this betrayal, the Indians continued their flight toward Lake Erie. In this brief skirmish, they became keenly aware of the full significance of this act of British isolation. Even in the midst of a battle, their British Father had refused to aid them. Thus the most stinging aspect of the defeat was psychological. According to Jonathan Alder, a twenty-four-year captive and adoptee of the Shawnees, this single act of British betrayal "did more towards making peace betwixt the Indians and Americans than any one thing."[150] In a few short years during the early 1790s, the Natives in the Ohio River and Great Lakes regions had come to rely on Britain for military and material support.[151] Now, with the exception of some sixty or so Canadian and Loyalist militia who had fought in the battle dressed in Indian garb, the confederacy's leaders found that they were fighting the Americans alone. The Indians would never forget this betrayal. One Shawnee messenger informed the Indian Department that, according to Blue Jacket and many others, "the English were [now] thought nothing of."[152] Blue Jacket had come to the same conclusion that Little Turtle had reached one battle earlier.

In November 1794 John Jay had come to terms with the British government, and the U.S. Senate ratified the resulting treaty the following summer, albeit by the bare two-thirds majority required. Highly controversial and unpopular among Americans at the time due to its pro-British flavor, Jay's Treaty nevertheless gave the United States a significant edge in matters of diplomacy. What the majority of white Americans could not grasp, the Indians understood quite keenly. Any entente with Britain meant diplomatic power for the United States.[153] For the allied tribes of the Maumee, nothing could have been worse than their British Father entering into a harmonious rapprochement with the confederacy's long-standing enemy. And though the treaty ostensibly acknowledged Indian trading rights on both sides of the Anglo-American border, there was no denying that the agreement had driven a wedge between the confederated tribes and their British allies. As a result, Jay's Treaty gave Anthony Wayne all of the additional diplomatic leverage that he needed to compel the former militant leaders to agree to terms.[154]

In the ensuing peace proceedings at Fort Greenville in August 1795, the Americans would have their way with the leaders of the former confederacy. Those who came to treat with Wayne were now completely isolated; the lone British agent (John Askin Jr.) who attempted to attend the peace council at Greenville ran afoul of Wayne and found himself treated as a spy, and ultimately locked in confinement at Fort Jefferson.[155] Not only had the British abandoned them, but the Great Spirit now seemingly favored the Americans. The Natives' attempts to gain spiritual power prior to Fallen Timbers, primarily through fasting, had proven disastrous.[156] Thus at the Greenville proceedings Wayne boldly declared to the vanquished "that the Great Spirit was on his side" and that "he [Wayne] never slept." In addition, the wily general even promised to someday return from the grave if the Indians ever again rose up against the United States. "And this the Indians believed," according to Jonathan Alder.[157] Hence, now believing that even the Master of Life opposed them, the Indians conducted themselves at the treaty processions with much grace and humility; one author has marveled at how "they handled themselves with extreme dignity."[158] In the end the Natives accepted the difficult terms that Wayne meted out, not only because they truly desired peace but also because they now knew "that there must be peace for ever."[159]

The Treaty of Greenville represented a pivotal turning point in the history of the Old Northwest for all groups, whether for the American, British, or indigenous inhabitants residing there. Of the former Maumee confederates, a number remained in northwest Ohio, hoping to live amicably with the Americans under the treaty's terms. A large portion of Shawnees and Delawares migrated westward, some settling in Indiana, while other Shawnees joined their brethren in the Mississippi Valley who had migrated there in the 1770s.[160] A few, choosing to maintain ties with their British Father, moved to Upper Canada. In 1796 the British government strove to shift its foreign policy in accordance to the new peacetime conditions brought about by Jay's Treaty and the Treaty of Greenville. While British troops prepared to withdraw from their longtime American possessions that summer, Lord Dorchester set about crafting a new set of Indian guidelines and instructions to reflect those policy changes shortly before his retirement. These alterations included an Indian policy that would attempt to further reduce expenses and deal with the Indians regionally, as opposed to stressing the importance of a confederacy. Indeed, peacetime retrenchment would bring many changes, marking the beginning of a new era in British-Indian affairs.

2

A New Diplomacy at Amherstburg, 1796–1803

In compliance with the terms of Jay's Treaty, British authorities relinquished the last of the Crown's possessions within American territory during the summer of 1796, including Detroit, Mackinac, and Niagara.[1] With the British evacuation of these posts in the Old Northwest came the creation of three new forts on the Canadian side, located in corresponding proximities to the original posts—Amherstburg, St. Joseph, and George.[2] The move marked a new phase in British-Indian relations, the implications of which would be explored by both parties to the old alliance in the years under consideration here, 1796–1803. During these years, British policy makers faced distinctive issues in the geographical areas within the sphere of influence of each of their western outposts: Amherstburg in the Detroit area; Fort George near present-day Niagara-on-the-Lake, Ontario; and St. Joseph, located on the island of the same name in northern Lake Huron at the mouth of St. Mary's River. Each of these three areas will be the subject of one of the next three chapters, beginning here with the story of British-Indian relations in the Detroit-Amherstburg area in the aftermath of British withdrawal from the Maumee and upper Wabash valleys, places that had been so hotly contested by the United States and Britain's Native allies, the Ohio Confederacy, during the mid-1790s.

British resources for continued good relations with the Crown's longtime Indian allies included a number of officers of the Indian Department who removed to new homes in the Western District of

Upper Canada. These individuals included, most notably, Alexander McKee and his son, Thomas; Matthew Elliott; George Ironside; and two of the three Girty brothers, Simon and James.[3] Relocating at or near Amherstburg, they worked to establish a British sphere of influence that eventually stretched as far west as the principal tributaries to the Mississippi: the Wisconsin, Rock, and Illinois rivers. Also, most tribal groups in the region that encompasses present-day northern Indiana and southern Michigan still sought closer ties to the British in the late 1790s. However, by 1795 the British no longer held significant influence in several areas where they had previously been strong: the Wabash, Maumee, Sandusky, and Auglaize river valleys. For the most part, these areas now fell under U.S. hegemony, due not only to American annuity payments to the Indians who lived there but also to Wayne's strategic placement of Forts Wayne and Defiance, which sat at the sites of the former intertribal villages of Kekionga and the Glaize, respectively.

Just as the withdrawal of British outposts from the Old Northwest ended a direct British military presence there, so too, the death throes of the old Ohio Confederacy in 1794–95 produced significant changes among the tribes that had long considered the British their allies. Intertribal disputes led many former coalition members to regroup in smaller villages, and factionalism divided many tribes. While living as refugees at Swan Creek (near the mouth of the Maumee River) from 1794 to 1796, the former Shawnee militants failed to come to a consensus over diplomatic strategy, and any remaining vestige of tribal unity soon disintegrated. Typical of intratribal factionalism was the case of the Shawnee leader Blue Jacket, once a leader of resistance to U.S. expansion, who now made his peace with the Americans, creating a schism with other Shawnee chiefs who thought he had usurped their peace-making authority. Of the five Shawnee divisions—Chalaakaatha, Mekoche, Thawikila, Pekowi, and Kishpoko—Blue Jacket belonged to the Pekowi, but it was traditionally the role of the Mekoche leaders to take the initiative in matters of diplomacy and to conclude peace agreements.[4] Other factions from Swan Creek remained aloof, recognizing neither British nor American sovereignty. Tecumseh, a Kishpoko Shawnee, led such a group, consisting of approximately 250 followers.[5]

Among the militant Shawnees, the bands of Captain Johnny and Blackbeard formed the only significant faction to maintain close ties with the British and consequently chose to relocate with them to Upper Canada. Like the Shawnees, the Potawatomis dwelling in northeastern Indiana and those near Detroit attempted to abide by the terms of the Treaty of Greenville, but other Potawatomis who lived farther west in northern Indiana and southern Michigan held out against U.S. control.[6] Among the Miamis, Little Turtle and his adopted white son, William Wells, also shifted from a British to an American orientation.[7] These examples simply suggest why many tribes and prominent leaders who had been bulwarks of the old Ohio Confederacy would not figure significantly among the Indians who came into the Amherstburg sphere of influence. Largely missing from the tribal groups that figure in this chapter, therefore, would be the Miamis and Delawares and the Shawnee factions under Blue Jacket and Tecumseh. The tribes remaining more closely associated with the British at Amherstburg after 1795 included the Wyandots at Brownstown, the Shawnee bands of Captain Johnny and Blackbeard, the Potawatomis along the St. Joseph River and the southern shores of Lake Michigan, the Ottawas of the Maumee River, and the Ojibwa peoples scattered throughout southern Michigan and Upper Canada.[8] The Sauks and Potawatomis of northern Illinois would also seek closer ties to the British at Amherstburg near the turn of the nineteenth century.

British Gift-Giving Policy Debates, 1796–99

Once the agreed-upon withdrawal of their forces was completed in 1796, British officials had to decide what sort of relations they would attempt and be able to maintain with their former allies of the old Ohio Confederacy. The possible choices were many. It had never been clear in the past whether those indigenous nations that dwelled within Britain's North American possessions should be considered the Crown's subjects or allies. The Indians' legal status became even more ambiguous after 1796, when many of them who lived within the territory of the United States sought to maintain their former ties with their British Father as they continued to visit His Majesty's posts in Canada. Were the indigenous nations independent of Euro-American sovereign powers? Even if British authorities considered these groups to have never been anything more than allies, the question still remained whether future British policy should be structured in a manner that would cultivate closer connections with the Indians who now lived under American jurisdiction. Should Whitehall take steps to strengthen these groups' political and economic ties with the British government as a means of promoting Upper Canada's stability and security? During peacetime, these questions would become more pressing, and which of these strategies represented the best interests of the Crown was not altogether obvious. Nor did British officials agree on which strategy to pursue, as the debates among British authorities from 1796 to 1799 revealed all too clearly.

Whatever the strategy, British leaders did not know how the Natives would respond to new policy measures. In the autumn of 1796, British traveler Isaac Weld gained a glimpse of the disposition of Britain's Indian allies, who now lived in the Western District of Upper Canada. Weld made his visit to the township of Malden (including Fort Amherstburg) and to the American post at Detroit only a short time after McKee resettled the few remaining Indians from Swan Creek to nearby Bois Blanc Island, situated in the Detroit River, a short distance off the shoreline from Fort Amherstburg. Although Weld did not name them, his Indian informants certainly would have included those who had recently emigrated from Swan Creek, possibly even Captain Johnny and Blackbeard. From his Indian hosts and other Natives in the vicinity of Detroit and Malden, Weld learned much about such recent events as the struggle in the Maumee Valley and the battle of Fallen Timbers (August 1794). According to Weld, the sentiments of his Indian informants reflected a much stronger dissatisfaction and concern with the Americans than with the British, in spite of the acknowledged British betrayal at Fort Miami.[9] At this stage the continued relationship between British leaders and these remnants of Britain's former allies from the Maumee Valley lay not so much in the Natives' love for and fidelity to the British, but in feelings of frustration due to the failure of the United States to deliver annuity goods as promised. Weld described the Indians' frustration, and its causes, well: "The American officers here [Detroit] have endeavoured to their utmost to impress upon the minds of the Indians, an idea of their own superiority over the British; but as they are very tardy in giving these people any presents, they [the Indians] do not pay much attention to their words. General Wayne, from continually promising them presents, but at the same time always postponing the delivery when they come to ask for them, has significantly been nick-named by them, General Wabang, that is, General To-morrow."[10] In addition to this grievance, Weld's account generally conveyed the relentless pressure the Americans imposed on the refugee Indians, and it implied that the frontier struggle could never be peacefully resolved. Weld also believed that the Indians received better treatment in Canada, explaining that the "English settlers" understood the "necessity of treating the Indians with respect and attention."[11]

Building on the Natives' anti-American feelings, Alexander McKee sought ways to continue strong British-Indian relations during the postwar period. Well aware that the British evacuation from the American side of the border in 1796 led to a loss of influence in the British Indian Department among Natives at such traditional meeting places as Brownstown and the Foot of the Rapids, McKee hoped to restore the confederacy by the establishment of a new general council fire on the Canadian side of the boundary. With permission from John Graves Simcoe and Lord Dorchester, McKee purchased a twelve-square-mile parcel from the Ojibwas, just north of Lake St. Clair on the Canadian side of the border at the confluence of the Rivers St. Clair and Chenail Ecarte—the reserve took its name from the latter river—and on August 30, 1796, in his first speech at Chenail Ecarte, McKee declared the site as a new location "for a General Council fire for all Nations." In addition to the loyal bands of the recently beaten tribes from the Maumee and Detroit regions that McKee hoped to resettle at Chenail Ecarte, the new council fire, he stated, would include "the Six Nations, the Nations of Canada and all the Nations of Tribes to the Northward and the Mississippi."[12] Indeed, McKee hoped for a grand council fire under British auspices along the lines of Brownstown, through which he and other British leaders could once again influence a restored confederacy. Lord Dorchester also had high hopes for the new reserve, anticipating an intertribal population, as he put it, of "Two or Three Thousand."[13] Had these estimates ever been realized, the new community would have been larger than either Kekionga or the Glaize in their heydays. Although this was not to be—none of the pro-British Shawnee leaders, such as Captain Johnny and Blackbeard, moved to Chenail Ecarte, and very few of the militants from Swan Creek ever accepted the invitation—by offering its defeated allies a refuge at Chenail Ecarte, Great Britain attempted to demonstrate good faith.[14]

In his speech at the site, McKee tried to make the case that his government's dealings with the Indians had been honorable. Regarding the British withdrawal from the American posts in 1796, McKee asserted that this was an act of "the Justice of the King" toward the Americans, who "have at last fulfilled the Treaty of 1783." In this transfer of power, McKee continued, the king, far from betraying his Indian allies, had always "taken the greatest care of the rights and independance [sic] of all the Indian Nations who by the last Treaty with America are to be perfectly free and unmolested." The veteran Indian agent also asserted that the king's desire to resettle "all his Indian Children" demonstrated the king's "paternal regard" for them, and that he had an equal affection toward them and "His own people who have fought and bled with you," many of whom the king had also resettled throughout southern Upper Canada. Finally, McKee promised that the king would never "abandon" them "so long as they behave like good and obedient children."[15] By his choice of rhetoric, the

Indian agent attempted to make it seem that the British government had always acted with consistency and in good faith, and that if British-Indian relations had been altered, it was due to the Indians having drifted away from their British Father, not vice versa. Under these circumstances, therefore, McKee argued that future British-Indian interaction would depend solely on the Natives' attitude and conduct.

Despite his confident paternalistic tone when addressing the Indians at Chenail Ecarte, McKee was pursuing a concept of British-Indian relations not shared by his superiors at Montreal and Quebec. In an attempt to sustain close ties with the Indians, McKee hoped to continue these former allies' dependence on the British for war matériel and additional gifts and provisions that had characterized that relationship during the many years of intermittent warfare. Writing to his superior, Sir John Johnson, in January 1797, McKee alluded to past British policy when requesting additional provisions intended for those groups moving to Chenail Ecarte: "During a long period of difficulties among the Indian Tribes and pending the evacuation of the Posts and those parts of the Indian Country from whence their sustenance was generally drawn, the humanity & Policy of Great Britain through the Commander in Chief Lord Dorchester directed their distresses to be relieved as well in Provisions as in an extra allowance of Cloathing, untill [sic] they shall be enabled to plant for their own support."[16] McKee's request did not meet with much sympathy from Johnson, who did not respond. Johnson had recently returned from a four-year sojourn in Britain, and being keenly aware of his country's wartime commitments in Europe, seemed to understand that peacetime retrenchment in the Indian Department and the reduction of the military budget in Upper Canada would never permit the increase in the Indian expenditures that McKee proposed. Only three weeks prior to McKee's letter, Johnson had written to his subordinate officer, instructing him to cut costs and disapproving of McKee's intention to add additional staff to the Indian Department's payroll:

As I cannot but look upon the present Establishment of the Indian Department as on too great a Scale, particularly should there be no Occasion for the Services of the Indians In the War [in Europe, against revolutionary France] that we are engaged in, and of which there is little prospect at present. . . .

I must request that you will be particularly attentive to the Necessity of the Service in the expenditure of Provisions and presents, and that your Requisitions will be made accordingly.[17]

As the highest-ranking official in the Indian Department, Johnson more easily understood the need to reduce expenses in the Indian budget from his distant and comfortable vantage point at Montreal. Conversely, Johnson's officers in the field—namely McKee and his son, Thomas; Elliott; Ironside; the Girty brothers; William Claus; and others—realized how disillusioned their former allies were with the British withdrawal. More than ever before, the British needed to act graciously if they wanted to maintain a "Chain of Friendship" with these nations formerly allied to the Crown.

The Indian Department's officers on the local level did not prevail. By the summer of 1797, the refugee Shawnees who had moved from Swan Creek to the island of Bois Blanc began to notice a diminishing flow of rations from the agency at Fort Amherstburg. These bands chose not to remove to Chenail Ecarte, and McKee, having moved to a new residence on the River Thames, was no longer present to administer to the Indians' needs on a regular basis. In council one day at Amherstburg, four Shawnee chiefs—Blackbeard, Captain Johnny, the Borrer, and the Buffaloe—met with the commandant, William Mayne, and laid out their complaints: "Colonel McKee who for many years had been our great friend told us that he was still so & that he would always pay attention to us & would see that our great Father King George would take great care of us. It appears to us friend that Col. McKee does not now take notice of his children. We know that the greatest part of the fine presents that our great Father sends to us he keeps behind for his own use. . . . [Furthermore] Capt. Elliott does not take pity on us as formerly he did."[18] Ironically, these loyal Shawnee militants believed that the British government had kept faith with them, and that the reduction of gifts could only be explained by corruption in the Indian Department. The Shawnee delegation did not realize that the men they accused were among the few who still advocated a return to a more liberal Indian policy and an increase of gifts to those tribes in the old Chain of Friendship.

Indeed, Captain Mayne, also under orders to reduce expenses, chose to ignore the Shawnee delegation's complaints. Mayne and his successor, Captain Hector McLean, the two commandants who served at Amherstburg during the years 1796–1801, took it upon themselves to question the practices of the Indian Department, to curb its power, and to expose any form of corruption within its ranks. McLean imposed a rigid form of accounting for all goods distributed to the Indians, a radical departure from wartime practices. Since the Indian Department in Upper Canada had just come under civil authority in 1796, theoretically this heightened pressure from the military should not have mattered, but the military still financed the Indian budget, and Dorchester's successor as governor-general, Robert Prescott, also favored military authority over Indian affairs. Feeling the pressure from the added scrutiny of the Indian Department and the necessity to reduce expenses, even McKee finally recommended that his colleague Elliott urge "these Indians . . . to cross the Lake [to the American side] & endeavour to feed themselves" in order "to lessen the quantity of Provisions required."[19] Had Captain Johnny, Blackbeard, and the other pro-British Shawnees known of McKee's instructions, they certainly would have understood them as a confirmation of their suspicions when they had gone to Mayne a few months earlier and accused the Indian agent of betraying them. In asking Elliott to encourage entire groups of Natives to return to the American side of the border, McKee probably had come to realize the hopelessness of his dream of a restored confederacy with a new council fire at Chenail Ecarte.

Yet McKee had little choice but to conform to the new standards; perhaps he already knew that Elliott's conduct was coming under closer observation. When Hector McLean took command at Amherstburg, the new commandant quickly asserted his authority, determined to reduce the Indian Department to what he believed was its proper peacetime status. McLean recognized that the department operated more "by custom than by any Instructions," and he resented it that Elliott and the other agents at Amherstburg carried on their affairs independently of the garrison's army officers, technically a violation of the regulations Dorchester issued a decade earlier in 1787.[20] Furthermore, McLean was annoyed to find that Elliott, a low-ranking Crown official with a meager annual salary of one thousand pounds, owned up to fifty slaves and lived lavishly on his farm a mile south of Fort Amherstburg, supposedly at the expense of the army, which financed the Indian Department.[21] The commandant also discovered that Elliott daily sent his slaves to the fort's bakery to pick up twenty to twenty-five loaves on every trip, supposedly for the Indians, but in truth as provisions for his family and plantation staff.[22]

By themselves, these abuses probably would not have merited Elliott's dismissal from the service, but McLean's opportunity for a coup d'état against Elliott and the Indian Department came in October 1797, when Elliott, following McKee's orders, submitted a requisition for goods necessary to supply the Indians wintering at Chenail Ecarte. Elliott's order for provisions assumed that 534 Indians lived at the reserve, which supposedly included some absent bands at the time of Elliott's rough census. McLean sent an officer to determine the actual number of Indians living there, which resulted in a count of only 160.[23] When the principal leader at Chenail Ecarte, the Ojibwa chief Bowl, confirmed this latter figure, it seemed that Elliott had intentionally falsified his earlier return. This discrepancy, coupled with McLean's earlier charges of irregularities against Elliott, was all that Governor-General Robert Prescott needed to unceremoniously dismiss the Indian agent in December, without even the dignity of a further investigation or public hearing.[24] McKee's son, Thomas, replaced Elliott as Indian superintendent at Amherstburg.

A full retelling of the McLean-Elliott controversy is not necessary here; for the purposes of this study, the incident's significance lies in how it represented the changing British Indian policy at the time, and how this in turn affected British-Indian relations in the West.[25] Previously, during the years of intense frontier conflict when Britain's continued presence in the upper country sometimes depended on the field agents in the Indian Department, Elliott's conduct and activities would have been regarded as necessary perquisites to the agents, but in this new era they were treated as abuses, and Elliott's dismissal enabled McLean to reduce the peacetime power of the Indian Department. Far more than a personal setback for Elliott, the agent's dismissal demonstrated the diminishing importance of the entire department, and it meant that the army would now exercise greater control by rigidly enforcing regulations and monitoring the Indian Department's budget. The firing of Elliott served as a warning to the other agents, most of whom were equally guilty of engaging in the peculation and irregularities that had caused Elliott's downfall. McKee in particular had spent an entire career conducting Indian affairs in an informal manner, rarely accounting for his large expenditures.[26] For the remaining agents in the Western District, the consternation of witnessing Elliott's forced departure and the department's having to succumb to military and political authorities must have raised concerns about their future role as agents in His Majesty's Indian service.

The agents were equally concerned with how their former Native allies would respond to the changes, and whether the Indian Department could continue to cultivate close relations with them. Indeed, the very lack of interest among the Natives in settling at Chenail Ecarte prior to Elliott's dismissal may have already signaled a defeat in the Indian Department's ideological struggle regarding the future of British Indian policy.[27] Previously upset by the British betrayals at Fort Miami and in Jay's Treaty, the Shawnees, in particular, reacted negatively to the firing of Elliott, a longtime friend and adopted brother who had married into their tribe. Even McLean, while apt to deny the far-reaching extent of Elliott's influence among the tribes that the former agent had once served, conceded that Elliott still carried some weight with "that contemptible tribe called the Shawanese," with whom "the whole of the officers of the [Indian] Department are indeed in some shape connected . . . either by Marriage or Concubinage."[28] Still, McLean's bitter remarks did not acknowledge the degree of dissatisfaction with British policy that prevailed among members of the former confederacy. Little more than a year after Elliott's removal, the Indian Department and the government of Upper Canada began to notice the effects among the Indians. At the beginning of February 1799, Lieutenant Governor Peter Russell wrote to Prescott: "Captain [Joseph] Brant [also a paid member of the Indian Department] took me on one side and mentioned to me in Confidence that Capt. Elliott was so universally beloved by the Indians that his dismissal had given them great uneasiness; and that the Shawanese had it in Contemplation to send a Deputation to his Majesty to move the Throne in his behalf, which he prevented.—I find by his last letter that the same uneasiness subsists among the other Tribes."[29] The agent's swift removal during a time of transformation and retrenchment in British-Indian affairs could only have caused greater distrust and suspicion among the Indians in regard to British intentions, and the incident may have further dampened Native interest in Chenail Ecarte.

At the center of the McLean-Elliott controversy lay opposing philosophies regarding the future of British Indian policy, which to some degree exposed the differing attitudes among British leaders toward the Indians. While Elliott and McKee wanted to increase the distribution of provisions to the Indians at Chenail Ecarte and elsewhere in hopes of restoring a British-Indian alliance, Captains Mayne and McLean and Governor-General Prescott endorsed the opposite policy, a reduction of Native dependence now that the alliance was no longer necessary. In keeping with McKee's strategy, Elliott's inflated order for provisions represented an effort to induce greater numbers of Natives to Chenail Ecarte, a place that British Indian agents hoped would become the site of a new intertribal council fire under British auspices. By distributing extra gifts among their former allies, the Indian Department could instill in them a greater sense of dependency, the very thing that Mayne, McLean, the army, and civil authorities feared at the time. According to McLean, the Indian Department had "lavished" far too many gifts on the Indians, causing a "total dependence on Govt.," discouraging "every other means of subsistence." Arguing that "the Bounty of Govt. has been an injury to many of them by encouraging indolence," the commandant recommended a gradual diminishing of this "consumption . . . so as in the course of time to abolish it altogether."[30] Prescott supported McLean, insisting that the "present posture of Indian affairs" cannot "Warrant . . . this additional Expence."[31]

Alarmed at the extensive requests for provisions that McKee continued to submit, the governor-general "gave strict injunctions" to McLean "to guard against increasing expences at Amherstburg."[32] Prescott also concurred with McLean's assertion that Elliott had encouraged the high frequency of Indian visits to the post, and that not just Elliott, but the entire Indian Department tended "to promote their own interested views."[33] Prescott could not understand why the Indians should be encouraged to visit the posts, sometimes from great distances, and he saw no reason why "the Issues of Provisions of the present day" should be "of equal extent with those of former years." Therefore, like McLean, the commander in chief believed that Indian distributions should be vastly reduced from the expenditures that characterized the years of frontier warfare, and that any attempt by the Indian Department to impede this reduction was "highly reprehensible."[34]

With Elliott out of his way and with Prescott's support, McLean transformed the system of distributing gifts to Indians, strictly adhering to Lord Dorchester's regulations and to a tighter budget. The peacetime policy of reducing gifts to Indians exposed further unsettled issues inherent in British imperial strategy involving the Indians. Did the gifts represent compensation for the Indians' past allied services, or did they constitute a form of rent and acknowledgment of Britain's continued presence in Indian country? Or were gifts to Indians simply the British government's method of controlling and manipulating a dependent people, a policy that was no longer urgently needed in peacetime North America? Dorchester's predecessor, Sir Frederick Haldimand, had adhered to the former theory, that the Indians deserved compensation for past services.[35] By contrast, McLean's desire to someday "abolish" giving gifts to Indians altogether, and Prescott's belief that the Indian Department should not distribute provisions equal to that of previous years, indicated a new outlook, one that no longer found it necessary to compensate the Indians based purely on the merit of past services.

McLean and Prescott did not grasp that their actions could mean far more than merely reducing a budget. Though the gifts themselves held material value, the solemn act of giving and receiving them symbolized much more to the Indian recipients. By doling out gifts to their former allies, the British, though they did not fully appreciate the significance of their act, demonstrated to the Indians a father's love for his children, strengthening the familial bonds between them and thus brightening the metaphorical Chain of Friendship.[36] Therefore the act of gift-giving symbolized mutual reciprocity in which the British acknowledged the dignity of their friends and allies, in spite of the hard facts of growing dependency. To flout this tradition was to court disaster, and the British had paid a horrible price in 1763 for harboring just such an attitude before the intertribal alliance led by Pontiac and others nearly ousted the British from the upper country.[37]

Nevertheless, by mid-1797 McLean and his superiors viewed the entire system of giving Indians gifts not as something their government owed to these past allies, but rather as a symbol of the king's goodwill and generosity. When complaining about the conduct of those in the Indian Department, McLean wanted to eliminate any misunderstanding on the part of the Natives, hoping "to Show the Indians Clearly that it is the bounty of Government, . . . [and that they are] receiving it out of the King's stores, instead of getting it from the hands of an individual, & supposing it their Gift."[38] From

Whitehall, the Duke of Portland, home secretary to William Pitt "the Younger," the British prime minister, concurred. In a matter regarding a misunderstanding with the Mississaugas of Upper Canada, Portland emphasized to Lieutenant Governor Peter Russell the importance of making the Indians realize that the gifts were certainly not theirs by right, nor was the British government obligated in any way to grant them. Instead, Portland maintained, "the Messessaugues ... [must be] impressed with a due sense of the obligations they are under to His Majesty for the Presents they annually receive."[39] By 1800, Russell's successor, Peter Hunter, also took this stance in his dealings with Brant, informing the Mohawk leader that "[the] King's Bounty to the Indians must not be considered merely as a reward for their past conduct but that it entirely and absolutely depends on their endeavours to promote to the utmost of their power the King's interests."[40]

This new imperial perspective of 1797–1800 was not without internal contradictions, notably the desire to achieve more control over Natives while giving them less in return. In order for the British administration in Upper Canada to wield the dominance over indigenous peoples that Portland envisioned, British leaders would need to make the Indians more aware of the latter's dependence on the Crown. Indians, Russell wrote, would need to be instilled with "a proper sense of the Obligations they owe to His Majesty," in return for the gifts "to which they are in no way entitled, but are indebted for them."[41] In a "Secret and Confidential" letter sent to all of the Indian Department's superintendents in the upper province, Russell ordered them to distribute gifts to Indians in such a manner "as ... to leave the strongest impressions on their minds of their Dependence on His Majesty's Bounty."[42] But this goal was to be implemented simultaneously with the Russell-Portland policy of instructing field agents to reduce Indian distributions and decrease budgets.

Such a contradictory policy could only lead to further confusion among both British personnel and tribal leaders, particularly when Captain Hector McLean, commandant at Britain's largest Indian agency at Amherstburg, already had made it clear that he believed that gifts to Indians should eventually be abolished.[43] Far from wanting to make the Indians more dependent, McLean worried that the Indians were beginning to rely too heavily on British gifts, and that too many would settle at Chenail Ecarte and other reserves, where they would become a permanent "burden upon Government." Moreover, McLean predicted that if Britain continued to dole out presents to Indians, this would cause the recipients to "turn effeminate & indolent," since "a total dependence on Govt. for the means of subsistence . . . relaxes their exertions to provide for themselves."[44] Consequently, McLean took steps to reduce this burden, entailing both a reduction in gifts and a limited schedule as to when the presents would be distributed. Like Governor-General Prescott, McLean also could not understand why "Indians from so great a distance" should be encouraged to visit the post.[45] Furthermore, although neither Portland nor Russell ever made a policy distinction between Britain's actions toward Indians living within the boundaries of Upper Canada and those living without, McLean believed that the government had virtually no obligations to those Indians living on the American side of the border. The commandant instructed Thomas McKee that "Indians of that description . . . should not be permitted to approach the Garrison until the purport of their Visit is known," and they are "to obtain permission previous to their being admitted to this side [of the Detroit River]." McLean justified this, arguing, "I do not conceive that we are at present in want of their aid or alliance."[46] From this perspective, Indian nations outside of British territory should always be considered as sovereign principalities and potential wartime allies, but not wards of government.

Both the Indian Department and the Natives protested McLean's reductions of Indian provisions. Thomas McKee wrote to William Claus, his superior in the department, complaining that McLean's restrictive measures were an "extraordinary deviation from a system which has been pursued here ever since Pontiac[']s War." The younger McKee also predicted that "this breach of so old a custom may greatly operate to the diminution, if not the total extinction of our influence and may infinitely prejudice His Majesty's Indian Interest in these parts."[47] Although McKee may have been prudent in not wanting to alienate the Indians, much had changed in the years since Pontiac's War in 1763, as the tribes in the vicinity of Detroit and Amherstburg had grown far more dependent on British goods and were in no position to stage another revolt. When Superintendent Sir John Johnson visited the upper posts in the spring of 1799, Shawnees living near Amherstburg assured him of their "steady Attachment to the King their Father." But they then went on to complain of their poor condition. The cause, they told Johnson, was that they were "surrounded on all sides by the White People, and their hunting ruined."[48] The regions of the Western District, the Detroit frontier, and northwest Ohio no longer teemed with an overabundance of wildlife, at least not enough to fully sustain independent Native peoples as McLean had hoped. Rather than a reduction in provisions, the Indians needed more protection and support, but as of 1799, British policy had moved in the opposite direction, toward reduced expenditures on gifts and annuities for their Indian neighbors and former allies.

Realities Intrude, 1798–1803

Despite all the discussion among British policy makers about cutting expenses for provisioning Natives, and all the complaints from Indians about reductions in British support, the realities of the situation were more complex. While the policy that emanated from Whitehall was intended to gradually diminish the government's Indian burden and to perhaps eventually terminate British-Indian relations altogether, increasing numbers of Indians turned to Britain for aid, hardly what McLean and his superiors wanted. In fact, figures indicate that in the years following the defeat at Fallen Timbers and the subsequent Treaty of Greenville, the tribes in the regions of Detroit and Upper Canada's Western District relied more heavily on British gifts and provisions than they had in the past. Between 1798 and 1803, the Indian agency at Amherstburg served a growing number of Native visitors, averaging 5,548 each year. By 1803, 6,207 Indians received provisions there, representing an increase of 1,038 over the total for 1798, a jump of more than 20 percent during the five-year period. Only once within this stretch—1802—did the totals decrease from the previous year's numbers, but the numbers quickly rebounded to the five-year high recorded the following year.[49] However, these statistics do not tell the whole story of British-Indian relations within the territories that fell into Fort Malden's (Amherstburg's) sphere of influence, for the conflict between, on the one hand, Britain's initial goal of reduced gift-giving and the Natives' complaints about that policy and, on the other hand, a continuation of strong British-Indian relations was simply a reflection of a complicated game of give-and-take in which Natives of diverse tribal backgrounds and infighting among British officials all played significant roles.

While the British continued to seek a sphere of influence in the region around Amherstburg during this period of peace, there were some key changes in the composition of the groups seeking assistance at the time. In any given year throughout this six-year stretch (1798–1803), at least 86 percent of those receiving provisions belonged to one of five nations—the Ojibwas, Ottawas, Potawatomis, Wyandots, and Shawnees—most of whom were scattered across southern Michigan, throughout Upper Canada's Western District, and among the tributaries of Lake Huron. Of these peoples, more than 40 percent of the total were Ojibwas alone, and the predominantly Ojibwa reserve at Chenail Ecarte showed no signs of a diminishing populace, as McLean and the government might have hoped; instead, the numbers increased in the years immediately following Elliott's dismissal in 1797.[50] These five tribes eventually provided the backbone of the British-allied tribes south of the Great Lakes and along the Detroit frontier in the War of 1812. Hence, just after the turn of the nineteenth century, many of those peoples who would fight for the Crown a decade later demonstrated their continued fidelity to the British, despite a stingy British policy and the attitude of Captain McLean, who did not leave his post at Amherstburg until 1801.

In spite of these indications of apparent healthy ties between Britain and several Native communities in the southern Great Lakes region, a pro-British orientation was not typical of every tribe. The

Miamis and Delawares, two of the nations that had once comprised key segments of a powerful triumvirate (with the Shawnees) in the Maumee Valley during the 1790s, rarely visited Amherstburg anymore. Only a few dozen Miamis still received annual gifts from Amherstburg, and visits by Delawares temporarily ceased in 1801. Similarly, when in the wake of Fallen Timbers Alexander McKee had invited the refugee Indians temporarily living at Swan Creek to relocate to places farther north, particularly Chenail Ecarte and Bois Blanc Island, fragments of the Shawnees did so, but the Miamis and Delawares generally returned home to places nearer to the expanding American settlements.[51] The Miami and Delaware villages that dotted the White and Wabash rivers during the early years of the nineteenth century were mainly under the influence of chiefs and former war leaders, such as the Miami headmen Little Turtle, Le Gris, and Pacanne, and the Delaware Buckongahelas, all of whom now cooperated with American officials.[52] That these villages were beyond the British sphere of influence was confirmed in a report by Matthew Elliott in September 1797. Elliott's findings showed that the Indians who visited his agency were from locations far north of the Wabash and its tributaries, where American influence had grown considerably.[53] The limited number of Miami and Delaware visits to Upper Canada, therefore, could be a by-product of closer ties with the Americans, as well as the westward migration of several Delaware bands.[54] Nevertheless, despite having, on the whole, grown distant from the British, the Miamis and Delawares never fully severed ties with their former father. In 1803, 162 Miamis and sixteen Delawares visited Amherstburg. Moreover, several hundred "Monseys" (Munsees), loosely considered a component of the larger Delaware nation, still received provisions at the post annually.[55] Consequently, after all this time, it seems that the British in Upper Canada could count on either the support or neutrality of most Indians in the southern Great Lakes region, leaving open the possibility for a renewed confederacy in the future.

The above statistics do not mean that Britain's Indian expenditures remained high during this period, but rather that significant numbers of Natives continued to visit Amherstburg in spite of receiving much smaller rations there. After the dismissal of Elliott and the implementation of stricter guidelines, Governor-General Prescott expected post commanders to oversee and account for all distributions of provisions to Native visitors. At Fort Amherstburg, Captain McLean did so with a vengeance, as he continued his efforts to trim the power of the Indian Department while simultaneously reducing the government's obligations to the Indians. McLean hoped to accomplish this by discouraging Indians from visiting the post, and he began to deny gifts and full rations to those who came. The commandant maintained that

> all their [the Natives'] whims and unreasonable desires ought not to be so much attended to as hitherto, when the best reason that coud [sic] often be assigned for giving them any unnecessary article was, that they ask'd for it. If all the Curiosities and Luxuries that [the] human heart can invent were deposited in the Indian Store and that they saw them, they would ask for them, but it does not follow that they are necessary or that they ought to be gratify'd. They may indeed address us emphatically with the term Father, as they artfully do for we certainly humor them like little children in all of their unreasonable requests.[56]

Consequently, in May 1799 McLean instructed agent Thomas McKee that each Indian should have a "Belly full" and nothing else "exceeding two days Provisions." This amount was intended merely to provide a little food for the visitors' homeward journeys. Moreover, gifts were to be distributed only once a year, when the shipment of Indian stores arrived in October.[57]

Behind McLean's attitude lay the complex issue of the Natives' ambiguous status in Britain's ever-evolving frontier policy. Were the Indians subjects or allies? Some military officers and civil officials maintained that the Indians were both. William Dunn, civil administrator in Quebec in 1807, implied this dual understanding when he wrote, "I have always understood that the Indians were not considered by the [C]rown merely as subjects, but as Military allies." Dunn further argued that this was why "all the expenses attending" the Indians were "to be paid out of the Extraordinaries of the Army."[58] McLean also adhered to this logic as he developed his own rationale in supporting his actions at Amherstburg. Though previously having been considered both subjects and allies, the Indians who now lived on the American side of the boundary no longer qualified as subjects, and McLean believed that there was no reason to retain those Indians as allies. Why keep an alliance during peacetime? The commandant reasoned that His Majesty's government had "nothing ever to fear from the Indians while at peace with America." McLean's confidence was partly due to the good relations that prevailed at the time between his government and a Federalist-led United States, but in the unlikely event of another British-American war, the captain argued that, whenever necessary, the British could easily restore a Native alliance, inasmuch as "the Indians being totally guarded by Interests & not principal will side with the best bidder."[59]

In applying this rationale, the rigid commandant carried his policy as far as he could before his superiors intervened. Russell and his administration in Upper Canada were not prepared to go as far as McLean in severing ties with their former allies. Agents Thomas McKee and William Claus, fearing the repercussions of McLean's restrictive measures, warned Russell of the danger. McKee claimed that the commandant's tampering with "a system [of gift distribution] which has been pursued here ever since Pontiacs War" had caused "great dissatisfaction" among the Indians, and he predicted the possible "extinction of our influence" and loss of the "friendship of the Indian nations."[60] Claus concurred, claiming "that Captain McLean is going too far with us."[61] Not yet willing to greatly alter Britain's Indian relations, Russell heeded these warnings and ordered McLean to "immediately suspend" his "plan of withholding Provisions from the Indians" lest this lead to "consequences not only injurious but dangerous to the safety of this Province."[62] Russell's crucial decision, coming near the end of his term as lieutenant governor, helped prevent the eventual dissolution of British-Indian relations in the Great Lakes region and Upper Canada. On the brink of a new century and during a period of relative calm in Canada, McLean and the military had seemingly gained the upper hand over the Indian Department, making the latter powerless apart from Russell's or Prescott's intervention. However, the aging Russell, a former soldier and lackluster administrator, prevented further extreme reductions, a policy that would remain in force until a successor administration once again actively prepared for war in 1807.[63]

Russell's interference in Indian affairs should not be construed as a shift in policy, despite the fact that McLean believed that he had merely been efficiently following orders by attempting to restrict presents and provisions to Indians. While Russell advocated a reduction in expenditures, he also sought to preserve the age-old Chain of Friendship with the Natives who visited the posts. The issue then was not whether the British should follow a policy of retrenchment, but rather how and to what degree should such a policy be implemented? Considering the weak state of the upper province at the time and the Indians' nebulous status (whether subjects, allies, or both), it was not clear exactly what peacetime retrenchment should entail.

Like Russell, other leaders in Canada ultimately took the view that the policy of retrenchment merely meant a continuation of former ties with the Indians, but on a reduced budget. The Executive Council of the upper province agreed with this interpretation, advising Russell "to take such steps as he [Russell] shall Judge proper (by writing to Captn. McLean or otherwise) for the purpose of preventing any change in the old system until the Pleasure of the Commander in Chief [Prescott] is known."[64] A month later Prescott made his "pleasure known" when he supported Russell, ordering McLean "to issue Presents and Provisions to the Indians in the manner customary at the Post" previous to his alterations in May 1799, "and in conformity to the existing regulations." Prescott also later informed the captain that he was not to "interfere . . . as to the mode or manner of conducting the business of the [Indian] Department."[65] Such language coming from the man who sacked Elliott and who also wanted to discourage excessive Native visitors at Amherstburg indicated that leaders in Canada still considered the value of maintaining relations with the Indians. To these leaders, then, retrenchment was not intended as a means to phase out Britain's Indian relations, but rather as a way of preserving ties with the Crown's former allies during a time of fiscal cuts.[66]

Prescott, who had earlier supported McLean in the latter's feud with Elliott and the Indian Department, understood the necessity of retaining some diplomatic ties with the Indians. The governor-general's concerns about the treatment of Indians at Amherstburg probably also stemmed from a letter he had received from Sir John Johnson only weeks prior to Russell's injunctions against McLean. Johnson informed Prescott of the discontent among the Indians he had encountered there while on his visit to the post in the spring of 1799. The bands that lived near Amherstburg at the time—primarily Shawnees, Ottawas, Delawares, and Wyandots, once the nucleus of the confederacy in the late war against the Americans—now wintered near the post at Amherstburg, where they could continue to receive at least a fraction of the aid the British had once given them when they lived at Kekionga and the Glaize.[67]

During Johnson's 1799 tour of the Western District, the leaders of these bands reaffirmed their loyalty to Britain, but did so as a preface to informing the superintendent of their needs. The Shawnees even asked Johnson to help them secure passage to England, where they could present their case directly to the government, in order "to find out what they had to depend on."[68] The Shawnees also informed Johnson that the Spanish had offered them a place to reside west of the Mississippi, where numerous Shawnees already dwelled, and that the tribe also intended to send a delegation to the Spanish king to further consider the offer. The Shawnees, realizing that Spain and

Britain were presently at war, probably hoped that the threat of their defection to the Spanish would stir Johnson, McLean, and other British leaders out of their complacent attitudes toward them. Although the Natives near Amherstburg most likely understood the extent of their dependence on the British, and consequently probably never considered rebellion as their fathers had done in 1763, they did, however, seem to understand their value as potential allies, or at least the formidable threat they still posed when allied to an enemy. Johnson, not wanting to lose the long-standing relationship between the British and the Indians of the upper country, tried to reinforce the idea that the Indians still had only one "Father," and the superintendent ordered Thomas McKee and the other agents "to point out [to the Indians] the Impropriety" of "sending a Deputation to Spain."[69] Thus the possibility of the Shawnee defection, in spite of McLean's assurances of Native weakness and military impotence, is most likely what grabbed Prescott's attention and led him to order a continuation of gifts to the Indians.

For a time the British, especially the officers in the Indian Department, seriously considered this threat. Logistically, they knew that a Franco-Spanish invasion up the Mississippi Valley was possible, particularly with Indian support. During the American Revolution less than twenty years earlier, a mixed British-Indian force set out from Mackinac and raided the Spanish territory near St. Louis, albeit with only moderate success.[70] The elder McKee was also aware of the importance of the passage through present-day Wisconsin via the Wisconsin and Fox rivers, but he believed "the Sakies [Sauks] and Fox's [sic]" were sympathetic to British interests, and thus could be "induced to resist any attempt of the French[,] Spanish or unfriendly Indians to pass through their Country."[71] British agents understood the need to maintain ties with these distant tribes, and McKee believed that French and Spanish agents regularly circulated war belts among the Indians of the Mississippi and western Great Lakes regions; only days before his death on January 15, 1799, the ailing agent dispatched an informant, Joseph Jackson, to the lower Mississippi. But Jackson found little evidence of any potential invasion brewing in that region; the Indians informed Jackson that neither French nor Spanish agents had solicited their service within the previous two years. However, Jackson did believe that although "very large Bodies of Indians of the Creek[,] Cherokee & Choctaw Nations are under Spanish influence," the Natives would only participate in an invasion if the Spaniards were to produce a substantial army in the lower Mississippi; such a force never appeared.[72]

True or not, the reports were of special interest to those who wanted to see a restoration of the Indian Department's wartime status, and perhaps a revival of Britain's Indian alliance. Writing to Russell, Mohawk leader Joseph Brant, also warning of a possible invasion from the West, firmly believed that "the French are busy among the Indians, and they will (if possible) Invade the Country." Brant feared that a renewed French influence might shake the western nations from their longtime allegiance to the British. He also ascribed some of the disillusionment among the Indians to "some new arrangements . . . in the Indian Department, which they are not acquainted with," adding, "they seem to be jealous."[73] The "new arrangements" to which Brant alluded most likely referred to both the reduction in the Indian budget and Elliott's dismissal. With the possibility of either the French or the Spanish having become active among the Indians, Brant could not think of a worse time for Britain to reduce its Indian commitments. Moreover, the Mohawk leader, who for several years had clamored to gain exclusive territorial rights and sovereignty for the Natives living at the Grand River Reserve, could enhance the Six Nations' sovereign status and possibly even improve his own position if the British were to once again acknowledge the Indians as indispensable allies. Matthew Elliott similarly predicted a French-led invasion into the upper province, originating from the upper Mississippi and Lake Superior.[74] Like Brant, Elliott had a vested interest in these matters, and his warnings of an invasion came at the very time that he submitted personal memorials to his superiors, listing his past services and hoping for reinstatement.[75]

When none of the dreaded western invasions materialized, Captain McLean took pleasure in discrediting the rumors, and the commandant pointed out that with the exception of Brant's, all the exaggerated reports seemed to filter through what he regarded as untrustworthy sources in the Indian Department's branch at his post. McLean charged that "these reports have without doubt originated with the Dept. themselves," for the purpose of adding "to their weight and influence in Upper Canada."[76] The commandant soon became more specific in his accusations when he discovered that one of the informants, a Shawnee chief, lived "with Mr. Elliott and is entirely under his influence, from which it may be easily conjectured how the reports are generated and the motives which gave rise to it [sic]."[77]

Without knowing for certain whether the reports contained any truth, McLean's haste to discount the stories tends to reveal his motives. In fact, according to previous British informants, Indians living on the Mississippi had already admitted that Spanish agents had made overtures to them a few years earlier. But McLean worried that the smallest threat of an invasion might create a wartime footing in which the officers in the Indian Department would once again have autonomy and control over Britain's frontier activity and Indian relations, a situation that would only increase the military spending allocated to the Indian budget at a time when McLean's superiors wanted him to reduce costs. In spite of his recent success against Matthew Elliott, McLean knew that he could still lose his struggle with the Indian Department if the department's officials convinced Lieutenant Governor Russell to acquiesce to their goals and to restore the Indian Department to its previous standing. Russell did not understand Indian affairs as well as his illustrious predecessor, John Graves Simcoe, and to a large degree the new administrator had to rely on the information and advice of his subordinates.[78] In McLean's mind, this made the lieutenant governor even more susceptible to being duped by those who wanted to "impose a belief on" Russell of "the importance of the Crisis . . . of a pretended invasion."[79] When Russell eventually ordered the captain not to withhold gifts or provisions from the Indians, the frustrated McLean fretted at how "astonished" he was that "Mr. President Russell has been deceived ... by false information from this quarter," but the captain agreed to comply with his orders and promised "that the Indians shall have whatever the Superintendant [*sic*] asks for them."[80]

Whether the province was ever in a state of danger by 1799 as Russell and Prescott feared is beyond knowing for certain. However, the future course of British-Indian relations had reached a crisis point at this critical time, and unbeknownst to most British leaders, the delicacy of Indian relations possibly even affected Britain's future hopes of remaining in Upper Canada. Although McLean believed that the Indians no longer had any bearing on the future of Britain's Canadian empire, higher British officials were not so sure. In any case, although the possibility of an enemy invasion from the West seemed remote, British leaders in Canada made the crucial decision not to let their relationship lapse with those Natives who lived in U.S. territory, a decision that would later pay dividends.

McLean's cooperation did not come any too soon. In early July 1799, barely two weeks after Russell ordered McLean to stop turning away Indians, a large delegation of Fox and Sauks from the upper Mississippi descended on Amherstburg. Apparently, this group of fifty warriors had discovered that the late Alexander McKee and others were concerned about the extent of Spanish influence among them, and the Indians therefore wanted to prove their loyalty by visiting their "Father" in order to "brighten and strengthen the Chain of Friendship" and to "strengthen the confederacy with our Brother Nations in this quarter."[81] McLean particularly resented tribes from distant regions who continued to rely on British gifts and provisions, but he must have taken some satisfaction when the Fox and Sauk delegation seemed to corroborate his repeated assertions that the invasion rumors from the West were all unfounded. Due to the deputation's unannounced visit and to the government's efforts to reduce expenses, Thomas McKee found little in the storehouse to give to the loyal sojourners, and the agent was forced to send them away "Naked" and unsatisfied, giving them only ammunition.[82]

The appearance of a large delegation at Fort Amherstburg from a distant region was significant. It demonstrated that in spite of a reduced Indian budget and weakening relations with the Miamis and Delawares, the British still held the fidelity of the nations where it mattered most at the time, in the Spanish borderlands. The presence of the Fox and Sauk visitors also indicated the effectiveness of messengers whom Alexander McKee had sent west within the previous year. British Indian policy from Amherstburg had been a success in that it had managed to maintain ties with groups from the southern Great Lakes all the way to the Mississippi Valley. The Fox and Sauk delegation went to Amherstburg to restore a relationship that seemed to be waning. At a time when British leaders hoped to lessen the government's Indian obligation, the distant Fox and Sauk tribes wanted to see a greater commitment from Britain, including a restoration of a wartime alliance.

In council with Thomas McKee, McLean, and other officers at Amherstburg, the Fox and Sauk emissaries reminded the British leaders of their peoples' attachment to the British cause during the American war and lamented that "our Father did not consider us in the Peace he made." Nevertheless, the western delegation faithfully contended that "we have never considered any as our Father but one," and "should you require our services, you may send for us." Hardly viewing themselves as a neutral power, the chiefs also asked specifically for British traders to be sent to their country, because "we desire no benefit from the Americans, neither in presents [n]or in the way of trade."[83] Had he survived, the late Alexander McKee would have taken much delight in witnessing this scene and hearing these words of loyalty from nations so distant. In part, the continued British influence among them stands as a tribute to his life's work.[84] Yet his son, Thomas, knew that the Fox and Sauk professions "of their Ancient attachment to Great Britain" would not continue unless his superiors saw "the propriety and necessity of treating all Nations as well distant as present with every mark of regard & friendship."[85]

Others of Britain's former Indian allies also reaffirmed their friendship and loyalty at this time, hoping to continue the past relationship with their British Father. Just a month after the Fox and Sauks visited Amherstburg, the principal Wyandot chiefs from Brownstown and Sandusky also held an important council there. The Wyandots at both communities, though ostensibly neutral regarding Britain and the United States after 1795, remained on cordial terms with the British. These leaders, while protesting the Amherstburg garrison's excessive cutting of timber on Bois Blanc Island and elsewhere, used the council to affirm a permanent bond between them and the British. Moreover, the Wyandots, formerly the first nation in the Western Confederacy in times of war, claimed to still speak for the leaders of the triumvirate of neighboring nations, "those of the Ottawas, Chippawas, and Poutawatamies."[86] In the name of all four nations, the Wyandot leaders then offered a large gift of land lying adjacent to the town's district, enabling the garrison to continue gathering necessary timber and firewood. The delegation wanted the king to know of their faithfulness and generosity; as a token of their gift, they gave four strings of black wampum, to "be seen by our Great Father beyond the Great Lake."[87] However, like the Fox and Sauks before them, the Wyandots also wanted evidence of continued good faith on the part of their longtime European ally, concluding their speech with an appeal to "receive . . . what you have always given us."[88]

In this context of affairs, Blue Jacket, formerly one of the most important leaders of the Western Confederacy, once again demonstrated his support for the British after living quietly for several years. In August 1800, barely five years since he had repudiated his British military commission and signed the Treaty of Greenville, the aging Shawnee leader secretly met with Thomas McKee.[89] McKee, the man who had once threatened to kill Blue Jacket for making peace with the Americans, now listened attentively as the old warrior disclosed private information entrusted to him by the American commandant at Detroit, who predicted an alliance between France and the United States.[90] Thomas Hunt, the American officer, apparently expected Blue Jacket to return to Detroit bearing key information from his interview with

McKee. Though Blue Jacket found himself in a position to act as a double agent, his loyalties seemed to fall with the British, for he potentially had much to lose by confiding in McKee. The Shawnee continued to receive annuity payments from the American government, and he had a "Son at School among them [the Americans]."[91] Blue Jacket may have anticipated another Anglo-American war, or, like other Natives in the southern Lakes region, he may have begun to grow dissatisfied with the Americans and thought that the British might once again be useful if such a struggle were to occur. Thus, in a sense, Captain Hector McLean had been right. While at peace with the Americans, the British really had nothing to fear from the Indians, and even if another Anglo-American war should commence, Britain's former allies, being "rather prejudiced against the Americans," would once again gravitate toward the British.[92]

The eighteenth century ended with the future of British-Indian relations uncertain. Alexander McKee's death in January 1799, an irreparable loss, symbolized the state of British-Indian affairs at the time. The illustrious leader's passing further indicated the Indian Department's loss of status and power. Yet the Indians among whom McKee had labored for so long demonstrated their devotion to their late adopted kinsman, just as they continued to proclaim their loyalty to the king. In a separate ceremony several months after McKee's extravagant funeral, hundreds of Indians wanted to pay their own respects. In a ritual conducted at the gravesite, located on the property of Thomas McKee (a couple of miles north of the fort), these faithful friends danced for well over twenty-four hours in honor of their late brother, "White Elk." Thomas and several of the officers from Fort Malden, recognizing the supreme tribute intended by those conducting the ritual, are said to have joined in the dancing. Simon Girty later recalled that in all of his many years among the Indians of the Ohio frontier and the Western District of Upper Canada, only twice before had he witnessed ceremonies that rivaled this one. Girty also claimed that the Indians would only bestow such an honor on "men of distinction among them."[93]

In honoring Alexander McKee, the Indians lamented that they would never again know such a distinguished leader or a friend who was so mindful of their interests, and they recognized this as the passing of an era. In the decade after 1794, these peoples saw themselves reduced from a formidable ally of Great Britain, a nation that once supported their cause, to a dispossessed set of refugees who had become wards of the state. McLean had even tried to make them less than that. With McKee gone and Elliott forced out of service, Britain's former Native allies no longer knew what to expect. Yet in spite of their hardship and suffering, thousands of Indians from the former alliance along the Detroit frontier and Upper Canada steadfastly clung to the idea of maintaining the old Chain of Friendship, hoping to preserve a remnant of a passing way of life.

3

British-Indian Relations in the North, 1796–1802

Jay's Treaty required the British to withdraw from Mackinac Island in the summer of 1796, but they strategically established a new post at nearby St. Joseph Island. Britain had multiple reasons for deciding to maintain a presence in the area. Like the old post at Mackinac, Fort St. Joseph continued to protect the British fur trade, as the North West Company and its competitors continued to expand farther west and into the Mississippi Valley. A northern military post also served diplomatic and strategic purposes. At St. Joseph, the British could continue relations with Natives who lived in the western Great Lakes, the upper Mississippi Valley, and even the northwest regions in the direction of Lake Winnipeg and the Red River. This vital link would enable the Crown to foster ties with the northern Ojibwas and Ottawas, Winnebagoes, Menominees, Fox, Sauks, and Dakota Sioux. This chapter describes the most distinctive cultural and political traits of some of these groups and examines the evolution of British-Indian relations in the North.

Like the previous post at Mackinac, Fort St. Joseph remained isolated from much of the rest of the upper country; no sailing vessels or communication could pass to or from these places for several months out of every year when weather and ice made navigation impossible. Although remote and isolated, the outpost held significant geographic importance. Since 1763, Mackinac had served as the westernmost military post and, later, Indian agency, in a long, thin line of communication that stretched eastward all the way back to Halifax, then across the Atlantic to Whitehall in London. Mackinac rested on the edge of an empire, and Britain's sphere of influence north and west of the Great Lakes depended on a continued British presence there. Without a military presence west of this site, only private civilians and fur trade interests existed among the Indians deeper in the western hinterlands. Thus British control of the Straits of Mackinac protected channels of commerce with traders, both British and French, who lived in places scattered throughout the regions of present-day Wisconsin, Minnesota, and Manitoba. Some of these key locations included Prairie du Chien, La Baye (Green Bay), Arbre Croche (Little Traverse Bay), the Falls of St. Anthony (Minneapolis), Fond du Lac (Duluth), the Red River (of Lake Winnipeg), Milwaukee, the St. Joseph River of southern Lake Michigan, and elsewhere. Furthermore, by remaining on the Straits of Mackinac, British authorities could more easily monitor activity to and from the key portages that separated the water networks of the Great Lakes and the tributaries of the Mississippi.[1] Any potential French or Spanish invasion from the Mississippi would in all likelihood cross the Wisconsin-Fox portage before slipping through the Mackinac corridor and attacking Upper Canada from the rear.

British-Indian Relations in the North Prior to 1796

Prior to 1796, British policy in the North, compared to that in other regions, was characterized by relative indifference on the part of the British leaders. The years of warfare in the Ohio country and the Treaty of Greenville had had little effect on the northern tribes, and these groups did not rely on the annuities that the American government distributed to Indians living near Detroit and northern Ohio. The predominant tribes of the region—most important, the Ottawas and Ojibwas—continued close ties with the British at St. Joseph. These tribes' villages dotted the shores and tributaries of Lakes Huron, Michigan, and Superior; the Ottawas' main village of Arbre

Croche was situated at the northeast end of Lake Michigan, near Little Traverse Bay, and the principal Ojibwa village sites included Sault Ste. Marie and Chequamegon, the latter resting on the southwest end of Lake Superior.[2] Other tribal groups that less frequently visited the post at St. Joseph included the Menominees, Winnebagoes, Santee Sioux (Dakotas), and Sauks. These nations' contact with British officials and traders from St. Joseph, especially in the case of the Dakotas, who were frequently at war with the Ottawas and Ojibwas, often occurred at outposts run by the North West Company and other trading companies in Indian lands far from Fort St. Joseph.[3] British leaders and the Indians of the northern Lakes both considered the region of the Mackinac Straits and the surrounding area to be of vital importance. As late as the War of 1812, Sir George Prevost, governor-general of Canada and commander in chief of British forces in North America, wrote to Earl Bathurst, explaining the continued significance of holding Mackinac:

The Island and Fort of Michilimackinac is of the first importance as tending to promote our Indian connexion and secure them in our interest; its geographical position is admirable; its influence extends and is felt among the Indian Tribes to New Orleans and the Pacific Ocean: vast tracts of country look to it for protection and supplies: and it gives security to the great trading establishments of the North-West and Hudson's Bay Companies by supporting the Indians in the Mississippi, the only barrier which interposes between them and the enemy.[4] From these observations Your Lordship will be enabled to judge how necessary the possession of this valuable post, situated on the outskirts of these extensive provinces, is daily becoming [for] their future security and position.[5]

The governor-general's remarks, while exaggerated in places, indicated the importance the British leadership in Canada placed on possessing Mackinac and its vicinity. Although written in 1814, Prevost's statement echoed a diplomatic perspective that had been central to vintage British strategy in the North since the 1780s, when leaders at Whitehall and Quebec viewed Britain's continued presence in the Northwest as essential for both the security of Upper Canada and the control of the Mississippi Valley.[6]

Long before Euro-Americans ventured into the region, the Ottawa and Ojibwa peoples in the vicinity of Mackinac regarded the area as vital to their interests, and possibly even necessary for their survival. For them, the region held spiritual, cosmological, and historical meaning. According to one myth, the island of Michilimackinac became the first piece of land restored by the manitous after the Great Flood, and consequently the home of the first peoples, or the Anishnabeg, ancestors to the Ojibwas, Ottawas, and Potawatomis. Later, the Great Spirit, or Gitchimanitou (also Kitche Manitou), sent an emissary, Nanabush, to dwell among the Anishnabeg people at Mackinac Island and to instruct them on how to live.[7] The people of these three nations descending from the Anishnabeg believed that the general vicinity of Mackinac was a perpetual source of power or metaphysical strength. Writing a history of his people, early Ottawa historian Andrew J. Blackbird told of a separate race of people known as the Mishinemackinawgos who dwelled on the island, and from whom the locale took its name, apparently after the Anishnabeg left. The Senecas then came and annihilated all but two of the Mishinemackinawgos, a pair of young lovers who escaped and became spirit beings who assisted the Ottawas and Ojibwas. According to Blackbird, "Whoever would be so fortunate as to meet and see them and to talk with them, such person would always become a prophet to his people, either Ottawa or Chippewa [Ojibwa]." Blackbird maintained that "every Ottawa and Chippewa believe to this day [1887] that they are still in existence and roaming in the wildest part of the land."[8]

According to traditional Anishnabeg beliefs, Michilimackinac also marks the core or focal point from which the three nations diverged in their separate routes of migration.[9] Eventually the Ojibwas, numbering far more than the Ottawas and Potawatomis combined, lived mainly in the regions that became Michigan's Upper Peninsula, Saginaw Bay, northern Wisconsin, southern Canada, and eventually northern Minnesota. The Ottawas dwelled largely in the northwestern part of Michigan and on Manitoulin Island, while the Potawatomis, farther south, occupied the regions of present-day southern Michigan, northern Indiana, northern Illinois, and southeastern Wisconsin.[10] By the mid-sixteenth century, this diaspora took the Ojibwas from northern Michigan into the areas of Lake Superior, where they initially encountered stiff resistance from multiple enemies, usually Fox and Dakotas, while still fending off occasional Iroquois war parties as well. These encounters touched off centuries of hostilities between the Ojibwas and the Dakotas, but according to William Warren, mixed-blood Ojibwa historian of the nineteenth century, his ancestors gradually prevailed, "gaining foot by foot" as they pushed onward "along the southern shores of the Great Lake [Superior]."[11] In about 1680, from within this conquered territory, the Ojibwas established a religious and cultural center, forming their principal western village of Chequamegon and uniting all of their bands into a single and distinct people.[12]

Prior to the end of the seventeenth century, this new site became the core location of the Ojibwa Grand Medicine Society, also known as the Midewiwin, an order of medicine men supposedly endowed with extraordinary spiritual power and wisdom. The movement may have constituted a religious revitalization movement, or may have been a conservative cultural response to years of warfare, migration, and initial European contact.[13] Henry Rowe Schoolcraft, nineteenth-century ethnologist and U.S. Indian agent, described this society as "an association of men who profess the highest knowledge known to the tribes," whose primary purpose "is to teach the higher doctrines of spiritual existence, their nature and mode of existence, and the influence they exercise among men."[14] These religious leaders could potentially wield much power over others, and the Ojibwas both feared and revered them. The priests of the Midewiwin generally instructed, healed, and called on the manitous for favors and blessings, but they remained secretive regarding the full extent of their power and actions.[15] By the mid-eighteenth century, the Midewiwin created social cohesion among the scattered Ojibwa bands, consisting of as many as twenty-five thousand people who dwelled in the northern Great Lakes region prior to the British arrival at Michilimackinac.[16] Though the Ojibwas recognized no form of external authority and had no central polity, Chequamegon, the Midewiwin's place of origin, became a de facto center of tribal activity and interaction.[17] Schoolcraft later pointed out that the Midewiwin gave the Ojibwa a sense of "national pride," and he even referred to it as a "grand national society."[18] The Midewiwin's authority was such that one observer concluded that the Ojibwas' civil affairs were "much mixed with their religious and medicinal practices."[19]

The unifying effect of the Midewiwin and the resulting clusters of northern Ojibwa communities helped to facilitate the tribe's interaction with Europeans. The French who arrived in the late seventeenth century and the British who replaced them in 1761 showed a keen awareness of Ojibwa society by establishing posts at the primary sites of Ojibwa culture and commerce: Michilimackinac, Chequamegon, and La Baye (Green Bay).[20] By the time of the British arrival, the previous century's trade and interaction between the Indians and the French had significantly altered Ojibwa lifestyles, making them reliant on European goods. The Ojibwa success in wiping out the British garrison at Michilimackinac during Pontiac's Conspiracy was not a true index of the tribe's circumstances after such a long history of contact and trade with Europeans. In 1765, when trader Alexander Henry visited Chequamegon, a place he "regarded as the metropolis of the . . . O'chibbuoy," he found the people there naked, starving, and desperate. No longer did these northerners want to expel the British from their country; rather, they wanted to reinstate the fur trade, and they compelled Henry to extend them credit in goods "to the amount of three thousand beaver-skins." His Ojibwa hosts at Chequamegon claimed that without the immediate use of Henry's merchandise, "their wives and children would perish."[21] Eager for trade, the Ojibwas at the island of La Pointe, adjacent to the peninsula of Chequamegon, sent deputations in 1764 and 1765 to Sir William Johnson at Niagara, seeking peace and requesting a restoration of the fur trade.[22] The British soon regarrisoned Fort Mackinac, and numerous independent traders, following in Henry's path, began to barter and live among the Ojibwas and Ottawas. This began a period dominated by individual traders in the North that lasted until 1783–84, when the North West Company was organized.

The fur trade became even more deeply entrenched in the North by the 1790s. The third article of Jay's Treaty between Britain and the United States in 1794 permitted the British, Americans, and Indians "to pass and repass" to either side of the border for the purpose of "trade and commerce," ensuring that the British would continue to dominate the fur trade and thereby maintain their nation's longtime influence and intervention in Native communities.[23] Pro-British traders enjoyed greater influence among their clients, and the latter generally tried to maintain good faith with the traders (that is, make good on their credit and provide them with shelter at times) and to generally assist the traders in every way possible, enabling them to remain in operation near their villages. Traders also depended heavily on the Indians, who acted as crucial middlemen in the trading process, leading to some degree of mutual interdependence.[24] Consequently, the traders came to be trusted friends and sometimes kinsmen. Most of the traders either married Indian women or took them as mistresses, and nearly all of the men who actively traded with the North West Company at one time or another lived with a Native woman in some capacity.[25] All of these factors gave traders a certain degree of political power among the peoples whom they served.[26] Particularly among the Ojibwas, a nation without any central polity or unifying element apart from its Midewiwin religion, traders could enjoy significant de facto authority among smaller bands of followers. A trader at times could even induce the members of his retinue to attack an enemy or a rival.

From the Ojibwas' perspective, the fur trade benefited all parties. With virtually no restrictions placed on fur traders in the Great Lakes region during the later eighteenth and early nineteenth centuries, the Ojibwas received favored treatment from competing fur trade interests and individuals who paid reasonable and competitive prices. During the trade's heyday, particularly between 1790 and 1811, traders at times even extended credit to their clients and distributed additional alcohol among them, which the Indians considered a valuable article in spite of its negative effects. Also, the more successful trading groups such as the North West Company and its temporary rival (from 1798 to 1804), the XY Company, established posts nearer to Indian communities in order to better accommodate their customers.[27] Although the trade would eventually work to impoverish the Natives as they increasingly depended on European goods, the Ojibwas and Ottawas briefly prospered during the trade's zenith, and at the turn of the nineteenth century they had an abundance of material goods, including guns, ammunition, clothes, blankets, kettles, utensils, knives, and cloth; they sometimes demonstrated their wealth by adorning themselves in jewelry, silver brooches, and scarlet cloth.[28]

Ties through trade meant much more than an economic exchange; the Indians also viewed it as a form of mutual reciprocity, indicating a level of trust, friendship, and loyalty. John Tanner, the famed thirty-year captive among the Ojibwas, felt betrayed when a lone trader denied him standard credit that he needed to procure blankets for his wife and family before the onslaught of winter.[29] It should not have mattered that the Ojibwas had less to offer in a material exchange; as long as they continued to profess and demonstrate their loyalty and devotion, the traders had an obligation to meet their needs. The Ojibwas and Ottawas extended this understanding of a two-sided, mutual obligation far beyond their connections with the traders; they perceived all of their relations with the British in this context. Furthermore, they understood the role of a father as that of someone who would take pity on them and care for them, regardless of how destitute or dependent they became. The Indians believed that their condition should never alter that role, or lessen the responsibility of their British Father. As a captive youth, Tanner described his relationship with his adopted Ojibwa father, Tawgaweninne, explaining that the latter "was always indulgent and kind to me, treating me like an equal, rather than as a dependant." Tawgaweninne provided for all of Tanner's hunting needs, and when the youth failed in his attempts to construct marten traps, Tanner recalled, "my father began to pity me . . . [s]o he went out and spent a day in making a large number of traps, which he gave me, and then I was able to take as many martins [*sic*] as the others."[30] Tanner understood that his adopted parents both loved him, but his mother bore the separate responsibility of disciplining him, while his father's role was to protect, guide, and assist his son.

Tanner's experience hints at how his adopted family and the Ojibwas in general viewed their familial ties with the British: a provider from whom they could expect pity and assistance. Some studies have shown that Ojibwas approached powerful and wealthy whites in the same manner that they would address a manitou, doing so with a gracious and humble disposition.[31] Whether seeking a vision or a material necessity, Ojibwas always appealed to the pity of a manitou or spirit guardian. Similarly, they could potentially share in the power of traders and agents by petitioning them accordingly, believing that some whites held significant influence among the manitous.[32] In his memoirs, Alexander Henry recalled that his Ojibwa captors believed that he possessed a certain foreknowledge of events and became suspicious of him when he denied their assertion.[33] Moreover, the northern Indians looked upon British agents and traders as servants of the British king, a distant person whom they regarded as a near deity, one who would always consider their needs and take pity on them. From his missionary work among the Ojibwas and Ottawas of Michigan during the 1820s, Peter Jones noted:

> The ideas entertained by the Indians generally of the King of England, with regard to his power riches, and knowledge, are most extravagant. They imagine his power to be absolute, and

his authority unlimited; that his word is law, to which all his subjects bow with implicit obedience. . . . They also consider that his riches and benevolence are unbounded, the whole resources of the kingdom being at his command, a portion of which he grants to those of his subjects who are needy. With regard to his wisdom, they conceive that he knows everything that is going on in the world; that even the speech or talk of an Indian chief delivered to a Superintendent of Indian Affairs in the wilds of Canada is made known to him.[34]

For their deference and devotion to British agents and authorities, the Ojibwas and Ottawas expected much in return, and according to St. Joseph's storekeeper, Thomas Duggan, often "the sole purport of their speeches was begging their Father would shew them Charity."[35] By reciprocating with lavish amounts of provisions, Duggan and his cohorts then fulfilled their fatherly responsibilities. In keeping with Tanner's description of his own foster father, the northern Indians expected the British to act as a genuine father by providing for his children and treating them as "equal[s], rather than as . . . dependant[s]," even when the power in such a relationship was skewed to one side.[36] Despite the minimal worth of the items that the northern Natives gave to the British, the actual act of exchanging gifts was more important to the Indians. It symbolized deeper ties and commitments than that of a mere economic partnership.[37]

British participants saw gift-giving from a different perspective. The officers in the North and West hoped to reinforce the Indians' belief that they participated as pseudo-equal partners by using official gift-exchanges, which often took place in formal council settings. The British conducted these events with much solemnity and always in the presence of the post's officers, who wore full-dress uniforms. Not really needing any material items from the Indians, and hardly thinking themselves under any obligation to continue to grant provisions, the British considered all distributions of gifts as an investment of sorts in the expectation of future Native support and loyalty. This represents a slightly different rationale than the one to which the Indians were accustomed; the Natives would have regarded their gifts as both compensation for past services and as a loving father's act of benevolence. In truth, however, promises of future Native fidelity made these exchanges more equal than the Indians' past services or any tangible gifts from them ever could. Lord Dorchester understood this principle, and in 1787 he considered the future benefits that could be derived from the Indians by psychologically making them dependent upon the British. The governor-general ordered that on every occasion, the Indians' "requests if reasonable, are to be complied with. Should they, as is customary on these occasions, lay down Presents of any kind, they are to be taken up with thanks, and in return, Presents exceeding the value of theirs are to be given, in which case the Chiefs are always to be distinguished."[38] The sobering and subtle truth in this policy was that, despite the guise of mutual reciprocity, these gift distributions, and any form of British trade for that matter, could be terminated at any moment. Among Dorchester's opening remarks in his new policy of 1787, he instructed his agents to assure "the Indian Nations . . . of the King's paternal care and regard as long as they continue to merit them, by acting as good and obedient Children ought to do."[39]

Ultimately, British-Indian relations in the North would more closely epitomize what Dorchester envisioned, in contrast to the course of British-Indian diplomacy elsewhere in Upper Canada. Unlike the other regions discussed in this study, the diplomacy in the North was marked by a period of continuity from 1783 until long after the War of 1812. Although British leaders and northern Indians may have interpreted their relationship differently, both sides, relatively unaffected by events to the south, sought a continuation of previous ties. Though some Ojibwas and Ottawas from the greater Detroit region had fought against Anthony Wayne, most groups farther north did not fully share in the military defeat of the Miamis, Shawnees, Delawares, and Wyandots at Fallen Timbers, a defeat that resulted in the loss of British trade and influence in the region of Detroit and southward. Pro-U.S. chiefs there who had signed the Treaty of Greenville, such as Tarhe, Little Turtle, and Black Hoof, came to rely on U.S. annuities and dealt with traders licensed by the American government.[40] The continuity of the British fur trade in the North did much to maintain long-standing British-Indian relations there, and the traders benefited from these consistent diplomatic and commercial ties. However, the British government did not view the trade itself as a reason to continue ties with the Natives or to maintain a presence in the region. The Crown partially subsidized the fur trade, and even at its peak, the enterprise never offset the expenses Britain incurred by governing the region and supplying the Indians' material needs.[41] Furthermore, the fur trade is not what gave the Indians diplomatic leverage in their dealings with British leaders. It was the British desire for future Native fidelity that prompted Dorchester to attempt to ingratiate the Natives, and in the North the Indians' loyalty was never in question.

British-Indian relations in the North grew stronger in spite of the two sides' differing perspectives on the meaning of those bonds. Ojibwas and Ottawas at St. Joseph continued to view British gifts as marks of their father's benevolence, generosity, and rewards for past services; the lopsided mismatch of any exchange did not matter. The Ojibwas and Ottawas believed that by giving any small gift, and by doing so in an attitude of humility and loyalty, they merited the gifts the British gave them. In this sense, the Indians did not merely consider British presents as free gifts. This strong Indian notion of reciprocity was lost on Captain Peter Drummond, commandant at St. Joseph, in an incident late in 1799. After two Ottawa bands from Arbre Croche visited his post in October, Drummond commented to his superiors, "I cannot comprehend what they [the Ottawas] mean by saying they never receive presents at this Post, but rather buys [sic] what they get." Yet in the same letter Drummond acknowledged that "the Ottawas receive much larger presents in proportion to their numbers than any other Indians, in some respects they deserve it, as they present more sugar & corn for the use of government than any other Indians."[42] Drummond did not grasp that the Ottawas viewed their relationship with the British as one based on bartering and kinship.

Differences between Indian and British understandings of the gift exchange could lead to confusion, conflict, and, in the 1780s and 1790s, corrupt dealings. The northern Indians' insistence on a relationship of reciprocity helped to encourage a string of abuses in the Indian Department that spanned many years. Some Indian agents at Mackinac and St. Joseph's, realizing that the Indians there expected to trade something for their gifts, attempted to profit from the situation. Once the formal councils had ended, the poverty-ridden Natives traded for additional goods from the Indian store with packs of furs and additional gifts of corn. John Dease, cousin of department superintendent Sir John Johnson, eventually lost his position as Indian agent for receiving bartered goods and furs from the Indians in this manner. Johnson had originally sent Dease to Mackinac in 1786, hoping that his cousin could negotiate a peace between the Dakotas and Ojibwas, who were constantly at war. Dease not only failed in that difficult task, but he came under fire for allegedly embezzling goods from the Indian store and conducting personal trade with Ojibwas and other tribes in the Great Lakes and Upper Mississippi. Dease's activities came to light not because of Indian complaints, but because those attempting to trade legally complained that Dease competed unfairly in this market, underselling them by bartering stolen government goods.[43] Due to inconclusive evidence and contradictory reports, Dease gained an acquittal.[44] Yet he never regained his post in the Indian Department, nor did his powerful cousin clamor for his reinstatement.[45]

Dease's activities most likely influenced Lord Dorchester's decision in 1787 to expressly forbid all "persons belonging to, or employed in the Indian Department" from being "permitted to trade, directly or indirectly, or to have any share, profit, or concern therein."[46] Nevertheless, subsequent storekeepers Charles Gauthier and Thomas Duggan continued to abuse the system by lending stores to traders, appropriating the goods for their own use, and/or using them to barter for furs and other goods.[47] Eventually, Duggan's unscrupulous behavior became excessive, causing the Indians to complain and leading to the storekeeper's suspension in 1802.[48] Until then, however, British army officers at Mackinac and St. Joseph had been more lax about monitoring the distribution of Indian goods at their posts. These conditions at Fort St. Joseph during the closing years of the century contrasted the rigid regulations implemented at Amherstburg at the time, and the activities of Gauthier and Duggan were reminiscent of Matthew Elliott's peculation prior to Captain Hector McLean's crackdown at the latter post. The fact that the officers and agents at St. Joseph continued to conduct Indian affairs in a loose manner is indicative of the continuity in British-Indian relations in the North, and British-Indian ties remained steady there as the fur trade continued to expand in the 1790s. As of 1796, the trade's negative repercussions and the corruption in the Indian Department at St. Joseph had not yet become issues deemed worthy of scrutiny, and in the meantime neither the northern Indians nor the British wanted to alter the nature of their relationship, which had existed for decades.

An incident that occurred in the autumn of 1796, shortly after the British had moved their northern garrison to St. Joseph Island, indicated the Native desire for continuity. In early October, Duggan noted the arrival of an Ojibwa chief, Meatoosikee, who came to apologize for his band's rough treatment of some traders who had visited his village late the previous year. Duggan did not indicate the cause of the frustration of Meatoosike's band, but the incident occurred around the time of the series of events that included the Treaty of Greenville, Jay's Treaty, and the subsequent British withdrawal from the American posts. Whatever the reason for Meatoosike's village's temporary displeasure with the British, this band soon came to understand its need for traders' goods. Duggan warned "that if they [Meatoosike's band] should ever be guilty of the like again the Traders would be taken from them." Meatoosikee "hoped his father would have compassion on him and forgive him and his Young Men and that They would be sure to listen to their Father's advice in [the] future and be good Children."[49] Thus, regardless of changes that had occurred on the frontier in the late eighteenth century, Meatoosikee, like most of his northern brethren, sought to maintain the long-standing ties between his people and the British.

The continuity in the North at this time stood in stark contrast to circumstances at Amherstburg 350 miles to the south, where only remnants of the shattered Western Confederacy still sought to maintain their Chain of Friendship with the British. A few of the pro-British Shawnee and Delaware bands had removed to new homes in Upper Canada by 1796, but a large number of the former confederates in the greater Maumee Valley would now be receiving American annuities at Detroit and Fort Wayne.[50] The Ojibwas and Ottawas in the North did not warmly welcome the arrival of the Americans at Mackinac, and unless these northern bands made annual pilgrimages to Detroit, they would not share in their tribal annuity disbursements from the Americans, which went to those bands dwelling nearer to Detroit and the Western District of Upper Canada. Therefore, the northern groups did not cultivate the ties with the Americans like some of the bands living in the regions of Detroit, Brownstown, and northwest Ohio. The tribes in the northern Great Lakes never considered themselves partisan to the confederacy's defeat at Fallen Timbers, and they no longer held a common interest with their former allies to the south. Furthermore, the bitterness felt between the northern Indians from Mackinac and Saginaw and the southern Maumee tribes, which had resulted from their quarrel during the campaign against Fort Recovery in the summer of 1794, probably still lingered.[51] Finally, the fur trade would continue to support the peoples living in the North for some time, whereas the regions of Detroit and northern Ohio were experiencing a steady decline in the fur trade that had begun decades earlier.[52] These divergent paths would continue to shape British-Indian relations in the two regions.

The North, 1796–1802

When the British withdrew from Fort Mackinac in the summer of 1796, neither they nor the Indians of the region fully knew what to expect from these changes. Aware of how the United States had recently expanded into the Ohio country and had attempted to usurp Britain's role as the Indians' overseer and protector, the northern tribes were understandably alarmed. What would become of the British? Would this signal the decline of the British fur trade? Did these changes indicate that British influence in general would decline in the North? Would the area Indians now deal with two fathers? Despite these initial concerns, British-Indian relations in the North proved as stable as ever during the next several years, and the North West Company had some of its best returns during this period, hardly feeling the effect of American competition as company men and other British traders expanded deeper into Spanish and American territory.

In June 1796, as the British prepared to evacuate Mackinac in the ensuing weeks, the Ojibwas and Ottawas grew concerned regarding the departing officers and personnel. These Native visitors believed that the moral obligations of a father bound him to those who depended upon his provisions. On his final visit to Mackinac while it was yet under British sovereignty, Amable, an Ottawa chief, expressed his "concern for the English evacuating the upper Posts, and his apprehension of his Nation being abandoned by them and left to the mercy of the Big knives."[53] Once Amable and the Indians in the area learned that the British intended to maintain a presence in the North, they were no longer distressed; they realized that their relationship with their British Father could continue as it always had, and they would not be compelled to deal with the American newcomers. Yet until the Indians knew for certain that their relations with the British would not change, the situation remained tense.

Initially, things appeared grim to the British as well, and they worried about the local Natives' response. Major William Doyle, former commandant at Mackinac, even wondered if the Indians would commit hostilities against British troops. In the summer of 1796, when Doyle and his garrison were relieved by a very small force ordered to take command at Fort St. Joseph in June, the commandant expressed his concern to Lieutenant Governor Peter Russell. Doyle feared that Indian discontent in the North would increase once the Natives realized that the British intended to maintain only a token military force of a dozen soldiers at St. Joseph, a post relatively smaller than Mackinac. Such a reduction in strength, when compared to the growing American military presence at Mackinac and the Old Northwest, would probably be interpreted as a sign of British weakness and a possible harbinger of a complete British withdrawal from the upper country. Russell relayed Doyle's concerns to Governor-General Robert Prescott, fearing that such circumstances in the North "may lead to contempt [by the Indians], contempt to insult (for it is well known that Savages are ever influenced by appearances) and should insult once begin, no man can say when it may end. In Short Major Doyle thinks that Ensign Brown and his small party are in very serious danger, from the present temper of the neighboring Indians."[54] Prescott immediately responded to this alarming news by sending an additional detachment of forty soldiers to reinforce the post at St. Joseph Island.

Doyle's fears proved unfounded. The departing officer had most likely witnessed a brief spasm of frustration by bands visiting Mackinac Island and by groups who probably had just learned that the British intended to leave the site. Only days prior to the evacuation of Mackinac Island, and therefore very close to the time of Doyle's alarming report, Duggan wrote, "I was given to understand that the Indians would be very troublesome here in the Spring and Summer; I am happy to tell You, that it is quite the contrary, and that They have been since last fall to this Moment remarkably quiet."[55]

Far from wanting to destroy Ensign Brown and his handful of troops, the Natives hoped to preserve a relationship that had existed for more than a generation. As the weather grew colder in the autumn of 1796, and with the small British garrison facing its first winter at St. Joseph, Ogaw, an Ojibwa leader, promised the officers that "he would protect us against any Bad people who wanted to disturb us[,] that they knew no other than their English Father[,] that They would never go to see the Big Knives [Americans] and would winter near us to protect us."[56] Ogaw shrewdly implied that the British also depended on the Ojibwas, suggesting that their relationship was one of mutual benefit. Early in 1797, the leader of an Ottawa delegation at St. Joseph's picked up on the same theme, proclaiming to Duggan and the officers, "I hold you by the hand and I'll never let it go, I shall be always near You ready to assist you if you should want me—here is the mark of my Tribe presenting the Belt[.] All my Nation seeing it will know it and assist you in time[s] of trouble." In keeping with Dorchester's instructions, the following day the post commandant responded in council, promising continued aid to the Indians but making it plain that the British were the more powerful party in the relationship.[57]

By the following summer of 1797, new post commandant Captain Peter Drummond reported that "the Indians in this Quarter, visits [sic] this Post, the same as they formerly did at Michilimackinac, and appears [sic] to be as friendly as usual."[58] Clearly, British apprehension regarding Native discontent had been exaggerated.[59] When reporting to Storekeeper General Joseph Chew the following summer, Duggan, while conceding that "our Indian Friends" did not have "a favourable opinion of us at the time of our Evacuating the Post at Michilimackinac," also reported that "they appear to be as much attached to us as ever, & I have the pleasure of informing you that the Indians since our coming to this Post [June 1796] have conducted themselves entirely to our satisfaction." If these statements were correct, then only days prior to the British evacuation of Mackinac Island the northern Indians were not at all displeased, and they expressed no dissatisfaction in the immediate wake of the occupation of St. Joseph Island.[60]

Once both the British and their Native allies got over the apprehensions prompted by the British withdrawal from their former posts mandated by Jay's Treaty, and once both had declared that they wanted to remain friendly after the move, a variety of issues unique to the St. Joseph's milieu surfaced for British policy makers. Four such issues arose in which conditions at Fort St. Joseph required distinctly different policies from those at Amherstburg. First, St. Joseph's military officers intervened in tribal affairs to appoint chiefs, a practice the Natives in St. Joseph's sphere of influence accepted. By contrast, it would have been unusual for British officials at Amherstburg to appoint tribal leaders, and any effort to do so would have offended Native sensibilities. Second, authority over Indian affairs, for reasons particular to the area, shifted from officers of the Indian Department to military officers much more rapidly at Fort St. Joseph than at Amherstburg. Third, the threat of competition from, or military action by, Britain's French and Spanish imperial rivals was greater at St. Joseph than at Amherstburg. Finally, intertribal rivalries unique to St. Joseph's sphere of influence, most notably hostility between the Ojibwas and the Dakota Sioux, posed a significant challenge to the British goal of maintaining peace among Britain's Indian trading partners and allies.

Army officers at St. Joseph enjoyed more influence in the affairs of the Ojibwas and Ottawas dispersed throughout the region than the officers at Amherstburg exhibited in their dealings near Detroit and even Brownstown. The northern Natives who so readily gave their allegiance to the traders among them also extended their loyalty to the officers and military personnel in the upper country. The Natives well understood that the post commandants and Indian agents served as the king's representatives and thereby possessed the power to remove the traders at any time. The Ojibwas and Ottawas carried this loyalty even further. They not only demonstrated an eagerness to obey military officers and Indian agents, but they also sought to derive their authority and political power over their own bands from the British.[61] In their egalitarian society, which lacked a clearly defined political infrastructure, northern Ottawas and Ojibwas grew accustomed to the notion of British-recognized leaders among them.[62] British officials installed or recognized chiefs by giving them medals and sometimes flags or officers' gorgets. The Native leaders appreciated these symbols of honor and authority, and they viewed them as a continuation of a practice begun by the French and one necessary to maintain their relationship with the British who succeeded the former power. One Ottawa leader, Eethsaguam, specifically asked for a medal to replace the "one he got in the time of the French."[63]

In the same manner, the northern Natives also looked to British

officers and Indian agents to remove a chief if necessary. On one occasion at St. Joseph's in the summer of 1798, during which time a
group of Ottawa leaders received medals, this delegation requested
that the officers remove from authority one of their fellow Ottawa
leaders (also present at the council) for having murdered some fellow
villagers at Arbre Croche. Significantly, the Ottawa delegation themselves did not attempt to remove the dishonored leader, but Duggan
wrote that interpreter "Mr. Langlade" took the guilty chief's medal
"from him at the desire of all the other Chiefs present for murdering
two of their Own Nation[,] One of them a Chief."[64] Apparently, the
chiefs had specifically sought the authority of Captain Drummond,
who in turn ordered Langlade to strip the chief of his medal.[65] The
Ottawa leaders had permitted the murderer to accompany them to St.
Joseph, where he was publicly stripped of his rank and status. Apart
from the anticipated revenge to be taken by the victims' families, the
Ottawa delegation expected the British not only to establish authority but to mete out justice as well. Since the murderer, Shaushauguaw,
had suffered much disgrace and public humiliation in the eyes of the
Ottawas, the British hoped that would be enough for everyone's satisfaction. Duggan and the officers advised restraint, and they distributed "Seven Strings of Wampum . . . to the Chiefs to speak to the Relations of the Indians Who were killed by Shaushauguaw to pacify
them, [and] presents were also delivered to them [presumably referring to the victims' families, since the rest of the delegation already
had received their gifts and provisions]."[66]

By expecting the British to delegate authority and administer justice among them, the northern Ottawas and Ojibwas showed their
regard for their British Father, who, by fulfilling the role of a media-
tor, acted as a leader in Ottawa/Ojibwa culture.[67] Although in certain instances British-delegated authority may have been more apparent than real, Natives who disregarded such distinctions of authority
could conceivably be cut off from receiving future British gifts. As
a result, the British found it a much simpler task to manipulate and
control Natives in the North than they did elsewhere. By creating

chiefs, they not only fostered loyalty, but the British also tended to gain the cooperation of those whom they did not make chiefs. British officers expected the men they made chiefs to wield authority and to control their people, but, most important, to keep their people loyal to British interests.

On at least two occasions, Major William Doyle, the last British commandant at Mackinac prior to the American occupation in the summer of 1796, even issued written commissions to men whom he made chiefs. On May 8, 1796, Doyle presented Keekwitamigishcam, an Ojibwa leader, with a British commission which in part read, "In consequence of your attachment to the English, of which you have given repeated proofs . . . I hereby constitute and appoint you a Chief of the Chippewa Indians residing at the said Sault St. Mary [Marie]."[68] Less than two months later and in his final few days at Mackinac, Doyle presented another written commission, this time to an Ottawa leader, Nangotook, who had asked for a commission in order to assume the position of his deceased father, "who had been made Chief in the time of the French." Doyle granted this request, issuing the young man a commission that stated: "In consideration of the fidelity, zeal and attachment testified by You to the British Government, . . . I do hereby confirm You the said Nangotook a Chief of Kishkacon [band] . . . of the Ottowa Nation, willing all and singular the Indians Inhabitants thereof to obey You as such."[69] With coincidental timing, Doyle issued these commissions just as he and his men prepared to deliver their post to the Americans; the commandant hoped to strengthen British loyalty among these longtime allies. However, Doyle need not have been concerned about the northern Indians' disposition, for the Ottawas and Ojibwas still drew their authority, not to mention their trade goods, from the British.

The practice of creating chiefs among the Ojibwas and Ottawas was unique to the northern British Indian agency. In the other regions examined in this study, British authorities ordinarily did not confer such authority on individual leaders. While British agents on the Maumee—such as Alexander McKee, Matthew Elliott, and the

Girtys—had all held significant influence in the councils of the Miamis, Delawares, and Shawnees, they did so as delegates representing their king and government; they also attended these meetings by virtue of their status as adopted kinsmen, but this did not give them authority over other leaders in Indian councils. The Native leaders in the coalition formed at Brownstown, and temporarily located at the Glaize, considered Britain a joint member of their confederacy. At no time would any British agents on the Maumee have had the power either to install or to remove a chief. In fact, in an incident in 1793 a Delaware war chief, Big Cat, upbraided Matthew Elliott after the agent had merely inquired as to the business of a pro-American Indian delegation sent to confer with the confederacy's leaders. Big Cat reprimanded Elliott: "Did you ever see me at Detroit or Niagara, in your councils, and there to ask you where such and such white man come[s] from? or what is their Business? Can you watch, and look all around the earth to see who come[s] to us? or is what their Business? Do you not know that we are upon our own Business?" Big Cat then added, "Eliots [sic] mouth was stopd [sic] immediately. Then the other chiefs laugh at him to scorn."[70]

In the North, however, clear limits to the British role in creating or confirming tribal leaders appear never to have been established, and the extent of British authority among the northern Ojibwas and Ottawas remained undefined. At Mackinac, when it seemed expedient to grant commissions to Native leaders, Major Doyle did so without hesitating. Apart from rare exceptions such as Joseph Brant's case, almost never did the British government issue commissions to Indian leaders elsewhere.[71] The tribes in the Ohio Valley would not recognize British-imposed authority or distinctions, particularly if these did not conform to the proper Shawnee, Delaware, or Miami political hierarchy. In the North, such an understanding did not exist among the Ojibwas and Ottawas, and the British at Forts Mackinac and St. Joseph encountered much less resistance to their meddling in tribal affairs.

Another distinctive feature of British-Indian relations at Fort St. Joseph, setting it apart from circumstances at Amherstburg, was the degree of involvement of its regular army officers in Indian affairs. When Alexander McKee first discovered that Doyle had granted a commission to a Native leader, the "astonished" Indian agent immediately notified his superiors. McKee, however, did not protest the actual granting of Indian commissions per se, for he saw no danger in meddling in Indian affairs, or wielding such an authority over them. Instead, McKee complained that Doyle, a regular army officer, had usurped a role and privilege reserved for the Indian Department by issuing a commission to an Indian. Doyle had prevented "the Principal officers of the Department" from fulfilling their duty and from increasing "their influence by the Selection of proper characters for chiefs."[72] Joseph Chew agreed, claiming that whenever the army commissioned chiefs, it "Surely will have a Bad Effect with Regard to the Influence the Officers of the department ought to have with Indians."[73] For McKee and Chew, Doyle's actions threatened the Indian Department, because they viewed the department's role as that of a permanent liaison between the government and a people who should be kept in a state of continual dependency, and the agents viewed the Indian Department as best suited for continuing to cultivate that sort of relationship. In his grievance, McKee complained that Indians receiving direct commissions from army officers would "be freed from that dependence on the Department which has hitherto constituted all the Influence and friendship so happily established between the British Nation and all the Indians in this Country."[74]

These statements show that McKee and Chew did not fully grasp the circumstances at the northern post, nor could they foresee the imminent changes at McKee's own Amherstburg agency. Not only did McKee think it improper for army officers to interfere in Indian affairs, but the agent was soon further dismayed when regular army officers began to eclipse the Indian Department at Amherstburg. This, of course, occurred when the events that led to Matthew Elliott's dismissal in 1797 left Captain Hector McLean wielding substantial authority over Amherstburg's branch of the Indian Department. The role of the military in Indian affairs theoretically should have been reduced when Indian affairs had come under civil author-ity in 1796, since this gave the lieutenant governor supreme authority over the Indian Department in the upper province. Therefore, prior to the McLean-Elliott controversy at Amherstburg, Doyle's granting of Indian commissions in the North would have appeared as an even greater usurpation of the Indian Department's role.

What the elder McKee did not realize was that the British military command at Mackinac and St. Joseph in 1796 held principal authority over the Indian agency there. Conversely, the Indian Department at Amherstburg still functioned in a virtually autonomous manner un-til late in 1797. One reason why the military leadership at St. Joseph extended its authority over the Indian Department there was because that branch of the department remained disorganized and short-handed, as it had been prior to its move from Mackinac. McKee had appointed his own son, Thomas, as deputy superintendent at St. Jo-seph, but the younger McKee never bothered to reside at his assigned post.[75] Except for short visits, Thomas McKee never spent any time at his agency, choosing instead to remain near his Amherstburg home. In order to cut costs, Governor-General Prescott rescinded Alexan-der McKee's appointment of an additional interpreter at the post, and at one point the agency employed an interpreter who was not even fluent enough to adequately communicate with the Indians.[76] In-dian agent Thomas Duggan doubled as storekeeper and clerk, but he eventually ran afoul of the post commandant when he began drink-ing heavily and purportedly expropriated and traded Indian goods from the storehouse.[77] Further complicating matters, Charles Cha-boillez, Duggan's French-speaking replacement, could not understand English.[78] Under these conditions, army personnel assumed control over Indian affairs at St. Joseph, and Major Doyle considered himself justified in issuing commissions to certain Indians in rare instances. He could easily defend this practice, not only because special circum-stances merited these favors but also because no person of adequate rank who could confer such an honor served in the northern branch of the Indian Department at the time.

Perhaps the military authorities heeded Alexander McKee's complaints. For whatever reason, it does not appear that Doyle's successors issued any additional commissions. Nevertheless, representatives in the Indian Department at St. Joseph, under the auspices of post commandants, continued their practice of creating chiefs within the small bands of Ottawas and Ojibwas that regularly visited the post. The elder McKee had no objections, as long as the Indian Department played a key role in the ceremonial process of establishing a chief. Thus the department's officials at St. Joseph continued to present each newly created chief with a medal and usually a Union Jack for the chief's band to hang above their village, an indication that those receiving these items took great pride in the distinctive status they symbolized.

The British needed to use caution, taking care not to recognize more chiefs than necessary for their purposes, or to award too many medals. Had they carelessly distributed numerous medals, the Indian agents might have inadvertently created a chief whom the prospective leader's people deemed less deserving and less experienced as a hunter and a warrior. Such a situation would only foster jealousy, having the opposite effect of the medal's intended purpose of cultivating loyalty to a British-controlled headman. Moreover, a distribution of too many medals would diminish the value of their distinction and undermine the respect due those who wore them. Therefore, British officials at Fort St. Joseph always attempted to present them to older, established bandleaders, or to men who were acknowledged as leaders since "the time of the French." In the summer of 1797, when Eshkan, an Ottawa man from Arbre Croche, requested a medal for his son, Duggan "thought [it] prudent to wait for Colo. McKee's further directions with respect to giving Eshkan's Son a Medal as [neither] he nor any of his Predecessors, Relations, were ever known to be Chiefs." In the meantime, the storekeeper pleased the young man by giving him a gorget instead. Duggan explained, "The reason of my being of the opinion of giving the gorget instead of a Medal was because Mr. Langlade who knows all the Ottawas at Arbre Croche well, said that it would offend all the other Chiefs of that place if a Medal was given."[79]

Langlade had good reason to be concerned. Arbre Croche, one of a cluster of villages just north of Little Traverse Bay on the northwest shore of Michigan's Lower Peninsula, had served as the Ottawa nation's most important community and the center of Ottawa affairs since 1742.[80] In May 1798, less than a year after Eshkan's band visited St. Joseph's, a much larger Ottawa delegation arrived from Arbre Croche, this time bearing fifteen Union Jacks. After presenting Duggan, Langlade, and the officers with "Forty three Makaks of Sugar," the principal leader among them, Keeminichaugan, expressed his concern that the British system of establishing chiefs was undermining tribal unity:

> Father, Since our old Principal Chiefs deaths the Young Chiefs hold Councils by themselves constantly, this is the reason We are not all come together, I am sorry We are not all united as formerly, there are different parties among us, It is your fault, Father, in not following the Ancient Customs of Your Children the Ottowas, You make too many Young Chiefs this is the Cause of the differences among us and the reason We are not all come together, besides You received Several of your Ottowa Children last year in small Bands[;] this is another reason why We did not come together.[81]

Immediately after voicing these concerns, Keeminichaugan asked for additional gifts and ended by reaffirming his people's loyalty, stating, "Father, remember our Ancestors behaved well and We follow their examples."[82]

Keeminichaugan's remarks indicate that Langlade's previous concerns regarding developing jealousies and factionalism at Arbre Croche were perceptive. The British-installed leaders had indeed divided the community at Arbre Croche, and as the older chiefs died, this allowed for a turnover in Ottawa leadership. Although British intervention may have caused temporary competition and disunity, the Ottawas had never had any form of centralized governmental authority prior to French and British meddling, and former Ottawa leaders held power based merely on their level of influence and ability to persuade. Since the Ottawas, like the Ojibwas, were politically organized in bands and not as a single tribe or nation, British-based authority may have actually served to unite the bands in the long run. In any case, despite Keeminichaugan's concerns over the loss of Ottawa unity, his people later demonstrated that they could rally around a common cause whenever necessary, as in their struggles against the Sioux. At no other known time did the Indians in the North complain about British meddling in their affairs.

British influence among the leaders of northern Ojibwas and Ottawas ensured that any Franco-Spanish invasion force would have little chance of gaining the Indians' loyalty and cooperation. Any army would have great difficulty in advancing up the Mississippi Valley, across the Indian-held portages, and through the Mackinac corridor without the support of the indigenous British trading partners. Because of the Indians' general pro-British sentiments and ties, nobody in the North had reason to suspect an invasion. Captain Drummond seemed surprised when Russell and Military Secretary James Green warned him of French attempts to enlist the Indians in their cause prior to an anticipated French-led attack. Drummond responded to Green, claiming that he "had not found any dissatisfaction as yet among the Indians who resort to this Post, they always appear pleased at what Presents they get, and Declares [sic] their attachment to the British Government."[83] No attack followed. Consequently, the British flag continued to follow its traders into American and Spanish territories, and these latter two governments found that they could not break the stranglehold of British trade and influence over the Indians of the western Great Lakes and the upper Mississippi Valley.[84]

Drummond and other British officials in the North worried less about a potential French invasion than they did about the incessant hostilities between the Ojibwas and the Dakota Sioux. This, more than other Euro-American powers, threatened to disrupt British trade and influence in the North. At times the Menominees and Winnebagoes also had altercations with the Ojibwas.[85] The British at St. Joseph's tried in vain to broker a permanent peace between these nations, but they merely achieved a series of temporary truces, beginning with John Dease's diplomacy between the Sioux and Ojibwas at Mackinac in 1787. Yet the Sioux, Menominee, Winnebago, Fox, and Sauk tribes would not be manipulated by the British to the same extent as the Ojibwas and Ottawas. Due largely to geography but also partially to their tribal structure, the Ojibwas and Ottawas had much closer ties to the British at St. Joseph's, while the Natives in Wisconsin and the upper Mississippi Valley visited St. Joseph's much less frequently.[86] Despite less contact with the western groups, the British still held considerable influence over them through their numerous traders along the rivers of present-day Wisconsin and Minnesota, and the officers at St. Joseph could rely on traders for reconnaissance just as well as they could the Indians. When Lieutenant Governor Russell initially wanted a report of any activity on the upper Mississippi, Captain Drummond explained, "It will make it more difficult to get Intelligence from the Mississipy [*sic*] as the Chippawas & Ottawas are at war with the Indians in that Quarter, having no Intercourse with one another. The Surest Information will be by the Indian Traders."[87]

Drummond referred to the traders in a region south and west of Lake Superior, an area that included a number of private British traders and encompassed the important Fox-Wisconsin River portage. The traders there generally operated independently, or in small combinations, belonging to neither the North West Company nor the XY Company.[88] These men helped to maintain a British sphere of influence by cultivating relations with those tribes who did not often visit British posts, by encouraging them to prefer British goods, and by preventing American and Spanish attempts to develop a trade network. One such trader, Robert Dickson, established ties with the Dakotas and married a chief's sister.[89] After more than two decades of living among his wife's people, Dickson was instrumental in recruiting his clients and kinsmen into the British cause in the War of 1812. In the absence of more formal ties, such as the Chain of Friendship that the British had cultivated with nations farther east, the informal individual bonds between the traders and the Sioux cemented British-Dakota relations at the turn of the nineteenth century. More important, as a result of these links, the Sioux recognized the British as kinsmen, in spite of the ongoing relationship the British maintained with the their enemies, the Ojibwas, both at St. Joseph and through the North West Company.[90]

Sir John Johnson, superintendent of Indian Affairs, had an unrealistic perception of the nature of British relations with the Native groups farther west, particularly with the Sioux and their hostility toward the Ojibwa nation. Johnson regarded the continuing warfare that pitted the Ojibwas and Ottawas against the Sioux "merely as a private Quarrel," ever since Amable, an Ottawa chief from Arbre Croche, visited him at Montreal, claiming that some distant traders had fomented "[h]ostilities . . . between the Sioux and them."[91] The superintendent mistakenly believed that British power and influence, via the Indian Department, extended to that region in the same manner that it had evolved southwest of Detroit. On multiple occasions in the late 1790s, Johnson naively referred to "the Peace that was Settled with them by Mr. Dease [Johnson's cousin]" more than a decade earlier.[92] Johnson simply could not believe that the western nations, whom he considered under British auspices, would defy a British-mandated peace without having been under an external and devious influence. The head agent went on to accuse "our remote Traders . . . [of being] the Instigators of those Predatory Wars from Interested Motives," and he instructed his field agents and the commandant at St. Joseph's to remind the Indians of Dease's peace settlement "with those nations . . . when they promised in the most Solemn manner never to break it, and a very Large Belt with my name and the year upon it, was left with the Chippewas to remind them of what was agreed upon."[93] Johnson must not have realized that hostilities between the Ojibwas and the Sioux had continued uninterrupted for more than a decade.[94] The Sioux-Ojibwa wars persisted for another half-century.

Johnson erred twice. First, he had imagined the British regime in the North strong enough to compel the cooperation of nations as far away as the west side of the Mississippi; second, Johnson mistakenly blamed the traders for the continued hostilities. In fact, it was the activities of these very men that kept the western tribes backing British interests. Due to the traders' continued influence and the expansion of the North West Company, the Indians who lived in the upper Mississippi Valley, in both Spanish and American territories, continued to fly Union Jacks over their villages during the early years of the nineteenth century.[95] The traders possessed far more influence than their own government, and they certainly did not want continued intertribal conflicts. The incessant warfare between the Sioux and the Ojibwas often hindered trade, and it also threatened the lives of the traders, particularly those who worked alone and lived near the bands with which they dealt.[96] These men had virtually no protection. Even those traders who belonged to the larger companies found that they also were vulnerable, and a few of them lost their lives.[97] Even though rivalries often grew intense, traders did not tend to foment wars that might endanger their own lives and fortunes; indeed, Michael Curot, an agent with the North West Company, sought refuge with his rival, before he was killed at his own post the following year.[98]

Although the Sioux-Ojibwa wars persisted, the Ottawas seldom participated in these conflicts. The Ottawa leader Amable, who initially complained to Sir John Johnson that distant traders planned to instigate hostilities between his people at Arbre Croche and the Sioux, was either confused or manipulative, because he did not represent the sentiments of his community. Three months after Amable's visit with Johnson near Montreal in the summer of 1797, Captain Drummond held a council at St. Joseph's with an Ottawa delegation from Arbre Croche, confronting them directly about the rumors of "considerable difficulties among themselves . . . instigated by the Traders." The chiefs resoundingly "answered they had no knowledge of any thing of the kind and were certain no such speech had been sent by their Nation[.] They then begged their Father would not listen to any bad reports, that there was no truth in them and hoped he would never think of them again."[99] For good measure, the following June an Ottawa delegation from Arbre Croche returned to St. Joseph on their way "to see their father Sir John Johnson." Their leader, Keeminichaugan, "begged hard," asking Duggan to write a letter for him to present to Johnson, stating, "Father, since We heard of the bad Bird's conduct in lower Canada We have been very sorry, We thank you for writing our father [Captain Drummond] last fall. . . . We were not concerned in any of that bad Bird's transactions, he makes us very much afflicted at what he said—We shall send down in a few days a Canoe well manned to meet him, when he sees our people he will contradict every thing he said of us."[100] The Ottawas at Arbre Croche remained firmly attached, both in their loyalty to the British and in their dependence on the traders sent among them.

One can only speculate as to Amable's motives for fabricating stories to Johnson regarding the actions of the traders in Indian country, but perhaps the Ottawa headman had valid cause to resent the traders, both those at his village of Arbre Croche and those who lived among the Sioux. Even if the traders did not actively attempt to foment a war, Amable knew that they dealt weapons to his enemies, and the mere fact that British traders bartered weapons to belligerent nations already at war endangered lives on both sides. The British had begun to cultivate relations with the Sioux similar to those that they had established with Amable's people more than a generation earlier, and the Sioux would now also fight to defend the British traders on whom they depended. A month prior to Amable's meeting with Johnson, Duggan reported that some British "Traders were nearly pillaged by the Sacques [Sauks] and Renards [Fox] headed by some [Spanish] Traders around with authority from the Spanish Commandant at St. Lewis. [F]ortunately for those interested, a party of Scioux were at La Prairie due Chien which overawed the other Indians and the property is . . . out of danger."[101] Amable might have perceived that the British were attempting to establish symbiotic ties with the Sioux as they had with his own people, and perhaps the Ottawa leader feared that the Ottawas had become the pawns of empire as they faced a debilitating future of dependence and poverty resulting from the trade.

From 1800 until after the War of 1812, British relations with Natives in the North and West would continue to be marked by a pattern of trade and dependence, but British attempts to quell warring nations there would never fully succeed, because British officials did not possess the authority and control over the Sioux to the same extent that they managed to influence the Ottawas and Ojibwas. The perpetual struggle that persisted between these groups became an accepted way of life, and by the turn of the nineteenth century British leaders in the North no longer made seeking peace there a pressing priority. In the summer of 1799, Captain Drummond wrote to Military Secretary Major Green, cavalierly stating, "I am happy to inform you that most of the Mississipy [sic] Traders are arrived at Mackinac, and bring no news of Importance, only the old Quarrel between the Chippawas and the Seus [Sioux] is still kept up as usual, but nothing of any consequence has happened only a few Scalps taken, which is the case every year."[102] Despite the ongoing hostilities, Duggan happily reported in 1801 that all Indians in his "quarter appear very well affected to [the British] Government."[103] Thus British-Indian relations in the North continued in a unique manner in which trade and familial ties defined British relations with indigenous nations, some of which were at war with one another. Conversely, British authorities at Amherstburg, where trade volume was much less, strove to decrease their ties with the Natives and lessen the Natives' reliance on British support. Also, British policy elsewhere in Upper Canada at the turn of the nineteenth century was geared toward creating intertribal division, rather than encouraging unity of the sort that British officers, agents, and traders had attempted to cultivate at Fort St. Joseph and in the upper Mississippi Valley.[104]

4

A New Society on the Grand River, 1784–1801

A third locale of British-Indian relations after the American Revolution was the Grand River, a tributary in Upper Canada flowing into the northeastern end of Lake Erie, set aside by Governor-General Sir Frederick Haldimand in 1784 for the Six Nations and their dependencies who had fought for the British during the war. At Amherstburg and in the North, Britain had maintained a sphere of influence mainly through trade and Indian gifts, though in the 1790s at Amherstburg, British officers reduced all gifts and annual presents to their former Native allies. The Grand River community was distinctive in that it was a large grant of territory intended as a place of settlement for the loyal refugee tribes, including Mohawks, Cayugas, Onondagas, Senecas, Tuscaroras, and Delawares, most of whom were from New York.

This chapter explores how the terms of the Haldimand Grant became a contested subject between British authorities and the Natives. It first examines the period from 1784 to 1797, during which both tribal and British leaders attempted to define the nature of the grant on terms favorable to their respective interests. The key issue was whether the Indian residents of the Grand River would be allowed to sell land to white settlers. British resistance to such proposals contributed to a virtual deadlock between the British and Indians regarding land sales by the end of this period, and the stalemate fueled a dispute over the extent of Six Nations' sovereignty and legal status of Natives in Canada in general.[1] The Six Nations at the Grand River stressed that they were the king's allies, nothing more. They tended to view their community as a self-sufficient, separate political entity that could deal with outside nation-states and individuals independently of Great Britain's interference. Conversely, for Great Britain, Native autonomy in Upper Canada presented a potential security threat, and Whitehall was not prepared to grant Indian demands pertaining to sovereignty, or to permit greater Native autonomy in land matters. The original Haldimand Grant made no provision for the Indians to alienate any of their land, and even the subsequent amended land patents always gave the British government the right of preemption, acknowledging only Crown sovereignty. The Grand River case was the first internal Indian crisis in Canada that the British faced after the United States gained independence, but it would influence subsequent British colonial jurisprudence and Canadian Indian policy down to the present time.

The chapter also examines British relations with the Grand River Indians and related tribes from 1797 to 1801 and will show that a series of controversies, less broad than the Grand River land sales issue but still significant, further undermined friendly relations between British officials and their former Indian allies. The common thread running through these struggles was the greater issue of Iroquois sovereignty, which remained nebulous as both sides were compelled to compromise during these crucial years at the Grand River. The Six Nations' legal status in Canada would remain undefined long after the close of the period covered by this study.

The Six Nations' Bid for Sovereignty, Brant's Struggles, and the British Response, 1784–97

Upon its establishment in 1784, the Grand River settlement was by no means the only Iroquois community in Canada. For instance, the principal Iroquois villages of the St. Lawrence Valley, such as Caughnawaga, Kanesatake (Oka), and Akwesasne (St. Regis), had begun under French-Catholic auspices as mission communities in the seventeenth and early eighteenth centuries. These eventually comprised a portion of the groups that the British collectively referred to as the "Seven Nations of Canada."[2] Moreover, in addition to that of the Grand River, a second refugee Iroquois community was established in Canada in 1784, when roughly two hundred Mohawks settled at Tyendinaga near the Bay of Quinte along the northeast shore of Lake Ontario. Led by John Deserontyon, a Mohawk and Joseph Brant's rival, this community did not recognize Brant's authority.[3] Finally, the Six Nations' residents at the Grand River would also face a growing diplomatic challenge from the Iroquois groups within the United States, most notably the Seneca community at Buffalo Creek in western New York and its leader, Red Jacket, a career-long antagonist of Brant. In spite of these concerns, the Grand River community had the largest populace of any indigenous reserve in Canada at the time, and its principal leader possessed the most experience in dealing with the British and American governments.

When various bands of Indian refugees originally settled along the Grand River, the community was composed of a diverse set of peoples. A census taken in 1785 indicated that 1,843 loyal Natives from nineteen different tribes or bands had settled at the Grand River. In addition to elements of the Six Iroquois Nations, other groups found at the new reserve included Delawares, Nanticokes, Montours, Creeks, Cherokees, Tutelos, Oghguagas, and Canadian Iroquois from Akwesasne.[4] Nevertheless, more than two-thirds of the entire community were Iroquois, and the Mohawks alone numbered nearly a quarter of the total populace.

These figures helped Mohawk sachem Joseph Brant maintain a greater level of influence at the Grand River intertribal community than other Native leaders there, and Brant soon became the community's principal spokesperson and primary leader. His record as a war chief during the American Revolution certainly enhanced his standing as a capable leader, but his other qualities and attributes are what made him the Six Nations' principal spokesperson during this era. Brant's longtime ties to the family of Sir William Johnson and his captain's commission in the Indian Department gave him an edge that other Native leaders lacked. Consequently, in spite of never having possessed any hereditary authority in Iroquois councils, Brant's position and experience had made him the most important liaison between the Six Nations and the whites when the Grand River Reserve was established.[5]

After their move to the Grand River, Brant and his people came to understand that their traditional modes of existence, namely hunting and subsistence farming, would not be enough to sustain them on the reserve, not even with the additional Crown gifts and presents given to them on occasion. In spite of future British claims of Brant's speculation and graft, the strategy of selling or leasing blocks of land in order to create a substantial revenue made sense at the time. Furthermore, Brant had a number of white Loyalist friends, some of whom had served under him during the American war, willing to invest in Grand River lands on the Mohawk leader's terms.[6] If successful, the scheme would not only generate a significant profit for the Six Nations at the Grand River, but Brant and his supporters believed that limited white settlement there would promote the establishment of model farms and foster modernized economic development.[7]

Early in 1787, Brant and the Six Nations' leaders made their first Grand River land transactions by selling several thousand acres to ten Loyalist friends. Apart from the Haldimand Grant, the Six Nations possessed no other legal title to these lands, but they acted independently, without including the government in the transaction. For some time the transactions went unnoticed by both the Indian Department and Governor-General Lord Dorchester. However, when Dorchester learned of these land transfers more than a year later, he vowed to "order all the white people off the Lands."[8] The governor-general instructed Sir John Johnson to inform all concerned parties that "the King will never confirm their [the Loyalists'] Grants nor allow the Individuals to keep possession."[9]

Brant was incensed that the British now seemed to be reneging on the stipulations of the Haldimand Grant. Much of the conflict stemmed from the vagueness of the Haldimand deed, which, while not expressly restricting the alienation of Native lands, did not sanction the transferring of land either. According to the Haldimand Grant, the Indians were "to take possession of and settle upon the Banks of the [Grand] River."[10] Though the government's intent behind the proclamation was later often debated, Brant assumed that by this document, the Crown offered land to the Six Nations on an equal basis with any other grants of land that the government awarded to whites in Canada. The United Empire Loyalists, for example, had fought for the king in the war and subsequently settled in Upper Canada at the government's expense; many later sold their land to whomever they chose. In other words, the Six Nations expected a written deed that acknowledged their full ownership of the Grand River lands, or a title in fee simple, held in common by all of the reserve's Native inhabitants.

The controversy was intertwined with the greater issue of Iroquois sovereignty. Brant and the Six Nations, while desiring full possession of their lands, knew that they could not adequately argue their case from the perspective of the United Empire Loyalists or other whites, because these settlers were acknowledged as British subjects, while the Indians viewed themselves as autonomous Crown allies. If independent, then the Grand River community could sell or lease their lands to whomever they pleased, whether to French, American, or British settlers, without the consent of Whitehall or any leaders in Canada. Brant believed that the Iroquois had always possessed this degree of mastery over all of their affairs. In response to Dorchester's restrictions against the Six Nations' sale of Grand River lands, the Mohawk sachem argued that the Iroquois are "on the same footing on which we stood previous" to the American war, adding, "your government well knew . . . they had no right to interfere with us as independent nations."[11]

The British held quite another view. Ever since the Canadian discoveries made by the Cabot family in the latter part of the fifteenth century, overall sovereignty of British possessions in North America had always rested with the English (and, after 1707, the British) monarch. Of course, the Indians within these vast domains had still enjoyed the right, known as the right of usufruct, to dwell upon and use the land, but this did not give them full title. Whenever the Indians ceded their lands by treaty, the British government maintained that the tribes had actually surrendered their usufructuary right to the land, but that was all, since the Crown had already possessed sovereign authority over those lands.[12] Contrary to Brant's claims, the British had never acknowledged any different status for the Iroquois lands in colonial New York, and the government viewed the Indians' postwar exodus to the Grand River as a continuation of a centuries-old understanding.[13] At the new site, the Six Nations again possessed their usufructuary right, just as before. Brant seemed to be the innovator in wanting to alter this long-standing tradition. Furthermore, the British government could not recognize Iroquois sovereignty over the land because British leaders, when forming government Indian policy, did not consider indigenous groups as political entities, but rather as separate racial classes, or groups, that were to receive special consideration or treatment.[14]

With such radically different notions of the Six Nations' legal status, conflict was unavoidable. Although Lord Dorchester never evicted the first wave of white settlers to move to the Grand River as he had threatened to do in 1788, Brant would not rest until he and the Grand River Council possessed a deed acknowledging the Six Nations' full ownership, a title in fee simple. Until that happened, the British government would never have to concede that the Haldimand deed meant anything more than a mere license of occupation for the Indians dwelling at the Grand River Reserve. For several years the matter hung in limbo and received less attention, as Canadian authorities were more concerned with the brewing crisis on the Maumee when the advance of Wayne's army nearly drew the British into another American conflict. Furthermore, the Grand River question grew more complex when the British Parliament restructured the

Canadian government in 1791, creating the province of Upper Canada and thus an additional bureaucratic layer of government with which Brant would have to contend in his efforts to gain the land title and the Six Nations' legal status that he sought.

When John Graves Simcoe, a distinguished veteran and officer who served in the American Revolution, became the upper province's first lieutenant governor in 1792, Brant immediately petitioned Simcoe for the Grand River deed that he had persistently sought for the previous seven years. The land issue ensured that relations between the two men would remain strained until Simcoe's departure in 1796.[15] Brant regularly clamored for a proper deed, while Simcoe at the same time continued his efforts to talk Brant out of engaging in any future land deals. The lieutenant governor and other British leaders feared that Brant would deal parts of the reserve to "Land Jobbers," who would in turn sell these tracts to any set of buyers, many of whom lacked loyalty to the British government or to British interests. The standoff continued, and Brant informed Simcoe that the Indians "were not always to be fools because they had once been such."[16]

Neither Simcoe nor Dorchester wanted to concede to the Six Nations the right to sell or lease their lands, so Simcoe finally issued a new patent to the Six Nations in January 1793, carefully defining and circumscribing the Indians' rights to the land: "IT IS OUR ROYAL WILL AND PLEASURE that no transfer, alienation conveyance sale gift exchange lease property or possession shall at any time be made or given of the said District or Territory or any part or parcel thereof." In spite of the full restrictions preventing the Six Nations from alienating any of their lands, Simcoe left an opening to Brant by including a clause providing for land sales under the condition that these "always . . . shall be purchased for Us [the British government], our Heirs and Successors at some public meeting . . . to be holden for that purpose by the Governor, Lieutenant-Governor or person administering Our Government."[17] Hence, Simcoe did his best to please everyone, including both Dorchester and Brant, by restricting any free alienation of Iroquois lands, while simultaneously permitting the Grand

River Six Nations to sell portions of their territory to the government alone whenever it became absolutely necessary. Yet the Six Nations' council believed that Simcoe had done little more than undermine Iroquois sovereignty by giving the British government the sole right of preemption over the Grand River lands. Such a policy mirrored that practiced by the fledgling United States, and it usually meant that the Indians would not receive a competitive price for the acreage, since the land was not sold on the open market; the government also wanted to turn a profit in reselling the land. Furthermore, Simcoe's patent still maintained a premise of Crown sovereignty, describing the Six Nations' reserve as a "Tract of Land under our protection."[18]

Brant rejected the patent outright, arguing that it violated the spirit, intention, and purpose of the Haldimand Grant. From that point onward, the Six Nations' Grand River Council has always claimed that Simcoe's deed could never be binding upon them.[19] If the Six Nations had merely wanted to sell the lands without seeking any additional legal status, then Simcoe had technically made it possible for them to do so, but Brant wanted more. Yet the Mohawk leader needed to use caution in seeking greater autonomy, because his sentiments could have been construed as seditious. After rejecting Simcoe's deed, the chief poured out his heart to his soon-to-be estranged friend, Alexander McKee, describing the breach between him and the British: "I am Sorry to inform you that we the Grand River Indians are . . . greatly disapointed [sic] of not having been able to obtain such Deeds we would have wished to have . . . it hurt my pride and feelings extremely. . . . I cannot hardly reconcile myself to Live on Such Situation I never did expected [sic] that my attachment to the English should any time Shake[.] I am totally dispirited."[20]

Knowing that Brant's loyalty to the British had been shaken, leaders in Canada soon believed that they had further cause to question the Mohawk's fidelity. Late in 1793, Simcoe informed Lord Dorchester that the Six Nations' leader communicated regularly with representatives in the American government, and that "Brant has said that the offers of [the U.S.] Congress to him, were a Township for himself, as much lands as he chose for the Indians, and a guinea a day for himself for life." Brant probably exaggerated the American offer, but even so, the chief's statements indicated that his loyalty to the British had its limits. Simcoe concluded, "My opinion of Brant is, that he is true to the Indian Interest, and honorable in his Attachment, where that is not concerned, to the British Nation."[21] To Simcoe, Brant's priorities were unacceptable, particularly when Britain was embroiled in a European war against revolutionary France and facing the possibility of another American war.

Although neither Brant nor Simcoe trusted the other, the lieutenant governor could not afford to alienate Brant while war with the Americans appeared imminent. The chief's influence over both the Six Nations and the Western Confederacy could help to determine Britain's future in Upper Canada. Yet Simcoe justifiably feared that the Six Nations' headman would exploit this to the Indians' advantage by playing off Britain and the United States.[22] Frustrated in his efforts to gain Six Nations' sovereignty, Brant could still perhaps utilize this potential diplomatic leverage in order to play off the two powers, just as his ancestors had done, with a degree of success, with the British and the French. The only trouble was that in 1793, two key parties with whom Brant dealt—the Western Confederacy and the Americans—were already at war, lessening his diplomatic leverage in an effort to broker a peace to the Six Nations' advantage. Nevertheless, Simcoe still feared that Brant would either manipulate matters to draw Britain into a war against the United States, or that the chief would merely continue attempting to play off Britain against the United States. Remarking to Dorchester about Brant's machinations, Simcoe explained "that he [Brant] sees the Calamities [the Indians are to experience] which in all probability must ultimately attend the Continuance of the War, unless by some means or other Great Britain shall take a direct part on the protection of the Indians."[23] Simcoe demonstrated his suspicions of the chief's disloyalty when he sided with Alexander McKee in the latter's dispute with Brant over a potential peace with the American commissioners. Though a misguided attempt to preserve Indian unity, Simcoe's decision to support McKee over Brant did quite the opposite, helping to divide the Western Confederacy and ultimately proving fatal to its war effort against the Americans. Thus, in little more than six months, Brant was twice thwarted, once by Simcoe at the Grand River, and later by McKee, with Simcoe's support, at the Miami Rapids.

Alarmed at Brant's growing belligerence, Simcoe considered "the use He [Brant] has made of his Power to be the subject of just alarm and that it is necessary by degrees and on just principles that it should be diminished."[24] By "just principles," Simcoe meant that he intended to reduce Brant's authority gradually through official channels. The lieutenant governor hoped to avoid an overt and permanent schism between Brant and the British and sought legal means by which to reduce Brant's authority, including a fresh interpretation indicating why the Six Nations could not sell or lease Grand River lands. Having already questioned Brant's motives and loyalty to the British, Simcoe now claimed that the chief's land schemes were simply "illegal in respect to the Customs and Laws of Great Britain."[25] The lieutenant governor reminded Brant that, according to British law, if the Indians were indeed allies, and not subjects, then the Six Nations, not being subjects, could not lease or sell lands to British subjects.[26] This determination still weighed heavily on Brant nearly three years later, when he complained about this unique interpretation in a speech near Fort George (near Niagara) in 1796.[27] By having the ambiguous legal status of dependent allies, the Six Nations had neither the full rights and privileges enjoyed by British subjects nor the liberty to conduct their affairs as a sovereign power. Simcoe also delayed any determinations on the land issue for as long as possible, informing Brant that any permanent decision in this matter would be made at Whitehall by the king's ministers. The lieutenant governor then promised Dorchester, "In respect to the lands on the Grand River, I shall do my utmost to procrastinate any decision on them."[28] Meanwhile, Simcoe took measures to appease Brant to some degree by visiting the Grand River in

FIG. 3. *Joseph Brant*, by Charles Willson Peale, 1797. After Brant's intertribal influence among western Indians had diminished in 1792 and 1793, he spent the rest of his life struggling with British and Canadian officials in an unsuccessful attempt to gain full sovereignty for his people at the Grand River in Upper Canada. Courtesy of Independence National Historical Park.

1794 and allocating the necessary funds and resources to assist the Six Nations in the building of a new council house. The government of Upper Canada also promised a future pension for Brant's wife, Catherine, in the event of her husband preceding her in death, and in 1795 Simcoe even approved of a measure that granted Brant 3,450 acres of land on Burlington Bay as personal property, land that he had previously requested.[29] Simcoe's concessions were significant, indicating that the government, while distrusting Brant and refusing to acknowledge Six Nations' sovereignty, thought it important to continue amiable ties with them in an effort to secure their traditional fidelity and support. The delicacy with which Simcoe and other British leaders dealt with Brant shows their continued respect for the Mohawk's enduring influence among both Natives and whites, not only at the Grand River but throughout Canada and among American officials as well.

Prior to his departure from Upper Canada in the summer of 1796, Simcoe made one final attempt to solve the land issue by drafting yet another land patent that incorporated a more clearly worded provision by which the Six Nations could lease land, albeit only to the government.[30] Brant and the Six Nations rejected the new document because they still found it too restrictive, and the patent's wording did not necessarily confine the leasing rights strictly to the Iroquois at the Grand River. It implied that other remnants of Six Nations' enclaves, such as those at Buffalo Creek in New York and John Deserontyon's band at the Bay of Quinte, could also share in the revenue generated from any leased lands at the Grand River.[31] For Brant, this would have defeated the purpose of attempting to generate revenue specifically intended for his people's survival and independent use at the Grand River. Still at an impasse, Brant continued to illegally lease Native lands in hopes of one day having the legal right to sell the title to those lands.

After Simcoe's departure, his successor, Peter Russell, for a time also attempted delaying tactics regarding the Grand River lands, but

FIG. 4. *Joseph Brant's Home at the Head of Lake Ontario*, by Edward Walsh, 1804. Brant's life-style demonstrated that he remained an important figure in both Indian and white worlds. Courtesy of William L. Clements Library, University of Michigan.

unlike Simcoe, Russell was forced to come to a more definitive reso-lution of the matter.[32] The new administrator, with little knowledge of Indian affairs or policy, had inherited a diplomatic quagmire that had begun before Simcoe's administration and was growing worse. Brant immediately pressured Russell to speedily resolve the issue in the Indians' favor. Russell asked Brant to outline in writing precisely which lands the Six Nations wanted to sell or lease, and to whom.[33] The new lieutenant governor then promised to lay all of the requested information before Upper Canada's Executive Council for its consid-eration. Brant responded with lightning speed; he issued the report to Russell only two days after the lieutenant governor had requested it, and the Mohawk leader informed Russell that he expected the entire matter to be resolved "in the course of Ten days."[34] Russell was not prepared to expedite matters in the manner that Brant expected. Due to the poor health of several members of the Executive Council, and the fact that the legislative session had ended, Russell did not have to comply with Brant's "ten days," and the legislature could not meet until spring. The delay enabled Russell to further consult Whitehall, particularly the Duke of Portland, home secretary. While awaiting instructions from home and carefully pondering his response to Brant and the Six Nations, Russell confirmed that all of the prospective buyers of the Grand River tracts were loyal British subjects, indicating that Brant did not want to subvert British authority in Upper Canada.[35]

When Brant learned that the Executive Council would not meet again during the fall of 1796, and did not plan to reconvene until the following May, he interpreted the postponement as another intentional delaying tactic, similar to the methods Simcoe had employed against him for four years. The chief bitterly exclaimed,

> We are at a loss what to think of our Great men here [British officials in Canada].... We cannot from their conduct towards us ... learn what their Intentions are, nor what we are to expect from them.... It is not what we expected nor what we deserved.
>
> Be assured that we have spoke[n] for the last time to the great men here on this subject; as they have from their Conduct gave us plainly to understand that it is not their Intention to do any thing for us.... Surely our Father their Master [the king], never intended that we were to be trifled with in this manner. I repeat it again, that is not what we deserve.[36]

Brant had come to the end of his patience, and, as he stated, he intended to never again deal with British leaders in Canada on the issue. The frustrated leader instead resolved to travel to Britain himself in order to secure a proper deed for his Grand River Reserve. But, short of funds, he never made the trip, and, contrary to his declaration, he continued to wrangle with leaders in Canada on land matters until his death a decade later.

Brant hoped to drive a wedge between Whitehall and the Canadian authorities, and he tended to stress the Six Nations' loyalty and devotion to the king, often in exaggerated terms. In November 1796 Brant restated his peoples' loyalty, declaring, "We pride ourselves by the losses we have suffered in the good cause of our Great Father the King of England . . . and are firm in our Attachment to our Great Father, the King of England. . . . [T]he ill Treatment we met with from Individuals sent to [this] Country to rule, shall never wean our Affections from that Government that sends them here." The Mohawk leader even claimed that his peoples' fidelity and attachment exceeded that of Loyalists, adding, "this Disappointment in not obtaining our Grant would (were we white men) shake us in our Loyalty and Attachment for the King of England our Father. . . . [I]t would leave a wound not easily to be healed. But we are Indians."[37] On numerous other occasions in his public statements, whether written or spoken in council, the Mohawk leader was always careful to reaffirm this loyalty, promising that his "affection and Loyalty to the King shall never be shaken."[38]

Brant's opponents understood what was at stake. Russell's attorney general, John White, pinpointed the crux of the problem when he connected all of the government's legal difficulties with the Grand River Reserve to "the Principal [difficulty, which] was that the Six Nations do not acknowledge the Sovereignty of the King."[39] Despite all of Brant's rhetoric about loyalty, the specter of a potential Indian rebellion in the vulnerable young province was empowering to the Indians, and Brant knew it. Therefore Brant played up the threat of an invasion of Upper Canada, and he did his best to intimidate Russell. Years later, William Claus, the late Alexander McKee's successor as deputy superintendent general, cynically remarked,

> Whoever pretends to a moderate knowledge of the 6 Nats. and their politics in a War between two powers of white people which may affect their Country . . . will allow that their first and principal view . . . is to find out which of the two contenting [sic] parties is the best able to supply them with their Necessaries in Trade as well as best able to bribe them. . . . During the interval of the Conflict they make no Scruple of Conscience

... when Opportunity serves to take what they can ... by carrying Lies.[40]

Claus understood that there was a limit to the Six Nations' loyalty toward the British, as Simcoe had previously surmised.

In 1797 Russell personally experienced the Six Nations' diplomatic pressure. The lieutenant governor informed Portland that Brant and the Six Nations, with their patience exhausted, "took upon themselves to conclude ... the Sale of Part of these Lands without waiting for His Majesty's Sanction." Russell did not immediately dispute the independent sales, regarding it as "impolitick [*sic*] in the present weak state of this Province to provoke Insult even from an Indian Tribe."[41] Thus the administrator chose not to openly reject Brant's propositions, while still maintaining that no "alienation of the lands [is] ... valid without the Consent of the King," and that the Six Nations "have placed themselves under His Majesty's Protection by taking up their Residence within this Province."[42]

Russell's letter to Portland hinted that the diplomatic vise was beginning to tighten. Neither Russell nor his superiors were prepared to recognize Six Nations' sovereignty, but the weak condition of the army and small population of the upper province prevented the government from flatly denying Brant's demands. Moreover, as tensions between the government of Upper Canada and the Natives at the Grand River escalated during the early months of 1797, the home government at Whitehall, from its distant vantage point, did not have a clear grasp of the seriousness of the situation. The Duke of Portland did not think it necessary for British leaders in Canada to compromise on the matter.

In March Portland wrote to Russell, adamantly insisting that the Six Nations "are positively restricted from alienating or disposing of" their land "to any other Persons whatever." Moreover, the duke pointed out that the original intention of the Haldimand Grant was never to permit the alienation of any of the Grand River domain. He observed that the Grand River's geographic location in the heart of the province was in itself "proof of the prudence and foresight" of the Haldimand Grant, "which dictated the Provision against the most remote possibility of such an important Tract of Ground ever becoming the Property of any other Persons, without His Majesty's Special assent being obtained for that purpose."[43] Nevertheless, Portland wanted the Six Nations to understand "the Parental regard which His Majesty feels for them and of his desire to meet their wishes in any manner in which it can be done, consistently with the principle on which the original Grant was made to them." Therefore the duke instructed Russell to determine a monetary figure equivalent to the projected proceeds of the Six Nations' anticipated land transactions, an amount that the government could then subsidize as a supplementary annuity to the Six Nations in lieu of any land sales or leases.[44]

The Duke of Portland had missed the point. Money was not the issue, but rather, as Upper Canada's attorney general John White had already pointed out, the Six Nations insisted upon wielding independent control over all of their affairs. In the spring and summer of 1797, Brant continued to conduct the Six Nations' affairs in an autonomous manner, and, as Russell had feared, the Mohawk leader also continued to exploit the fact that Upper Canada was weak and defenseless. In April Brant traveled to Philadelphia to meet with Robert Liston, British envoy to the United States; Brant also spoke to anyone else who would listen to him. While in Philadelphia, the sachem voiced his complaints at the inn where he lodged, purportedly asserting "with great resentment of the treatment he had met with from the King's Government of Canada, and threatened, *if he did not obtain redress through me*, that he would offer his services to the French Minister Adet [French envoy to the United States], and march his Mohawks to assist in effecting a Revolution, and overturning the British Government in the Province." Liston patiently listened to Brant, but the British envoy wrote to Governor-General Robert Prescott, warning him of "the possible event of an Insurrection in the [Upper] Province," hoping "to avert so serious a danger."[45] On June 18, only days before the Executive Council would meet, Brant wrote to Upper

Canada's surveyor general, D. W. (David William) Smith, exclaiming, "We wish to be on the same footing with [the] Government [as] we were before the War [American Revolution] . . . we look upon it that what we formerly called the covenant chain is in some danger of getting rusty."[46] The very next day, the Six Nations' chief also sent a similar letter to Russell, expressing his distress that unless the Six Nations could "enjoy the lands here . . . in the same independent and unlimited manner [as they supposedly had done in the Mohawk Valley prior to the war]," then the ancient British-Iroquois friendship would be in peril.[47] Brant insisted upon this point, and in late June three hundred angry warriors accompanied him to York (modern Toronto), the capital of the upper province, to forcefully demonstrate the importance of the matter while the Indians awaited a decision.[48] Indeed, Brant's behavior during the spring and summer of 1797 did not reflect the degree of loyalty he had proclaimed the previous autumn.

Brant's tactics brought a measure of success to the Grand River Indians' endeavors.[49] Acting on his own authority, but with the unanimous support of the Executive Council, and hoping to ward off an Indian rebellion, Russell evaded his orders from home and confirmed the land sales that Brant had already transacted. Fearing imminent hostilities, Russell made this decision before he could receive final instructions on the matter from Portland, even though the home secretary's previous correspondence strictly forbade any alienation of Iroquois lands in Canada.[50] Since Russell had already determined to disobey his instructions, there was no longer cause for delay, which at that point could only risk exacerbating the already-strained relations between his government and the Six Nations. In addition to confirming the Six Nations' prior sales, the lieutenant governor provided a way for the Six Nations to conduct future land transactions, but only with the king, who retained the right of preemption.[51] Therefore Russell believed that in spite of his having neglected his orders, all parties would ultimately be satisfied that he maintained peace and tranquility and entitled the Six Nations to conduct future land transactions strictly with the government.

Russell's hopes were soon dashed; neither Brant nor Portland was completely pleased. The duke "lamented" the lieutenant governor's handling of the matter, and he feared that this show of British weakness might develop into "a most dangerous tendency."[52] For his part, Brant thanked Russell for his efforts thus far, but he complained, "I am sorry the mode adopted is not yet satisfactory, because this is not the footing *we were upon before*." Furthermore, the chief gave another subtle threat regarding the possible demise of British–Six Nations relations, remarking that the government's continued intervention "is entangling the Chain we so long kept hold of, which I should be sorry to be the case."[53]

Brant's response stunned Russell, who summoned another meeting with the Executive Council before meeting with the chief personally on July 21, 1797. Russell nearly revoked his previous offer to Brant, explaining to the Mohawk leader that the king's ministers would have to determine the Six Nations' legal rights regarding their land, and that His Majesty's government would provide an annuity to meet the Six Nations' material needs in lieu of any alienation of lands, precisely what Portland had already proposed.[54] "Brant appeared . . . greatly affected by" this, and he passionately explained to Russell that had his people known that "the lands on the Grand River were given to them upon any other footing than that on which they formerly possessed those on the Mohawk River," then they never would have accepted them, and he emphasized that the Six Nations "were a free & independent Nation."[55] Russell, fearing that Brant "was very capable of doing much mischief," relented and again extended the same offer he had presented to the chief earlier in the month.[56] The government of Upper Canada therefore confirmed the land sales that the Grand River Indians had already made, but in the future the Crown would possess the right of preemption, and the king's ministers would serve as trustees on any further relinquishments of Grand River lands. Knowing that he had better take what he could get, Brant this time responded favorably. He thanked Russell and said, "This Sir, is every thing we wanted, we have no desire just now to dispose of more land, as this will be enough for our immediate wants."[57] Three days later, Russell met in council with the leaders of the Six Nations, all of whom "marked their satisfaction & Approbation in the most distinguished manner," and Brant emphatically declared "that they would now all fight for the King to the last drop of their Blood."[58] Russell thought that the matter was finally settled.

The acting lieutenant governor discovered otherwise the next day, when he was "not a little mortified" to receive a new speech from Brant, supposedly written on behalf of the Six Nations' leaders and expressing the Six Nations' dissatisfaction. They again specifically requested that Russell "empower them to continue to sell at their pleasure without waiting for His Majesty's approbation."[59] When Russell held his ground, threatening to end all agreements regarding the confirmation of the current land sales, Brant again backed off, explaining that the Six Nations did not expect Russell to acquiesce, but that the lieutenant governor should interpret this latest written speech as a matter of tribal protocol, in which the Indians needed to voice their sentiments.[60] In other words, the Six Nations' council did not want to completely accept Russell's offers without first officially submitting the Six Nations' objections and misgivings. Brant's point was simply that, although his people would accept Russell's terms on this occasion, they did so only grudgingly, and that the Six Nations still believed that the British had an ethical obligation to eventually recognize their full sovereignty.

Brant, like Russell, found himself in an impossible predicament. The Mohawk sachem derived his nonhereditary authority from a people who still believed themselves to be free and independent, and he was caught between them and the British, who would never grant this degree of autonomy. Brant frequently faced critics and had to deal with quarreling factions at the Grand River, but as long as he kept the pressure on the British regarding land matters, his leadership authority among his people would remain intact. Thus, while facing similar plights, Brant and Russell needed each other in order to effect a compromise that would keep the peace, permit a degree of latitude for the Iroquois, provide a future method of meeting Six Nations' material needs, maintain provincial security, and preserve dignity on both sides, allowing both men to retain their positions. Russell's position was particularly delicate. The administrator understood that after disobeying Portland's instructions, he might be dismissed, and as Russell anticipated, the home secretary was not pleased with Russell's actions. In utter disbelief that Russell would permit "Brant, or any other Chief or Body of Indians, to interfere with the . . . Government of His Majesty's Province," the duke wrote that he considered this "a most dangerous tendency, and the necessity of giving way to it, [and] allowing such necessity to have existed, can only have arisen from not pursuing a proper line of conduct towards the Indians, who, in consequence of the assistance they derive, and can only derive from the king's bounty, should be given explicitly to understand, that they owe every return, which can be expected from the warmest gratitude, and the most unshaken fidelity."[61] The Duke of Portland saw no reason why the British should have to compromise with Natives who derived their material support from the king. The home secretary could only conclude that if the Indians had a mistaken understanding of this relationship, then Russell had not properly implemented sound Indian policy. Russell knew better. Portland did not grasp the dangerous political climate in Upper Canada, and he did not seem to have a full understanding of just how weak the British position in the province was at the time. Most important, because the duke believed that British leaders in Canada could act from a position of complete hegemony, he saw no reason to compromise, and he assumed that mandates could be unilaterally imposed on Native people, even though the Indians still considered themselves sovereign. But Russell realized that if he handled the affair in this manner, he might ignite the rebellion that everyone hoped to avoid. The beleaguered president wrote to Governor-General Robert Prescott, explaining this "dangerous dilemma to which I am reduced: Disobedience of His Majesty's Commands or an Indian War, and tho' I should choose the former, I am not certain I shall escape the latter, for it appears . . . from the offence Joseph Brant has taken without cause that he meant to pick a German quarrel with us and only seeks a feasible excuse for joining the

French should they invade this Province."[62] Clearly Russell and the British government in Canada did not have the level of dominance and control within the upper province that Portland imagined from his vantage point in London.

Portland's view of distributing gifts to Indians also differed sharply from that of the Six Nations. While Portland considered the "King's bounty" a means of pacifying the Natives and securing their future cooperation, Brant and the Six Nations always regarded British gifts as compensation for past services, and they never thought that by receiving the king's presents and provisions they had forfeited their independence.[63] By accepting the gifts as compensation for previous services rendered, the Iroquois understood the transfer of goods as a solemn gesture symbolizing British faithfulness and indicating that the bond of friendship, or the Covenant Chain, between the British and the Six Nations could never be broken. The Duke of Portland's narrow understanding of Indian affairs signaled further conflict with the Grand River community.

Continuing Struggles at the Grand River, 1797–1801

As the summer of 1797 passed, it became clear that Russell's compromise on the land issue had produced a temporary truce only, since it failed to address the real issue of Native sovereignty. British leaders and the Grand River peoples would continue to hold diametrically opposed views regarding the legal status of Indians in Upper Canada. In addition, other issues arose at the Grand River Reserve in which, as in the case of the land crisis, Brant and the Six Nations continued to strive for greater autonomy. Among these were the Six Nations' bid for a resident clergyman, their intertribal dealings with the Mississaugas, a French nobleman's attempt to settle on a land grant from the Mississaugas, and Brant's overtures to the U.S. government and to tribes dwelling within U.S. borders.

As Lieutenant Governor Russell's failure to resolve the land grant issue became increasingly evident, Brant, frustrated but resolute, sought new ways to strengthen his position in hopes of one day arguing his case to the king that his people should receive a land patent bearing a title in fee simple. Meanwhile, Portland, troubled by Brant's machinations, sought for the rest of Russell's administration and beyond to check at every turn Brant's seemingly expanding power. Portland's main fear was that the Mohawk sachem, having extorted a compromise from Russell, would subsequently be encouraged to seek to expand Native power even further. Consequently, the duke wanted leaders in Canada to keep the indigenous nations of the upper province and the Great Lakes divided and dependent upon the British, thereby undermining all of Brant's endeavors. As the home secretary put it in a letter to Russell, it was necessary to give "strict attention to every possible means of preventing connections or confederations from taking place between the several Nations, and . . . the rendering them dependent on your Government, and keeping them as separate and distinct as possible from each other, should be laid down by you as a system."[64] Indeed, Portland's instructions marked a sharp departure from the policy that Simcoe had pursued merely two years earlier, when the former lieutenant governor attempted to encourage a vast confederacy that would theoretically serve as a buffer to protect Upper Canada from American expansion. The difference between 1795 and 1797 was that the Americans no longer posed a threat, and, ironically, Portland and Russell now believed that the Indians themselves presented the real danger to the internal peace and security of Upper Canada.

Realizing that Portland had ample reason to remove him from his post should the duke want to do so, Russell consciously strove to comply with every aspect of the home secretary's instructions for the remainder of his administration. Consequently, Russell now became more active than ever in attempting to curb Brant's power and influence, and he carefully monitored all matters pertaining to the Grand River. Early in 1798, less than a year after the heated land disputes of the previous summer, another issue arose that brought Russell's intervention. Toward the end of 1797, Brant had petitioned Superintendent General Sir John Johnson, requesting a permanent resident clergyman of the Anglican faith to serve the Six Nations on the Grand River.[65] The Indians there had not known the benefits of a resident minister since the Reverend John Stuart departed in 1789, and Brant grew concerned regarding the future spiritual well-being of his people.[66] The Mohawk leader had already selected a potential candidate, Davenport Phelps, a former lawyer who had studied for the ministry and now sought ordination.

As with the other issues concerning the Grand River Reserve at the time, the subject of procuring a resident clergyman soon became linked to the question of the Six Nations' fidelity. From the start, authorities in Canada expressed concern, not so much over Phelps's spiritual qualifications, but regarding his political sympathies. The bishop of Quebec, Jacob Mountain, emphasized the important role of an Anglican clergyman at the Grand River, "not only in . . . Religious and Moral" affairs, "but [also] in a political point of view."[67] Russell questioned the loyalty of Phelps, who had once served as an officer in an American militia and who, as an attorney in Upper Canada, had purportedly helped rally a group of seditious farmers in a march on a provincial courthouse in support of a man accused of treason. The administrator said he considered it his "duty to guard against the introduction of Persons to situations of that nature (wherein they may do mischief) whose attachment to the British Constitution, I have the slightest cause to suspect."[68] Yet Russell also noted "that the placing of a discreet & respectable Clergyman of the Church of England among the five [Six] Nations would be a most usefull [sic] measure in every point of view, whether religious, moral, or Political."[69] The Duke of Portland later agreed, arguing that the Grand River Indians should have a "resident Clergyman. . . . But . . . that the choice should be entirely independent of them, and that they and the Clergyman should know and feel, that they neither have been, nor ever will be, consulted on the subject."[70]

Both Russell and the bishop were probably aware of the role the American missionary Samuel Kirkland had played in splintering the Iroquois Confederacy by turning the Oneidas and Tuscaroras against the British in the Revolution. Kirkland's actions helped extinguish the league's council fire at Onondaga in 1777, and Kirkland also succeeded in undermining the fabric of British-Iroquois relations. Even if by chance both Russell and the bishop of Quebec had forgotten about Kirkland's influence in drawing the Indians away from the British, Sir John Johnson certainly would have remembered these difficulties between his late father and the politically biased missionary.[71] The bishop of Quebec denied Brant's request to ordain Phelps, arguing that no person is "fit to be their [the Indians'] Spiritual instructor who would be disposed to unsettle their notions of loyalty & obedience & weaken their attachment to the Governments under which it is their happiness to live."[72]

To no avail, Brant, himself a staunch Anglican, complained to Russell, noting Phelps's purported "Testimonials of his Moral Character and Loyalty." Brant further reminded Russell of the assistance that the archbishop of Canterbury had promised to him in the king's presence twelve years earlier in London.[73] The Mohawk naturally assumed that the provincial leaders would want the Six Nations to have a resident minister, since they had encouraged the teachings of Anglicanism among his people for nearly a century. Despite these efforts, a suitable and willing candidate never materialized, and the Grand River Reserve never acquired a resident minister until 1827.[74] Embittered, the Mohawk chief threatened to invite "a Romish Priest" to settle at the Grand River.[75] The decision to override Brant's request in this matter was another blow to the Six Nations' quest for autonomy and, more specifically, to the chief's authority.

Preventing Phelps's appointment was actually a single measure in a much larger secret policy whereby British authorities worked to reduce Brant's power so gradually that he and his supporters would not be alienated from loyalty to the Crown. Robert Liston, British emissary to the United States, believed that "every movement on the part of Brant . . . must naturally give rise to suspicion." Considering the "delicate nature" of "the crisis" of Six Nations' dissatisfaction in the face of a potential French invasion of Upper Canada, Liston thought it best "to temporize" with Brant, believing that the British should "damp his [Brant's] hopes by degrees, [rather] than at once to extinguish them."[76] The Duke of Portland concurred, and he advised Russell to "temporize with Brant, even if you have reason for thinking unfavorably of his Conduct."[77]

Accordingly, Russell clandestinely took measures to reduce the chief's influence. The Duke of Portland feared the possibility of Brant "endeavouring to form a Combination of Indians . . . adverse to His Majesty's Interests," and he therefore ordered Russell to follow "the general line of Policy" that he had previously given to the administrator "in order to defeat such Combinations."[78] In making these remarks, Portland referred to his instructions to Russell from the previous November, when he directed the lieutenant governor to keep the Indians "as separate and distinct as possible" in order to prevent "connections or confederations."[79] Russell ordered agent William Claus at Fort George "to do everything in his power (without exposing the object of this Policy to Suspicion) to foment any existing Jealousy between the Chippewas [Mississaugas] & the Six Nations; and to prevent as far as possible any Junction or good understanding between those two Tribes."[80] In addition to giving Claus these instructions, Russell had appointed a new agent, James Givens, whom he ordered to oversee Mississauga affairs, hoping to remove this tribe from Brant's influence.[81] Since the Mississaugas had grown accustomed to participating at the Six Nations' Grand River council fire and receiving their gifts from the British there, Russell feared this growing intertribal connection. Thus the administrator attempted to put a halt to this growing fraternization by ordering Givens to move the Mississaugas' council fire to the mouth of the River Credit, some fifty miles away from the Grand River and nearer to Givens's agency at York.[82] From the new site, the Mississaugas would receive their annual presents directly from the British.[83]

The Mississaugas realized that it was in their best interests to maintain a close connection with Brant and the Grand River community at the time. When compared to the Six Nations, the Mississaugas were poorer and more migratory, dependent primarily on seasonal hunting, gathering, and fishing.[84] By contrast, the Six Nations were more sedentary, dwelling in permanent villages and practicing a more advanced form of horticulture than most indigenous peoples. The Iroquois in Upper Canada were also more numerous than the Mississaugas, who had consisted of barely one thousand individuals in 1790, a small number that continued to diminish as white settlers moved into the region north of Lake Erie.[85] Moreover, the Six Nations had far more experience in dealing with the British Empire, and Euro-American leaders generally respected them more than they did the Mississaugas.[86] Finally, the Mississaugas had been pressured to cede most of their lands in the southern portion of the upper province in the final quarter of the eighteenth century, giving them stronger incentive to enlist the support of the Six Nations in an effort to retain a remnant of territory.[87]

Russell anticipated some difficulty in separating the Mississaugas from the Six Nations. At the time, relations between these groups were very amiable, and, more important, the Mississaugas had attempted to place themselves under Brant's leadership.[88] Russell therefore knew he would have to contend with the Mississaugas' protests when he attempted to divide the indigenous nations in his province. Relations between the British and Mississaugas had still not fully recovered after a tragic incident in the summer of 1796, when, as a result of a spontaneous misunderstanding, Wabakenin, the principal Mississauga leader, lost his life in a drunken scuffle with a British soldier.[89] For the Mississaugas, the loss of a competent leader strained relations with the British and led them to turn to Brant, whom they appointed "the sole guardian of our Nation, and as our Agent . . . [and] Attorney for us," giving Brant control over all of their affairs and dealings with whites. In their speech to Brant, the Mississauga chiefs also reaffirmed "the connection between our Nations, which we hope you have not forgot."[90]

Although Brant had not orchestrated this arrangement, his willingness to accept leadership over the Mississaugas was precisely what the British had feared. Just as Brant had always desired, the new position made him the principal Native leader and sole liaison between the British and the Indians in Upper Canada. Furthermore, this could potentially have given Brant significant influence with the bulk of the Ojibwas and Ottawas of the Great Lakes. Quite simply, such developments threatened a British policy of acting unilaterally in Indian affairs. Any growth of Brant's influence with the majority of Indians in Upper and Lower Canada at a time when the upper province remained weak raised the specter of Brant and the Six Nations gaining the necessary diplomatic leverage to compel the British government to meet their demands. Lieutenant Governor Russell, alarmed by these possibilities, noted to Governor-General Prescott that Brant's activity among the Mississaugas "Militates most strongly against the Policy which the Duke of Portland recommends."[91]

Just as Simcoe and McKee five years earlier had prevented Brant from gaining the ascendancy over the Western Confederacy, thereby blocking the chief's attempts to negotiate a peace between the confederacy and the Americans at the time, Russell and the officers in the Indian Department now took all necessary measures to bar Brant from Mississauga affairs. As in 1793, British intervention divided the Indians by overcoming Brant's influence, only this time the British intentionally hoped to foster the division. Brant suspected the British motives in appointing Givens and moving the Mississauga council fire, and in a letter to Russell the chief claimed that the new policy had made the Mississaugas "apprehensive" and "uneasy," and "they think it done with an intent to disunite us."[92]

In the ensuing council, the Mississauga chiefs voiced their concerns and complaints regarding the new policy, adding that they had registered these complaints with Brant.[93] After the Mississauga leaders mentioned Brant, Claus "immediately answered," trying to put their minds at ease regarding their concerns; without mentioning Brant's name, he implicitly denounced the Mohawk leader, claiming that he (Claus) could not "but believe that you have been urged to say what you have now spoke, and that it does not come from yourselves." The agent also wanted to use this opportunity to foster the division that Portland and Russell had ordered, so he ended the council, exclaiming that those who had told them these things "were bad people."[94] The Mississaugas did not seem convinced, mostly because Claus never gave them a satisfactory explanation of why they were compelled to move their council fire. Instead, the agent twice told them that the only reason for the change was that "the Government looked upon it to be for their good."[95]

The removal of the Mississaugas' council fire to the mouth of the Credit River did not end the collaboration between Brant and the Mississaugas. The latter continued to seek the Mohawk's advice in the wake of Wabakenin's death (1796), a time when the leaders in Canada were pressuring them to make further cessions. Brant complied with the Mississaugas' wishes, continuing to advise them on land matters, further irritating Russell, Claus, and other British authorities. Shortly after Russell had ordered the removal of the Mississaugas' council fire, Brant invited all of the Mississaugas to visit the Six Nations on the Grand River, where they renewed their friendship in May 1798. The Mohawk leader viewed himself as the "guardian to their lands," claiming that he assumed this role in order to fulfill a promise he had made to the late Wabakenin and his people.[96]

By 1799 the Mississaugas had grown very concerned over the government's intentions. According to Brant, the Mississaugas had come to believe that the government wanted all of their lands and was even willing to terminate their long-enduring friendship in order "to deprive them of it [their lands] wantonly." Brant wrote William Claus that he would advise the Mississaugas to maintain faith in the British, but the chief added a complaint of his own. He could not understand why his actions should spark "the jealousy of Government," when he had, as he put it, always sought to "promote the Welfare of the Country" and its "attachment to Government." If British-Indian relations had become strained, therefore, this was in Brant's view due to the fact that the British "in Several instances ... seem[ed] to put aside the Covenant Chain."[97]

The frustrated Mohawk also complained to Claus that the British method of dealing with the Indians had come to mirror that practiced by the American government, and it appeared to him that the Crown would henceforth always exercise its "preemptive right" in acquiring Native lands. The government might pay lip service to the Indians' supposed status as "free and Independent people," but the words meant nothing as long as the government did not allow them sole and full authority over their lands, including the right to dispense with them as they so chose. By denying the Indians the right "to Sell or give as they please," the government would eventually "take the Whole . . . at as low a rate as possible." Near the end of his indictment, Brant expressed surprise and shame "at this conduct of our friends, so nearly resembling the Yankies [*sic*]."[98] Thus, in airing his grievances, Brant had come full circle back to his perennial concern. In a letter that had begun as a defense of his role as protector of Mississauga interests, Brant managed to end with an assertion of the Natives' right to sell lands freely, and of his people's absolute sovereignty over the Grand River lands.

In response to these rising tensions, British authorities temporarily ceased their attempts to acquire additional Mississauga lands. Rather than bluntly inform Brant that he could not serve as agent and protector of the Mississaugas, Governor-General Prescott instead thought it "highly expedient" for Russell "not to attempt to enter into any Treaty whatever with the Messissaguas" for a while. Although he still planned to appropriate more Mississauga territory at the time, Russell backed off from immediately pursuing further negotiations. Russell and Prescott hoped to discredit Brant in the eyes of the Mississaugas, demonstrating to them that their lands were secure.[99] The Duke of Portland concurred, advising Russell "not to shew any . . . eagerness" regarding that tribe's lands "until the Messessaugues are impressed with a due sense of the obligations they are under to His Majesty for the Presents they . . . receive." The duke anticipated "that in due time an opportunity will arise of purchasing" the Mississauga lands.[100]

In spite of Portland's instructions to wait for a better opportunity to purchase additional Mississauga lands, the matter could not be so easily set aside. A cadre of Mississauga chiefs, with Brant as their spokesperson and adviser, had already begun plans to complete a cession, only this time one supposedly favorable to Indian interests and one in which they were demanding exorbitant terms. Years earlier, Simcoe had considered a land grant to an exiled French nobleman, Count Joseph de Puisaye, who had supported the British in their struggle against revolutionary France. Like so many of the French *noblesse émigré*, de Puisaye and his people did not expect to return to their homeland any time soon, and the Frenchman had already begun discussions with Brant and the Mississaugas to acquire a substantial tract of land in Upper Canada. Therefore in April 1799 Brant gave Russell a touching proposal, arguing "it was in the Cause of Loyalty this Nobleman and his unfortunate followers had suffered," and since the Six Nations "had suffered in the same Cause," the Mississaugas were now willing to part with a five-mile strip of choice lake-front terrain at the northwest end of Lake Ontario.[101] The Mississauga chiefs, at Brant's urging, hoped to compel the British to pay the Indians' requested price of one shilling threepence per acre, Halifax currency, for the entire 69,120 acres.[102] Thus, in spite of his warnings to the Mississaugas regarding the British desire to expropriate their lands, Brant pushed forward with the proposal, hoping this time to control the negotiations and manipulate them to the Indians' advantage.

Russell sensed Brant's intentions, and he attempted to circumvent the chief's plan by informing the Mohawk that if the British engaged in further negotiations for Mississauga lands, these would be handled through the agency of Superintendent General Sir John Johnson. Even if the Mississaugas had earmarked the land for the Count de Puisaye, the government reserved the right to alter or deny this agreement. The governor also pointed out that it was Brant, and not the British in this case, who had pushed for dispossessing the Mississaugas of their land.[103] In truth, however, Russell simply wanted to remind Brant of protocol, realizing that the proposed transaction would not occur, and that Johnson's services would therefore be unnecessary in this instance. Russell and his Executive Council thought the Mississauga proposal absurd, considering it "Injurious to His Majesty's Interest & consequently improper to [be] acceded to, not to mention the extreme Indecency of their [the Mississaugas'] presuming to shackle their cessions to the king by any condition whatsoever."[104] Even if the government had wanted to, it could not have paid an amount close to what Brant and the Mississaugas demanded, particularly at a time when the Indian Department budget had already been drastically slashed and when the war with France continued to drain the home government's treasury. Russell explained the abortive agreement to the disappointed Count de Puisaye, emphasizing the impropriety of the Mississaugas' "Innovations derogatory from the King[']s dignity," and the administrator found it ironic "that Indians being ever inclined to express strong attachments to old usages, ought assuredly [to] be the last in attempting thus to introduce new ways in their Transactions with us."[105] For the time being, the count and his followers would remain homeless, and the British still refused to recognize Brant as a spokesperson for the Mississaugas.

Russell did not even bother to inform Brant of the Executive Council's decision regarding the Mississauga lands. From the British perspective, Brant's repeated attempts to challenge the British government seemed to substantiate Portland's warnings regarding the hazards of the government's attempts to compromise with Indians. They also demonstrated the apparent wisdom behind the home secretary's cautioning against the dangers of permitting the existence of intertribal confederacies and coalitions during this period of peace with the Americans. When Brant finally inquired a few weeks later, the lieutenant governor curtly shot back a response the same day that he received Brant's letter, exclaiming that "it was the Unanimous opinion of the Board that this offer ought not to be accepted because it is contrary to past Usages with Indian Nations who have not before (that we have heard of) fettered their cessions of land to the King with any *Conditions* whatsoever."[106] Moreover, as Russell had done in his correspondence with Brant a month and a half earlier, he again insisted that Sir John Johnson would handle the government's future dealings with the Mississaugas.

In his struggles against British leaders in Upper Canada, Brant had lost, and he knew it. Throughout years of striving for the diplomatic leverage that could one day guarantee his people their sovereignty, he found himself checkmated at every turn. Beginning with Alexander McKee's undermining of his influence and authority among the Western Confederacy at the Miami Rapids in 1793; continuing with the further humiliation Brant experienced when Simcoe, Russell, Dorchester, Portland, Liston, and Prescott all worked to deny him and his people a full title in fee simple to their lands; and after leaders in Canada and at Whitehall combined to deny him a resident clergyman at the Grand River, Brant was finally thwarted in his attempts to serve as the Mississaugas' agent, in spite of that nation's request. After this string of defeats and humiliations, Brant could bear it no longer. Yet when the Mohawk's anger boiled over, Russell merely ascribed the disgruntled chief's behavior to either a case of too much "liquor or his extreme Impatience of Control."[107] Although the crestfallen Mohawk for the time being refused to fraternize any further with the British leaders in Upper Canada, he decided to make a last-ditch attempt to sway Prescott's opinion. Brant again stated his grievances, complaining not only of matters pertaining to the Mississauga lands but the Grand River case as well. The chief got nowhere with Prescott, who told him that he would have to petition Russell on these matters. Additionally, Prescott attempted to do Russell a favor by defusing any of Brant's remaining hopes and explaining, "that whenever any Lands were wanted from Indians by the Government, they would be consulted respecting them according to ancient Customs, and they would be purchased from them in the manner prescribed by the Established Regulations and in no other way."[108] The governor-general's remarks dealt Brant a crushing blow, not only because the chief had appealed to the highest authority in all of Canada but also because Prescott's words presumed Native subservience to the British, precisely what Brant had striven to overcome ever since his people's migration to Canada.

Brant returned from his visit with Prescott no less perturbed and resentful than before. By December 1800 he even seriously entertained the notion of resettling his people within the boundaries of the United States. Brant wrote a "secret and confidential" letter to an American friend, Thomas Morris, asking to make "a purchase of the Western Indians" from within the jurisdiction of the United States in order to perhaps "move there," where "we would desire to be under the protection" of that government. In this letter, Brant revealed that he had not given up on his dreams of an autonomous status for his people, and he even hinted at the possibility of gaining an authoritative role over the western tribes within the United States.[109]

In the summer of 1801, only months after his letter to Morris, Brant addressed some of the western Indians within the boundaries of the United States, specifically Ojibwas, Ottawas, and Potawatomis from the greater Detroit region.[110] In possibly his most inflammatory public speech ever, Brant sharply denounced the British while attempting to rally these western tribes under his leadership. He informed their leaders that they "have been misled by the advices [*sic*] of your [British] Father and the mistaken Ideas of the Shawanies & Wyandotts." The Mohawk leader included the Shawnees and Wyandots in his indictment against the British because of their continued close ties to the British at Amherstburg and Brownstown, respectively. Using intentional sarcasm directed at the Shawnees and Wyandots, Brant informed his listeners that he would not address those two tribes because "they consider themselves wise enough to guide their own conduct." In truth, the chief still smarted from the rebuff he had received from those nations when they had heeded Alexander McKee's advice in council at the Foot of the Miami Rapids eight years earlier, when McKee had urged them not to compromise with the American peace commissioners and to insist upon the Ohio River as a permanent boundary between the confederacy and the United States. The Shawnees and Wyandots had not only opposed Brant's proposal, but they also managed to undermine the leader's influence among the majority of the confederacy at that time. Now the angry Mohawk reminded the headmen of the Ojibwas, Ottawas, and Potawatomis that "had you listened to my advice [at the Rapids in 1793] instead of attending to that of the English Shawanies the United States would have had their limits more circumscribed, and you would not have lost your country."[111]

Brant did not stop there, choosing to further vent his grievances against the British, particularly against the government officials in Canada. He informed the western Indian leaders that they only had themselves to blame for "listening to the foolish advice of those petty Officers at the different Posts who call themselves your Father." At this point Brant exempted the king from his harangue against the British, assuring his Indian audience "that the king has no confidence in them [the leaders in Canada]; they are unexperienced [*sic*] and do not deserve attention and the British Government altogether has shewn great ingratitude to those [Indian allies] who have rendered it the greatest services." Finally, Brant boldly claimed that "I am a greater Man than them all, the Commander in Chief not excepted," and "I myself have done more for that [British] Government than any of those whom you call Father."[112] This speech represented a turning point in Brant's diplomacy. Having grown weary of dealing with leaders in Canada, he now sought external support, whether from the U.S. government, the tribes dwelling on the American side of the border, or from the British monarch directly.

Nevertheless, the chief still wanted to form a coalition of tribes that could coerce the Euro-American powers to recognize an autonomous Native state. In this respect, Brant considered his plight similar to the Indian nations that he addressed on the American side of the border and therefore attempted to identify with them. He believed himself dispossessed of his land by the British authorities, in spite of the Haldimand Grant and his position as Grand River agent and captain in the Indian Department. Now he hoped to form a new confederacy and proposed to the leaders of the Ojibwas, Ottawas, and Potawatomis that they meet him in council at Buffalo Creek with the Iroquois who lived on the American side of the boundary.[113] Nothing appears to have come of this invitation, nor did the U.S. government respond to Brant's overtures via Morris to establish a new home for his people in U.S. territory. Consequently, after 1801 the Six Nations' leader apparently abandoned his American scheme, and he resolved to formulate a strategy of ultimately presenting his Grand River case to friends and government leaders in London. Brant still retained a kernel of faith in the home government. Wanting to believe that Russell and Prescott had always acted on their own, the Mohawk remained unaware of the extent that leaders in Canada had taken their orders from Whitehall. The Duke of Portland constantly sought ways to reduce the chief's influence, and when the duke regularly laid Russell's letters before the king, there is no evidence that George III, though having met Brant personally, ever intervened on the chief's behalf. Instead, the home government grew more confident in its dealings with Brant as the threat of a French invasion dissipated. The Duke of Portland and other British leaders at Whitehall knew that the French would have much difficulty in transporting an army to North America. Britain's continued naval supremacy drastically limited French strategy after the string of decisive British victories over several French and French-allied fleets at Ushant, Camperdown, Cape St. Vincent, and the Nile.[114] As a result, in December 1798 Portland denied Prescott the military reinforcements that the governor-general had requested, and from Philadelphia, British envoy Robert Liston also happily informed Russell of the reduced threat to Canada, stating that "nothing can be effected there [in Canada] against His Majesty's Government without external assistance, and the late destruction of the French Squadron by Admiral Nelson . . . will probably damp the ardour of the enemy for distant expeditions."[115] The predictions of Liston and Portland proved prophetic, and by 1800 Britain's naval supremacy had virtually ended France's hopes for a restored North American empire.

The fortunes of war had also made the British leaders in Canada more bold in matters pertaining to Indian affairs. The passing of the French threat meant an end to any diplomatic leverage that Brant had once enjoyed in his efforts to intimidate Upper Canada's leaders. Such conditions meant that provincial leaders now had no reason to give in to the chief's demands, as Russell had done in 1797. In 1800, for example, Peter Hunter, Russell's successor as lieutenant governor of the upper province, used less tact than his predecessors when he "told [Brant] that I would not permit him to act as an Agent for the Mississagaus."[116] Then in September 1801, shortly after the Mohawk's inflammatory speech at Detroit, Brant received a letter from his longtime friend and nephew by marriage, Sir John Johnson. In a manner simultaneously caring and stern, the superintendent informed Brant that the government could not permit him to take on the role he sought, whether with the Mississaugas or any other nation. Johnson instructed him "to give up all concern in their [the Mississaugas'] affairs, and desist from assembling the different nations in distant parts of the country, and only attend to the business of your settlement, except when called upon by government to do otherwise; as it gives opening to the world to put unfavorable constructions on your conduct, which must tend to lessen your consequence in the opinion of those at the head of affairs; and I much fear may do you serious injury."[117]

Deeply hurt by Johnson's words, Brant interpreted this language as a veiled threat. Indeed, Johnson probably would not have sent such a letter four or five years earlier, when provincial security seemed at risk due to rumored invasions and strained relations between Britain and the United States. In his response, Brant vehemently defended himself and his loyalty, and he complained of the government's "change of politics," arguing that there was once a time when his efforts at uniting the Indians "formerly gave satisfaction," but this "has now quite a different effect."[118] The frustrated chief wrote two letters to Johnson in such a vein, but neither drew a response. Having endured war, dispossession, and a forced migration from the Mohawk Valley, this friendship, after nearly fifty years, was over.[119]

By the turn of the nineteenth century, little had changed at the

Grand River Reserve since the Six Nations' refugees had moved there in 1784. Apart from Russell's compromise in recognizing some of Brant's land transactions with private buyers in 1797, the British had made virtually no concessions to the Grand River community. Consequently, the struggle for sovereignty would continue, and Brant proved himself both resilient and relentless in this quest. The aging Mohawk never abandoned his dreams, and in the first years of the new century he would look increasingly to his talented protégé, John Norton, and to some old friends in London, hoping to finally obtain for his people what he believed was already theirs.

5

John Norton and the Continuing Struggle at the Grand River, 1801–12

In the history of the intertribal community at the Grand River, the years between 1801 and 1812 divide into two broad periods. From 1801 until his death in November 1807, Joseph Brant, the Mohawk chief, remained the dominant figure in the community. But as described in this chapter, John Norton, a younger leader whose career was promoted by Brant, came to prominence at the Grand River in this period. Together, Brant and Norton attempted to defend the rights and future of the residents of the Grand River. Brant's passing inaugurated a new phase of the community's history. From 1807 to 1812, Norton was Grand River's most prominent local leader, even though his leadership was challenged by leading British officials in Canada and also by some Native opponents. As the War of 1812 approached, certain factions emerged at the Grand River, particularly those favoring British interests, neutralists, and even a handful of Grand River residents who might have cooperated with a successful American invasion of Upper Canada. In spite of considerable opposition from leaders in Canada, never would John Norton's career be more important to the future of British Canada than in the years following Brant's death. Hence, the years between 1801 and 1812 were a time when the future nature of the Grand River community was debated and its very survival often at stake.

As described in the previous chapter, British leaders in London, other officials in Canada, and the Indian Department's agents had worked in conjunction to thwart Joseph Brant at every turn. Realizing the limitations placed upon him, Brant altered his approach in dealing with Canadian and British authorities after 1801. The Mohawk leader no longer corresponded regularly with William Claus, Sir John Johnson, or any other officials in the Indian Department, nor did he continue to file grievances with the lieutenant governor's office after Peter Hunter, who had succeeded Russell, admonished the chief about his efforts to head the Mississaugas and illegally lease Grand River lands.[1] Having a clearer idea of his opposition, he became more reserved in openly discussing matters pertaining to the Grand River, except in formal council. Although he did not abandon the fight to gain a proper land patent for his people at the Grand River, the chief now understood that he could never attain this through the conventional channels of the Indian Department and the office of Upper Canada's lieutenant governor. In the meantime, Brant focused his attentions on improving the internal conditions at the Six Nations' reserve and on completing the still-outstanding land transactions involving the sales of the six large "Blocks" of land along the Grand River that President Peter Russell and the Executive Council had approved, albeit under duress, in the summer of 1797. If he could confirm some of these sales, Brant believed that this would produce enough income to temporarily alleviate the Six Nations' impoverished condition.

During the early years of the new century, Brant came to rely heavily on John Norton as an ally in all of these endeavors.[2] Born about 1770, this talented mixed-blood of Cherokee-Scot parentage first met Brant during the 1790s, when Norton worked for British trader John Askin Sr. in the Detroit and the Maumee Valley regions.[3] Norton possessed a plethora of abilities; he proved an articulate writer and a fine orator, and he purportedly had mastered English, French, Spanish, and German, in addition to a dozen Native American languages and dialects.[4] While visiting England and Scotland on separate occasions, Norton became acquainted with many significant individuals, including the Duke of Northumberland, the Earl of Moira, the Earl of Camden, Lord Castlereagh, John Owen, George Canning, Sir Walter Scott, William Wilberforce, and other members of Wilberforce's Clapham Sect.[5] Under the direction of Wilberforce and with the support of Owen, who was the secretary for the British and Foreign Bible Society, Norton translated the gospel of St. John into the Mohawk language.[6] He later wrote a history of the Iroquois League, adding his account of the league's participation in the War of 1812.[7]

Brant sensed these talents many years before Norton's travels abroad. In 1796, after the conclusion of hostilities in the Maumee Valley and the British withdrawal from their occupied posts in American territory, Brant, hoping to utilize Norton's abilities, recommended him for an appointment as an interpreter in the Indian Department, to be employed primarily in matters pertaining to the Grand River.[8] Subsequently, Norton accepted an offer to join the department and took up residence near the newly constructed Fort George late in 1796. Brant envisioned a much larger role for the new appointee. By this time, Brant had already experienced his falling out with Alexander McKee at the Foot of the Rapids, and Lieutenant Governor Simcoe had grown distant in all matters, including the Six Nations' attempts to secure a proper land patent. Therefore the chief anticipated that he could use another ally in the ranks of the Indian Department, and Norton demonstrated strong sympathies for the Native cause. Norton made such an impression on Brant that the latter adopted him as his nephew and made him his personal deputy and messenger while Norton was still serving the Indian Department as an interpreter.[9] By 1799 Brant and other leaders at the Grand River had named Norton as one of their war chiefs, after which Norton resigned his position in the Indian Department lest it cause a conflict of interest with his new role.[10]

Although some of Norton's critics and enemies would later attempt to undermine his authority as an adopted chief, claiming that Norton was an imposter and a usurping white man, by Iroquois standards he met the criteria that empowered him to function as their chief.[11] According to traditional Iroquois practice, whenever a civil chief died, top matrons of the deceased chief's clan would choose a successor, usually a son, to fill the vacated position.[12] However, men of significant bravery and skill could be named war chiefs, regardless of family or clan status. Therefore Norton, a Mohawk by virtue of his adoption by Joseph Brant, was eligible to be selected as a war chief independent of the clan matrons' selection process for creating civil chiefs. In a statement made in 1805, Norton implied that war chiefs generally possessed more talent and held more influence than civil chiefs, and that only those civil leaders with the best oratorical skills could aspire to the higher honor of becoming a war chief.[13] Perhaps Norton chose to present the distinction this way because of his own war-chief status, but his view was consistent with the great importance war chiefs had in the Six Nations' Grand River society. Initially a group of wartime refugees, the Natives living at the Grand River had always looked to war chiefs to handle their affairs after their removal from New York. Their principal chief, Joseph Brant, had never been named a civil chief, holding all of his authority and influence by virtue of his martial feats and former connections to the Johnsons and by his position as a captain in the Indian Department.[14] Technically, both Brant and Norton were war chiefs, but at the Grand River they handled all of the affairs that civil chiefs would have managed in the days of a united confederacy in New York.[15]

Though sharing much of Brant's vision for improvements at the Grand River community, Norton had hopes and expectations that transcended those of the elder leader.[16] Brant had at one time imagined an autonomous and self-sustaining Six Nations as independently allied to the British and situated at the helm of a united Western Confederacy, a position he believed his people had enjoyed for generations prior to the American Revolution.[17] Now with these hopes virtually dashed and his influence reduced, Brant concentrated his efforts on gaining full control over Iroquois land for the purpose of generating revenue through legal land sales and leases that would slow the growing poverty at the Grand River.

Norton shared this goal, but he also envisioned much more, desiring to wholly transform Native society. His schemes would come to resemble the assimilationist programs ordinarily associated with the Jeffersonian benevolence that the United States practiced during these early years of the nineteenth century in an attempt to transform Native cultures and lifestyles.[18] Although he was circumspect about revealing the details of his acculturationist ideas to the community at the Grand River, the chief made no secret of his plans when he petitioned the support of important leaders in England. In a lengthy letter to his friend John Owen, he described the Six Nations' plight and asked the secretary and his colleagues to finance nothing less than the transformation of the Grand River community. To begin with, Norton proposed that the society send "a Missionary or an Instructor, a Farmer, a Blacksmith, a Wheelright [sic], a Spinster and Weaver, a Tanner[,] Saddle & Harness Maker" to the Grand River Reserve. From this cadre of support, he continued, "a good farm should be immediately formed, sufficiently stocked with Cattle & the means for carrying on its cultivation to perfection; the Young Men might be employed to work on it, & it be formed into a kind of seminary for the Boys & Girls who at the same time should be instructed in letters of those useful branches of industry." Norton's request also called for "some indulgence [to be] shewn their parents or relations to encourage them to be instructed, a little bribery used for the promotion of religion and industry may perhaps be excused and leave us only to regret that the blindness of the bulk of Mankind sometimes may reduce us to that necessity."[19]

Norton's description of a seminary and educational farm resembled the mission stations that the U.S. government encouraged among Native peoples at the time. Norton probably knew of the activities of Quakers, Moravians, and Presbyterians who ran government-supported missions among the Iroquois in New York and among the Cherokees, Shawnees, Delawares, and Muskogees.[20] Furthermore, in attempting to convince Owen of the benefits of such programs, the chief even praised "the System of the United States to keep friendly & contented the Indians."[21]

This praise and optimism regarding U.S. Indian policy probably stemmed from Norton's knowledge of the successful transition toward a commercial agricultural economy made by his father's people, the Cherokees.[22] Just how much the American government was responsible for these developments among the Cherokees is debatable, but Norton believed that the government had "sacredly observed and guaranteed the Treaty [of Hopewell, 1785]" and with good results.[23] After Norton's visit to Cherokee country, he praised that nation for retaining "the appearance of Independence," and for making vast improvements in agriculture, including both "Cultivation" and "great herds of cattle." He also lauded Cherokee women for their skill in spinning and weaving.[24] The mixed-blood chief hoped to duplicate these successes at the Grand River, but he understood the fragility of developing societies, and he especially feared the external pressure that encroaching European settlements placed on Indian communities attempting to acculturate. Even for the mighty Cherokees, Norton predicted that it would require at least a century of uninterrupted development before "they might become a flourishing, civilized Nation."[25]

Norton's zeal for acculturationist reforms stemmed in large part from his genuine Christian faith. He considered himself an Anglican, a faith shared by many Mohawks at the time, but Norton had internalized and personalized his faith to a much greater degree than most Mohawks. Wherever he went, he sought opportunities to worship with other Christians, and he was determined to eventually bring all Native peoples to the knowledge of the beliefs he had adopted. Shortly after his return from his first trip to England in 1804-5, he distributed five hundred copies of his translated gospel of St. John at the Grand River, and when he later stopped at the Cherokee village of Willstown in present-day northern Alabama, he addressed the chiefs in council there, "lay[ing] before them, that which is due from Man to God; the frailty of the one, the Great Mercy of the Other, a brief account of the Creation; the Fall, and the Redemption of the World by our Lord Jesus; with the duties he inculcates, and their application in life."[26] Also along this southern journey, Norton stopped at a Moravian mission in northern Georgia and "joined in the devotions of these worthy people." He described them as "Missionaries, who are blest with the feelings of true religion. May the Almighty, bless and prosper the pious labours of these worthy Christians, who sojourn with a strange nation."[27]

Despite Norton's enthusiasm for transforming Indian communities into Christian societies, a large number of Natives, both at the Grand River and elsewhere, did not embrace his ideas. In a letter to Owen, Norton confessed that "religion does not flourish as might be wished—there is too much catching at the shadow and neglecting the substance."[28] Part of the problem, as Norton later complained, was that "there is no proper minister to instruct them in the word of God." Since the leaders of Upper Canada and Whitehall had denied Brant's request for a resident clergyman in the late 1790s, an ordained minister visited them only about twice a year.[29] Norton feared that legitimate conversions would not occur on these rare occasions, because "it is only the ceremony that is perceived," and he lamented that "the established Church of England do [sic] not take upon themselves" the style of missions that the Moravians practice.[30] Rev. Clark Kendrick, a visiting minister from the Massachusetts Baptist Missionary Society, corroborated Norton's fears, exclaiming, "You may see the natives returning from the whisky shops, when they appear and act more like incarnate devils than Christians."[31]

The lack of a resident clergyman at Grand River may have hindered the spread of Christianity, but other obstacles impeded this as well. The Grand River Reserve was an intertribal, multicultural community, containing a number of religious orientations. On a visit to the Grand River villages in 1800, Rev. Samuel Kirkland encountered a Mohawk prophet who experienced visions and prophecies from "the *Upholder of the Skies*."[32] The Mohawk holy man also had reintroduced the Iroquois White Dog ceremony with considerable success at the Grand River and elsewhere. Brant was grudgingly compelled to permit this prophet's sacrifices and rituals, because the latter's teaching had "gained almost universal credit in the settlement."[33]

The Mohawk's prophecies and practices bore similarities to the teachings of the Seneca prophet Handsome Lake, whose new religion had a significant impact throughout all Iroquois settlements in the same period. Handsome Lake viewed his teachings as a restoration and purification of a traditional Iroquois religion.[34] His tenets derived from a series of visions in 1799 and 1800 in which the Creator instructed Handsome Lake to revive a number of religious rituals that had nearly lapsed among the Senecas and other Iroquois nations. The Creator's revelations also entailed the observance of a strict moral code, calling for abstinence from drunkenness, wife abuse, infidelity, promiscuity, gambling, theft, witchcraft, bickering, and gossiping.[35] Handsome Lake's people needed to adhere strictly to the observance and practice of this modified faith, lest the world come to an end. These teachings appear to have gained some adherents at the Grand River.

Brant, Norton, and other Christians at the Grand River indirectly benefited from the spread of Handsome Lake's religion of the longhouse, for the Seneca prophet espoused a number of the ideals regarding lifestyle and culture that the Christian missionaries also championed. In addition to his rigid moral code, Handsome Lake spread a message of peace, denouncing every form of conflict and warfare, and he even announced that Iroquois men should now take up agriculture for a living.[36] These precepts departed radically from Iroquois cultural practices of merely a generation earlier, when warfare had been a necessary component of Iroquois life in the ongoing struggle to preserve the League and extend the Covenant Chain, and when agricultural pursuits were reserved strictly for women. Handsome Lake further struck a blow at long-standing Iroquois tradition when he called for the formation of male-led nuclear families, which would mean an end to matrilocal family settings and a decreased significance of the matrilineal clan system, further diminishing the role of women in Iroquois society.[37] While the new religion revolutionized Iroquois life and resembled elements of Christian culture, its purpose was to preserve the Iroquois community intact against the onrush of Christian culture.[38]

In light of such sweeping changes by respected religious leaders from within the former League, Norton's own acculturationist schemes appear less radical. Like Handsome Lake, the adopted Six Nations' leader did not believe that agricultural labor diminished a warrior's honor and dignity. As Norton once remarked, "The most industrious at the plough, generally shew themselves the most persevering at the chase, when in Winter they throw aside the hoe and take up the gun."[39] Norton also believed, as he put it, that "possession of property is the basis of civilization," and that "little hopes can be entertained of their [the Six Nations'] improvement either in Christianity or agriculture" without the tribes' adoption of a private property system.[40] Norton, like Handsome Lake, was very concerned about the further loss of Native lands, and he feared that unless the Six Nations chose to adapt and privately use the land, they would eventually lose it to scheming people.

Norton resented the pattern of white encroachments and Native land dispossession that tended to accompany the Jefferson administration's assimilationist programs and Christian evangelization. The establishment of mission stations and forced land cessions always followed in the wake of Native defeats. But Norton rejected the idea that Natives could not become Christians while they were still thriving cultures and independent peoples. He believed that genuine Christian missions should attempt to bolster the Natives' quality of life and independence and prevent the Indians' slide into the status of wards. However, Norton believed that the negative white influence in undermining Native cultures had particularly prejudiced indigenous peoples against "the Light of *the Gospel*."[41] But the most striking difference between the young Mohawk chief's ideas and those of numerous others interested in acculturation programs was his view that the Indians should retain all of the land that they currently held, and that they should not be compelled to move.

Nevertheless, as a last resort, Norton contemplated the scheme of moving the Grand River community farther away from the whites in an effort to retain the integrity of the Six Nations' culture and political autonomy.[42] The prospect of building a modernized, agriculturally based pan-Indian state had appealed to Norton for some time, and if positioned farther west, this intertribal community could be expanded to include the Ojibwas, Ottawas, and Potawatomis. With these nations in mind, Norton wrote to John Owen, requesting that Owen and the Bible Society "without delay secure a patent" for them at a site near Lake Huron in order to establish Christian schools and agricultural missions among those groups before white encroachments severely tainted their communities.[43] Norton predicted that this "attempt at civilizing them" would "become a general benefit to the whole" of all the Indians living in the Michigan peninsula and Upper Canada. He further believed that the Six Nations, who relied more heavily on agriculture and who were more apt to think in terms of owning private property than the western tribes, would play a significant role in the establishment of this society.[44] Here, Norton argued, the Six Nations could potentially unite with "Chippawas, Ottawas, Poutawattamies, Shawanons, Wyandots, Miamies and others from the Southward," forming a confederated Native state.[45] The mixed-blood leader further reasoned that his scheme would also benefit British interests, arguing that the assembled tribes of the upper country "would be more for the good of the Empire in case of war."[46] Such thinking, though noble and visionary, could never prevail at a time when the Crown feared Six Nations' sovereignty and Whitehall had taken pains to prevent any intertribal connections, as Brant had discovered.

Norton's ambitious scheme to create an independent confederacy of acculturated tribes illustrated the widening gulf between his thinking and that of British officials as both sides pondered the future role of Indians in Canada, and this gulf foreshadowed further conflict between Norton and the Indian Department.[47] Norton came to resent the department as the primary obstacle preventing the process of acculturation and political autonomy for the Indians dwelling in Upper

Canada. The schism grew worse when Norton had somehow gained knowledge of the department's previous attempts to divide the Natives when Portland and Russell had issued secret orders to William Claus and his subordinate agents to foment as much division as possible between Upper Canada's tribes.[48] Conversely, the Indian Department believed that Norton posed a genuine threat. Thomas Douglas, the Fifth Earl of Selkirk and humanitarian who founded the Red River colony (today's Winnipeg, Manitoba) in 1812, recognized that Norton's plan, if successful, "would be opposed by the officers of the Ind[ia]n Department as it would render many of them useless."[49] Much of the remainder of Norton's career at the Grand River involved an ongoing conflict with the Indian Department, a struggle that would eventually reach its climax in a leadership schism between Norton and Claus during the War of 1812.

As time passed, Norton's resentment of the Indian Department grew. He fully grasped the one-sided and incongruous relationship between Britain and its former Indian allies, one in which British leaders strove to reduce their Indian expenses and obligations while simultaneously continuing to assert their authority and influence in Indian affairs and refusing to recognize any actual Native sovereignty. He was also frustrated by the hierarchical structure of government in Upper Canada, which would not formally hear any grievances or complaints by the Indians unless they filed them specifically through the official channel, the Indian Department.[50] Hence, in dealing with an organization whose best interests lay in preventing reforms of the government's Indian policy, and without recourse for submitting appeals in Canada, Norton understandably saw the Indian Department as the primary impediment to reform, regardless of how much the department merely represented an extension of the overall government's policies.

Without gaining adequate redress from officials in Canada, Norton articulately and colorfully aired his grievances to his friends in London. Writing to Robert Barclay in 1806, he described the Indian Department and its measures as running counter to all forms of advancement and philanthropy. He complained that this organization merely encouraged "idleness & corruption," and "unless the system is changed & its efforts be united with yours [that of Barclay & Owen] it will resemble two men jumping into a canoe & paddling against each other," causing the canoe "to remain in the same position."[51] Again writing to Barclay nearly four years later, Norton more pointedly described the department, this time likening it to "a bad tree that not only brings forth poisonous fruit, but is also of such pernicious influence that even in its shade no wholesome plant can thrive."[52] Norton presented these concerns to Owen, arguing that the department's "principal object seems to be our ruin."[53] He asked the Bible Society's secretary to use his influence with the government in order to, if possible, eliminate the Indian Department altogether, requesting that Owen "eradicate this opposition at the fountain head."[54] The Mohawk leader further suggested that the "Government . . . turn the vast expence [sic] of the Indian Department towards the end . . . of bettering the situation of the Indians," which would have entailed rechanneling all of the agents' current salaries into mission programs and material necessities for the Indians.[55]

Norton's struggle with the Indian Department eventually degenerated into a running battle between him and William Claus. Previously, the two had always been at odds, and as early as his appointment to the position of deputy superintendent general of Indian Affairs, Claus had begun to evince his distaste for Norton.[56] Norton had at one time worked as an interpreter under Claus at the department's Fort George agency, and later while Norton was still working there, Brant appointed him his personal deputy in handling official Six Nations' affairs. This in itself must have annoyed Claus, who, as acting agent at Fort George, was technically the liaison between the Six Nations and the government. Norton's fluency in as many as a dozen Native languages and dialects aided him in these endeavors, and in a rather short time he gained the trust and confidence of the majority of the Indians at the Six Nations Reserve.[57]

Conversely, the people who looked to the adopted Norton as their

FIG. 5. William Claus (unknown artist, circa 1800). The grandson of Sir William Johnson, Claus served as deputy superintendent general of Indian Affairs in Canada from 1800 until his death in 1826. An able administrator, he became one of the key figures in preventing the Six Nations in Canada from gaining greater sovereignty. Courtesy of the Niagara Historical Society and Museum.

leader did not feel much affinity for Claus, a former regular army officer in His Majesty's Sixtieth Regiment who had not spent much time among the Indians the way his grandfather and father had done.[58] Norton's meteoric rise and unexpected influence posed a constant threat to Claus, who continued to visualize a leading and significant role for the Indian Department comparable to the one it had achieved in the days of his family predecessors. By the time Claus became the deputy superintendent general in 1800, the department had severely suffered from the government's retrenchment and from fiscal reductions in its Indian policy. But Norton's clamors (and Brant's) for Six Nations' sovereignty and his desire to completely transform Britain's Indian policy happened to come at the very time that Claus wanted to restore the Indian Department to its past glory, and the agent understood that Norton's schemes endangered the organization's very existence.

Shortly after his promotion in 1800, Claus warned Canadian officials of possible Six Nations' disloyalty and treachery after Brant had allegedly made his seditious speech to an audience of Ojibwas, Ottawas, and Potawatomis in Detroit. Regarding land matters, the deputy superintendent general firmly informed the Six Nations that any further sales or leases (other than the six "Blocks" previously confirmed by Peter Russell) were "quite out of the question" and "cannot be allowed."[59] But despite these bitter clashes between Claus and the Six Nations, the history and role of the Indian Department and the predicament of the Grand River nations would have probably caused a breach, regardless of who served as deputy superintendent general at the time. Given this conflict of interests and Claus's inherent bias against compromise, the Six Nations could expect few favors from him.[60]

By February 1804 Norton was on his way to Britain, where he and Brant hoped he would obtain redress for all of the Six Nations' grievances. Claus and Lieutenant Governor Peter Hunter soon learned of Norton's mission, and these two officials bitterly resented Norton's attempt to circumvent their authority. Indeed, the breach separating

Claus and the principal Grand River leaders became virtually irreparable once Norton began his diplomatic journey to the home government. Prior to this time, Claus's refusal to further listen to Six Nations' grievances had merely dampened relations between the government and the Indians at the Grand River. But once Norton departed, the deputy superintendent general actively interfered in Six Nations' affairs, overstepping his authority in his eagerness to thwart Norton.

In the spring of 1805, with Norton still absent, Claus convened a meeting of various Indians from the Grand River, most of whom were not chiefs, and many of whom Claus knew would relish an opportunity to challenge Norton's and Brant's authority, with Claus hoping that the council would disavow Norton and his mission.[61] The agent also invited dozens of Senecas from Buffalo Creek and various other Iroquois from the American side of the border, all of whom were openly hostile to Brant's leadership at the Grand River. Previously, Iroquois leaders still living within the United States never held any authority in matters pertaining specifically to the Grand River, but now Claus endeavored to use them against the Brant-Norton cadre of leaders.[62] This dubious delegation from Buffalo Creek included Brant's longtime rival, Red Jacket. While en route to Claus's council in early April 1805, this group, temporarily detained by ice on the Niagara River, waited on the American side at Fort Niagara, where four American officers later testified that they had heard these forty or so Senecas claim that "they were going into Upper Canada for the express purpose of breaking Captain Brant."[63] Most of the chiefs who supported Brant and Norton, and who by this time disdained Claus, refused to attend such a sham meeting, a decision that played into the agent's hands because it enabled him to secure the council's disavowal of Norton.[64]

Claus ordinarily did not interfere so blatantly in Native councils or manipulate their leadership to this degree. On the contrary, despite not advocating Native sovereignty, he generally respected the integrity and independence of the Six Nations' councils. But in this case, Norton, by petitioning in person for support from powerful individuals in

London, posed a serious threat to the status quo of Upper Canada's Indian policy and to the Indian Department itself. Brant had given Norton letters of introduction to the Duke of Northumberland, the Earl of Moira, and Sir Evan Nepean.[65] After his arrival, Norton became acquainted with several other leading figures in the British government, including the Earl of Camden, Lord Castlereagh, and William Wilberforce, and Camden worked to bring Norton's Grand River case before the Privy Council. The chief's petitioning also prompted Camden to write to Lieutenant Governor Hunter, instructing him to look into the Six Nations' affairs and to give them any redress to which they were entitled.[66] While awaiting responses, Norton met Owen and Barclay and used this opportunity to complete his Mohawk translation of the gospel of John. On Christmas Eve, 1804, he addressed the Bath and West of England Agricultural Society.[67] Having gained a hearing from and approval of some of the most powerful individuals in the country, Norton appeared on the verge of success.

Claus and Hunter sensed how close Norton was to succeeding and fought back. Hunter responded to the Earl of Camden, reporting Norton's public disavowal by the Six Nations' chiefs in council. When this news arrived in London in the summer of 1805, it raised many questions and virtually destroyed Norton's hopes of gaining the Six Nations' coveted title to the Grand River lands.[68] The government's leading ministers, including Camden and the Privy Council, suddenly became more concerned with Norton's identity and his credentials than they were with the status of the Grand River lands. In July Norton wrote detailed letters to Camden and Castlereagh, defending his position and qualifications, and he submitted a full report to the Privy Council, detailing the history of the Grand River case and the Six Nations' grievances.[69] Despite the chief's continued efforts, Camden and the Privy Council became evasive. Furthermore, Norton had failed to bring a copy of the Haldimand Grant at the outset of his journey from the Grand River, and the administrators in Britain informed him that they could not make any decisions on the matter without a copy of the original grant.[70] With dwindling resources, the chief was soon compelled to return to North America, arriving in Quebec in mid-November 1805. The strategy of Claus and Hunter therefore had its desired effect, preventing the possibility of Six Nations' independent status, and indefinitely preserving the status quo of Indian Affairs in Upper Canada.

Back at the Grand River, Norton joined Brant in reasserting their authority over the Six Nations' affairs, and they disregarded any of the claims made by the Iroquois councils under Claus's auspices while Norton was in London. Brant, his authority temporarily undermined by the dozens of makeshift "chiefs" that Claus had briefly brought over from Buffalo Creek, now denounced these Seneca rivals for having received pensions from the American government, which, he argued, compromised their loyalty and disqualified them from issues pertaining to the Grand River Reserve. Claus disagreed, but Brant had the support of the majority of Grand River chiefs, who had previously remained silent during the councils held with the Buffalo Creek faction. This show of support for Brant enabled him to continue as the Grand River's principal agent in spite of the wishes of the deputy superintendent general.[71] But apparently Brant never again visited any of the Six Nations at Buffalo Creek, and a permanent split developed between the two groups.

Along with the reconfirmation of Brant as head chief and agent at the Grand River came the restoration of Norton's chieftainship, a necessary procedure since Claus's bogus councils had disavowed him. In council at York on September 3, 1806, Six Nations' leaders upbraided Claus, exclaiming, "You know that he [Norton] was made a Chief in a public manner, you received the Wampum on the occasion."[72] Five weeks earlier, in a series of heated speeches delivered at Fort George, another leader from the Grand River, Benjamin Okoghsenniyonte, rebuked Claus for meddling in Six Nations' matters, and he denied that Claus had the authority to create chiefs, particularly those from Buffalo Creek: "Brother—The right of being chief according to our customs arise[s] either from hereditary line on the female side or from having distinguished by meritorious conduct so as to be accepted as such. This has not been the case in the last appointments you sanctioned—one of them [Red Jacket, or 'Cow Killer' perhaps?] we know to whom you pay great regard has been distinguished in your opinion for some things we have not been accustomed to pay that respect to."[73] In addition to this support, Norton drafted a twenty-six-page memorial defending his qualifications, which he read as a speech during a council held at the Onondaga village at Grand River on February 12, 1807.[74] In this lengthy address, he noted that when the letter of the Six Nations' supposed disavowal of his activities in London arrived at Whitehall, he suspected "it to be some misrepresentation from Fort George [Claus's headquarters]." He went on to praise "the greater part of the Grand River people, particularly those who were Chiefs," who "could not be led into the error" of supporting Claus.[75]

In spite of Six Nations' leaders' repeated rebukes, Claus continued to resist Brant's leadership and Norton's reinstatement. By early April 1807, shortly after Norton's speech at Onondaga, Claus wrote to Francis Gore, the new lieutenant governor of Upper Canada who had replaced the recently deceased Peter Hunter. The agent wanted to convey to Gore the identity of the man he believed was their primary antagonist in Indian affairs, asserting that "John Norton is such a Character that any thing he does will not surprise me." Claus went on to deride all the Six Nations' leaders, ridiculing the headmen's claims that the Indian Department refused to relay their grievances to the lieutenant governor. Most important, the deputy superintendent general repeated to Gore the vow he had made to an old Onondaga chief a year earlier: "I would not take notice of any thing from them [the Six Nations] in which Norton was concerned."[76]

Yet Claus would find it difficult to disregard Norton's claims to leadership. Only twelve days after Claus's letter to Gore, Norton delivered another speech at the Grand River, supporting Brant and expressing the Six Nations' grievances regarding the delays and poor handling of several land sales that Peter Russell had approved ten years earlier. Norton also admonished Claus for not recognizing the proper leaders at the Grand River, and concluded by expressing his

FIG. 6. *Major John Norton*, by Thomas Phillips (circa 1816). As a Cherokee-Scot who became the adopted nephew and protégé of Joseph Brant, the talented John Norton spoke many languages, and he would ultimately become Brant's successor. Like Brant, he struggled for Six Nations' sovereignty at the Grand River, but he would temporarily enjoy virtually sole control over Indian affairs there during the War of 1812. Collection of the Duke of Northumberland, Alnwick Castle/Syon House. Photograph: Photographic Survey, Courtauld Institute of Art, London.

hope that, as he put it, "a practice so improper may be dropped for the future."[77] Judging from the council records of 1806 and 1807, and from numerous statements made by Brant and Norton during these years, it is clear that the majority of the Indians at the Grand River believed that Claus had overstepped by manipulating their councils, and that he had no right to discredit Norton or to discount Norton's status as chief. At the time of Brant's death in November 1807, therefore, Norton was poised to succeed Brant as chief of the Six Nations at the Grand River, and the majority of leaders there hoped for this succession.[78]

The Grand River Community, 1807–12

After Brant's death, Norton became head chief at the Grand River. In May 1808 "the chiefs & principal Warriors of all the Five [Six] Nations living on the Grand River" appointed Norton "solely to be at the head of their Councils." Knowing that this decision would not be popular with Canadian authorities, Norton insisted that the tribal council "first make known to [the] Government this their determination." It was not the most promising beginning to what proved to be a long career as the Grand River community's leader, but it was a realistic gesture on Norton's part given, as he put it, "how obnoxious I am to [the] Government."[79]

One thing, however, was not realistically possible. Norton would not be recognized as Brant's successor as the Six Nations' agent in the Indian Department.[80] This mattered not at all to Norton because his view of the department was so negative that he had no wish to be associated with it. Moreover, neither he nor Claus could have tolerated working with each other as fellow agents. Initially, therefore, the chief did his best to avoid further direct confrontations with either Claus or Gore. Norton did try to influence British policy by writing letters to friends in London, continuing to petition for their support of his plan to evangelize and acculturate the residents of the Grand River community. Although never sufficient by themselves to bring about the kind of Indian society that the chief envisioned at the Grand River, these letters brought the plight of the Six Nations to the attention of some of the highest-ranking leaders in the empire and thereby did much to keep the pressure on the home government to compel Canada's administrators to relieve the Indians' distress.

The impact of Norton's efforts and those of his supporters in Britain was most evident when Secretary of War Lord Castlereagh wrote to Governor-General Sir James Craig in April 1809, inquiring as to the status and condition of the Indians of Upper Canada. The tenor of Castlereagh's letter indicated that he did not personally trust Norton, referring to him as someone "who calls himself an Indian," who had come to Britain "without any regular Deputation, and without any previous Communication with the Lieut. Governor of Upper Canada." The secretary further alluded to Claus's report, in which "the Indian Chiefs disavowed Mr. Norton's Journey and the objects of it."[81] But in spite of his skepticism regarding Norton's identity, Castlereagh went on to indicate that Norton had powerful supporters in the government and that those lobbying for him were on the verge of success. According to Castlereagh, several of the king's ministers wanted to investigate the Haldimand affair to determine the feasibility of implementing significant policy reforms regarding the Indians, possibly even to the extent that Brant and Norton had long envisioned.[82]

Despite this apparently renewed interest on the Grand River case, Castlereagh's instructions to Craig contained a request that indicated his reluctance to undertake any substantial reforms. The secretary of war sought the opinions of the top officials in both Upper and Lower Canada regarding the proposed reforms, indicating that the home government was not prepared to impose radical reforms in Britain's Indian policy in Canada over the objections of their administrators there. For their part, Claus and Gore were resolutely opposed to such sweeping reforms. From their perspective, Upper Canada remained simply too weak to allow any significant degree of autonomy or union among the Indians. Gore predicted that if the Indians had sovereign control over their lands, they would fall victim to "an unprincipled set of Land Jobbers, who in their unrestrained Intercourse with the Indians, would in the first Instance, teach them to despise the Government that protected them, and in the next, would defraud them of their Land."[83] With much of the populace of Upper Canada already possessing less than a lukewarm loyalty toward Britain, and with more American immigrants constantly streaming across the border, the government in Canada could ill afford to relinquish sovereign control over Native territory.

These concerns represented only a portion of Gore's response to Castlereagh. Since Castlereagh had asked for their opinions, Gore and Claus seized this opportunity to further discredit Norton, taking their revenge on him for reasserting his rights as chief upon his return from Britain. The prospect of placing the Natives under the supervision or control of Norton was precisely what Upper Canada's leaders sought to avoid. Consequently, Gore cast Norton as an imposter of humble birth, stressing that "he is a Scotsman by Birth and came to Canada, a private soldier."[84] In addition to attempting to demean Norton's identity, Gore (basing his allegations mainly on information provided by Claus) proceeded to suggest that Norton had corrupt motives for attempting to handle the Grand River affairs.[85] Gore alleged that Norton, like the late Brant, practiced "extensive sums of corruption," hoping to pocket much of the revenue generated from forthcoming land sales if the Six Nations could begin to alienate their lands.[86]

Gore's allegations against both Brant and Norton were very serious. In truth, Gore had only lived in Upper Canada for a short time, and he consequently knew little about the matter; he merely relayed information that Claus had given him. The fact was that Brant had handled his business affairs too poorly to have had any great chance of succeeding at the large-scale intrigues of which he stood accused. Without adequate education or the experience necessary to engage in the sophisticated type of business that he had attempted to transact in the sales of the approved blocks of land at the Grand River, the late chief often became confused and worked at odds against his appointed trustees.[87] For his part, Norton exhibited even less of a desire to accumulate wealth than Brant had, and at certain times the younger chief demonstrated apparent lapses of thought in financial matters. He had previously fallen into debt to his former employer, trader John Askin Sr., and he also ran up big debts during his trips to Great Britain.[88] Even when Norton permanently left the Grand River region in 1823, he showed no concern about collecting his continuing pension payments.[89] Claus and Gore never understood Norton, nor did they discern his true motives. They probably remembered the cases of Matthew Elliott and John Dease, both of whom embezzled Native goods, and they assumed that almost anyone would practice such graft, or worse, if only given the opportunity. Thus they failed to see any difference when Brant and Norton clamored for Six Nations' sovereignty and control over Grand River lands.

In addition to this distrust of Norton's motives and concerns for Upper Canada's security, the government had another reason for being unwilling to allow Indian autonomy or to permit any significant reforms at the Grand River, and this was their skepticism regarding the Native capability of maintaining intertribal unity. In his letter to Castlereagh, Gore discouraged alterations in Whitehall's Indian policy, arguing, "It is impossible for a large body of Indians to subsist together, for any Considerable time, in any one part of the Country—they would soon disperse, and form themselves into small Bands."[90] Gore's thoughts may have contained an element of truth regarding the Natives' reluctance to abandon their former lifestyles and take on a sedentary existence, but he showed no desire or willingness to ever give Grand River's residents a choice. Furthermore, the tone of his remarks, often cynical, indicated that he had no confidence in the Indians' ability to adapt, and the lieutenant governor offered no sort of alternative plan to help foster Native people's future survival. Gore's opinion stood in stark contrast to Norton's; the latter believed that his people at the Grand River, like the Cherokees, would make any changes necessary for their future survival and integrity as a confederacy. But the administrator derided the efforts of the philanthropists in London and spoke condescendingly of the Indians in his province. Writing to Lord Camden's undersecretary, Edward Cooke, MP, Gore complained, "I only wish Mr. Wilberforce and his benevolent associates, had a little practical knowledge to guide them in their philanthropic views respecting these Peoples—They would soon be satisfied, that these Gentry [the Indians] would consider themselves very little obliged to them for any attempt to abridge their National or Personal Independence; . . . —To gain their Lands individually, with the unrestrained Power of Alienation, would be to supply them with the means of gratifying their Passion for Rum."[91]

Gore, while resisting any significant measures of reform, at least acknowledged the failure of the prevailing Indian policy that Whitehall had implemented after 1796. As discussed in earlier chapters, the peacetime policy of retrenchment, entailing a significant reduction in government Indian expenditures, simply could not strengthen British-Indian ties while simultaneously ending British obligations to their former allies. The lieutenant governor bluntly stated that "the System of gradually reducing the Presents to the Indians of Upper Canada . . . preceding my arrival, appears to me, neither to have been founded on a sound Policy, nor agreeable to justice." According to Gore, Native leaders were not shy in telling him, "You are very kind, when you want us to fight for you but when that Service is performed, you shut the Store door in our Faces." Apparently the gifts had dwindled to such small portions that "very many of the most respectable and gallant Nations" no longer even bothered to visit "the King's Posts to receive the trifling quantity."[92]

Gore made his observations about the negative consequences of the shortcomings and inconsistencies in British Indian policy as tensions rose once again between the United States and Britain. In 1807 the British warship HMS *Leopard* violated American maritime rights and nearly ignited a war in the so-called *Chesapeake* Affair by violently seizing four naval deserters off of an American vessel and killing three American sailors. In December of the same year, Jefferson's economic embargo was a hard-line response to both Britain's and France's restrictions on American merchant shipping.[93] This growing international crisis led Gore to seek measures to reduce Upper Canada's internal instability and to prepare his province for the possibility of war. Logically, then, the lieutenant governor wanted to try to appease the Indians, even if merely by increasing their gifts, lest the Indians take advantage of Britain's weakness in a time of war in order to secure their own sovereign independence.

Such an outcome stood as a distinct possibility in Upper Canada at the time. With the bulk of the British army having just begun a difficult campaign under the Duke of Wellington in the Iberian Peninsula in 1807, Canada's upper province was virtually unprotected. Fewer than 1,400 British regulars remained in Upper Canada.[94] Judging by such minimal troop strength, the British government had obviously not given significant forethought to the defense of the province, and as early as 1807 Governor-General Craig even considered the possibility of withdrawing the British presence from Upper Canada in the event of war, abandoning it to the Americans. Acting on orders from Castlereagh, Craig considered "the preservation of Quebec as the object of my first and principal consideration, and that to which all others must be subordinate." Furthermore, the governor-general predicted that "if the Americans are really determined to attack these Provinces, and employ those means which they may so easily command, I fear it would be vain for us to flatter ourselves with the hopes of making any effectual defence of the open Country."[95] Having therefore conceded that any British forces stationed in Upper Canada could not ward off an American invasion, Craig and others concluded that the only hopes of preserving that sector would depend on Canadian militias and, most important, support from Britain's former Indian allies scattered throughout Upper Canada and the Great Lakes. Craig and Castlereagh both believed that "if a war takes place," the Indians "will not be idle—If We do not employ them, there cannot exist a moment's doubt, that they will be employed against us, and in that event . . . [t]he chain of our Connexion which has subsisted for so many years [with them] would be broken."[96]

Accordingly, Gore, in compliance with Craig's wishes, began to make efforts to determine the temper of the Indians throughout the

Great Lakes. In addition to increasing the Crown's gifts to the Indians in his province, Gore sought to reestablish ties to Britain's former allies who dwelled on the American side of the border. He dispatched Claus to Amherstburg early in 1808 to summon leaders of the various nations to council in hopes of reestablishing the old Chain of Friendship that had nearly lapsed after Fallen Timbers fourteen years earlier. Claus did not have to petition very hard; Indians throughout the Great Lakes, northern Ohio, and Indiana Territory, and from west of Lake Michigan, rapidly answered the king's call. During the spring, various groups continued to filter in. In June the Shawnee leader Tecumseh and some of his followers also visited the post, where they met Claus, opening communication between the Indian Department and the growing intertribal confederacy at Prophetstown on the Wabash, which gave the British a link to the multiple nations living there.[97] The next month Gore personally held a council at Amherstburg, where he addressed approximately one thousand warriors and one hundred chiefs, including Tecumseh, who had returned with many of his followers from the Wabash.[98]

The positive response of Natives living in the United States to British overtures was not immediately shared by those living at the Grand River. American expansion seriously endangered the future of the tribes beyond Canada's borders. By contrast, the Six Nations at the Grand River did not face an immediate territorial threat, and therefore had much less incentive to fight for the Crown. As Gore had commented in his lengthy letter to Castlereagh in 1809, many of Upper Canada's resident Indians hardly bothered any more to visit the posts in order to receive the king's bounty.[99]

Precarious conditions in Upper Canada—namely the uncertainty of the Six Nations' support and the question of the loyalty of the militias—caused a curious aberration in Sir James Craig's Indian policy. Canada's administrators and agents knew that they could rely on Indians from across the border, but they now needed to be careful that those aggressive-minded groups did not drag Britain into a war with the United States too soon, particularly when Canada's leaders did not have the internal support necessary to hold the upper province. As a matter of necessity, then, Craig and Gore ended the policy of peacetime retrenchment and adopted a wartime stance in their dealings with the Indians.

For the Natives at the Grand River, the new policy temporarily meant additional gifts; for Norton, it eventually led to a wartime commission and significant autonomy as agent and commander of the Six Nations during the upcoming conflict. Though Claus and Gore both despised him, they recognized that Norton continued to hold considerable influence over the Six Nations, and they temporarily avoided provoking or alienating the chief any further lest he discourage those at the Grand River from supporting Britain in its anticipated struggle. As a result, Upper Canada's leaders avoided interfering significantly in Grand River affairs between 1810 and 1812.

Just how far would the British government go to gain Indian support, particularly that of the Grand River nations, in the face of the new international crisis? Certainly, some type of fair and permanent understanding with the Indians was desirable; British leaders did not want to have to periodically rely on questionable Native fidelity every time a crisis arose. As war drew near, all hopes of compromise grew dim, and the Indian agents in Canada reverted to their old practice of increasing gifts to Indians and tenaciously pressuring the Indians to fight for the Crown if necessary. As always, this policy tended to blur the extent of mutual obligations in the Anglo-Native relationship. Were the Indians subjects or allies? Craig continued to pursue the dual stance of telling the Indians to prepare themselves for war, while informing the Americans of his country's neutrality.[100] These contradictory actions could only lead to further distrust on the part of the Natives or the Americans, or both.

The approach of war also brought other changes in Canada. In the autumn of 1811, Norton received favorable news regarding a change in Upper Canada's leadership. In his journal, Norton stated that Major General Isaac Brock "arrived at York, to take the command of the

Troops in the Upper Province,—and also assume the civil Government under the Title of President, at the same time that Francis Gore Esqr.—Lieut. Governor, took his Departure for England." Regarding this transition, which entailed the removal of Gore, one of Norton's principal antagonists, the chief wrote, "This change was very well received throughout the Province." Further emphasizing the contrast between Gore and Brock, Norton added that Brock displayed "discernment, candour & rectitude," qualities that "confounded the spirit of Party, and exposed the Mystery of Calumny."[101]

Brock's arrival may have prevented Norton from leaving Canada. Discouraged by the belief that his vision of reform would never occur under Gore's leadership, Norton had decided, as he put it, "to retire to the South West, to prepare an establishment where we might live undisturbed by factious disputes."[102] But Brock's arrival gave Norton new hope, and soon after, the general summoned the headman to York to discuss the mood of the Indians at the Grand River and to ascertain what was needed to secure their aid should war break out.

Norton seized this opportunity to apprise Brock of the Six Nations' history and grievances at the Grand River, informing him that the people there desired, above all else, a proper land title. Though the general remained noncommittal, he maintained a "favourable Disposition" toward the Grand River people, and in a subsequent letter to Norton he expressed a "disposition to favour their requests" as much as was in his power. Claus once again attempted to prevent the Six Nations' leaders from submitting the land question to Brock, but Norton claimed that "this time" the agent's intrigues were "without effect."[103] Perhaps for the first time since the creation of the upper province more than two decades earlier (1791), the Six Nations' leaders at the Grand River had the opportunity to address a lieutenant governor who earnestly desired to hear their pleas, and to do so without interference from the Indian Department. Norton was quite taken by Brock's caring and thoughtful response, and upon hearing the general give his honest assessment in interpreting the Haldimand Grant as a full, exclusive land title for the Six Nations, the chief immediately threw his support behind the military governor. "From the time that he made this candid avowal," Norton wrote, "I became opposed to insisting any further on the Land Matters, until we should see the end of expected hostilities."[104]

Norton was probably a bit surprised by the officer's verbal concession on the point of Six Nations' land rights. Brock may have been the first British leader ever to acknowledge Six Nations' sovereign rights over the Grand River lands, if that is in fact what he intended to say when he spoke with Norton. Norton's unhesitating devotion to Brock also rested on the fact that the general confided in the chief, looking to him to provide key information regarding the sentiments of the nations dwelling at the Grand River, and the general hoped that the chief's loyalty would inspire those who continued to waver.[105] In choosing to deal directly with Norton and the Six Nations, Brock circumvented the Indian Department, and Norton leaped upon this rare opportunity.

Not all residents at the Grand River shared Norton's enthusiasm for supporting the British in another conflict. A division among them became apparent in June 1812 after a deputation of Seneca-led Iroquois chiefs from within the American boundary arrived at the Grand River, hoping to dissuade their northern brethren from going to war. Little Billy, a Seneca chief among the delegation argued, "Why should we again fight, and call upon ourselves the resentment of the Conquerors? We know that neither of these powers have [*sic*] any regard for us." "In the former War," Little Billy continued, "we espoused the cause of the King, We thought it the most honourable. . . . Experience has convinced us of their neglect, except when they want us. Why then should we endanger . . . the existence of our families, to enjoy their smiles only for the Day in which they need us?"[106] The delegation then repeated the uselessness of joining in the conflict on either side, since the Americans claimed not to need their services; if they were to join the British, their people living in New York would suffer reprisals from the American government. In his closing remarks, Little Billy added, "We are in their [the Americans'] power, but we do not wish to join them in war."[107] These arguments had a strong effect, causing the people of the Grand River to hesitate for two days in forming a response. Ultimately, a majority chose to remain idle, hoping that peace might continue.[108]

Challenging this opposition, Norton did his best to rally the Grand River consensus in favor of the Crown. Arguing eloquently, the mixed-blood leader acknowledged that the Iroquois peoples living on the American side of the border should remain at peace, but with regard to the Canadian Iroquois, he maintained, "Our situation is very different." For those at the Grand River, it was a matter of honor and security to resist an American invasion, and Norton alluded to the Americans' past treatment of Indians, even of those who attempted to remain neutral, reminding his audience that the Americans "have always been the Enemies of the Aboriginal Nations."[109] He added that an American conquest of Upper Canada would destroy the Grand River Reserve, despite its inhabitants' claims of neutrality.

Ultimately, Norton's attempts at persuasion proved futile. Until the British government satisfactorily resolved the question of the status of the Grand River lands, little support could be expected from the Six Nations in Upper Canada. Without a clear title to their land, the warriors at Grand River had little incentive to fight. And as always in Iroquois societies, each man would individually decide whether to take up arms, based mostly on how he perceived this affecting his personal interests. When the war began, Norton and a mere sixty warriors, representing only a small minority of the Grand River's more than four hundred able-bodied men, arrived at Niagara in July 1812 to help repel an anticipated American attack. Cheered to see Norton, Brock eagerly inquired as to the current general sentiments at the Grand River, but the chief could only reply: "They are unfortunately divided into parties, and there are some plausible men, who succeed in retarding their coming forth,—but when they engage, I have no doubts they are not so depraved as to be faithless."[110] Norton's predictions would later prove correct, but until then, neither he nor Brock could depend on the majority of the Six Nations' warriors. When the chief and his small party of warriors departed from Niagara to assist in the upcoming brief siege of Detroit, his followers dwindled yet further, and by the time his band reached the Moravian mission of Fairfield on the Thames, only thirty-eight men still accompanied him.[111] The majority of the Six Nations' leaders and warriors chose to remain neutral at the war's outset, and the Mississaugas followed suit, withholding their warriors as well.[112]

Although Brock thought highly of Norton and respected his efforts, he interpreted the Six Nations' lukewarm response to British overtures in a highly negative way. Despite Norton's optimism that the bulk of the Six Nations would yet prove faithful to Britain, Brock remained unconvinced. Judging by the small turnout of warriors at Niagara, the commander correctly reasoned that the Natives living in Upper Canada had little confidence in Britain's ability to protect the province against American aggression. Their unwillingness to fight infuriated Brock, who trusted neutral Indians even less than he did the many potentially disloyal whites in his province. He, like his predecessors, believed that Indians could never remain idle during warfare and assumed that they would eventually join one side or the other. "To expect that this fickle race would remain in the midst of war in a state of neutrality," Brock wrote, "is truly absurd."[113] The Indians' refusal to fight further complicated Brock's problems, because most of the available white male inhabitants who lived near the Grand River refused to join the militia once they learned that the majority of the Six Nations' warriors had refrained from entering the contest. The white inhabitants, like Brock, believed that the Indians would not remain neutral for long, and that the warriors of the Grand River would soon take up arms against whichever side stood at a disadvantage. The whites, as Brock put it, were "unwilling to leave their families to the mercy of 400 Indians, whose conduct affords such wide room for suspicion."[114]

Brock's feelings stemmed from the fact that he, contrary to the Native perspective, viewed all Canadian Indians as British subjects, rather than independent people who could freely enter the conflict as the king's allies, if and when they chose to do so. Shortly after Norton first informed Brock of the Six Nations' reluctance to fight, the general met with Upper Canada's Executive Council on August 3, 1812, requesting permission to impose martial law.[115] Among his reasons for seeking such a measure, Brock included the seditious conduct of both whites and Indians, specifically claiming "that the Indians on the Grand River . . . had withdrawn from their Volunteer Services and declared for a neutrality, which, in respect of them, was equally inadmissible [sic] as with the King's other subjects."[116] In viewing the Indians as reneging subjects, Brock seemed to believe that unless they fulfilled their duty, the Natives should forfeit the rights and protection that they possessed under the Crown. On August 4, the day after the Executive Council voted to suspend habeas corpus, giving Brock virtual dictatorial powers, the general wrote to a fellow officer, suggesting that as soon as the government had the power to do so, "the first step ought to be to expel the Indians from their present residence and place them out of the reach of doing mischief."[117]

Norton probably never knew of Brock's strong sentiments regarding the Indians, their obligations, and, perhaps most important, the military governor's conception of the Indians' status with respect to the British Empire. Clearly, the commander believed that the Native warriors living in Canada had a moral obligation to defend the king's territories and interests, a duty that stemmed primarily from their hypothetical status as British subjects. Such an interpretation of the Natives' situation indicates that Brock had not fully grasped the meaning of the Grand River council's earlier stipulations regarding their control and possession of land that the council proclaimed as the necessary prerequisites needed to induce them to take up the king's cause. At that time, it probably did not occur to Brock that the Indians' request for a land title in fee simple also entailed the distinctive free and independent status that Brant and Norton had always espoused. But Norton's unhesitating devotion to Brock from that point forward suggests that the chief also misunderstood British policy, insofar as he believed that Brock agreed with him on the issues of land, sovereignty, and the Six Nations' legal status. Convinced that Brock understood "the true Intent and meaning of General Haldimand's Grant," Norton was content to trust the commander, and thus the Mohawk leader decided not to raise the issue of Six Nations' grievances again, "until we should see the end of the expected hostilities."[118] Yet due to the fortunes of war involving Brock's untimely death late in 1812, this misunderstanding never surfaced, and the land issue would remain unresolved after the war.

Brock's rationale in dealing with the Indians was based on several factors. While regarding the Indians in Upper Canada as British subjects, he sincerely wanted to address their grievances, but more than this, his situation was quite desperate.[119] Perhaps as many as 60 percent of Upper Canada's population were either born in the United States or were direct American offspring.[120] As Brock wrote to a fellow officer, "My situation is most critical, not from anything the enemy can do, but from the disposition of the people.... The population, believe me, is essentially bad.... A full belief possess them all that this Province must inevitably succumb."[121] Given these dire circumstances, Brock was extremely anxious to gain Native support, and he would have been inclined to agree to nearly anything Norton said in council regarding the Haldimand Grant.

Knowing that the opening phase of the war could prove pivotal, and realizing that numerous Natives and whites alike needed to have a sense of anticipated victory before committing themselves to the conflict, Brock boldly took the initiative. He believed that if he could provide a psychological lift to the inhabitants of Canada, they would rally to the king's cause. Accordingly, the immediate captures of Michilimackinac and Detroit in the summer of 1812, combined with the destruction of Fort Dearborn in mid-August, helped unify the Indians in those regions in their support of the British, and these early successes provided the inspiration that Canadians sorely needed.[122] And to Norton's relief, the Six Nations finally lived up to his prediction that they were "not so depraved as to be faithless."[123] Brock's bold strategy immediately galvanized the Grand River chiefs and warriors, and by the beginning of September 1812 the Six Nations' leaders were nearly unanimous in rallying to the British cause.[124] Nothing more was said about neutrality, and Brock believed that the Indians, embarrassed by their earlier refusal to fight, now "appear ashamed of themselves, and promise to whipe [sic] away the disgrace into which they have fallen by their late conduct." Barely two weeks after the Americans had surrendered Detroit, most of Upper Canada's Native warriors turned up at Fort George. The major general commented that three hundred Indians had arrived at the post, and he anticipated the arrival of two hundred more.[125] These figures account for nearly all of the available fighting men at the Grand River, combined with some Mississaugas and Moravian Indians as well.[126]

Although Brock believed that his military successes, especially the capture of Detroit, had shamed the Six Nations into fulfilling their duty to the king, the sudden shift in attitude at Grand River, while remarkable, does not necessarily convey a growing sense of obligation on the Indians' part. At no time did all of the Grand River's warriors fully embrace the king's cause.[127] The delayed decision to fight the Americans did not indicate that the Indians suddenly acknowledged their status as subjects; it merely meant that the Six Nations, acting as a neutral power, needed time to assess the fortunes of war before determining how to best safeguard their own land and liberties. After the initial hostilities opened in favor of the British, the Six Nations, still regarding themselves as an independent force, deemed it best for their future status and landholdings to ally themselves with the British.

The ensuing war extinguished the final glimmer of hope for the Indians of Upper Canada to attain an autonomous status. After their initial hesitation prior to the capture of Detroit, the Six Nations fought with a purpose, distinguishing themselves on multiple occasions. These included some of the most critical moments of the war for Upper Canada, particularly the battle of Queenston Heights in October 1812 and the battle of Beaver Dams the following summer, in which the Indians were instrumental in twice thwarting enemy invasions.[128] On the former occasion, Brock lost his life, but Norton's contingent of warriors turned the tide against a far superior army of Americans, leading to the destruction or capture of the entire invading force.[129] Although Brock's untimely death meant that the misunderstanding between him and Norton on the land issue was never resolved, the general went to his grave much admired by Natives and whites alike.[130]

The war and its inconclusive outcome mirrored the Six Nations' fortunes and status in Canada. After a difficult struggle, little was resolved. When the Anglo-American powers agreed to cease hostilities in accordance with terms amounting to status quo ante bellum, the Six Nations lived under the same nebulous conditions that they had known prior to the war. Moreover, with the advent of peace, the independent status and land patent that the Grand River people had coveted for so long were now out of reach. At war's end, the British government had less reason than ever to grant these terms. In 1816 the Crown once again placed Indian affairs in Canada under military jurisdiction, a branch of government that faced another peacetime period of retrenchment. As the white population around them grew increasingly dense, the Six Nations could only try as best they could to maintain their collective integrity. Years later, in 1841, as squatters heavily encroached on Iroquois lands along the Grand River, the government eventually saw the necessity of consolidating the remaining lands of the Haldimand Grant in order to protect the remnants of the reserve; by 1848 the Crown assigned one hundred acres to each male head of household among the Six Nations there.[131] The Indians of Upper Canada had effectively been absorbed as British subjects, though they would periodically continue to deny this status.[132]

6

Restoring the Chain of Friendship in the West and in the North, 1801–12

After the turn of the nineteenth century, as Joseph Brant and John Norton continued their struggle for autonomy at the Grand River, British-Indian relations elsewhere proceeded along different lines. As a result of their defeat and subsequent events that occurred in the 1790s, tribes residing in northwest Ohio and the Wabash Valley depended less on the British. The former Western Confederacy that once thrived in the Maumee Valley, including significant numbers of Shawnees, Wyandots, Miamis, and Delawares, sought not only peace with the Americans but in some cases also a degree of acculturation to Euro-American lifestyles. By the commencement of the War of 1812, very few of the Native leaders who once supported British interests in rallying the Western Confederacy against the Americans in the late eighteenth century could still be counted among Britain's supporters.[1] By contrast, renewed Native resistance to American expansion developed more extensively from within the ranks of tribes situated farther west, including the Potawatomis from the present-day regions of Illinois, northern Indiana, and southern Michigan; the Kickapoos from Illinois; and the Winnebagoes in Wisconsin. They were joined by militant Ojibwas and Wyandots from the region surrounding Detroit and Brownstown, along with Ottawas from the Detroit region, some of whom had continued dwelling along the Maumee after the Treaty of Greenville. Together, these communities formed a new alliance that

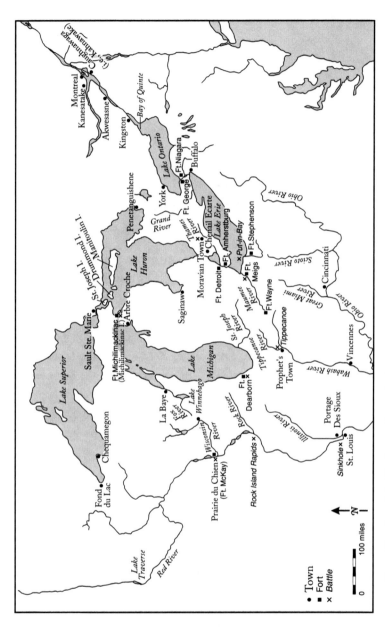

MAP 2. Upper Canada and the Northwest, circa 1796–1815

gained much of its early unity and strength from the Shawnee Prophet's revitalization movement, between 1805 and 1811. These changes represented a revolution in Indian leadership along the Wabash Valley and Detroit frontier, causing further uncertainty in the already nebulous state of Britain's relations with the Natives of that region.

Conversely, British relations with the northern Ojibwas and Ottawas dwelling in the northern Great Lakes region, and with the Sauks, Fox, and Menominees in northern Wisconsin and the upper Mississippi Valley, generally continued as they always had. Hardly affected by Anthony Wayne's defeat of the Ohio tribes in the 1790s, these nations maintained closer ties to British traders and agents in the northern country and upper Mississippi Valley.[2] The expanding fur trade, conducted primarily by the North West Company, the xy Company, and a handful of private British and French interests during this period, increased Native economic dependency without presenting an immediate threat to the cultures and social structures of those nations involved. Their escalating commercial ties to the British, coupled with a greater distance between them and the Americans, placed these northern nations in a position nearly opposite to that of Indians to the south, who, after 1808, gathered on the Wabash in support of the Shawnee Prophet and his brother, Tecumseh. In fact, most northern Natives eventually spurned the Shawnee brothers' revitalization movement altogether, giving British-Indian relations in the North further continuity and greater stability.[3]

An Uncertain Alliance in the West, 1801–6

In 1801 the British leaders at Amherstburg continued to strictly observe the government's Indian policy of retrenchment that Whitehall had begun five years earlier, attempting thereby to further reduce Britain's obligations to its former Native allies. Captain Hector McLean, still serving as the post's commandant, kept a tight control over Indian affairs there, and his superiors in Quebec and at Whitehall never wavered in their support of his control over Amherstburg's branch of the Indian Department. Indeed, all authorities continued to support McLean's earlier decision to dismiss veteran Indian agent Matthew Elliott, and none granted Elliott the dignity of either a formal inquiry or a public hearing. In this political climate, the commandant enforced a parsimonious accounting of Indian goods, and, as much as possible, he discouraged Native visits to his post. While McLean served at Amherstburg, the average number of Indian visitors to the post remained steady at a little more than five thousand per year.[4]

During McLean's command, the post experienced fewer visits from those tribes with whom the British had been more closely associated prior to the Western Confederacy's defeat at Fallen Timbers in 1794. Very few Miamis continued to receive British gifts, and there is no record of any Delawares at Amherstburg between 1798 and 1803.[5] Moreover, the Shawnees and Wyandots had fragmented, and while several bands still visited Amherstburg each year, most of them resided within U.S. territory, and both nations came to rely more heavily on U.S. annuity goods.[6] Several of these Shawnee groups had formed a new pro-American community at Wapakoneta, Ohio, under the leadership of the village chief, Black Hoof.[7] In addition to Black Hoof's village, other former war leaders such as the Miami Little Turtle, the Delaware Buckongahelas, the Wyandot Tarhe, and the Potawatomi Five Medals had all come to favor accommodation with the Americans after 1795.[8] Finally, significant numbers of Shawnees and Delawares had begun migrating west to communities along the Mississippi River during the 1780s and 1790s, further decreasing British contact with the Crown's staunchest Native allies of previous decades.

While these old allegiances weakened, British Indian agents at Amherstburg continued their communication with Wyandot leaders directly across the Detroit River at Brownstown, the symbolic center and council fire for the former confederacy. From this site, longtime Wyandot peace chief Adam Brown remained firmly attached to British agents and leaders. In September 1803, after a year of bad crops throughout the Detroit region, agent Thomas McKee specifically requested that additional provisions be sent to Brown and a few others still residing at Brownstown whom he considered "deserving of His Majesty's bounty."[9] Four years later, when another British-American war seemed imminent in the wake of the *Chesapeake* crisis, Adam Brown warned McKee and his fellow agents that the Americans intended to execute any captured member of the British Indian Department in the forthcoming conflict. Since Brown considered "Captain McKee ... a very good man" who "had always treated him in the handsomest manner, he [Brown] would do everything in his power to have his [McKee's] life saved."[10] Although the Brownstown community would profess an official stance of neutrality as the War of 1812 approached, these enduring ties between British agents and influential leaders at Brownstown would prove crucial to Britain's prospects of retaining Upper Canada.

Despite maintaining close ties with some of the bands in the region of Brownstown, the British had no way of gauging the degree of allegiance the Natives would show them in the next war. Although Brownstown still served as a central meeting place, the Brownstown confederacy no longer existed in the form that it once had, and the Indians were less inclined to view their British Father in the same manner that they had when Britain participated in that confederacy. Consequently, British Indian agents rarely attended the councils still held at Brownstown, and British officials found that the only remaining Native confederacy worthy of the name to be represented at Brownstown's councils was the one emerging among Indians who dwelled farther west, usually along the Wabash, Illinois, and Mississippi rivers. As early as 1801, British agent George Ironside had informed his superiors of a possible restoration of the Brownstown council fire, only this time the proposed confederacy would be composed of Sauks, Fox, Potawatomis, Shawnees from the Wabash and Mississippi, and even a few western Cherokees. The former Shawnee war leader Blue Jacket, apparently envisioning a return to the days of his past glory, worked to bring this about.[11]

Although British leaders in Canada did not yet seek a restored intertribal confederacy (an indifference that contributed to the failure of Blue Jacket's scheme), Blue Jacket's brief attempt at Indian unity had foreshadowed the restored British-Indian alliance of the future that would derive more from regions farther west and north of the core of the former alliance. From the late 1790s, British agents had worked to maintain ties with the leaders of the Ojibwas, Ottawas, and Potawatomis, including those Potawatomi groups dwelling throughout Lake Michigan's southern tributaries.[12] By 1801 the Potawatomis who dwelled near Chicago and Peoria learned of American intentions to erect a post at Chicago, and they appealed to officials at Amherstburg for advice and support. They also requested that their British Father "would be as indulgent to us as to those of your children who live nearer [to you]."[13] In subsequent years, Potawatomi delegations from this region continued to appeal to their British Father at Amherstburg, making allusions to past alliance obligations and their own proven loyalty.

In the summer of 1805 the Potawatomis from Chicago returned to Amherstburg, this time accompanied by a delegation of Sauks, Fox, and northern Ottawas. A Sauk speaker opened the council, giving the British a message from the Sioux of the upper Mississippi region; a symbolic war pipe accompanied the Sioux message. The Sioux sought to unite all of the tribes against the encroachments of "the new white Nation," and they informed their British Father: "Your answer will govern the conduct of the young warriors who are anxiously waiting for it."[14] The Sauk speaker then added that their confederacy "now consists of Ten Nations," and the Potawatomis from Chicago and the Ottawas from Arbre Croche reported that their village chiefs had turned over tribal affairs to their war leaders, who now stood poised to join with the Sioux, Sauks, and the others.[15] All must have been disappointed when Thomas McKee answered two days later, explaining, "Your great Father has strenuously recommended peace and good neighbourhood between the Indians of this Country and the peoples of the United States."[16]

After the United States purchased the Louisiana Territory from Napoleonic France in 1803, the new American presence along the

Mississippi River and at Fort Dearborn near the mouth of the Chicago River served to unite the tribes there even as it presented the British with an opportunity to lead a new Western Confederacy. Soon after the Amherstburg council of 1805, trader Robert Forsyth of St. Louis wrote to Thomas McKee, informing the agent that anti-American sentiment in the West was spreading and that now the Kickapoos also "did not like the Americans and . . . were determined to strike them."[17] The following summer a delegation of western Potawatomis again visited Amherstburg, reminding the British that they still awaited their British Father's instructions, pleading that "our eyes [are] always turned towards you."[18] There was little of a specific nature that McKee could say to Native delegations seeking a renewed British-led alliance. This time the agent answered that he had indeed forwarded their request from the previous year to Upper Canada's governor at the time, Peter Hunter, but as McKee explained, "It has pleased . . . the Master of Life to remove him [Hunter] from this world before he had an opportunity of sending his directions and answer which you expected."[19] McKee's creative response temporarily succeeded, but the British could not demur forever. They now had a growing Native confederacy on their hands, one that was nearly ripe for hostilities long before any of them could have anticipated another British-American war.

Both the nature and the timing of these continued Native visits to Amherstburg are significant for several reasons. First, they demonstrated a growing anti-American disposition among the Natives throughout present-day Illinois, Wisconsin, and the Mississippi Valley long before British leaders in Upper Canada became cognizant of what was happening there. As of yet, Britain had not done anything to encourage a renewed alliance with any of those nations to the west, and agents and officers in Upper Canada had in fact done their best to discourage such an arrangement. When William Claus learned that the Dakotas from the upper Mississippi contemplated sending a delegation to Amherstburg in 1805, the deputy superintendent advised them "not to venture a visit to their English Father at present."[20] Leaders in Canada and Great Britain did not want any further trouble with the Americans, particularly after the resumption of their wars against Napoleon in 1803, only a year after the signing of the short-lived Peace of Amiens. Initially, it was the Indians, not the British, who sought a renewed alliance.

American leaders, however, thought that the British were the source of Native exasperation and hostility. As early as 1805, Indiana's territorial governor, William Henry Harrison, who no doubt keenly remembered British involvement with the Indians in previous wars, spoke of the necessity of "cutting off" the Indians' "communication with every foreign power."[21] In June of the following year, U.S. Indian agent William Wells, the one-time captive youth who was raised by Little Turtle and had married the chief's daughter, warned Harrison of the growing anti-American sentiment among the tribes. Wells believed that the Ojibwas, Ottawas, and Potawatomis were at the center of a new confederacy instigated by the "perturbation" and "intrigues of British agents and other mischief makers."[22] Already suspicious of British frontier activity, American leaders became convinced of its existence after the *Chesapeake* crisis in June 1807. Governor Harrison publicly warned his fellow citizens, exclaiming, "for who does not know that the tomahawk and scalping knife of the savage are always employed as the instruments of British vengeance. At this moment, . . . as I sincerely believe, their agents are organizing a combination amongst the Indians within our limits, for the purposes of assassination and murder."[23]

Harrison's words deeply impressed numerous Americans, many of whom tended to imagine British intrigue at the root of every Indian depredation committed on the frontier. In subsequent years, such American political and military leaders as Henry Clay, Thomas Jefferson, James Madison, and Andrew Jackson adopted this rhetoric in order to justify a forced expulsion of British presence from North America. Theoretically, once Canada rested safely in the hands of the new republic, the Indians would live harmoniously with its frontier inhabitants.[24] Neither the Americans nor the British fully grasped the degree and the cause of the growing Native discontent, but the Americans understood it the least.

In retrospect, the Native solicitations of British support at Amherstburg between 1801 and 1806 not only tend to diminish the credibility of American allegations of British manipulation among the Indians during these early years but are also significant in other ways. The Indian councils held at Amherstburg indicate that the western nations, namely the Potawatomis, Kickapoos, Sauks, Dakotas, and Winnebagoes, sought to form a militant confederacy and a British alliance before the religious revitalization movement of Tenskwatawa, or the Shawnee Prophet, and Tecumseh had gained much momentum. For example, the Amherstburg councils of 1805 and 1806 occurred before Tecumseh began his journeys to augment the number of converts in his brother's fledgling prophetic movement. The western nations that had previously begun to discuss a new confederacy needed only a unifying agent to bring it to fruition. When the British refused to fulfill this role, remaining noncommittal and attempting to placate the war-minded tribes that solicited their support, these nations became fertile ground for the spread of the subsequent nativistic religious movement, and the Prophet gained many converts from among them. A bit later, in 1810, William Henry Harrison recognized the increased devotion that the Shawnee Prophet enjoyed among the tribes to the west. The governor informed Secretary of War William Eustis that "the Prophet's principle, that their lands should be considered common property, is either openly avowed or secretly favored by all the Tribes west of the Wabash."[25] Like Harrison, the British did not fully grasp the far-reaching extent and significance of the religious movement's impact among the western nations until 1810 or 1811. But by then British officials in Canada had come to view the growing confederacy as a potential asset in wartime, rather than a peril to continued peace, and while still cautious, the British no longer spurned Native pleas for support.

While several of the tribes from Illinois, Wisconsin, and the Mississippi River valley sought British support in the early years of the nineteenth century, British relations with Natives from northwest Ohio and the Wabash Valley remained negligible. Much of this neglect resulted from the westward migration of some of those bands, but the primary reason for the diminishing ties between Britain and its former allies was the American policy of acculturation that followed the Treaty of Greenville and the resulting social upheaval that led to a revolution in leadership within the tribal ranks.[26] The American annuities were insufficient to fully sustain even those Native communities that sought acculturation, causing further dissatisfaction. The inadequacy of government annuities was further exacerbated as declining game and the waning fur trade south of the Great Lakes hastened the advent of a crisis. Tribal leaders struggled to adapt to these rapid changes just as new rounds of disease, hunger, and alcoholism ravaged their communities. As the Indians' impoverished condition grew worse in the first years of the nineteenth century, they became increasingly disillusioned with any leaders who seemed to benefit by cooperating with the Americans. Tecumseh and the Shawnee Prophet successfully wooed thousands of followers who no longer recognized the authority of such chiefs as Little Turtle, Black Hoof, Tarhe, Five Medals, and Buckongahelas.

The open rebellion against these traditional leaders crystallized in the form of the Shawnee Prophet's nativist revitalization movement, which began with his visions along the White River in 1805.[27] The Master of Life warned the Prophet of the Indian peoples' pending destruction if they did not return to their pristine lifestyles, which they had abandoned due to their contact with whites. An explicit target of this critique was the leadership of the chiefs who signed the Treaty of Greenville and favored agricultural development via government-sponsored "civilizing" missions, and who had grown increasingly dependent on annuity distributions from the U.S. government.[28] In obedience to the Great Spirit, Tenskwatawa lashed out against these government chiefs, depicting them as wicked traitors and minions of the Americans, whom he considered "children of the Evil Spirit."[29]

Events along the White River in 1806 demonstrated the Prophet's growing intertribal influence and the rapid expansion of the nativist prophetic movement. The local Delawares sought to purge their community of "witches" in order to purify their culture, not an uncommon phenomenon within nativistic movements. Like other Indian communities in crisis, the Delawares had experienced an extraordinary level of disease, poverty, and drunkenness, ripe conditions for a conservative cultural revolt. In this atmosphere, accommodationists who compromised with American officials and who wanted to adopt white ways of life came under heavy suspicion of sorcery and witchcraft. As tensions mounted, Delawares in the White River villages polarized into nativistic and accommodationist elements.[30]

In March 1806 Tenskwatawa arrived on this scene, seizing the opportunity to demonstrate his power by identifying several witches. The proceedings that followed resulted in the execution of four pro-American Indians who lived along the White River and closely fraternized with the Moravian missionaries there. The victims all shared a belief in the benefits of cooperation and accommodation with whites, and one of the executed, the Delaware leader Tatapaxsit, had signed the Treaty of Greenville and subsequently made further land cessions to the Americans. Like other pro-American chiefs, Tatapaxsit favored the government's civilizing missions.[31] Similarly, Tenskwatawa also attempted to purge witches elsewhere. In 1807 the Prophet determined that the pro-American Shawnee leader Black Hoof was a witch, and Tenskwatawa's followers assassinated two of the old chief's villagers from the government mission community at Wapakoneta.[32] In addition, the Wyandots of the Sandusky River conducted a purge in 1810, executing three accused witches.[33]

While scholars may differ on the full meaning of the Prophet's movement and its links to militant resistance, the new faith marked a turning point in British-Indian relations south of the Great Lakes.

The previous level of Native discontent from the West between 1801 and 1806 indicated that a militant anti-American confederacy was brewing prior to Tenskwatawa's prophecies. However, before the Prophet's revitalization movement, the confederate militants sought and expected British support until 1806; after the advent of the Prophet, they did not, and the militants remained aloof of the British for several years.[34] When British support was not forthcoming between 1801 and 1806, the new faith provided the unifying catalyst for a resistance movement. Moreover, although the British at first failed to understand the meaning of the religious movement, it soon became apparent that the prophetic doctrine and its religious zealots were at odds with American leaders, and British agents would attempt to exploit this by making efforts to influence the confederacy's leaders after 1807, directly contrasting previous British policy. Thus the Wabash prophetic movement became the most important aspect of Native resistance south of the Great Lakes after 1806, largely because it peaked just when British and Canadian leaders began to anticipate a war with the United States, giving the nativists and their future British allies a common interest.

Of all the events indicating the shift in power away from the institutional chiefs to the Prophet's nativists, none was more important than the brief encounter between the Miami leader Little Turtle, the most powerful pro-U.S. government chief, and Tenskwatawa near the Mississinewa River early in 1808. Determined to prevent the Prophet's entourage from moving to the Wabash, Little Turtle threatened to kill Tenskwatawa if he and his followers made the proposed move.[35] Not the least bit intimidated, the Prophet scoffed at Little Turtle and condemned all the "Chiefs [who] had abandoned the Interests of their respective nations and sold all the Indians['] Land to the united [sic] States."[36] According to Little Turtle, the Prophet added that "his plans had been ... sanctioned by the Great Spirit and that it was not in the power of man to interrupt them ... nothing could stop him."[37] Little Turtle's meeting with Tenskwatawa had quite the opposite effect from what the older chief had anticipated. It confirmed the success of the

Prophet's coup d'état, and it did nothing to slow the expansion of the revitalization movement, which challenged the influence of the government chiefs.

The nativists' revolt against conventional tribal authority reflected a rift between the chiefs and their followers that had been widening for years. As early as 1801, William Henry Harrison noted that the tribes on the lower Wabash had murdered a number of their headmen, lamenting that the "Chiefs and . . . nearest relations fall under the strokes of their [followers'] Tomhawks [sic] & Knives." The governor further emphasized that "there is scarcely a Chief to be found amongst them."[38] Harrison's words demonstrated that Indian communities had begun to experience political disarray long before the origin of Tenskwatawa's prophetic movement. The Treaty of Greenville in 1795 and the subsequent government civilizing programs had not brought the harmony and stability that American leaders hoped they would. In spite of the inviolable boundary line established at Greenville, American settlers encroached upon Indian territory and threatened to encircle Native enclaves well beyond the line. The threatened tribes began to understand the bitter reality that the government could not protect their lands and lifestyles, and that, as one historian puts it, "the [U.S.] policies formulated in the first two decades of the new nation facilitated rather than curbed American expansion."[39] Harrison's attempt to remedy the instability of the Native communities entailed efforts to make the Indians more dependent on the United States, which meant an increase of Native debts followed by a series of rapid government land acquisitions.[40] However, the flurry of treaties that Harrison negotiated not only failed to reduce U.S.-Indian tensions, but the agreements intensified Native frustration with their leaders.[41] Consequently, Harrison's policy had quite the opposite effect than what he and his superiors intended, further destabilizing tribal communities throughout Indian territory.

Of all of Harrison's treaties with the Natives in Indiana Territory, his sixth and final pact as governor proved to be the most damaging to U.S.-Indian relations. Negotiated at Fort Wayne in the autumn of

1809, this treaty involved the Delaware, Miami, Potawatomi, and Eel River nations, and it entailed a land cession of nearly three million acres, a portion of which extended west of the Wabash River, cutting an enormous swath from the remaining Native territory in Indiana and southern Illinois.[42] Only a year earlier, the Prophet and Tecumseh and their followers had moved to the new village of Prophetstown near the confluence of the Wabash and Tippecanoe rivers, largely for the purpose of guarding these very lands. In fact, Tenskwatawa had told Little Turtle that the Indians intended to unite at the new location, where "they would then be able to watch the Boundry [*sic*] Line between the Indians and white people—and if a white man put his foot over it that the warriors could Easly [*sic*] put him back."[43] The cession under the Treaty of Fort Wayne of such a large area that the growing nativist confederacy specifically hoped to retain produced an angry response among the Prophet's followers and led the prophetic movement to become even more militant. The following spring, while in a heated discussion at Black Hoof's village, Tecumseh angrily snatched a letter written by Harrison (addressed to the Shawnees) from the hands of Baptist missionary Stephen Ruddell and threw it into the fire. The war leader then declared that he would do the same to Harrison if the governor were present. After convincing a few of the formerly pro-American Shawnees to join the gathering confederacy, Tecumseh continued his recruiting efforts among the Wyandots.[44] Then in late August, while speaking in council with Harrison at Vincennes, Tecumseh threatened "to kill all the chiefs that sold you the land."[45]

Clearly, the Treaty of Fort Wayne had further impaired relations with the Indians, and the nativists had no intention of honoring any agreement made by leaders whom they considered to have abdicated. But the aftermath of the treaty also marked a more significant turning point within Native politics. It represented the moment at which the nativist confederacy began to wield its maximum political strength, and the moment at which the majority of Natives throughout southern Michigan, Indiana, northwestern Ohio, and Illinois fully rejected

FIG. 7. Tecumseh. Taken from Benson J. Lossing's *Pictorial Field-Book of the War of 1812* (1869), this only known engraving of Tecumseh depicts the legendary Shawnee as a British ally donning an officer's coat. While Tecumseh might have possessed a scarlet military coat, he never held an officer's rank or commission, nor was he eager to rekindle a British alliance until it became an absolute necessity between 1810 and 1813. Taken from the Library of Congress, General Collections, E354.L88.

the authority of the government chiefs, giving allegiance to the Shaw-nee brothers and the prophetic movement on the Wabash. Prior to this time, the fiber of the confederacy had been mainly spiritual, but after 1809 the prophetic movement began to also crystallize and function as both a political and military entity. In 1810 Tecumseh, without any hereditary authority as a village chief, boldly proclaimed to Harrison, "I am authorized by all the tribes. . . . I am the head of them all." The Shawnee leader also explained that his nativist followers needed to "destroy [the] village [government] chiefs," in order "to let all our affairs be transacted by [genuine] Warriors."[46]

Some scholars argue that the nativist movement became secular and political after the Treaty of Fort Wayne, and that Tecumseh eclipsed his brother's authority at this point.[47] However, Gregory Dowd replies that while Tecumseh did indeed gain influence, indicating a stronger intertribal political structure within the confederacy in the aftermath of the Treaty of Fort Wayne, this did not necessarily coincide with a decrease of either his brother's status or the spiritual revitalization movement in general.[48] In fact, Tecumseh's increasing popularity after 1809 indicated the growing disillusionment of the younger warriors with the government chiefs, and not so much a shift in the confederacy's ideology; Tecumseh's rise did not alter the Prophet's original tenets and prophecy, which dated from the movement's origins on the White River.

Since the confederacy grew out of a religious revitalization movement, its principal war chiefs were generally thought to possess the spiritual powers required to act as leaders in such a movement, or, at the very least, they were loyal followers of the Prophet, who directly foretold their fate. Tecumseh, while often thought of as a political and secular war chief, was perhaps the greatest proponent of the revitalization movement. More than merely possessing talents of warfare and inspirational rhetoric, Tecumseh also purportedly wielded much spiritual power; those who followed him believed that the Great Spirit and the manitous favored the war leader. Throughout Tecumseh's southern journey in the autumn of 1811, Creeks and Seminoles claimed to have witnessed his rituals and miracles, and even his immense "power to deal with the evil spirit."[49] In the North, the Winnebagoes also regarded Tecumseh as an invincible war leader.[50]

Other important war leaders during this era also functioned as both war chiefs and shamans. Some of these included the Potawatomi Main Poc and the Creek Josiah Francis, and perhaps to a lesser extent the Ottawa-born, Potawatomi leader Shabonee, along with the Wyandot chief Roundhead and the Sauk leader Black Hawk. Main Poc held significant sway over the Indians in the Indiana and Illinois territories; many feared him, since his followers claimed that their leader "was not born of a woman but that he was got by the Great Spirit and sprang out of the ground."[51] As a *wabeno*, or the most powerful type of shaman short of being a prophet, Main Poc allegedly could change the weather.[52] Although Main Poc never joined the Shawnee Prophet's following, he invited the Prophet and Tecumseh, along with their entire entourage, to move from Ohio to what became the site of Prophetstown near the confluence of the Wabash and Tippecanoe rivers early in 1808. At about the time that the Shawnee Prophet and his devotees made this move, U.S. Indian agent William Wells at Fort Wayne considered Main Poc "the greatest warrior in the west . . . the pivot on which the minds of all the Western Indians turned. . . . [He] has more influence than any other Indian."[53] Wells, Little Turtle's son-in-law and arguably the most important Indian agent serving the Americans, believed that the key to good relations between the United States and the Indians depended on the government's dealings with Main Poc, and that he could control the nativists in the Wabash prophetic movement by controlling Main Poc. Ultimately, Wells's efforts failed to turn Main Poc, and the Potawatomi *wabeno* became an important British ally along the Detroit frontier in the War of 1812.

Among the other key figures mentioned above, the Creek prophet Josiah Francis, also known as Hildis Hadjo, led the Muskogee religious revitalization movement between 1811 and 1814. Known as the "Redsticks," Francis's Creek followers had initially drawn much of their inspiration from Tecumseh, and these militant revivalists initiated a civil war among the Creek towns that did not join their religious movement and cultural revolt.[54] Francis, a mixed-blood, became perhaps the most important Native prophet in the South during the Creek civil war and also during the War of 1812, when the Redsticks ardently resisted white culture and American expansion.

In the North, Shabonee and Roundhead both became war leaders who sought sacred power from within the context of Tenskwatawa's prophetic movement. The adopted Potawatomi leader Shabonee, who had ties with Tecumseh since 1807, became a firm devotee and, like Black Hawk at the Thames in 1813, interpreted the Native defeat there as the ultimate will of the Great Spirit, after having experienced a loss of sacred power.[55] The Detroit Wyandot headman Roundhead, the only signer of the Treaty of Greenville to participate in the Native resistance during the War of 1812, joined the Shawnee Prophet's movement by 1807, even before the Prophet and his converts moved to Tippecanoe.[56] In September 1812 Roundhead, Tecumseh, and Main Poc, along with their warriors, accompanied Major Adam Muir on the abortive British expedition up the Maumee River in an attempt to capture Fort Wayne. When Muir decided to retreat after learning of an advancing American army, Roundhead urged him and his soldiers to continue the campaign because the divinations of Main Poc and other "conjurers" portended success against the Americans.[57] Furthermore, Tecumseh respected Roundhead as the most prominent leader in the nativist movement. A month earlier at the British-Indian capture of Detroit, General Isaac Brock demonstrated his gratitude to Tecumseh by giving him his scarlet sash. Tecumseh acknowledged Roundhead's rank and prestige by giving Brock's sash to the Wyandot, explaining that Roundhead was "an older, and . . . abler warrior than himself."[58] This cadre of leaders tended to have common goals, and they viewed themselves as members of a unified movement to restore a threatened culture and religion. Unlike the Native leaders who sometimes acted as culture brokers for Euro-American lifestyles among their people, the nativist war chiefs of the revitalization era did not accept leaders who sought compromise and accommodation.[59]

After this radical shift in leadership among the nations in the southern Great Lakes region and Wabash Valley, British officials in

Upper Canada, especially those at Fort Malden (Amherstburg), were compelled to cultivate ties with the nativist faction, or have no relations at all with the most vital elements in Native communities. Since most of these warriors had not served as confederacy war leaders at the Brownstown council fire, British attempts to restore their former alliance involved the challenge of reestablishing diplomatic ties with tribes that had ousted their institutional chiefs. From the years of the American Revolution through the mid-1790s, all tribal factions in the Old Northwest had generally been allied with Britain, but after the revitalization movement had brought about a new confederacy and new sachems, British agents really did not know where they stood with their former allies. Furthermore, Whitehall's policy of retrenchment in the Indian Department between 1796 and 1807, as implemented by Captain Hector McLean and other army officers, had drastically cut the practice of gift-giving that had long sustained British-Indian ties.

Having distanced themselves from the few remaining Native groups in Ohio and those in Indiana for more than a decade, British officials, no less than the Americans, were mystified by the Prophet's charismatic movement.[60] Late in 1807 William Claus, deputy superintendent general of British Indian Affairs, held the opinion that "that Rascal the Prophet" was a French agent.[61] Ironically, while Claus suspected French treachery, the Americans believed that the Prophet was a pawn of British intrigue.

Although Claus badly misread the prophetic movement, his suspicions of French involvement indicate that the deputy superintendent general had not fully dismissed rumors of French invasions from the West. Years earlier, leaders in Upper Canada had ridiculed Joseph Brant for supposedly fabricating stories of French incursions in order to further his own cause and perhaps gain Six Nations' sovereignty at the Grand River. Now Claus thought it best to seriously consider the plausibility of growing French influence among the Indians.[62] The agent was cognizant of Napoleon's stunning successes against the allied nations of the Third Coalition during the years 1805–7. And, despite the fact that Admiral Lord Nelson had previously demolished the enemy fleets at Trafalgar, Claus knew that Britain's growing military commitments on the European continent meant that Upper Canada could expect virtually no reinforcements from home in the event of a Franco-Indian insurrection in the Great Lakes.

The mood of the hotheaded Americans in the wake of the *Chesapeake* Affair gave Claus an additional incentive to begin making friendly overtures to the Prophet and other leaders associated with him. Harrison and the Americans were mistaken in their belief that the naval tragedy was somehow linked to British-Indian dealings on the frontier, and although the incident ironically did precipitate closer British-Indian ties, this came only as a defensive measure after hawkish American sentiments led the countries to the brink of war.[63] The changing diplomatic climate in the Great Lakes region compelled Claus and his superiors to take an assertive role in reestablishing their Chain of Friendship with nations that now fell under the influence of the Prophet, Tecumseh, Main Poc, Roundhead, and others. Claus, who ordinarily maintained his headquarters at Fort George near the mouth of the Niagara River, spent more than five months during the first half of 1808 at Fort Malden, where he attempted to ascertain the viability of a restored Native confederacy and its fidelity to British interests. Claus met with dozens of Indians passing through Amherstburg, but he most earnestly desired to speak with the Prophet. The agent sent a number of invitations to Tenskwatawa to meet with him at Fort Malden, and after receiving no response, Claus finally dispatched Frederick Fisher, another Indian agent, to journey to Prophetstown to deliver the invitation personally.[64] Fisher returned with favorable news, indicating that Tenskwatawa assured the British "of his friendship."[65] When the Shawnee Prophet still did not arrive after much anticipation, Claus sent a Fox runner specifically informing Tenskwatawa that "I [Claus] will be very glad to take you by the hand and as there will be several Nations with you I will be glad to take some of their chief young men by the hand also."[66]

Despite all of Claus's efforts to speak with the Prophet and to restore close ties with the Natives south and west of the Great Lakes, it does not seem that the Prophet visited Fort Malden until after the commencement of the War of 1812, long after his intertribal influence had seriously diminished. Tecumseh, however, answered Claus's call, and the elder brother, accompanied by five Shawnees, finally traveled to Malden, where they met with the deputy superintendent for the first time in mid-June 1808. At this initial meeting, Claus "had at least 3 hours conversation with" Tecumseh, but Claus, like most Euro-American leaders at the time, still regarded Tenskwatawa as the most important member of the Indian confederacy. The agent never referred to Tecumseh by name, but merely as "the Prophet's brother." No formal commitments were struck in this encounter, but both parties exchanged kind words, and the Shawnee delegation came away with "a handsome Present."[67]

Although both the Prophet and Tecumseh initially approached the British with caution and reserve, they chose not to fully reject Claus's overtures. The Shawnee brothers' recent move to Prophetstown had brought the risk of extreme deprivation and starvation; at the new site, the nativists no longer had access to any of the benefits that they had known in Greenville: partial annuity distributions, gifts from the Shakers of Turtle Creek, and produce and livestock stolen from white settlers.[68] While far from representing an immediate military alliance, Tecumseh's meeting with Claus in 1808 was the first step in reuniting British leaders with nativist factions south of the Great Lakes and in the Wabash Valley, paving the way for a future partnership in a common cause. The meeting also opened a new phase of diplomacy in which the British ardently pursued a wartime policy in their dealings with Natives dwelling on the American side of the border, and it marked the beginning of Tecumseh's career as a liaison between British officers and the nativist faction that would support them. Although it can be argued that a militant British-Indian policy had already been revived a year before this meeting with Tecumseh, British leaders had understood their own vulnerability if they did not gain the support of the growing nativist movement, which explains Claus's anxiety over the Prophet's disposition. Once Claus and the Indian Department's personnel had opened communication with these recalcitrants, they were no longer uncertain of the Shawnee brothers' position, and British officials could then work more earnestly to restore the Chain of Friendship.

Tecumseh and the British, 1808–10

Prior to his meeting with Claus in 1808, Tecumseh probably had never entered a British or an American fort.[69] He had never signed a treaty, nor did he possess any hereditary claims to leadership within the Shawnee infrastructure, a deficiency of credentials that led Black Hoof and the Mekoche Shawnee council at Wapakoneta to view Tecumseh as a usurping imposter and demagogue.[70] Black Hoof and the leaders of the Mekoche Shawnee tribal division traditionally held civil authority in Shawnee affairs and would certainly have resented any challenge to their authority from upstart Kishpoko leaders such as Tecumseh and Tenskwatawa. Though Tecumseh lacked the proper authority to treat with white officials, he seems, based on his tendency to separate himself and his small band from external forms of authority, not to have desired intertribal or international political power. He wanted to be free of all ties to British or American leaders, and he did not think that he and other Shawnees should yield to the authority of chiefs who had compromised with the Americans. Thus Tecumseh only became a de facto village chief in the years following Wayne's victory and the Treaty of Greenville; his followers most likely consisted of other Kishpoko Shawnees who also felt betrayed by their leaders who had signed the Treaty of Greenville and encouraged assimilation with the Americans.[71]

From the British perspective, Tecumseh was a godsend. With most of their former allied chiefs now dealing with the Americans, and the future of the Brownstown council fire uncertain, the British had little hope of warding off an American invasion. Unlike the era of the American Revolution, the British in Upper Canada could no longer expect all tribal factions to support their cause. Now they would have to rely specifically on the disaffected nativist elements, mainly those groups alienated by U.S. frontier policy. Even so, Claus and the Indian Department were stunned when more than five thousand of these Indians visited Fort Malden in the autumn of 1808, only a few months after Claus's departure from that place.[72] Such a large number of potential intertribal Native allies linked to so few leaders—Tecumseh, Roundhead, and Main Poc—was certainly more than anyone had anticipated, particularly when considering that British-Indian ties had nearly been severed due to the British betrayal at Fallen Timbers more than a decade earlier. Although these results were due in part to the Indian Department's renewed efforts to restore the old alliance, much of the Native enthusiasm can be attributed to the crystallization of the prophetic movement, and perhaps to the fact that the proselytes needed food as they faced their first winter at Prophetstown.

The potential connections with the nativist confederacy also appeared especially advantageous to the British after the *Chesapeake* Affair in June 1807, and from that date onward Canadian officials strove to restore an alliance with Natives living within the borders of the United States. But such a delicate task had to be done with discretion, since Britain technically stood as a neutral power between the U.S. government and the belligerent Indians in the Old Northwest. Blatant British activity among the anti-American tribes could itself precipitate another British-American war. Knowing that they could not send open overtures to their former allied chiefs who now dealt with the Americans, Claus and his staff favored opening a dialogue with Indians who wanted nothing to do with the U.S. government, keeping the diplomacy more discreet. Although the Americans suspected British involvement with the Indians, Prophetstown was sufficiently removed from both Vincennes and Fort Wayne that neither Harrison nor U.S. agent William Wells could determine the level of British-Indian contact.[73]

In the meantime, leaders in Canada pursued a dual Indian policy, one that constantly proclaimed neutrality and another that prepared for war in case the first failed. Governor-General Sir James Craig understood the crucial necessity of a British-Indian alliance, reasoning that Indians could never sit idle in warfare and would therefore be "employed against us," unless already in the king's service.[74] Thus Craig instructed his officers not to make any public commitments to the Indians, but to privately assure them of the king's friendship in order to gain their trust.[75] At the same time, the nativist allies were urged not to strike the Americans until their British Father was at war with the United States.[76] The pursuit of such a diplomatic line required experience, and Craig reinstated the aging Matthew Elliott after an eleven-year absence from service due to the agent's dismissal in 1797 for alleged misconduct. By 1808 his services were badly needed; not only did the Indians favor him, but he could carry out a duplicitous policy as well as anyone.[77] Although the Americans had exaggerated British tampering with the Indians prior to 1808, the secret policy carried out by Craig, Gore, Claus, and Elliott now gave credence to American allegations of British involvement.[78]

Like the British, Tecumseh and the nativist leaders also used discretion, refraining from wholehearted promises of military support in any forthcoming conflict between Britain and the United States. However, they definitely understood that a reestablishment of ties with their British Father in the face of an imminent crisis could work to their advantage. In July 1808 Tecumseh returned to Fort Malden, where he and dozens of chiefs, accompanied by hundreds of warriors, listened to hours of British rhetoric regarding friendship. Lieutenant Governor Gore personally delivered the capstone speech, reminding his listeners of the eternal bonds between them and the king and of past injuries done to them by the Americans. Gore also boldly informed them that the king still held sacred "the Treaty made at Fort Stanwix in 1768," which had prohibited white settlement north and west of the Ohio River.[79] This prohibition had been flagrantly violated by more than thirty years of American expansion, U.S. military conquests in the North, all the cessions made at the Treaty of Greenville, and the multiple subsequent treaties that Harrison and others had negotiated.[80] But Gore and his cohorts were desperate for allies. Two days later, the chiefs formally responded, reciprocating with statements of friendship, telling Gore that his speech had "brightened the Chain of Friendship," and adding, "we pray the Great Spirit to keep it bright and lasting."[81] However, these statements were not accompanied by any binding commitments.

After all of the public ceremonies and pleasant exchanges during the Fort Malden council, Claus and Elliott met privately with Tecumseh and a handful of other headmen. Of the Native leaders present, Tecumseh seems to have made the strongest impression on the agents and Lieutenant Governor Gore. The Shawnee remained friendly but noncommittal, stressing that the growing confederacy on the Wabash did not "intend to take part in the quarrels of the White People." However, Tecumseh affirmed that "if the Americans encroach on them, they are resolved to strike," and "if their Father the King, should be in earnest and appeared in sufficient force they would hold fast by Him."[82] It seems that Tecumseh had achieved with regard to the British precisely what Gore and the Indian Department had hoped to accomplish with the nativist Indians: the Shawnee clung to an official status of neutrality for the confederacy, while he temporized on the possibility of a British-Indian alliance. Before he would make such a commitment, Tecumseh first needed to know if war could be avoided between his nativist followers and the Americans. If not, only then would the Shawnee leader consider an alliance. Tecumseh happily paid lip service to the restoration of the Chain of Friendship, which was little more than a simple statement of goodwill. In so doing, the Shawnee scored a diplomatic victory in which he promised nothing, gained a potential ally, and came away with much-needed provisions for the growing intertribal community at Prophetstown. In a tribute to Tecumseh's diplomatic skills, Gore referred to "[t]he Prophet's Brother" as "a very shrewd, intelligent man."[83]

Tecumseh's main purpose was to remain neutral while strengthening the Wabash confederacy. In 1809, a year after his initial meetings with the Indian Department officials at Fort Malden, Tecumseh returned to that vicinity and visited several groups, including the Wyandots and Shawnees, and probably villages among the Ojibwas, Ottawas, and Potawatomis, yet all without stopping at the British post.[84] Tecumseh made it plain that he did not trust the British. During one of his early visits to Fort Malden, the Shawnee headman reminded Elliott and Claus of the British perfidy at Fallen Timbers in 1794, and "of the number of Chiefs who fell in consequence of that Fort [Miami] being shut against them."[85] Having personally fought in that action against General Anthony Wayne's U.S. Legion, Tecumseh vividly remembered not only having been abandoned by the British but also that the British did not even fire a shot in defense of their fort's perimeter. Still smarting from this betrayal, Tecumseh again alluded to "the treachery of the British" in his first meeting with Harrison at Vincennes in 1810. He informed the governor that the confederacy, without developing additional ties with the British, intended to use the restored Brownstown council fire to punish those chiefs who had sold land to the U.S. government. This formal council would also seek redress and land restoration from the U.S. government for those unauthorized sales.[86] At that moment, Tecumseh sincerely believed that he could accomplish his goals through skillful diplomacy and without British intervention.

Harrison's reply to Tecumseh's appeal that the United States should rescind the Treaty of Fort Wayne led to a sharp shift in the Shawnee's demeanor. The governor had begun to explain the legality and justice of the U.S. government's Indian policy.[87] After listening for more than fifteen minutes, Tecumseh could bear it no longer; he leaped to his feet and called Harrison a liar, angrily denouncing everything he had just heard.[88] He was furious because Harrison's legalistic statements made it all too plain that negotiations could never recover the lost treaty lands, and that Harrison did not recognize Tecumseh's authority as supreme among the Indians. Given these facts, the matter would probably come to blows, though Tecumseh did not immediately give up on defending his position and policies. The following day he again stated to Harrison, "I am alone the acknowledged head of all the Indians," and he concluded by warning that any American attempts to survey or settle the lands in question would certainly produce "bad consequences."[89]

Although Tecumseh had exaggerated his claims to possessing sole authority over "all the Indians," his remarks were not completely unfounded.[90] The British came to view him as the confederacy's principal spokesperson, and at Malden in the summer of 1808 they presented the Shawnee leader and his followers with a belt of wampum containing 11,550 grains.[91] The solemn gesture represented Britain's attempt to restore the Chain of Friendship of an earlier generation, only this time Tecumseh would serve as the principal liaison for any such alliance. Moreover, certain leaders at Brownstown must have also viewed the Shawnee in this manner; by 1809 the remnants of the Brownstown council entrusted Tecumseh with carrying the sacred belt of the old confederacy to Prophetstown.[92] This suggests that the Wyandot leaders at Brownstown viewed Tecumseh's leadership qualifications as preeminent among those living at Prophetstown, and that his prestige had eclipsed that of the former members of the Brownstown council who had since made compromises with the Americans. The Brownstown gesture also indicates that this most influential Wyandot community, which had led the first confederacy during the 1780s and 1790s, now approved of the Wabash movement's goals and sought to incorporate that community into a revived Brownstown confederacy.[93] The Wyandot chief Roundhead may have been instrumental in bringing about the Brownstown endorsement of the nativist movement, but the decision would have also included the approval of both Adam Brown and Walk in the Water, Brownstown's principal village chief and war leader, respectively.

Harrison understood the seriousness of the Wyandots' defection. After having been confident that they supported American interests, he lamented to his superiors that "the Prophet[,] knowing the great advantage he would derive from gaining over this Tribe to his interests[,] attempted it and has succeeded." Harrison also realized the significance of "the Great Belt which was the Symbol of Union between the Tribes."[94] The Wyandots had previously paid little attention to the nativist movement, and, indeed, their principal village of Brownstown rivaled Black Hoof's Wapakoneta to the degree that it fostered accommodation with whites.[95] The resistance movement's appeal to the Wyandots grew after Michigan's territorial governor William Hull concluded the Treaty of Detroit late in 1807, which effectively expropriated most of northwest Ohio and southeast Michigan for virtually nothing. These lands belonged not only to the Wyandots, but the treaty would also greatly affect local Ojibwas, Potawatomis, and the Ottawa peoples along the Maumee River.[96] The Wyandots apparently did not fully understand the transaction, because they were later troubled to learn that they no longer owned any of the tract, not even Brownstown.[97] The treaty's significance was also not lost on the Indian Department at Malden, where William Claus informed other tribes of its terms.[98]

While not all of the Wyandots joined Tecumseh and the British, most ultimately supported them. Years later, in August 1812, Wyandot support would prove crucial along the Detroit frontier, and one wartime observer noted that the entire Brownstown community "evacuated the place and crossed the [Detroit] river to place themselves under the British flag."[99] John Norton later remembered the Wyandots of Brownstown as "warriors of the best character," and that two Wyandot leaders, Roundhead and Walk in the Water, were instrumental in the capture of Detroit.[100] Moreover, after the British seized Detroit in August 1812, Roundhead and Walk in the Water continued in their support by attempting to intimidate the neutral French inhabitants at the River Raisin into taking up arms against the advancing American troops that hoped to recapture the post.[101]

Prior to the war, Tecumseh understood the pivotal role that the Wyandots might play in the forthcoming conflict. Thus, by the end of 1810, the Shawnee war leader, emboldened by his support from Brownstown and annoyed with Harrison, sought a full British alliance for the first time since the disaster on the Maumee sixteen years earlier. In November he met with Matthew Elliott and admitted to him "that at first they [himself and his confederates] intended to keep their plan a secret even from their [British] Father," but now "Governor Harrison has pushed them to make some kind of avowal of their intentions."[102] During this visit, Tecumseh formally presented the officers with a belt of wampum that the British had given to the Shawnee leaders nearly fifty years earlier, when the British "laid the French on their back" at the end of the French and Indian War.[103] Tecumseh claimed to have stolen the belt from his nation's chiefs five years earlier, and he considered himself authorized to conduct the tribe's international diplomacy, explaining that "we the Warriors now manage the affairs of our Nation."[104] Unlike his visits to Malden during the summer of 1808, Tecumseh this time did not speak of past betrayals. He and the cadre of nativist leaders now viewed war as imminent, and they petitioned for all of the help that they could obtain; suddenly the prospect of a mutually binding British alliance held stronger appeal for the Indians than it had previously. After three years of remaining aloof to British overtures, the belligerent Native coalition appeared poised for war and intent on dragging Britain into a conflict prematurely.[105]

The Northern and Western Peoples' Response to Revitalization, 1801–12

The period of Native revitalization that culminated in the Shawnee brothers' movement at Prophetstown early in the nineteenth century was less eventful for the tribes living in the northern Great Lakes region, northern Wisconsin, and the upper Mississippi Valley. These nations, specifically the northern Ojibwas and Ottawas, Sauks, Menominees, and Dakotas, did not have to grapple with the same issues faced by the other groups featured in this study. Although most of these tribes lived within the territorial boundaries of the United States, at this point they did not have to defend their sovereignty as the Six Nations did at the Grand River. Also, the northerners had not yet experienced American encroachments to the degree that those south of the Great Lakes had. With the single exception of a treaty involving the Sauks and Governor Harrison at St. Louis in 1804, neither Harrison nor Michigan governor William Hull ever negotiated any treaties with these northern groups or those of the Mississippi Valley.[106] Anthony Wayne's conquest of Ohio had a minimal effect on the tribes of the northern Great Lakes, and very few, if any, received American annuity distributions.[107] Moreover, the northern tribes had not experienced a revolution within their leadership ranks, and their younger warriors were not faced with the painful decision of whether to follow an upstart nativist leader or remain loyal to an older pro-American headman who advocated accommodation. Finally, the fur trade in the North continued to define British relations with the tribes there, whereas the nativists at Prophetstown eschewed such contact, fearing both their resulting economic dependence and the Master of Life's wrath.

Of all of these different regional circumstances, the fur trade was possibly the most crucial in influencing the Indians' decisions and in shaping their diplomacy. By comparison, neither the nativists on the Wabash nor the Indians of the northern Great Lakes region cared for the Americans, and both had previously fought against the "Long Knives," making the nativists' added aversion to the Americans at the time merely a matter of degree. The fur trade, however, set these Native groups apart and placed them on divergent paths. The expansion of the trade in the North coinciding with its decline in the Wabash Valley would generate opposing interests between these groups. As the Wabash group sought to depend less on white trade, the northerners wanted to escalate the trade and, through it, continued to define their relationship with the British.

By the turn of the nineteenth century, British and Canadian fur companies fiercely competed with one another in the Old Northwest, causing most competing interests either to expand or eventually merge with the competition. The North West Company expanded west through northern Wisconsin, the upper Mississippi Valley, north into Canada, and ultimately to the Rocky Mountains. It competed with several other trading interests, including the famed Hudson Bay

FIG. 8. *Two Ottawa Chiefs* (circa 1812, artist unknown). Since the Chain of Friendship remained stronger in the North, British officials there continued to enjoy better relations with Native peoples. As a result, the northern allies helped the British easily capture U.S. Fort Mackinac in July 1812, and they ensured that it would remain in British possession for the remainder of the war. Library and Archives Canada, Acc. No. 1981-55-41 Bushnell Collection.

enterprise and a number of smaller, newly formed partnerships such as the xy Company, the Michilimackinac Company, John Jacob Astor's American Fur Company, and scores of private traders. Unlike the situation nearer to Detroit and the Wabash, the northern fur interests experienced a time of overall growth, prosperity, and expansion during the first decade after the Treaty of Greenville, and the North West Company in particular continued to be profitable for significantly longer.[108]

In the latter years of the eighteenth century, the northern Indians had grown increasingly dependent on the trade, and the heightened competition among the rival companies accelerated this process.[109] By 1800 the fur companies held a strong influence over their Native clients, but this influence was not simply imposed by the companies. In a spirit of reciprocity, Native participants in the fur trade viewed the relationship as more than a business arrangement, interpreting the market transactions to symbolize bonds of friendship between them and their British Father.[110] The Indians along the upper Mississippi and near Lake Superior closely fraternized with the North West Company's traders, and they proudly wore medals of King George and flew Union Jacks above their villages. Early in 1806, when the American officer Zebulon Pike made this discovery during his Mississippi expedition, he "felt indignant."[111] The company agents whom Pike encountered treated the American lieutenant graciously, and one of them, Hugh McGillis, even apologized about the distribution of flags and medals among the Indians, but he assured Pike that these tokens merely symbolized commercial ties and not a political alliance.[112]

Pike appreciated the hospitality shown him by the company agents, but McGillis's statements failed to convince him of the innocence of the northern traders' activities among the Indians. The American officer had witnessed firsthand the devotion the Indians accorded British traders, and he knew that it went beyond commercial ties. Pike found it remarkable that "the Gentlemen of the N.W. Company" contented themselves in the "Wilderness for 10, 15, and some 20 years, by the attachment which they imbibe for the Indian Women."[113] Whether or not Pike ever realized the extent of these bonds of kinship, he sensed that British-Indian ties would not be easily severed.[114] In his official report on the North West Company, the lieutenant alerted his superiors to this danger, recalling the "almost unlimited influence the traders . . . had acquired over the savages" in all previous frontier struggles.[115]

Pike's concerns were well-founded. In his memoirs, John Tanner, a thirty-year captive among the Ojibwas and Ottawas, indicated that traders could at times spontaneously persuade Indians to take up arms for them.[116] Similarly, Black Hawk, after declining the Shawnee Prophet's invitation to move to the Wabash, and despite having informed the Americans that he and his party would remain neutral, enthusiastically joined the British when a British-employed trader arrived near his village with two boatloads of goods.[117] The trader in this instance, Edward La Guthrie, had earlier befriended Black Hawk and had worked as an associate to Robert Dickson, the most important British trader and Indian agent in the West. Dickson, who was the brother-in-law of Red Thunder, a Dakota chief, became the critical link in the British alliance with the western nations.[118] Both Major General Isaac Brock and Sir George Prevost, the military governor of Upper Canada and the governor-general of Canada, respectively, looked to Dickson to cement this alliance.[119]

As the groups in the northern Great Lakes region and the upper Mississippi Valley continued to develop stronger ties with the British through kinship and trade, members of the intertribal nativist coalition on the Wabash distanced themselves from such economic links and most other forms of interaction with whites. To those who believed Tenskwatawa's prophecies, the fur trade meant poverty, drunkenness, and dependence on whites. The Prophet expected his converts "to do without any [white] merchandise," and several of his primary tenets reflected an attempt to escape a market economy.[120] Decades of extensive overhunting by both Natives and whites had contributed to the Indians' destitute condition. As early as the 1780s, Moravian missionary David Zeisberger noted the excessive hunting in areas of Ohio and Indiana that resulted from intensive trade, and modern studies also document the long decline of the fur trade in the southern Great Lakes region in the late 1700s.[121] After 1796, the U.S. government further accelerated this process of decline by establishing federal trading houses at the sites of major Indian agencies, in hopes of competing with British trade interests and of increasing Native debt and reliance on the U.S. government.[122] After the many years of overhunting in the Old Northwest, this final push by the government eliminated much of the remaining game south of the Great Lakes and further alienated Tenskwatawa's followers, who faced a period of starvation shortly after their arrival at Prophetstown in 1808.[123] Clearly, those on the

Wabash did not have the opportunity to interact with the British in the same manner in which the northern nations did. With game still plentiful in the North, tribes dwelling in the upper Mississippi Valley and in the northern Great Lakes region had less reason to consider the fur trade's potential for negative effects.[124] Thus they continued to cultivate closer ties with the British, while those at Prophetstown resisted the Americans and remained ambivalent toward the British until Tecumseh directly petitioned their assistance in 1810.

The clash of ideology between the nativists and those tribes linked to the British fur trade became increasingly manifest between 1807 and 1809. Ultimately, the northerners would have to choose between accepting the Prophet's new doctrines or continuing their commercial ties to white traders. In fact, the Shawnee Prophet may not have sought to completely abolish the fur trade, but he certainly wanted to minimize it, control all economic transactions, and prevent excessive Native dependence on Euro-American commodities.[125] He knew, for example, that his followers would still need European guns and powder. However, by the time Tenskwatawa's message spread to northern Michigan in May 1807, an Ottawa prophet who claimed to serve as the Shawnee's messenger had interpreted the message much more stringently, calling for a total abstinence from the trade. This prophet, known as La Maigouis, or the Trout, insisted that his followers "kill no more animals than are necessary to feed & clothe you," and also encouraged all Indians to renege on their outstanding debts with traders. He warned that if the Indians persisted in the trade, then the Great Spirit would take the animals "back to the Earth that they may not come to you again."[126] With the fur trade so prevalent in the North, La Maigouis saw this as the primary evil and agent of cultural destruction.

The Ottawa prophet's speech presented the northern Ottawas and Ojibwas with a dilemma. Uncertain of the prophecy's authenticity, some may have hesitated, but if La Maigouis was correct, then the issue became a question of what the Indians feared most: the Master of Life's judgment or the wrath of their creditors. The fact that obedience to the Supreme Being in this case coincided with immunity from their debts may have made the Indians' decision easier, but whatever the reason, La Maigouis began to enjoy moderate success in spreading the revitalization movement among his people. For a time, the movement spread rapidly in the North, and agents of the North West Company, knowing that the "Doctrine is . . . prejudicial to the interest of the Traders," feared that it might even "extend to the Saulteux [northern Ojibwas] & Crees," much farther to the northwest.[127] Captain J. Dunham, the American commandant at Mackinac, sent a speech to the principal Ottawa village at Arbre Croche, denouncing the tribe's intention to cheat the traders, and Dunham sternly demanded that the Indians "pay them up."[128] The commandant also dispatched a party of soldiers in an unsuccessful attempt to arrest La Maigouis.[129]

There was little Dunham could have said that would have altered the natural evolution of the revitalization movement or the attraction to it that led numerous northerners to make pilgrimages southward to visit the Shawnee Prophet. By August 1807, just three months after La Maigouis delivered his admonitions to the Ottawas and Ojibwas of northern Michigan, U.S. agent William Wells informed Harrison that "Indians . . . from the Lakes near Mackinac" have passed Fort Wayne as they "flock to" hear the Shawnee Prophet. Wells added "that all the Indians in that quarter believe in what the Prophet tells them," and that "they appear to be deff [sic] to everything I say to them."[130] American officials at Green Bay, Chicago, and the upper Mississippi also alerted their superiors of increased activity in their sectors among the Ojibwas, Potawatomis, Winnebagoes, and Sauks. Charles Jouett, agent at Chicago, warned that "the Indians are crouding [sic] down upon us from the Green Bay on their way . . . to see the Shawonee."[131]

The hysteria, though temporarily significant, was short-lived. With the exception of the Winnebagoes, most of the northern and Wisconsin tribes soon abandoned the prophetic movement. A close examination of the Winnebago society at the time reveals a different infrastructure from that of the other Wisconsin tribes that ultimately rejected the Prophet's teachings. In comparison to the Ottawas, Ojibwas, and Menominees, the Winnebagoes had a government that was much more centralized. They maintained an elaborate hierarchical clan system, which served as the basis for their nation's political organization. Of the ten Winnebago clans, the Thunder clan was most powerful, and its chiefs held significant authority over the entire nation. The head chief of the Thunder clan presided over a centralized body of counselors who ruled Winnebago affairs, with the head Thunder chief theoretically holding more power than the council.[132] This centralized form of government enabled the Winnebagoes to maintain their political independence longer than the other Wisconsin tribes, who sought British recognition in the form of medals and flags as symbols of authority over their own bands. The Winnebagoes remained more insular, as they did not necessarily yield to the wishes of the traders with whom they did business on occasion. Thus, despite commercial ties between the British and the Winnebagoes, the latter could not be manipulated politically as easily as their neighbors who operated on a band level.

While the Ottawas, Ojibwas, and Menominees all maintained clan systems, none of these nations' clans operated as anything more than units of kinship, and they certainly did not serve as a basis for a political structure. For instance, none of the clan chiefs possessed any authority over the greater portion of the tribe, and despite having clans, these tribes functioned on a village or band level.[133] An ethnographic field study in 1824 listed the Ojibwa government as "republican in all its features," without "the least subordination known" among its warriors.[134] The same study also found that although the Menominees had a clan system that paralleled that of the Winnebagoes, the Winnebagoes had a much more centralized government.[135] No central body of counselors existed among the Menominees, and they, too, operated with a village and band level of government. Like the Ojibwas and Ottawas, then, the Menominees were much more susceptible to the external influence of a Euro-American power such as the British. Functioning at the band level, the Menominees developed economic ties and loyalties to individual traders, and this tribe, like their northern counterparts, was heavily influenced by pro-British traders who continued to control the fur trade in the Wisconsin region as they did with peoples farther north.[136] Furthermore, in comparison to these other northern nations, the Menominees did not show an initial interest in the Shawnee Prophet, not even when their neighbors were temporarily attracted to Tenskwatawa's teaching in 1807.[137]

In addition to their tribal infrastructure, Winnebagoes also followed the Shawnee Prophet for cosmological and spiritual reasons. Like the Shawnees, the Winnebagoes regarded Thunderbirds as among the most powerful deities, and these supernatural beings were thought to bless warriors with most anything requested, especially victory in war. Powerful leaders and shamans among the Winnebagoes claimed to be reincarnated Thunderbirds, and the Shawnee Prophet distributed sacred slabs illustrating that the Thunderbirds' role was to serve as gatekeepers to the Master of Life.[138] The Prophet's name itself, Tenskwatawa, was even interpreted as "the Open Door."[139] According to Winnebago cosmology, if Tenskwatawa himself were a reincarnated Thunderbird, or could at least converse with the Thunderbirds, then not only was the Prophet a direct link to the Great Spirit, but he was also a potential source of immense power for Winnebago warriors. Winnebago oral tradition indicates that their warriors who decided to visit the Prophet believed that they would "walk as the thunderbirds do . . . above the earth."[140]

Unlike the Winnebagoes, the other northern and Wisconsin tribes began to drift away from the Prophet by 1808. In early May of that year U.S. agent Charles Jouett reported that "those Indians from Green Bay . . . are . . . returning home," and they now "appear truly ashamed of their late infatuation relative to the prophet."[141] According to Black Hawk, the Sauks also generally rejected the Prophet's overtures, and John Tanner recalled that Tenskwatawa's "impression was obliterated" among the northern Ojibwas.[142] Why the sudden reversal and decline of the nativist frenzy in the North? Quite simply, the Prophet could not provide the food and material needs for all of the newcomers in a rapidly growing intertribal society. His closest followers usually subsisted on near-starvation diets, and when new converts arrived from the North, they could not be absorbed into the nativist community.[143] For a man who promised to end Native suffering and restore prosperity, this was not a good first impression in the minds of the sojourners from the North. In Tanner's own northern village, "famine began to be felt" among those who adhered to the Prophet's teachings, and the longtime captive concluded, "At this day he [Tenskwatawa] is looked upon by the Indians as an imposter and a bad man."[144]

Tanner's observation is especially significant, since it demonstrated that the Prophet's followers both in the vicinity of and far from Prophetstown experienced the negative effects of revitalization. More than half a century after Tanner wrote his recollections, Andrew J. Blackbird, an aging Ottawa, corroborated this in his personal history. When the Prophet's message came to his people, "a great many Ottawas believed and went far west," Blackbird explained, in order "to escape the habits of the white man." Of those who migrated west, "nearly all of them died out there" as a result.[145] The Ottawas, as was the case with the other northern tribes, lived in areas where the fur trade continued to flourish. Had the fur trade in the North been farther advanced and nearing its demise, the Prophet's message would have probably held a stronger appeal, but for the time being, the traders met their clients' needs and supplied their wants. The nativist movement collapsed in the North due mainly to the inveterate strength of the economic system that it had challenged there. Significantly, Tanner not only preferred to do business with the traders, but through his contact with them, he also came to view whites as superior in spiritual knowledge, making it easier for him to reject the Prophet's teachings. Tanner related, "As was usual with me in any emergency of this kind, I went to the traders, firmly believing, that if the Diety [*sic*] had any communications to make to men, they would be given, in the first instance, to white men. The traders ridiculed and despised the idea of a new revelation of the Divine will, and the thought that it should be given to a poor Shawnee. Thus was I confirmed in my infidelity."[146]

Though Tanner, as an Indianized white, was perhaps quicker than most to reject Tenskwatawa's teachings, his peers soon followed, and as with Tanner, the traders played a role in undermining the Prophet's teachings among other Ojibwas. In writing a history of his people in 1852, Ojibwa William Warren alluded to an incident in 1808 when trader Michael Cadotte turned back a huge party of Ojibwas who had set out to visit the Shawnee Prophet. Traveling in a cluster of 150 canoes, the group carried a dead child, hoping that the Prophet could restore the body to life. But when Cadotte met the party along the southwest shores of Lake Superior, the trader convinced them that the Prophet was a fraud.[147]

Several of the northern tribes had already begun to question the veracity of the Prophet's teaching, but the most serious breach between Tenskwatawa and his northern followers came in the winter of 1808–9 when an Ottawa band from Arbre Croche lost faith in him. This group had come from the same village as La Maigouis, the Ottawa prophet, and it most likely consisted of some of Tenskwatawa's most devoted disciples at the time. Many of these Ottawas and a few of the Ojibwas who had made the pilgrimage to Prophetstown in 1808 attempted to remain on the Wabash for the winter, but extraordinarily harsh weather conditions and the lack of food weakened the inhabitants. When an epidemic (most likely influenza) swept through the community, it selectively carried away 160 Ottawas and Ojibwas; very few members of the other tribes perished.[148] Stunned at their losses and the disproportionate figures of casualties, the surviving Ottawas and Ojibwas became suspicious of the Prophet. It seemed that the professing Shawnee holy man was a fraud, or that he had deliberately fomented the sickness among them. Either way, these northerners concluded that it was not in their best interests to remain at Prophetstown, and they returned to their villages in Michigan shortly thereafter.

The breach between Tenskwatawa and these northern bands widened when the disaffected groups decided to test the supposed shaman. Earlier, he had warned that no blood should ever be spilled at Prophetstown and promised that the Master of Life would destroy anyone who defied this warning. Anxious to determine its truth, a war party of Ottawas and Ojibwas secretly returned to Prophetstown, where, under cover of darkness, they tomahawked two unsuspecting Shawnees—a woman and her child. Unable to detect any afflictions attributable to Tenskwatawa's retaliatory power, the murderers triumphantly returned to Michigan. The brutal experiment had succeeded; the Michigan Indians were convinced that they had exposed a charlatan and would have no further contact with the Prophet or his revitalization movement. When Tenskwatawa sent messengers the following year to summon these dissidents back to Prophetstown, they flatly refused.[149] After this schism, only a wartime British alliance could unite the nativist faction to the tribes of the northern Lakes, and the peoples living in the North, namely the Ojibwas, Ottawas, Menominees, Sioux, and Sauks, all later fought the Americans as British allies, not nativists.

Shortly after the troubling incidents along the Wabash in 1808–9, the split between the Prophet and the northerners nearly took a turn that could have ruined the prospects of a future British alliance with both groups. With their anger not yet appeased, the Ottawas and Ojibwas conspired to destroy Prophetstown. Ironically, had it not been for the intervention of the U.S. government, the angry dissidents might have carried out their plan. But when Michigan governor William Hull learned that, as he put it, "the Ottawas and Chippewas [Ojibwas], on Lake Michigan, were preparing to make an expedition, against the Shawanoese Prophet, and his people, residing on the Wabash," he sent messages to the northern tribes "that the Shawanoese were under the protection of the U. States, and we should consider hostilities against them, the same as against us." Thus the Prophet's worst enemies—the Americans—shielded him from the wrath of his former partisans, doing the British an enormous favor in the process. Hull sent these messages reluctantly; the Michigan governor understood that the Prophet's "object has been to form a combination . . . in hostility to the U.S."[150] Harrison also expressed reservations about intervening to prevent intertribal conflicts, consistent though that was with Jeffersonian peace policies.[151] The response of these western governors raises some provocative questions: If the U.S. had not protected Prophetstown, would the village have been destroyed in 1809, making Harrison's 1811 campaign unnecessary? More important, to what extent would this have affected British attempts to reconstruct a general intertribal alliance among all of the tribes in the Great Lakes region and the Wabash Valley on the eve of the War of 1812? Without the support of the nativist coalition from the Wabash, the British prospects of successfully defending Upper Canada would have diminished significantly.

In the North, the rejection of nativist doctrine and the continued expansion of the fur trade, specifically the dominance of the North West Company, ensured that British-Indian relations there would continue as they had for decades.[152] Unlike the capricious relations between the Indian Department at Fort Malden and the Prophetstown community, northern British-Indian relations maintained a steady course in which British leaders at Fort St. Joseph's continued to play an assertive role in the affairs of the Ottawas and Ojibwas. After 1801 British officers in the North continued to distribute medals and create chiefs, very much in the manner that Major William Doyle and others had done prior to the British withdrawal from Fort Mackinac in the 1790s.

Doyle's successors could reduce a chief in status as well. After Major Alexander Campbell took command at St. Joseph's in 1806, he soon heard that an influential Ottawa chief from Arbre Croche, Little King, had allegedly sent his son to the Americans at Mackinac to present them with a string of wampum, indicating that the chief's "heart was American." When the Ottawa headman arrived at St. Joseph's in May 1807, Campbell immediately brought charges against him, but the commandant gave Little King an opportunity to reply formally to the allegations in council. Little King explained that his son had only given wampum to the American doctor at Mackinac as compensation for pulling a tooth for him. The chief also affirmed his loyalty to the British. The matter became so serious that the council even summoned the American commandant, Captain Dunham, to testify at the council. When Captain Dunham arrived at St. Joseph's, he corroborated Little King's defense, explaining that "he had always understood that the Little King had been firmly attached to the British government." Yet prior to Dunham's arrival, Major Campbell and the British tribunal had already informed Little King that he would be required "to return [his] meddals [sic] & Colours, and never more trouble us with your Presence."[153] Only the American officer's testimony ultimately cleared the Ottawa chief of the charge of disloyalty, and Little King was fully restored as chief.

Such an encounter goes contrary to the supposedly widespread practice in frontier diplomacy of Indian leaders "playing off" one Euro-American power against another. In some cases, particularly along the Detroit frontier, Indians did possess more diplomatic leverage, but in the North the dominance of British trade had made nations there both economically and politically beholden to British authorities. In theory, Little King should have had every right to have cultivated ties with both the British and the Americans simultaneously. The chief's village was situated in American territory, and the British had withdrawn from Mackinac more than a decade earlier. Moreover, the British and Americans were not at war, and Little King and his people should have enjoyed the rights of free passage and neutral diplomacy between both nations. Nevertheless, Little King did not have this liberty because he and the British had an understanding that both parties would work to continue the sacred bonds first sanctioned by the Chain of Friendship. This sacred Chain had never been broken in the North, while the defeat at Fallen Timbers in 1794, followed by the Treaty of Greenville the following year, had nearly severed the Chain's links between Britain and the Crown's allies there.

In the North, British commandants and Indian agents continued to assert their authority over the Ottawas and Ojibwas, a policy that their counterparts at Fort Malden could never carry out in the Detroit and Maumee regions. British officers and Indian agents at Malden were not in a position to bully chiefs and strip them of their medals, particularly when British officials there virtually begged the Wabash nativists for support after 1807. Little King may have also perceived the difference in attitude toward Indians at the two posts. In February 1808, barely eight months after narrowly being cleared of the disloyalty charges, the Ottawa leader arrived at Fort Malden to meet with William Claus. This meeting went quite differently than Little King's ordeal at St. Joseph's. The deputy superintendent general eagerly questioned the chief, just as Claus would later interview Tecumseh, in hopes of determining the Ottawas' disposition in the event of a British-American war. After having promised Major Alexander Campbell and the council at St. Joseph's the previous spring that he would "always be faithful to the British Government," Little King now remained evasive and noncommittal with Claus.[154] When the agent asked him about his people's disposition, the Ottawa leader replied, "The ground is smooth yet." Claus pressed the issue, but Little King merely stated, "You will know when it happens."[155] Such unforthcoming remarks at St. Joseph's might well have cost the headman his position with the British, who would have quickly sought to replace him at Arbre Croche with a leader they deemed as more loyal.

Although Little King equivocated, Claus felt confident that the chief and his band would either support the British or remain neutral in the anticipated conflict, since, according to Claus, Little King intimated "the Indians [were] decidedly opposed to the Americans."[156] Consequently, the question of neutrality became the key issue at that point, and Little King considered the option of separating himself and his people from both the British and the Americans by joining the

Shawnee Prophet's nativist movement. Perhaps Little King's rough treatment at the hands of Major Campbell and his fellow inquisitors at St. Joseph's had compelled the chief to rethink the consequences of his tribe's close economic and political ties with the British. In any case, Little King was among the hundreds of other Ojibwas and Ottawas who had resolved to join the nativists at Prophetstown prior to the tragic winter of 1808–9.

Although several of the northern groups had rejected Tenskwatawa's teachings prior to Little King's arrival on the Wabash, the Ottawa leader remained an influential voice in his band from Arbre Croche.[157] Some of his followers may have been reluctant to join their chief at the Wabash, but they acquiesced due to Little King's faith in the Prophet. The Ottawa and Ojibwa bands were therefore all the more distraught when the epidemic that struck them so severely at Prophetstown also carried off their beloved leader who had brought them there.[158] No wonder that the Ottawas from Arbre Croche and elsewhere wanted to destroy Prophetstown. Now embittered against the nativists, and always hostile to the Americans, the remnants of Little King's band returned to their homes at Arbre Croche. Having flirted with notions of Native revival, separatism, and neutrality, they reentered the only world they really knew, one dominated by British trade and influence.

John Askin Jr., storekeeper and interpreter at Fort St. Joseph at the time, claimed to have played a significant role in the return of the disillusioned northern Indians from the Wabash.[159] In a memorial listing his past achievements in hopes of gaining a promotion, Askin asserted that his contribution to retrieving the Ottawas and Ojibwas was one of his most important accomplishments while serving in the Indian Department. Writing to Claus, the northern agent took credit for "getting back a number of Indians of the vicinity of this Country who had followed the Shawnee Prophet & settled on the Wabash."[160] Although an exaggeration, Askin's claim provides valuable support for the idea that British leaders in the North typically thought it proper to intervene on a large scale in Indian affairs, and that they viewed

Tenskwatawa's prophetic movement as anathema to the northern people's lives, commerce, and culture. However, British policy on such matters differed greatly from region to region and tribe to tribe. For example, Claus, a British official in the southern Great Lakes, had viewed the nativist movement as a mechanism for Indian unity and the basis for a potential British-Indian alliance at the very time that Askin, in the North, had attempted to dissuade Indians from joining the Prophet.

Such examples of regional differences in British-Indian relations between 1801 and 1812 provide important windows into the complexities of the history of the time. British diplomacy was never monolithic. It varied by region, and it always reflected the differing perspectives of its participants, based on their respective positions in the hierarchy of command. Put another way, there was often a large gap in practice and belief between central administrators and agents living among and even intermarrying with Natives.[161]

The history of the tribal revitalization movement also shows regional diversity. At its zenith, Tenskwatawa's religious movement and cultural revival enjoyed its strongest support from the Kickapoos, Potawatomis, and Winnebagoes. The Kickapoos and Potawatomis, geographically located throughout southern Michigan, northern Indiana, the expanse of Illinois, and portions of southern Wisconsin, fit well within the Prophet's main geographical sphere of influence. The Winnebagoes appear to be more of an aberration, being the only northern group to show strong support for the Prophet. This nation occupied portions of central eastern Wisconsin near a major trade route, the Fox-Wisconsin rivers waterway. They, like their neighbors in the North, would have also had substantial contact with British traders, including private entrepreneurs and, to a lesser extent, men of the North West Company. Yet the Winnebagoes became the Prophet's staunchest supporters, and they did not desert him until many of their warriors died in the fierce action against Harrison's troops on November 7, 1811.[162] As previously shown, a possible explanation is that the Winnebago tribal structure and clan hierarchy did much to prevent that tribe from coming under the full extent of British economic and political influence, while the other northern groups were drawn into the British orbit by trade ties. In any case, the Winnebagoes were ripe for the Prophet's revitalization.

Once the Prophet and his movement were largely discredited at Tippecanoe in November 1811, all of the tribes that continued to resist American expansion during the War of 1812 did so as British allies.[163] It now meant little whether or not these allies had at one time been members of the Wabash nativist movement, and it became more difficult to discern the regional differences in British-Indian relations. These differences became even less evident when early British-Indian successes at the war's outset tended once again to unite disaffected factions of Natives. Nevertheless, some traces of these distinctions remained, and the British encountered multiple Native responses to British policy and actions as the war progressed.

Epilogue

Reassessing the Chain of Friendship, 1812 and Beyond

The thesis put forth in this study—that Britain's relationship with three different groupings of Indians of the Old Northwest and Upper Canada evolved along separate lines between 1783 and 1812, and that the nations of each of those sectors responded differently to British policy—is borne out by the subsequent events of the War of 1812. Of the three regions discussed, British agents and officers experienced their greatest difficulty in maintaining amiable ties with the remnants of the nativist faction from the southern Great Lakes region, those Indians ostensibly under the leadership of Tecumseh, the Potawatomi chief Main Poc, and the Wyandot leaders Roundhead and Walk in the Water. British officers found that they possessed virtually no influence or control over these warriors. Furthermore, tribal infrastructures had collapsed within the ranks of these bands and of the tribes that had once participated in the Shawnee Prophet's revitalization movement, and after the revolution in leadership brought by Tecumseh and the Prophet, a power vacuum remained. Though the above-named Indian leaders were influential, they probably did not command the intertribal support that Joseph Brant, Blue Jacket, and Little Turtle had enjoyed from the 1770s into the 1790s. Even Tecumseh, though popular, did not always possess the influence that the legend suggests, and neither he nor Roundhead could prevent the Indians from ravaging the area around Detroit in the days after the Americans surrendered that post in August 1812. The British-allied warriors also intimidated the Canadian populace across the Detroit River in the Western District of Upper Canada and even killed and scalped a man serving in an allied Canadian militia unit.[1]

During the War of 1812, the southern Great Lakes region became the conflict's most brutal theater. Events there helped to confirm old frontier stereotypes, and American leaders drew conclusions about British-Indian relations and motives based largely on these happenings. In 1838, many years after the wars in the Old Northwest had ended, William Henry Harrison completed his *Discourse on the Aborigines of the Ohio Valley*. In his study, the future president speculated as to why the Indians of the Northwest had previously clung so tightly to the British, and he surmised that His Majesty's agents had purchased Native loyalty with "arms and equipments, clothing and trinkets." According to Harrison, the Indians had accepted these petty gifts from the British because the Natives did not grasp the "enviable distinction" between British rule and the peace and justice that the United States offered them.[2] The retired general also pondered the possible British motives for maintaining close ties with the Indians into the second decade of the 1800s; Harrison could only conclude that Britain, in spite of acknowledging the independence of the United States, had "still indulged the hope, that ... it would be able to again reduce them [the United States] to subjection." "No other reason," Harrison mused, "can be assigned for the close connexion which they [the British] continued to keep up with the tribes within our territorial boundary, and their constant and liberal supply to them of the means of committing depredations upon our settlements."[3] In the near half-century since he had first served as a young officer in Anthony Wayne's U.S. Legion, little had changed in how Harrison perceived the Indians and their former British allies.[4]

Harrison's perception resembled that of numerous other American statesmen and military officers of his generation. For example, Lewis Cass, perhaps more than any other American leader of that era, condemned the British government for its dealings with the Indians. Cass, who was taken prisoner by the combined British-Indian force that captured Detroit in August 1812, subsequently served as an aide-de-camp to Harrison later during the war; he then spent eighteen years as Michigan's territorial governor before becoming secretary of war under President Andrew Jackson and secretary of state in James Buchanan's administration.[5] Like Harrison, Cass believed that the British had exploited the Natives. The Michigan governor summed up the relationship between the British government and its Native allies as one in which the Indians *"were useful, and were used, in war to fight, and in peace to trade."*[6] Furthermore, Cass regarded the British use of Native wartime allies as a tactic tantamount to terror, often indiscriminately employed against civilians. In his indictment against Britain, he passionately charged that "the nation which authorizes . . . [an Indian alliance], should be arraigned at the tribunal of Christendom. . . . And 'allies,' as the Indians may be, it is an alliance, to which posterity will look back with grief and indignation, and which will tarnish the brightest jewel in the crown of the *Defender of the Faith."*[7] Cass also believed that it was principally due to their dealings with the British during the years of intermittent warfare that the Indians resisted American attempts to acculturate them.[8] In 1827 Cass concluded that "not a vestige remains of any permanent advantage derived by the Indians" from their years of fidelity to the British.[9] Consequently, during his tenure as Michigan's territorial governor (1813–31), Cass became one of the leading advocates of the federal policy of Indian removal, arguing that the scheme was the Native peoples' only hope for survival.[10]

Both Harrison and Cass, like so many of their peers, formulated their opinions based on years of frontier warfare and diplomacy during a period in which the Indians of the Old Northwest demonstrated maximum resistance to all external influences that threatened their lifestyles and cultural traditions. Native determination in resisting American expansion reached its zenith shortly after the turn of the nineteenth century, when American policy successfully accelerated the process of expropriating Indian lands in Indiana, Ohio, and Michigan. Coincidentally, the strongest intertribal resistance to these measures occurred precisely when British-American relations once again turned sour, prior to the War of 1812, causing U.S. leaders to believe that the British were the actual source of Native discontent. Such thinking on the part of the Americans gave the British too much credit; it assumed that the Crown retained the influence among the tribes of the Great Lakes that it had enjoyed in previous times.

In truth, British-Indian relations in the Old Northwest had a much richer and more complex history than either Harrison or Cass realized. In 1794 the old Chain of Friendship that had once joined Britain to the nations of the southern Great Lakes was virtually severed by Anthony Wayne's victory over the confederated tribes at Fallen Timbers, a defeat that was confirmed by the terms of the Treaty of Greenville the following year. This marked the beginning of a twelve-year period of Anglo-American cooperation in which the tribes south of the Great Lakes dealt more directly with the Americans. Only with great difficulty after 1807 did the British Indian Department manage to restore a semblance of the Chain of Friendship as a defensive measure intended to protect Upper Canada from an anticipated American invasion. Yet by that time, American leaders were convinced that Britain's ties to its former allies had never been broken, and only by permanently eliminating the British menace from North America could the frontier be made secure. In the years preceding the War of 1812, Kentucky leader Henry Clay and his faction of "War Hawks" in Congress clamored for an invasion of Canada, and John Harper, a representative from New Hampshire, argued that Providence would sanction such an undertaking, bellowing, "The Author of Nature has marked our limits in the south, by the Gulf of Mexico; and on the north, by the regions of eternal frost."[11]

American rhetoric aside, Britons and Indians had always understood their relationship with each other quite differently. British agents, government officials, and Native leaders often spoke of the

Chain of Friendship as a unique understanding that had existed between them, albeit tenuously at times, since Sir William Johnson's years as superintendent of Indian Affairs in the mid-eighteenth century.[12] At various times since then, the Western Confederacy, particularly those Indians dwelling south of the Great Lakes in the intertribal villages of Kekionga and the Glaize, had made it clear that they would not accept American acculturation.[13] For Britain to have attempted any of the cultural reforms among its allies that Cass had accused them of neglecting would have meant an end to the Anglo-Native entente. Moreover, the Indians viewed their British Father as an allied member of the Brownstown council fire who would protect them from American attempts to expropriate their lands and impose new ideologies on them. Implicit within the Chain of Friendship agreement was a military alliance between sovereign powers, including an understanding that Britain would recognize and protect Native sovereignty for those tribes living within the boundaries of the United States.

When Britain failed in this role during the crisis and defeat of the Western Confederacy in 1794–95, numerous intertribal leaders in the Ohio Valley and along the Detroit frontier considered their Chain of Friendship with the British broken. Blue Jacket, the Confederacy's principal leader, relinquished his British commission and hoped to replace it with a similar title under the American regime.[14] The Shawnee war leader, along with the majority of Miami, Delaware, and Shawnee warriors, now "thought nothing" of their British allies, as the Indians made peace with the United States.[15] Within this triumvirate of nations that had once coalesced in the Maumee Valley, Britain never completely regained the Indians' trust, nor was this segment of the Chain of Friendship ever fully restored.

When Britain negotiated Jay's Treaty with the Americans in 1794—once again, as in 1783, acting independently of Native interests—it further weakened any remaining semblance of the Chain of Friendship with tribes of the Ohio Valley and the southern Great Lakes. When, under the terms of Jay's Treaty, the British evacuated their posts in American territory in the summer of 1796, it appeared that Whitehall had played a complicitous role in undermining the future integrity of indigenous cultures south of the Great Lakes by recognizing U.S. suzerainty in the Ohio country.

The Indians there remembered this, and only very gradually after 1808 did elements of the former Maumee and Wabash tribes again gravitate toward the British. However, all of the former principal leaders were gone, and by 1808 the British were forced to seek an alliance with an intertribal group of nativist Indians who were in the process of staging a cultural revolt. Led by Tecumseh and his charismatic brother, Tenskwatawa, the nativists attempted to purify their culture and religion, and at times they even encouraged the execution of those Indians who were overtly Christian or who had supported U.S. acculturation and land-acquisition policies.[16] The Indians participating in this revitalization movement would not have tolerated British attempts to reform them any more than they accepted American schemes. Extreme factions of this movement even attempted to compel the tribes living in the northern Great Lakes region to cease trading with the British and to renege on their outstanding debts.[17] In this light, Cass's criticisms of British dealings with the Indians appear ludicrous. Prior to the war, Tecumseh had made it clear that he did not trust the British, but he, like the British, restored the Chain of Friendship out of necessity when he presented the British officers at Fort Malden with a belt that the king's agents had given to his people nearly half a century earlier.[18] British relations with the nativist Wabash coalition remained tenuous throughout the War of 1812, and only grew worse after Tecumseh was killed (in 1813) and the fortunes of war in the southern Great Lakes and the Detroit frontier shifted in favor of the Americans. Thus this theater of war, the one from which Americans formed their conclusions regarding unethical warfare and the British-Indian relations ostensibly responsible for it, was clearly the region where those allied relations were the most strained.

In the North, British-Indian relations proved much more stable during the interwar period, and thus the assessments of Cass, Harrison, and other American leaders contain a kernel of truth when applied to the continuing influence that the British enjoyed among the Ottawa, Ojibwa, Menominee, Dakota, Sauk, and Fox peoples. The continuity of these ties, based primarily on trade, meant that the Chain of Friendship had never been significantly altered with the northern groups, and these nations remained virtually unaffected by Wayne's conquest of the Ohio country. At Mackinac and later at St. Joseph, British agents continued to exercise much influence among Ottawa and Ojibwa bands, often creating chiefs and even issuing commissions on occasion. Cass's assessment that the Indians were merely *"used"* by the British, *"in war to fight, and in peace to trade"* to some extent describes the Chain of Friendship in the North.

Yet Cass's remarks overlook the degree of mutual reciprocity in the northern British-Indian relations. Moreover, the charge that the British failed to implement cultural innovations among their Indian allies also entailed a false presupposition that Britain could unilaterally impose its ideals on Native peoples. The fact that the Crown met some of the Indians' material needs—and nothing more—was the secret behind Britain's success in maintaining its enduring friendship with the northerners. In not attempting to compel their allies to adopt Euro-American lifestyles, British agents and traders generally recognized the dignity and integrity of the northern tribes (with occasional exceptions), while asking for virtually nothing in return, apart from their clients' continued commerce and future wartime loyalty. This can be seen in the fact that although His Majesty's agents and officers could never mediate a lasting peace between the Ojibwas and Dakotas, they continued to trade with both belligerents. Though enjoying their best relations with the northern Indians, the British held only limited influence among them. American officer Zebulon Pike misread the situation when he returned from his expedition to the upper Mississippi Valley (in 1804–5) bewildered by the British inability to quell this ongoing struggle. Pike asserted that the United States could bring a lasting peace to the area through a more powerful show of force.[19] But had the British made such a heavy-handed attempt to pacify the distant northwestern tribes, the result probably would have been an immediate end to the Chain of Friendship there. In the end, British-Indian relations in the North proved so strong that they weathered not only the Dakota-Ojibwa wars but also all the efforts by the Shawnee Prophet's nativists to end the northern fur trade. Consequently, in the War of 1812 the northern tribes fought as Crown allies, and only incidentally as allies to Tecumseh's nativist coalition of tribes from the Wabash that had once participated in the Shawnee Prophet's revitalization movement.

In evaluating British-Indian relations, both Cass and Harrison implicitly assumed that the Crown maintained sovereignty over the Natives with which it dealt—even those tribes dwelling within the boundaries of the United States—and that Whitehall's and Canada's leaders had therefore misused their power in treating the Natives as allies rather than subjects. In truth, although the king's ministers argued the Crown's legal sovereignty over British North America, the Chain of Friendship could exist only if the Crown never attempted to assert this supposed right over its Indian allies. Only after the Six Nations at the Grand River Reserve in Upper Canada attempted to force Whitehall's recognition of Native land sovereignty did the British government more clearly define its stance toward the Indians living within its limits. Joseph Brant and the Grand River Council systematically rejected the land deeds offered to them by British leaders in Canada, since these ultimately gave the king final determination over the distribution of Six Nations' land cessions.[20] The Grand River nations did not concur with the notion that they were simultaneously British subjects and allies, and they tenaciously argued the latter status only. Moreover, by the outset of the War of 1812 (after Brant's death), the Grand River Council, attempting to act as a sovereign power, informed Isaac Brock, military governor of Upper Canada, that the Natives would remain neutral until their land question was satisfactorily resolved. Less than a few dozen warriors from the Grand River joined the British at the war's outset. Hence, by the commencement of the War of 1812, it proved easier for the British to form alliances with those tribes living within the United States, since British sovereignty was no longer an issue with them.

Here lay the dilemma, and indeed the flaw in Cass's argument. Even if the British government had wanted to do so, it could not support acculturation and at the same time expect Native peoples to accept extended Crown sovereignty over them. One might expect that by becoming agricultural and Christianized, the Indians would also accept government sovereignty, but such was not the case. The Six Nations, the most acculturated Native peoples of the groups featured in this study, were also the most vocal in claiming an autonomous status, independent of Whitehall. The more John Norton spoke of establishing a seminary and agricultural missions, the more he envisioned a new, politically independent Native community, one distant from British influence. Cass, who had criticized the British government for not promoting the advancements of civilization among the king's Indian allies, did not seem to grasp that such developments among the Natives would have altered the unique relationship between Britain and the Crown's allies, while simultaneously adding impetus to the Indians' desire for sovereignty. Ironically, Cass would later experience this difficulty himself when, as secretary of war to Andrew Jackson, he encountered the Cherokee situation; despite the advancements of Cherokee learning, agriculture, and Christian teaching, the secretary ultimately opted for removal after the U.S. government denied the Cherokees a sovereign status.[21] But the Crown's Indian policy was much more benign, and by the end of the eighteenth century the British had already set aside three reserves in Upper Canada.[22]

Cass, Harrison, Clay, and other American leaders could not properly understand British-Indian relations during the early years of the American Republic because they failed to consider the various tribes and regions with which the British dealt. Furthermore, Americans did not grasp that Whitehall's Indian policy was not static, and that the British government's frontier measures were always subject to an overarching foreign policy that often focused on France as the main concern. Moreover, memories of border warfare, and more recent naval incidents such as the *Chesapeake* Affair in June 1807, prevented American leaders, particularly the Jeffersonian faction, from discerning that Britain did not desire another British-American war.[23] After the *Chesapeake* crisis, American suspicions of British frontier intrigue seemed to be confirmed when the king's agents at Fort Malden and elsewhere earnestly attempted to restore the Chain of Friendship as a means of protecting Upper Canada from anticipated American invasions. Such renewed activity among the Indians was construed as offensively hostile, rather than as a defensive measure.

The better-documented atrocities that the Indians inflicted upon white Americans during the conflict were carried out by warriors from the southern Great Lakes, specifically, northern Ohio, southern Michigan, Indiana, and Illinois. This string of activities includes the actions remembered as the Fort Dearborn Massacre (August 1812), Pigeon Roost Massacre (September 1812), River Raisin Massacre (January 1813), Dudley's Defeat (May 1813), and Buffalo (December 1813); these incidents are what shaped the American postwar opinion, including the views of Cass and others, when reassessing British involvement with the Indians. Yet each instance demonstrated how little control the British actually exerted over the Indians south of the Great Lakes. No British personnel were present at the first two incidents, and at both the River Raisin Massacre and Dudley's Defeat, British soldiers were allegedly killed by their Native allies while bravely attempting to protect American prisoners from Indian vengeance.[24] After Tecumseh's death late in 1813, when the remnants of his former nativist confederacy had followed the battered British army eastward toward the west end of Lake Ontario, numerous warriors who had participated in the previous killings at the River Raisin and Dudley's Defeat accompanied a British expedition into American territory on the Niagara frontier.[25] When the British burned the towns of Black Rock and Buffalo on December 30, 1813, Ottawa leaders from southwestern

Michigan who had previously fought along the Detroit frontier later gave accounts of throwing live American children into the flames. After the Indians had burned three children, a detachment of British soldiers managed to save the remaining American civilians, but only after a British officer had been shot through his sword arm with an arrow and a significant body of cavalry had come to his aid. The episode once again nearly ended the rocky relationship between the British and their allies from south of the Great Lakes.[26]

Officers of the British Right Division—the army that was deployed along the Detroit frontier and Upper Canada's Western District—dreaded the consequences of an Indian alliance gone awry. Their overall commander, Major General Henry Procter, also feared his allies' instability, and what would become of the British forces and His Majesty's subjects of Upper Canada if his army was ever compelled to retreat. After learning of Fort Dearborn's fate and having personally witnessed the carnage following the actions at the River Raisin and Dudley's Defeat, Procter understood what his allies were capable of doing. At Fort Stephenson in July 1813, when the Indians refused to commit any of their forces until the British made a reckless frontal assault in which the latter sustained severe losses, Procter considered the futile attack as a necessary "Sacrifice . . . to Indian Opinion."[27] Although Procter was not popular with his men and other officers, most shared his concerns regarding the Indians.

At one point during the Right Division's ill-fated retreat in early October 1813, the aging Indian agent Matthew Elliott, an adopted Shawnee who had lived among the Indians for nearly fifty years, broke into tears, exclaiming that "he would not stay to be sacrificed."[28] Had Procter not stopped to give battle against the pursuing Americans in unfavorable circumstances, the British might very well have had to fight their own allies. At Procter's court-martial in December and January 1814–15, all of the testimonies given by Indian agents confirmed these fears, mainly that the Indians would either attack the British troops or that "they would fall upon the Country" and its inhabitants.[29] Colonel William Caldwell, a thirty-five-year veteran in the Indian Department who had also fought for the illustrious Loyalist outfit known as Butler's Rangers during the American Revolution, was convinced that these Indian allies would commit depredations against the local civilians, causing him to take the precaution of secretly moving his family. In addition to Caldwell, his adult mixed-blood son, Billy, and another experienced Indian agent, Francis Baby, testified that their allies on this retreat often grumbled about the British betrayal at Fort Miami more than nineteen years earlier.[30] Specifically, the elder Caldwell related, "They said to me this is like the peace of 1783, and again alluded to 1795 [1794] and said this is the second [third?] time we have been deceived by our father."[31]

In stark contrast to those often tense moments that characterized the alliance in the Detroit and southern Great Lakes regions, British-Indian relations in the North and in the upper Mississippi Valley progressed much more smoothly. Dakota leader Wabasha defined this relationship, leaving no doubt where his loyalties lay, when he proclaimed that "we live by our English Traders who have always assisted us, [and] have always found our English father the protector of our women and children."[32] Similarly, by the end of 1812 British leaders in Canada also grasped the importance of loyal traders in the North and West, and in January 1813 Governor General Sir George Prevost commissioned longtime trader Robert Dickson to serve as His Majesty's principal Indian agent west of the Great Lakes.[33] Dickson's role cannot be overemphasized, for it was primarily due to his influence, and that of a select group of his associates, that Britain was able to win the war in the northern Great Lakes region and upper Mississippi Valley. After having lived and worked west of the Mississippi River among the Santee Sioux (Dakota peoples) for nearly a decade by 1797, Dickson married the sister of Red Thunder, an important chief of that nation.[34] Thus familial ties helped to cement the Chain of Friendship in the West, as these relationships had previously done for Britain's Indian agents elsewhere. As with the illustrious careers of Sir William Johnson, Alexander McKee, Matthew Elliott, William Caldwell, the

Girty brothers, George Ironside, John Askin Sr., Jacques Baby, and John Norton, Dickson's liaison with a Native woman and his place of dwelling enabled him to achieve a unique position of trust among his adopted people. In Dickson's case, that trust carried with it an inter-tribal influence that stretched from east of the Great Lakes to west of the Mississippi River, well into Spanish territory. Though several places of the past, such as Johnson Hall of the Mohawk Valley, Keki-onga, the Glaize, Sandusky, Brownstown, and Tippecanoe, were no longer in the orb of British influence, Dickson would muster new al-lies from the regions of Lake Traverse, Green Bay, Saukenuk (present-day northwestern Illinois), Prairie du Chien, the Iowa River, the Falls of St. Anthony (now Minneapolis), Fond du Lac (near present-day Duluth), Arbre Croche, and elsewhere.[35]

In support of Dickson, other former traders from the Northwest would also strive to protect the Crown's interests there during the War of 1812. Specifically, William McKay and Thomas G. "Tige" An-derson commanded militias during the conflict, but both, proving in-valuable as liaisons to the Indians, received commissions in the In-dian Department by war's end.[36] The collective efforts of Dickson, McKay, and Anderson produced an effective wartime alliance remi-niscent of an earlier period when Joseph Brant and his pro-British Iroquois fought alongside units of Loyalists and Indian agents, effi-ciently laying waste to much of New York State during the American Revolution. Yet British military leaders during the War of 1812 relied much more heavily on the support of their far northwestern Indian allies, since authorities in Canada no longer recruited or trained white ranger regiments such as those that had served so well supporting His Majesty's Indian allies during the first American war.

Dickson's influence became apparent early in the summer of 1812 when he secured alliances with the Dakotas, Fox, Sauks, Winneba-goes, Menominees, Ojibwas, and Ottawas, helping to bring about the British captures of American posts at Mackinac and Detroit in July and August, respectively. In 1813 Dickson then led hundreds of these allies to the Ohio country, assisting the British war effort there. The expedition included many of Dickson's adopted Dakota peoples, who willingly traveled more than six hundred miles to fight the Americans. Finally, in July 1814 these western allies again made the difference in assisting Dickson, McKay, and Anderson in multiple actions along the Mississippi River, entailing the capture of the American post (Fort Shelby) at Prairie du Chien, which the British promptly renamed Fort McKay.[37] Only days after this success, the Indians severely defeated an American relief force moving upriver near the Rock Island Rapids, killing or wounding nearly fifty. The hot action at the rapids prompted McKay's praise, as he exclaimed that "this is perhaps one of the most brilliant actions fought by Indians only since the commencement of the war."[38] After McKay's departure, Thomas Anderson commanded Fort McKay throughout the remainder of the summer and autumn, relying on a coalition of western Indian allies to defend the position. In a final skirmish late in the summer, Sauk leader Black Hawk and more than a thousand Sauks, Dakotas, Winnebagoes, Fox, and Kickapoos defeated a substantial force of Americans under the command of future U.S. president Zachary Taylor, who attempted to ascend the Mississippi River in order to recapture Fort McKay.[39]

Elsewhere in the North, allied Menominees under their well-known leader Tomah defended Fort Mackinac in early August 1814 by beating back an American attack bent on reclaiming the island fortress. Had the post fallen, Americans would have controlled the vital straits between the Great Lakes and easily cut off the British supply line to Green Bay and Fort McKay. Thus Wisconsin and much of the Northwest would have been lost as well. Britain's Indian allies clearly made the difference in the North, and Tomah epitomized the vintage brand of Native leader there who had rejected the overtures of Tecumseh and Tenskwatawa, while remaining steadfastly attached to the British and their traders.[40] After the war, this highly respected Menominee leader could not abide a British peace that would once again permit an American presence in the North. Consequently, in 1817 Tomah apparently committed suicide at Mackinac Island, the place that he so ably defended for the British just three years earlier.[41]

In all these actions, Britain's northwest allies remained firmly attached to the Crown's war efforts in spite of experiencing perpetual hunger and a lack of supplies, due largely to the Indian Department's wartime logistical difficulties. In September 1814 the Kickapoo leader Barboullier sent a speech to Anderson at Fort McKay, promising, "I am yours. In everything you do, I wish to be with you. I can only die once, and the only death I look for is along side you. . . . I have hold of your hand, and will never let it slip; but will follow your road as long as I live."[42] Such Indian rhetoric in British councils was not heard in regions farther east along U.S.-Canadian borderlands by 1814, but the Chain of Friendship remained true in the North and West. Lieutenant Colonel Robert McDouall, British commandant at Mackinac, understood this. Soon after Tomah's Menominees had preserved McDouall's post and command with their defense of Mackinac in early August, the commandant wrote to Anderson at Fort McKay, reassuring him that "with the assistance of your Indians, I doubt not you will be able to repel any attempt of the enemy."[43] Within days, McDouall's words proved prophetic, when Britain's allies in the upper Mississippi region defeated the American expedition under Zachary Taylor that intended to recapture Fort McKay.

In the North and West, the mutual obligations and trust that British and Indians shared within their relationship under the Chain of Friendship were telling throughout the war; consequently, the better discipline of the Indians from those regions stood out. When Robert Dickson arrived at Detroit with hundreds of Native reinforcements to assist Procter in the summer of 1813, the general described them as "restrainable, tractable to a Degree that I could not have thought possible." But Procter feared that after several days they had begun to grow "contaminated, by the other Indians" from the Detroit region.[44] Like Procter, John Richardson, a "Gentleman Volunteer" from Upper Canada, also praised Dickson and the northwestern Indians, comparing the Sauks' "nobleness of feature" to that of the ancient Romans.[45]

More important, Richardson related an instance in which Dickson prevented a Sauk chief, Metoss, from taking the life of an American prisoner in order to avenge the death of the chief's son.[46] But Richardson's stories of American prisoners captured near Brownstown the previous year by tribes from the Detroit region demonstrated that, in those instances, not even the presence of a British Indian agent or that of army officers could prevent the ritualized killing of prisoners.[47] As they had always done prior to the war, Britain's Indian allies from the North and the far West continued to look to their traders and Indian agents for leadership and guidance. These tribes envisioned themselves in a symbiotic relationship with their British Father, one that would always protect them and provide for their material needs.

In his autobiography, the Sauk leader Black Hawk speaks of his relationship with the British agents in the Mississippi Valley and Wisconsin. In a meeting with Dickson at Green Bay, Black Hawk recalled that the agent *"could not consent to send brave men to murder women and children,"* and therefore would not permit the king's allies to raid defenseless settlements.[48] Instead, Dickson insisted that the Sauks and the other western nations accompany the traders and British officers to assist Procter in northern Ohio. According to the Sauk chief, he and approximately five hundred warriors happily complied with this request. Furthermore, while en route to Fort Meigs, Black Hawk demonstrated his humanity by advising other allied tribes to treat American prisoners well, and he credited himself with the distinction of intervening to end the slaughter of captive Americans at Dudley's Defeat along the Maumee in April 1813.[49] Black Hawk's cooperation with the British and his respect for the basic human dignity of his enemies were almost diametrically opposed to the attitudes of his Indian counterparts along the Detroit frontier.[50] Britain's ties to the Sauks and Dakota peoples of the upper Mississippi, along with its ties to the Ojibwas, Ottawas, and Menominees of Wisconsin and northern Michigan, provided the necessary support for the Crown's little army to hold key posts in those regions until the Treaty of Ghent in December 1814.[51]

As with the other groups covered in this study, the Grand River community of Upper Canada endured a wartime experience reminiscent of their prewar years. With their land question still unsettled, the Six Nations officially proclaimed neutrality at the commencement of hostilities, ostensibly until the British government would address their grievances. Nevertheless, after the initial British successes, coupled with the relentless urging of John Norton, most warriors from the Grand River once again allied themselves with the king's cause.[52] This time, however, they did so in hopes of receiving future redress from the Crown, and with the understanding that it was a matter of honor to repel an invader of their homeland. Unlike the other segments of the Chain of Friendship, the Iroquois at the Grand River did not fight to regain lost territory, but to retain the ground that was rightfully theirs, regardless of how the British government perceived their status on that land.

Once again, officials in Canada were forced to temporize with the Six Nations at the Grand River. Neither Prevost nor the military governor of Upper Canada, Isaac Brock, could make any promises to the Six Nations, nor could they undermine the Indian Department's position, which was still at odds with Norton and elements of the Six Nations. Nevertheless, Prevost, realizing that it was essential to keep the Six Nations actively employed in the war, compromised with the Grand River group by allowing them wartime autonomy and resources and eventually granting Norton a great deal of control over the distribution of gifts and war matériel at the Grand River.[53] In essence, Prevost had established a direct link between Norton and the upper levels of government and had given the mixed-blood leader significant control over military resources. Prevost's maneuver drastically undercut the power and influence of the Indian Department at the Fort George agency, particularly that of Norton's archrival and nemesis, William Claus, who resisted Prevost's orders throughout the war and took every opportunity to continue to malign Norton. Although Norton was eventually shoved aside by his adversaries at the war's end after Prevost's recall to England, the Grand River's wartime experience demonstrated that the British, while not prepared to fully grant Six Nations' demands, were in a position in which they were compelled to compromise with Iroquois interests.

In fact, after forcing Norton to retire in 1815, the government of Upper Canada recognized his continuing influence at the Grand River by granting him an annual pension of two hundred pounds plus rations, and the following year the British government bestowed upon him a permanent, nonserving commission as major in the army.[54] Making use of this prestige while traveling through England and Scotland in 1816, Norton seems to have circumvented the Indian Department one last time. Though no longer possessing the authority to distribute gifts to Indians at the Grand River, Norton convinced several important figures in the British government to permit him to present multiple models of custom-made rifles as gifts to those faithful Indian leaders at the Grand River who had served under him.[55] At one point in the process, the Prince Regent, future king George IV, even offered to personally cover the cost of manufacturing Norton's requested gift rifles.[56] Thus, despite his setbacks throughout his career, Norton maintained a steady influence at the Grand River for several more years, continuing in his important role there between Indians and whites.

Several aspects of the Chain of Friendship have been discussed in this study. Ties between the British government and the Indians of the Old Northwest and Upper Canada between 1783 and 1815 were often tenuous, and this relationship differed widely, depending on several varying factors, such as geographical position, Native relations with the United States, the fur trade, Indian intertribal relations, the degree of Native acculturation, indigenous religious beliefs, the influence of British Indian agents, and the constitutional issues of Native sovereignty and legal status. During the nineteenth century, few Americans, if any, grasped the reasons for the continuation of the Chain of Friendship alliance between Great Britain and its Indian allies, nor could Americans understand the complexities of these bonds. Perhaps

Henry Schoolcraft, ethnologist and U.S. Indian agent, came the closest when, in 1834, he publicly presented his study, "The Movements of the North Western Indians During the Late War," to the Historical Society of Michigan. At the time of his presentation, several of the Indians who had fought in the war were still living, and the Shawnee Prophet had moved to an Indian reservation in Kansas. While erroneous in places, Schoolcraft's study pointed out the regional differences between the tribes of the Old Northwest, and it emphasized that the northern nations had rejected the teachings of the Shawnee Prophet. The ethnologist also credited "the Agents of the North West Company" and Robert Dickson as key figures in preserving the northern alliance. Finally, rather than condemning the British for their participation and involvement in Native atrocities, as most Americans were wont to do, Schoolcraft pointed out that the British had not kept their promises to their faithful allies.[57] The U.S. agent, having worked among the tribes in northern Michigan for more than a decade, also managed to incorporate a degree of Native perspective in his scholarship, and in so doing helped to pave the way for further studies in British-Indian relations such as this one.

Schoolcraft's study also hinted at a key point, namely the Chain of Friendship's frailty. The uncertain level of British commitment to their Indian allies was further brought out in the Treaty of Ghent, which did not adequately protect Indian interests. This would have been forgivable if British officers and agents had not made promises to their allies regarding the restoration of their land and sovereignty. Little is known about what was actually promised to the Indians at the war's outset, but the Native postwar responses and a few quotes from key officers make it easy to conjecture. In 1815 Robert McDouall, from his post at Mackinac, lamented, "I shall to the latest period of my life, bewail the hapless Destiny of these devoted Nations who listened to our solicitations and confiding in our promises faithfully adhered to us during the war, but found the Peace which *promised* security to them and their Country only led to their utter ruin and annihilation."[58] McDouall often expressed the shame he felt regarding his nation's postwar Indian policy, saying, "After what I have told them [the Indians][,] what a superlative and unequalled——— they must think me."[59]

At Mackinac in June 1814, McDouall had informed the Indians that the king would assist them in recovering their "old boundaries." Great Britain, McDouall continued, would refuse to make peace until "your interests . . . be first considered, your just claims admitted, and no infringement of your rights permitted in the future."[60] At Fort McKay in the upper Mississippi Valley, where news of the Treaty of Ghent had not yet reached the British garrison by April 1815, Captain Andrew Bulger of the Royal Newfoundland Fencibles (who had replaced Thomas G. Anderson as post commandant the previous November) instructed his interpreters to inform both the Sioux and the Sauks that "it is *solely on their* account that the War is now carried on."[61] When news of the peace finally reached these distant outposts the following month, both officers were stunned. The treaty's terms called for the restoration of all conquered territories. The disillusioned McDouall could only conclude that "our negociators [*sic*], as usual, have been egregiously duped. . . . [T]hey have shown themselves profoundly ignorant of the concerns of this part of the Empire."[62]

The northern and western Indians who subsequently met with McDouall and the Indian agents at Mackinac and Drummond Island between 1815 and 1817 were thunderstruck as they began to fully grasp the implications of the peace. In July 1815 American troops reoccupied Mackinac Island as McDouall and his small garrison removed to a new post at nearby Drummond Island in northern Lake Huron. The following summer the Dakota chiefs Wabasha and Little Crow, accompanied by four hundred warriors, visited the new British post to express their dissatisfaction.[63] A Winnebago leader also made his way to the northern agency that summer, where he confronted Thomas Anderson, by this time a commissioned Indian agent, complaining "we . . . have always been deceived by you."[64] Black Hawk, too, visited the post for a few consecutive summers in an attempt to compel the British to make good on their earlier promises, exclaiming, "I many

FIG. 9. In compliance with the Treaty of Ghent that officially ended the War of 1812, British forces under Captain Andrew Bulger prepare to withdraw from Fort McKay (Prairie du Chien, Wisconsin) in May 1815. The Indians present, thought to be a Sauk band under Black Hawk, are firing their guns in a final salute to their British ally. *Captain W. Andrew Bulger Saying Farewell at Fort Mackay, Prairie du Chien Wisconsin,* 1815, by Peter Rindisbacher, watercolor and ink wash on paper, circa 1823, 14⅛ x 23⅞ inches. 1968.262. Courtesy Amon Carter Museum, Fort Worth, Texas.

times rubbed my eyes and cleared my ears, before I could believe what I saw or what I heard." If the British did not support the Indians, Black Hawk continued, "your red children . . . will be slaves to the Big Knives." When the Sauk leader grew aggressively angry, recently appointed agent William McKay forcefully silenced him: "I have your Great Father's orders to obey and all the Indians in the universe will not make me deviate from them. The council is Ended and you must withdraw." These remarks left Black Hawk "crying with rage."[65]

Of all the groups within the Chain of Friendship, the tribes in the North and West—those shown in this study to have been the more stable segment of the Chain—were the most vocal in expressing their anger with the British after the War of 1812. This was partly due to the fact that they still held out hope of resisting the Americans. The nations nearer to the Detroit theater of the conflict had relocated or had surrendered to the "Big Knives." Tecumseh and Roundhead were dead, and by 1816 Main Poc was gone as well.[66] Walk in the Water, one of the few surviving chiefs of the coalition from the southern Great Lakes, had begun to cooperate with the Americans much earlier. The warriors from the Grand River merely returned to their farms, and with the restoration of peace, they no longer stood to lose their land. But the nations in Wisconsin, northern Michigan, and the upper Mississippi Valley were beginning to experience the pressure of an expanding military presence in those regions after 1815, causing more consternation for the Indians there.[67] Finally, however, probably the most significant reason that the northern and western tribes so ardently expressed their dissatisfaction with the British stemmed from their understanding of the familial, symbiotic ties that had subsisted between them for so long. To these groups, their British Father was far more than a mere wartime ally, and since the nations in these distant quarters had not been greatly affected by events in either 1783 or 1794, they now began to experience this disappointment for the first time.

In truth, British officials and military leaders, both in Canada and in the home government, earnestly desired to protect their allies and make good on their wartime promises. After Tecumseh's death, the fallen warrior's sister and Tecumseh's teen-age son, along with nearly two dozen Indians from the Detroit region, visited Governor-General Sir George Prevost at Quebec in March 1814. Prevost compassionately expressed his condolences, telling the delegation of his sorrow upon previously learning of Tecumseh's death. To console the Indians, the governor-general reminded them that they and the British shared a common cause, and that "our Great Father considers you as his children and will not forget you or your interests at a Peace."[68]

Like Prevost, British leaders in England, including the prime minister, Lord Liverpool and his war secretary, Earl Bathurst, considered it a priority to negotiate a permanent Indian boundary and preferably a sovereign Native buffer state that would separate the U.S. territories from Britain's Canadian possessions. Furthermore, the British peace commissioners at Ghent exceeded their government's instructions by boldly demanding an Indian buffer state as a sine qua non of any peace agreement. The proposal was to include nearly all of the Indian territory lost since the Treaty of Greenville in 1795, and both the British and U.S. governments would theoretically be prohibited from purchasing or acquiring any Indian lands from within its boundaries.[69]

Such a lofty ultimatum by the British commissioners had no chance of succeeding. Any attempt to redraw the boundary separating Indian country from the United States at the old Greenville line would have first required the removal of more than one hundred thousand white settlers. In addition, John Quincy Adams, a member of the American peace delegation, pointed out that "no European power had ever considered the Indian nations as Great Britain appeared now to consider them."[70] Adams later told Henry Goulburn, Britain's undersecretary of state for war and the colonies at this time (1812–21) and the leader of the British peace commission, that to "condemn" so great a "territory to perpetual barrenness and solitude [so] that a few hundred savages might find wild beasts to hunt upon it, was a species of game law that a nation descended from Britons would never endure."[71] When the two countries' delegations informally met for dinner on August 23, 1814, Henry Clay, another of the American commissioners, explained to Goulburn that the British proposition regarding the Indians was "equivalent to a demand for the cession of Boston or New York."[72] Consequently, the Americans prepared to break off negotiations. Only Clay held out hope for reaching an agreement, but merely because he, renowned for his gambling and card playing, felt certain that the British were bluffing.[73]

The Americans ultimately had the better of the argument, for they were basing their perspective on the traditional Euro-American legal understanding that Natives were not sovereign over the lands on which they lived, but merely possessed the usufructuary right to the temporary use of the land. Americans had regarded the region of the proposed Indian buffer state as sovereign U.S. territory ever since the Peace of Paris in 1783. The proposal was more convenient for Britain.

Since Britain had ceded this region at that time, it was not as if the king's ministers were offering to carve a sovereign Native state from British territory. Certainly, the Grand River experience had demonstrated their aversion for such a concept. In any case, the Americans would never agree to any compromise unless the British were in a position to forcibly evict them from Indian lands. Even then, the war would probably never end. Adams believed that even if the U.S. government agreed to Britain's Indian proposal, "all its [the U.S. government's] force, and that of Britain combined with it, would not suffice" to prevent the American settlers from crossing the line.[74] Clay shared this view, intimating to Goulburn that the two countries' "united efforts would be inadequate to restrain that part of the American population which is to the Westward of the Allegheny, from encroaching upon the Indian Territory and gradually expelling the aboriginal inhabitants."[75] Amazed, Goulburn later concluded, "I had till I came here no idea of the fixed determination which prevails in the breast of every American to extirpate the Indians and appropriate their Territory; but . . . there is nothing which the people of America would so reluctantly abandon as what they . . . call their natural right to do so."[76] Thus the problem stemmed largely from the massive land cessions made in 1783 of areas that the Americans had never actually conquered, but which they had based their right to possess on a myth of conquest.

Rather than demanding an Indian buffer state, perhaps a wiser stratagem for the British commissioners to have attempted would have been to seek modest territorial gains in Wisconsin, Michigan, New York, and Maine, without mentioning the Indians at the peace talks. Then the Crown might have subsequently had the option of earmarking some of the conquered regions specifically for Native reserves. Instead, once President James Madison received news of the extravagant British proposals for an Indian buffer state, he released the substance of the confidential peace talks to the American public, further raising the ire and hatred of the populace against Britain and the Crown's faithful Indian allies.[77] Once the British commissioners had proposed the buffer state, the American government and its citizens were in no mood to make any territorial concessions at all, no matter how poorly American forces had fared in the war.

Even so, British officials contemplated a continuation and an escalation of the war and offered overall command of Britain's North American forces to the greatest military mind of the age, the Duke of Wellington. The "Iron Duke," though expressing his willingness to accept the command, could not promise further territorial conquests until the British had gained full naval superiority on the Great Lakes. Only then could he consider moving great numbers of troops south of the Lakes and dislodging the Americans from their remaining forts scattered throughout northern Ohio and Indiana, key locations that Procter's former Right Division had failed to capture. Without control of the Great Lakes, Wellington firmly maintained, "you have no right . . . to demand any concession of territory from America."[78] The duke's words helped temper Britain's zeal to continue to prosecute the war. Fortunately for both countries, Wellington remained in Europe to meet the revived French threat after Napoleon's escape from his temporary exile at Elba.

Wellington's opinion represented only a single factor influencing Britain to end hostilities in North America. After more than two decades of fighting France, a continued war with the United States would require additional loans and property taxes.[79] Furthermore, Europe's instability at the time and growing European sympathy for the United States made peace desirable. Years later, Henry Goulburn reflected on the final months of 1814, recalling that "the discussions at Vienna assumed a character which made it possible that there might be a renewal of hostilities in Europe & parties there speculated upon the embarrassment which an American war would cause to England."[80] Therefore British commissioners relented to American pressure for a peace based on the principle of status quo ante bellum, a restoration of all conditions and territories as they stood prior to the war. Thus, while officers and agents in North America such as McDouall, Bulger, Dickson, and others all recognized the familial ties that the Indians believed morally bound the British to the Chain of Friendship, the home government, though wanting to help the Indians, in the end shaped Britain's foreign policy to conform to its European geopolitical interests.

By all conventional standards, the Americans had lost the war but won the peace. Louise Phelps Kellogg, illustrious historian of the Old Northwest during the early twentieth century, most aptly concluded, "What Americans could not accomplish by force of arms, their diplomats obtained during the negotiations at Ghent."[81] Militarily, the United States had failed in all of its objectives, including its attempt to conquer Canada. In fact, American commissioners at Ghent never compelled the British peace delegation to address Britain's violation of maritime rights for which the war was supposedly declared, and at the war's end British troops occupied much more American territory than vice-versa. In Canada, the United States held only the Western District of Upper Canada, the southernmost slice of British territory in North America that encompassed Fort Malden.[82] Finally, the Americans held naval domination only on Lake Erie, albeit the most vital of all the Great Lakes. Yet the American diplomatic triumph in gaining a stalemate at Ghent, coupled with Andrew Jackson's brilliant postwar victory over a seasoned British army at New Orleans in January 1815, left Americans with the false impression that the former event was linked to the latter, and that they had therefore won the war, compelling Britain to agree to favorable terms. In a sense, it was the myth of victory in 1783 all over again; Jeffersonian Americans even regarded it as a second war of independence.[83]

As in 1783, the Crown's Indian allies were once again left vulnerable to American expansion. This time, however, British leaders had at least attempted to address Native concerns at the peace negotiations, and in place of the ill-fated buffer state proposal, Goulburn and his associates managed to persuade the American commissioners to add an article to the treaty as a token attempt to protect Native interests. In keeping with the principle of status quo ante bellum, Article IX of the Treaty of Ghent theoretically restored all Indian "possessions, rights, and privileges" to which they had been entitled in the year 1811. This, however, did not guarantee the Indians a sovereign status, and it did nothing to prevent the continuation of a process of relinquishing their lands to the United States through a rapid succession of treaties. Furthermore, Tecumseh and other significant leaders of resistance were now gone, and the British no longer attempted to intervene, so nothing hindered the accelerated process of American land acquisition. Short of continuing the war for many years in what promised to be a bloody, futile struggle for Lake Erie and northern Ohio, Article IX in the Ghent agreement was the best that the British could do for the Indians, given the circumstances and American temperament.

In spite of the broken promises and the drastically reduced government budgets earmarked for Indian expenses that followed the war, traces of the old Chain of Friendship remained. Numerous Indians who remained in the vicinity of Detroit continued to cross over each year in order to visit their British Father at Fort Malden through the mid-1830s, a practice that continued to annoy Governor Lewis Cass of Michigan.[84] And during the Mackenzie Rebellion in Upper Canada in 1837–38, Ojibwas from Lake Huron and nearly a hundred warriors from Upper Canada's Grand River turned out to assist in putting down the revolt.[85] Even Black Hawk, after having survived the bloody war that bears his name, by 1833 had seemingly forgotten about his harsh words and shouting sprees with British agents sixteen years earlier. In his autobiography, the Sauk leader recalled that "the *British* made but few [promises]—but we could always *rely upon their word.*"[86]

Yet the best examples of postwar continuity in British-Indian relations occurred in the North. The wartime careers of Robert Dickson, William McKay, Thomas G. Anderson, and Captain Andrew Bulger all accentuated the past while simultaneously portending the future. In the early 1820s Bulger went on to a successful stint serving as post commandant at Fort Douglas, Red River Colony (today's Winnipeg, Manitoba), providing stability and mediating disputes between white settlers, Ojibwa peoples, and traders of the Hudson's Bay

FIG. 10. Grand River Iroquois veterans of the War of 1812. Perhaps having once served under John Norton's contingent of British-allied Iroquois during the War of 1812, these veterans from the Grand River are photographed in 1886, when all three were in their nineties. Left to right: Jacob Warner, John Tutlee, and John Smoke Johnson. Courtesy of the Woodland Cultural Centre.

Company.[87] Robert Dickson retired from the Indian Department in 1815 and quietly lived out his final years among his adopted peoples in the Northwest until his death in 1823. McKay and Anderson enjoyed lengthy careers serving His Majesty's former Indian allies; the two agents continued to annually distribute gifts and provisions to Indians at the British post on northern Lake Huron's Drummond Island, before moving to Manitoulin Island in 1828, where the British government continued their Indian policy of gift-giving well into the 1840s.[88] Coinciding with the move to Manitoulin Island, the Indian Department of Upper Canada also transferred its central headquarters to Penetanguishene on the southern shore of the Georgian Bay. William Claus had died in 1826, and the vacated deputy superintendency was no longer maintained at Fort George. After McKay's death in 1832, followed by the retirement of Superintendent James Givens five years later, Anderson remained the lone figure in the Indian Department who had personally fought for the Crown and who could yet remember a unique relationship with the Crown's Indian allies, a relationship based on a mutual understanding of the meanings and significance of the Chain of Friendship.[89]

By the time of Anderson's retirement in 1858, this stalwart Indian agent and former commander at Fort McKay had seen Britain's Indian policy in Canada wholly transformed. No longer a mutual alliance that sought to preserve former Indian lifestyles and livelihoods linked to the fur trade, newer British-Indian relations entailed civilization programs based on agrarian and humanitarian concerns. In spite of the continuity that had for a time persisted in the North after the War of 1812, the fur trade was now greatly diminished, and the years of frontier warfare, alliances, council fires, and Indian revitalization movements had all passed.[90] In his final years, Anderson still possessed a keen recollection of the early days, recalling that he once "had . . . about five thousand Indians at my command."[91] But in 1814 one Dakota chief, Red Wing, who claimed to have seen the future three times, informed the agent that he would not fight the Americans. Though declaring to Anderson that "all the blood in my heart is English," Red Wing explained that his dream revealed that the "eagle" and the "lion will finally make up and be friends, and smoke the pipe of peace. The lion will then go home and leave us with our foes."[92] In his memoirs, the long-retired agent could only add, "And so things turned out; we left them to care for themselves."[93] At the time of Anderson's death—at age ninety-five—in 1875, few could remember that His Majesty's Indian allies had once saved Canada.

Notes

Introduction

1. Spain and the Netherlands were also drawn into the war against Great Britain in 1779 and 1780, respectively, but unlike France, neither of those nations immediately recognized American independence. The Netherlands formally recognized American sovereignty in 1782, but the Spanish only did so after the British officially acknowledged an independent United States in the general Peace of Paris in 1783. France had recognized American independence and sovereign status upon entering the war in 1778.

2. Linda Colley illuminates the national character of the British people during this period, emphasizing Protestantism, commercial interests, internal free trade, and anti-French patriotism as the key factors binding them together. Colley, *Britons*, 3–6, 85–100, 177–93, 368–72.

3. The best brief overview of the early development and original meanings of the Covenant Chain is found in Jennings, "Covenant Chain."

4. Proceedings of an Indian Conference, Detroit, December 3, 1760, in Sullivan, Flick, and Hamilton, *Papers of Sir William Johnson* (hereafter cited as *Johnson Papers*), 10:200.

5. Proceedings of an Indian Conference, Detroit, September 10, 1761, in *Johnson Papers*, 3:484.

6. The expression "Pontiac's Conspiracy" originated with early students and scholars of this war, among them Francis Parkman, renowned frontier author of the nineteenth century. Modern scholars have since shown that the Ottawa leader Pontiac was but a single, local participant in a much broader movement that was years in the making prior to 1763. Furthermore, while the preparation for the conflict did entail a vast and intricate "conspiracy," the end result was a full-scale war that ravaged the entire northern frontier eastward to the Appalachians and may have cost the lives of more than two thousand people. Dowd, *War Under Heaven*, 5–6; White, *Middle Ground*, 271–77.

7. White, *Middle Ground*, 305–7; Steele, *Warpaths*, 246–47; Dowd, *War Under Heaven*, 274–75. Also, Colin G. Calloway, in his definitive study of the Native American West prior to American expansion there, pointed out this fresh diplomatic landscape after Pontiac's conflict, asserting that "Britain . . . modified [its] vision of empire to fit the realities of the Indian West. By war and diplomacy, western Indians [that is, at the time, 1763–64, those in the Great Lakes] inserted themselves in the Covenant Chain alliance system between Britain and the Six Nations [Iroquois]." Calloway, *Winter Count*, 354.

8. Proceedings of an Indian Conference, Niagara, July 31, 1764, in *Johnson Papers*, 11:309–11.

9. Prior to 1796, these three agencies were located at the corresponding adjacent sites named, situated on the American side of the border at British Forts Detroit, Mackinac, and Niagara, respectively.

10. Created in 1791, the province of Upper Canada was roughly the expanse of present-day Ontario. The other province at the time, aptly named "Lower Canada" (now Quebec), is at a lower sea level.

11. Taylor won both the Pulitzer and Bancroft prizes for American History with his *William Cooper's Town: Power and Persuasion on the Frontier of the Early American Republic*.

1. *The Quest for a Just Peace*

1. The term "upper country" was used to describe the region of the hinterland's higher altitude moving up the St. Lawrence River and beyond, encompassing the areas of the Great Lakes, the Old Northwest, and Upper Canada. At the highest elevations of this upper region, a continental divide forms a natural watershed just south of the Great Lakes, separating the two principal river systems, which either flow southwest toward the Mississippi River, or northeast, emptying into the Great Lakes and the St. Lawrence.

2. Charles Gravier, count de Vergennes, to Antoine Raymond Jean Gualbert Gabriel de Sartine, count d'Abby, December 4, 1782, in Wharton, *Revolutionary Diplomatic Correspondence*, 6:107.

3. The Earl of Shelburne hoped to foster harmony and economic cooperation between Britain and the fledgling United States, and he envisioned a westward-expanding American nation tapping British markets. Shelburne also wanted to drive a wedge between the United States and Britain's other enemies by favoring American geopolitical interests over those of France and Spain when determining boundaries in North America. See Dull, "Foreign Relations," 374–75. Also, in the epilogue of a recent study, Calloway draws a comparison between this peace agreement and that of the first Treaty of Paris in 1763. On neither occasion were American Indians consulted or represented on matters pertaining to their homelands that they had so successfully defended. See Calloway, *Scratch of a Pen*, 168–70. In an expanded discussion

from much earlier in his career—beginning with a conference paper that became a published article—Calloway more thoroughly covered the Treaty of Paris of 1783, including its reasons and consequences for both the British and the Crown's Indian allies. See Calloway, "Suspicion and Self-Interest," especially 49–60.

4. Sir Frederick Haldimand to Sir John Johnson, May 22, 1783, MG 21 B 115, 106, Haldimand Papers, Library and Archives Canada, Ottawa (hereafter cited as LAC); Thomas, *Sir John Johnson*, 105–7.

5. "Johnson's Speech at Niagara, July, 1783," in Burt, *United States*, 89–90; speech originally taken from Colonial Office, MG 11 Q 21, 433–35, LAC.

6. It must be remembered that Sir John Johnson, like his Iroquois friends and allies, also lost his home and inheritance as a result of the war. This included the mansions at Johnson Hall and Fort Johnson, and the vast landholdings of approximately two hundred thousand acres stretching throughout much of the Mohawk River valley. Johnson, who had inherited his father's title of baronet, served with distinction throughout the war, successfully leading combined Loyalist and Indian invasions through the heart of New York. After the conflict, Johnson made his home in Montreal, and in 1782 he received his appointment as superintendent general and inspector general of Indian Affairs, a position he held until his retirement in 1828. Johnson died two years later at age eighty-seven.

7. "Transactions with the Indians at Sandusky, 26 August to 8 September," in Michigan Pioneer and Historical Society, *Historical Collections of the Michigan Pioneer and Historical Society* (hereafter cited as *Historical Collections*), 10:174–83. See also Nelson, *Man of Distinction*, 131–32. A few Iroquois also attended the McKee's council held at Lower Sandusky.

8. Allen, *His Majesty's Indian Allies*, 54. Good accounts of these actions are found scattered in several publications, most notably Nester, *Frontier War*; Waller, *American Revolution*; Cruikshank, *Butler's Rangers*; Graymont, *Iroquois in the American Revolution*; Potter, "Redcoats on the Frontier"; and Walker, "Northwest during the Revolution."

9. White, *Middle Ground*, 434.

10. Haldimand to North, November 27, 1783, Colonial Office, MG 11, CO 42, Vol. 46, LAC.

11. A full compliance with the terms of the Treaty of Paris would have required the American government to pay the nation's outstanding prewar debts to British merchants, and the separate state governments needed either to restore confiscated Loyalist property to its owners or at least compensate these loyal refugees for their losses. Far from regaining their property, most Loyalists still suffered harassment, ridicule, physical harm, and sometimes even death when attempting to collect their property in the former American colonies after the war. These violations represented breaches of Articles IV, V, and VI of the Treaty of Paris. Burt, *United States*, 95–98; Ritcheson, *Aftermath of Revolution*, 59–69, 80–87. The entire Treaty of Paris, includ-

ing a nonratified article of the treaty, is found in Bemis, *Diplomacy of the American Revolution*, 259–64.

12. "Haldimand Grant," in Graymont, *Iroquois in the American Revolution*, 299; Kelsay, *Joseph Brant*, 363.

13. Lord Shelburne, prime minister during the preliminary peace negotiations in Paris, defended his government's actions, arguing, "the Indian nations were not abandoned to their enemies; they were remitted to the care of neighbors, whose interests it was as much ours to cultivate friendship with them, and who were certainly the best qualified for softening and humanizing their hearts." Quoted in Graymont, *Iroquois in the American Revolution*, 262; Calloway also alludes to this excerpt in *Crown and Calumet*, 8.

14. Compare the "Haldimand Grant" in Graymont, *Iroquois in the American Revolution*, 299, to Haldimand's initial intention to retain the posts in the upper country in his letter to North, November 27, 1783, Colonial Office, MG II, CO 42, Vol. 46, LAC. In his attempts to protect the Indians by preventing "such a disastrous event as an Indian war," the governor saw the necessity in "allowing the posts in the upper country to remain as they are for sometime."

15. The Iroquois League consisted of the Mohawk, Cayuga, Onondaga, Oneida, Seneca, and Tuscarora nations.

16. Francis Jennings cleverly disassembles the myth of a perpetual Iroquois empire in *Ambiguous Iroquois Empire*, especially chapter 2. Jennings also provides an overview of the history of the Covenant Chain in "Iroquois Alliances," 37–65. An important eighteenth-century perspective supporting the notion of Iroquois dominance over their western neighbors is Colden, *History of the Five Indian Nations*.

17. Haldimand to Claus, December 17, 1783, Claus Papers, 3:277, MG 19 G 1, LAC.

18. "Memorandum Respecting the Public Matters in the Province of Quebec submitted for the consideration of the Right Honourable Lord Sydney by General Haldimand," March 16, 1785, Colonial Office, MG II, CO 42, Vol. 48, 251, LAC.

19. Prucha, *American Indian Treaties*, 46–48.

20. The most important western nations that continued to resist American expansion after the Revolution included the Shawnees, Wyandots, Delawares, Miamis, Ottawas, Ojibwas, and Potawatomis.

21. Kelsay, *Joseph Brant*, 312–13; Nester, *Frontier War*, 300; Cruikshank, *Butler's Rangers*, 96–97. Although Brant was technically not selected as a sachem under the traditional Iroquois protocol of matriarchal selection, he in effect assumed this role for the final thirty years of his life, beginning in 1777. More important, Brant's people recognized him as qualified to fulfill the role of sachem, and after functioning in this capacity for his career, Brant was formally—and hereditarily—replaced as a sachem by traditional means after his death in 1807. Stone, *Joseph Brant*, 2:500; Lydekker, *Faithful Mohawks*, 188–89. Key scholars have also indicated that the Mohawk leader was distinguished as a "Pine Tree chief," a category of civil chiefs who had lacked he-

reditary rights to leadership and were not chosen in the traditional matriarchal process. For Brant as a Pine Tree chief, see Tooker, "League of the Iroquois," 429; and Snow, *Iroquois*, 65, 139, 145.

22. Sword, *Washington's Indian War*, 37–40; White, *Middle Ground*, 433. This expeditionary force included Daniel Boone and Simon Kenton. Faragher covers their involvement in the campaign in *Daniel Boone*, 251–55. There are various other spellings for these two Shawnee villages, including Mequashake and Wakatomica, but those in the main body of this text are taken from Sword, *Washington's Indian War*.

23. Kelsay, *Joseph Brant*, 404.

24. Blair, *Indian Tribes*, 2:188.

25. Blair, *Indian Tribes*, 2:189. Historian Richard White contradicts Forsyth, arguing, "official British representatives were not present at Brownstown." White, *Middle Ground*, 434. In spite of this discrepancy between White and Forsyth (and probably an oversight by White), White agrees that the confederacy leaders at Brownstown maintained close ties with the British at Detroit and that the confederacy grew increasingly dependent upon the British after the initial council at Brownstown in 1786.

26. Blair, *Indian Tribes*, 2:188.

27. While the Wyandot peoples generally favored British interests, the Wyandot villages on the Sandusky River in central and northern Ohio would on occasion act independently of Brownstown in matters of peace and diplomacy.

28. E. A. Cruikshank, a late-nineteenth-and early-twentieth-century historian, described Brown as "[a] half-breed chief of the Wyandots," in Cruikshank, *Correspondence of Lieut. Governor John Graves Simcoe* (hereafter cited as *Simcoe Correspondence*), 3:183, n1. However, Emma Helen Blair, a contemporary of Cruikshank's, noted Brown's English colonial origins in Virginia, in Blair, *Indian Tribes*, 2:189, n67. According to Blair, Brown died sometime after the War of 1812.

29. Lord Sydney to General Hope, April 6, 1786, Colonial Office, MG 11, CO 42, Vol. 49, 59, LAC.

30. McKee to Johnson, February 25, 1786, Colonial Office, MG 11, CO 42, Vol. 49, 258, LAC.

31. Horsman, *Matthew Elliott*, 55–57; Nelson, *Man of Distinction*, 153–54.

32. Horsman, "British Indian Department and the Resistance to General Anthony Wayne," 270–71; Calloway, *Crown and Calumet*, 51, 64–65, 70–74.

33. Kekionga was the site of present-day Fort Wayne, Indiana; the Glaize, present-day Defiance, Ohio; and the Foot of the Rapids, present-day Toledo, Ohio. Roche de Bout sat a short distance upstream from the Rapids, near today's Waterville, Ohio. *Historical Collections*, 20:680, n60. For Kekionga and the entire Maumee region, see Tanner, *Atlas*, 85–89.

34. Excerpt from Little Turtle's speech at the treaty proceedings of Greenville, August 1795, quoted in Poinsatte, *Outpost in the Wilderness*, 1.

35. Le Gris and Pacanne were Miami leaders, and the other three, Shawnee.

36. Tanner, *Atlas*, 85, 88; Carter, *Little Turtle*, 24, 66; Sugden, *Blue Jacket*, 80.

37. Helderman, "Danger on the Wabash," 459.

38. Le Gris was an older, more established chief who presided over his own village and held much influence in matters of intertribal diplomacy during the 1780s and 1790s, whereas Le Gros was a younger warrior at the time. Nevertheless, Le Gros became an influential Miami chief in his own right, serving as one of Trowbridge's most important informants regarding Miami people and culture in 1824–25. This Captain Pipe was probably the son of the famed Delaware leader of the same name who fought against the United States between the 1770s and 1790s. Although Trowbridge did not indicate it, the elder Captain Pipe is thought to have died in 1794. The younger Captain Pipe was probably also involved in the conflicts of the 1790s. Wheeler-Voegelin and Tanner, *Indians of Northern Ohio and Southeastern Michigan*, 281; see also *Historical Collections*, 20:680, n67.

39. Anson, *Miami Indians*, 12; Trowbridge, *Shawnese Traditions*, 67. A good study pertaining to the intertribal communities along the Maumee at this time is Tanner, "Glaize."

40. Trowbridge, *Meearmeear Traditions*, 13–14.

41. Trowbridge, *Shawnese Traditions*, 11–12.

42. Delaware Manuscripts, MS/14d, Trowbridge Papers, Burton Historical Collection, Detroit Public Library.

43. Anson, *Miami Indians*, 18–19; Rafert, *Miami Indians*, 17–18; Howard, *Shawnee!* 87–90.

44. Howard, *Shawnee!* 100–101; for Delaware social organization, see Goddard, "Delaware," 225.

45. Howard, *Shawnee!* 109; Trowbridge, *Shawnese Traditions*, 12–13; Trowbridge, *Meearmeear Traditions*, 14–15, 26. According to Trowbridge, the Delawares had "[n]o female Chiefs." Delaware Manuscripts, MS/14d, Trowbridge Papers, Burton Historical Collection.

46. Trowbridge, *Shawnese Traditions*, 37; Delaware Manuscripts, MS/14d, Trowbridge Papers, Burton Historical Collection; Howard, *Shawnee!* 182. The Wyandots, an integral member of this Confederacy, also subscribed to the legend of the giant turtle. See Tooker, "Wyandot," 402.

47. Dowd, *Spirited Resistance*, 10–11; Howard, *Shawnee!* 176–78.

48. James Howard explains that the legend of the Giant Horned Snake is a dual myth shared by the Shawnees and Delawares, and he relates the Delaware account of how that tribe managed to kill one of these deities. Howard, *Shawnee!* 189–90. For the Miamis, this most feared underwater manitou took the form of a panther, called Lennipinja. Rafert, *Miami Indians*, 15.

49. Trowbridge, *Shawnese Traditions*, 42; Trowbridge, *Meearmeear Traditions*, 56.

50. Quaife, "Narrative of Life," 226.

51. Quaife, "Narrative of Life," 225.

52. Heckewelder, *Narrative*, 396–97.

53. The three Girty brothers—Simon, James, and George—were captured as youths and adopted into Indian families, and all three later served as agents and interpreters in the British Indian Department. They gained infamous reputations among white Americans who viewed them, especially Simon, as savage renegades. Yet Jonathan Alder, a young captive among the Shawnees, had a high regard for Simon Girty, who at times interceded on behalf of captives. See Nelson, *Jonathan Alder*, 52–55, 171–76; and Calloway, "Simon Girty," 38–58.

54. Quaife, "Hay Journal," 237.

55. Quaife, "Hay Journal," 255.

56. Quaife, "Hay Journal," 226.

57. Quaife, "Hay Journal," 222–23.

58. Quaife, "Hay Journal," 221–22, 223.

59. "Dorchester's Instructions for the good Government of the Indian Department. To Sir John Johnson, Baronet, Superintendant [*sic*] General and Inspector General of Indian Affairs, 27 March 1787," RG 10, Indian Affairs, Vol. 789, 6759–61, LAC.

60. In 1792 the British traders and Indian agents shared living quarters at the Glaize, the new location of the intertribal collection of villages that replaced those at Kekionga. See Tanner, "Glaize," 30.

61. "Dorchester's Instructions," RG 10, Indian Affairs, Vol. 789, 6760–61, LAC.

62. Calloway, "Foundations of Sand," 147–49.

63. Davidson, *North West Company*, 17–18, 272.

64. Calloway, "Foundations of Sand," 157–58.

65. Calloway, *Crown and Calumet*, 160, 188. Calloway refers to the fur trade as a "Trojan horse" to the Indians, "unleashing catastrophic forces at the same time as it delivered desirable gifts" (188).

66. Calloway, *Crown and Calumet*, 188; Calloway, "Foundations of Sand," 159.

67. "Dorchester's Instructions," RG 10, Indian Affairs, Vol. 789, 6759, LAC.

68. Quaife, "Hay Journal," 255.

69. Edgar, *Upper Canada*, 367.

70. Sword, *Washington's Indian War*, 102–3; Sugden, *Blue Jacket*, 100. The number of warriors to defend against Harmar had diminished so drastically that scholar Harvey Lewis Carter concluded—albeit mistakenly—that the ensuing victory was gained by the Miamis alone. Carter, *Little Turtle*, 93.

71. Sword, *Washington's Indian War*, 102.

72. Sword, *Washington's Indian War*, 106–8. In November 1790 Harmar gave two written accounts of the expedition, one to Henry Knox, secretary of war, November 6, and the other to Major John Hamtramck, U.S. post commandant at Vincennes, November 29. In both accounts Harmar attempted to claim victory, though acknowledging that his troops sustained heavy losses. Thornbrough, *Outpost on the Wabash*, 268–69.

73. Sword, *Washington's Indian War*, 117–19.

74. Trowbridge, *Shawnese Traditions*, 37; "Col. Boyd's Account," Chippewa Manuscripts, MS/14c, Trowbridge Papers, Burton Historical Collection. Far more than merely holding parallel cosmological beliefs, the Ottawas and Ojibwas shared a number of common links. They and the Potawatomis are thought to have a common origin, and the three form what some modern scholars refer to as the alliance of the Three Fires. Contemporaries recognized the cultural and diplomatic ties between them, and John Graves Simcoe, lieutenant governor of Upper Canada, collectively referred to this triumvirate as "the Lake Indians." Simcoe to Henry Dundas, November 10, 1793, in *Simcoe Correspondence*, 2:99–100. For a historical sketch of the common origin and culture of the Three Fires, see Fixico, "Alliance of the Three Fires"; see also Edmunds, *Potawatomis*, 3; and Clifton, *Prairie People*, 30–32. While contemporaries did not use the phrase "the Three Fires," the three nations did function in such a manner in the eighteenth century, and some modern scholars have therefore chosen to use the expression, including Ritzenthaler, "Southwestern Chippewa," and John Sugden in his definitive *Tecumseh*.

75. Speech of Blue Jacket, November 4, 1790, quoted in Sugden, *Blue Jacket*, 106–7.

76. Quaife, *O. M. Spencer*, 90–91. Blue Jacket was even thought to have worn a red coat in the action against St. Clair. See Sword, *Washington's Indian War*, 179; and Sugden, *Blue Jacket*, 123.

77. Sugden, *Blue Jacket*, 108.

78. Tanner, "Glaize," 16.

79. Quaife, *O. M. Spencer*, 78, 117.

80. Quaife, *O. M. Spencer*, 116.

81. Quaife, *O. M. Spencer*, 78–80. See also Tanner, "Coocoochee," 24–25, 28. The Ohio Iroquois, known as Mingoes, began migrating into Ohio in the 1740s and 1750s; Coocoochee's family relocated to Ohio sometime after 1768, the year in which the first Treaty of Fort Stanwix supposedly made the Ohio River a permanent boundary and acknowledged that the country north of the river belonged solely to the Indians.

82. A good analysis of the Iroquois Condolence Ceremony is found in Fenton and Hewitt, "Iroquois Condolence Council." See also Fenton, *Great Law*, 136–37, 178–79. Erminie Wheeler-Voegelin studied Shawnee death and burial customs, spanning the period from the late seventeenth century through 1938, and also compared the differences in the practices of the five separate Shawnee divisions. Wheeler-Voegelin, *Mortuary Customs*, 243–319. For the Shawnee version of a funeral and Condolence Ceremony, circa 1800, see Wheeler-Voegelin, *Mortuary Customs*, 268–69.

83. At this time the Shawnees held death feasts on the fourth night after death, the Iroquois on the tenth. Wheeler-Voegelin, *Mortuary Customs*, 268–69. The feast was intended to nourish the spirit of the deceased, helping to prepare it for its final journey, but without the ceremony, the spirit would linger. Howard, *Shawnee!* 286–87; Parker, *Parker on the Iroquois*, 57; Wallace, *Death and Rebirth*, 98–99.

84. Trowbridge, *Shawnese Traditions*, 42; Edgar, *Upper Canada*, 364; Wallace, *Death and Rebirth*, 98–101; Parker, *Parker on the Iroquois*, 126.

85. Quaife, *O. M. Spencer*, 95–96; Tanner, "Glaize," 17, 25–27.

86. Tanner, "Glaize," 17, 25–27.

87. Nelson, *Man of Distinction*, 158.

88. Nelson, *Man of Distinction*, 171.

89. Sword, *Washington's Indian War*, 182, 188; Horsman, *Matthew Elliott*, 69.

90. White, *Middle Ground*, 454; Allen, *His Majesty's Indian Allies*, 74–76. This excerpt from Allen contains a contemporary British account of the battle and its implications, found in an anonymous letter from Niagara three weeks later, November 24, 1791, Colonial Office, MG 11, CO 42, Vol. 88, LAC. The general engagement, known as St. Clair's Defeat, is best detailed in Sword, *Washington's Indian War*, chapter 17. Only Edward Braddock's defeat near the banks of the Monongahela in 1755 rivaled the magnitude of St. Clair's Defeat thirty-six years later.

91. White, *Middle Ground*, 454.

92. White, *Middle Ground*, 455; Horsman, "British Indian Department and the Resistance to General Anthony Wayne," 270–71; Calloway, *Crown and Calumet*, 51, 64–65, 70–74.

93. Simcoe to McKee, September 24, 1792; Simcoe to McKee, November 10, 1792, both in *Simcoe Correspondence*, 5:23, 25.

94. Simcoe to George Hammond, January 21, 1793, in *Historical Collections*, 25:522.

95. Simcoe to McKee, August 30, 1792, in *Simcoe Correspondence*, 1:208. Simcoe had many concerns, not only about how to best protect his Indian allies' interests and the fur trade without engaging in a war but also how to defend Upper Canada itself from American expansion. With virtually no army at his disposal, a peacefully negotiated Indian buffer zone seemed the best solution. For Simcoe's dilemma, see Fryer and Dracott, *John Graves Simcoe*, 123.

96. Confederacy's Address to Lieutenant Governor Simcoe, October 9, 1792, in *Simcoe Correspondence*, 1:229.

97. Speech from Lieutenant Governor Simcoe to the Western Indians, October 1792, in *Simcoe Correspondence*, 1:230.

98. Speech from Lieutenant Governor Simcoe to the Western Indians, October 1792, in *Simcoe Correspondence*, 1:230.

99. The captured American documents among General Arthur St. Clair's baggage taken in the battle the previous November confirmed Indian fears of American intentions, entailing a chain of military posts along the Maumee and a system of imposed agricultural reforms for the Indians. See Painted Pole's (Messquakenoe's) speech at the Glaize, October 7, 1792, in *Simcoe Correspondence*, 1:227; Nelson, *Man of Distinction*, 163; Sugden, *Blue Jacket*, 137–38; Sword, *Washington's Indian War*, 145, 148.

100. John Norton later mentioned that the Shawnees became leaders of the intertribal alliance prior to the action against St. Clair. See Klinck and Talman, *Journal of Major John Norton*, 177–78.

101. Proceedings at the Glaize, October 2, 1792, in *Simcoe Correspondence*, 1:220.

102. Proceedings at the Glaize, October 2, 1792, in *Simcoe Correspondence*, 1:220.

103. Proceedings at the Glaize, October 4, 1792, in *Simcoe Correspondence*, 1:222.

104. Proceedings at the Glaize, October 5, 1792, in *Simcoe Correspondence*, 1:224.

105. Proceedings at the Glaize, October 5, 1792, in *Simcoe Correspondence*, 1:224. See also Densmore, *Red Jacket*, 39.

106. Snow, *Iroquois*, 153–54.

107. Proceedings at the Glaize, October 7, 1792, in *Simcoe Correspondence*, 1:226.

108. Proceedings at the Glaize, October 8, 1792, in *Simcoe Correspondence*, 1:228.

109. Proceedings at the Glaize, October 7, 1792, in *Simcoe Correspondence*, 1:227–28.

110. Speech of the Shawanoes and Delawares at the Grand Glaize, June 11, 1792, recorded by Thomas Duggan, Clerk, British Indian Department, Native American Collection, Clements Historical Library, Ann Arbor MI.

111. Snake's Speech at the Foot of the Miami Rapids, October 28, 1792, in *Simcoe Correspondence*, 1:242.

112. Henry Knox to Joseph Brant, June 27, 1792, Northwest Territory Papers, Clements Historical Library.

113. Proceedings at the Glaize, October 7, 1792, in *Simcoe Correspondence*, 1:227.

114. Simcoe to McKee, August 30, 1792, in *Simcoe Correspondence*, 1:208–9.

115. Horsman offers a good analysis of the proceedings at this council in "British Indian Department and the Abortive Treaty of Lower Sandusky."

116. Captain Brant's Journal of the Proceedings at the General Council held at the Foot of the Rapids of the Miamis, June 3, 1793, in *Simcoe Correspondence*, 2:6.

117. Simcoe to George Hammond, September 8, 1793, in *Historical Collections*, 24:608; Sword, *Washington's Indian War*, 247.

118. Simcoe to Henry Dundas, November 10, 1793, in *Simcoe Correspondence*, 2:99–100.

119. Brant Journal, July 24, 1793, in *Simcoe Correspondence*, 2:8.

120. Brant Journal, July 24, 1793, in *Simcoe Correspondence*, 2:16.

121. Wallace, *Thirty Thousand Miles*, 19; *American State Papers*, 1:355; *Simcoe Correspondence*, 2:24, 33. McKee had consistently insisted throughout his career that the Ohio River was the only just boundary between the Indians of the Northwest and the United States, and he had always discouraged Native peoples from engaging in treaties with the United States long before the council at the Foot of the Rapids in 1793. Major John Hamtramck to Josiah Harmar, August 31, 1788, in Thornbrough, *Outpost on the Wabash*, 119.

122. Simcoe to McKee and Major John Butler, June 22, 1793, in *Historical Collections*, 24:555.

123. Simcoe to Major General Alured Clarke, July 10, 1793, in *Historical Collections*, 24:569.

124. Simcoe to Clarke, June 14, 1793, in *Historical Collections*, 24:549.

125. Simcoe to Henry Dundas, September 20, 1793, in *Simcoe Correspondence*, 2:59.

126. McKee to Simcoe, August 22, 1793, in *Historical Collections*, 24:595–96.

127. Simcoe to McKee, September 8, 1793, in *Simcoe Correspondence*, 5:72–73.

128. Simcoe to Henry Dundas, November 10, 1793, in *Simcoe Correspondence*, 2:100; Simcoe to Dorchester, November 10, 1793, in *Simcoe Correspondence*, 2:102.

129. Speech of the Chiefs of the Western Nations to His Excellency Governor Simcoe, late August 1793, in *Historical Collections*, 24:597–98.

130. Speech of the Chiefs of the Western Nations to His Excellency Governor Simcoe, late August 1793, in *Historical Collections*, 24:597–98.

131. Nelson, *Anthony Wayne*, 243–44.

132. Far more than mere rhetoric, Dorchester's passionate speech was genuine; he wholeheartedly believed that war with the United States was inevitable at the time. Nelson, *General Sir Guy Carleton, Lord Dorchester*, 223–28.

133. *Simcoe Correspondence*, 2:149–50; Wright, *Britain and the American Frontier*, 88–91; Sword, *Washington's Indian War*, 258–60; Ritcheson, *Aftermath of Revolution*, 309. Dorchester's speech was denounced in Parliament, and Whitehall disavowed both the speech and the government Indian policy that it implied. These disputed Native land cessions resulted from the earlier treaties of Fort Stanwix (1784), Fort McIntosh (1785), Fort Finney (1786), and Fort Harmar (1789).

134. Sword, *Washington's Indian War*, 261–62; Nelson, *Man of Distinction*, 167.

135. Simcoe to Dorchester, April 29, 1794, in *Historical Collections*, 24:660.

136. Nelson, *Man of Distinction*, 168–69; Sword, *Washington's Indian War*, 277–78.

137. Brant to McKee, May 8, 1794, in *Simcoe Correspondence*, 5:86–87.

138. Simcoe to Dorchester, 29 April 1794, in *Historical Collections*, 24:660.

139. Examination of two Shawnee warriors, taken prisoners on the Miami of the Lake, 20 miles above Grand Glaize, June 26, 1794, at Greeneville, by Anthony Wayne, Shawnee File, January–June 1794, Glenn A. Black Laboratory of Archaeology, Indiana University, Bloomington (hereafter cited as GABLA).

140. Examination of two Potawatomis, June 5, 1794, Shawnee File, January–June 1794, GABLA. According to another Potawatomi prisoner on July 21, "The British told all the Indian Nations to bring on all their Warriors and that then the British would bring more than all of them put together." The Examination of a Patawatime [*sic*] Warrior who was in the Attack upon Fort Recovery on the 30th Ultimo, July 23, 1794, Shawnee File, July–December, 1794, GABLA.

141. Cruikshank, "Diary," 640.

142. Sugden, *Blue Jacket*, 162; Nelson, *Man of Distinction*, 169.

143. Cruikshank, "Diary," 641; Sugden, *Blue Jacket*, 157, 162. The continued existence of such strong feelings surrounding this issue a year later indicated that Brant had held strong support in the council at the Rapids before being undone by McKee.

144. Nelson, *Man of Distinction*, 169; Sword, *Washington's Indian War*, 278.

145. McKee to Joseph Chew, July 7, 1794, in *Historical Collections*, 20:364.

146. The Ottawas and Ojibwas may have contributed more than six hundred warriors to the campaign effort against Fort Recovery, creating an enormous void in the Confederacy's fighting strength upon their departure. The mere 127 warriors who had pillaged the Maumee villages and violated the women there represented only a fraction of the overall contribution from the North. Sugden, *Blue Jacket*, 168; Edmunds, *Potawatomis*, 130.

147. Colonel Richard England to Simcoe, July 22, 1794, in *Simcoe Correspondence*, 2:334.

148. Carter, *Little Turtle*, 132–34; Sword, *Washington's Indian War*, 291; Rafert, *Miami Indians*, 54; Anson, *Miami Indians*, 128–29.

149. An account of the Jay Treaty proceedings and how these related to events on the frontier can be found in Bemis, *Jay's Treaty*, especially chapters 1, 8–10, and 12. See also Burt, *United States*, 82–165.

150. Nelson, *Jonathan Alder*, 115. See also Gaff, *Bayonets*, 325–27, 364–65.

151. White, *Middle Ground*, 467.

152. Thomas Smith to McKee, October 11, 1794, in *Simcoe Correspondence*, 5:113.

153. Wright, *Britain and the American Frontier*, 95–100.

154. White, *Middle Ground*, 472; Nelson, *Anthony Wayne*, 282–85. Jay's Treaty was also the diplomatic trump card that helped the United States negotiate the Treaty of San Lorenzo (Pinckney's Treaty) with Spain in 1795, settling a boundary dispute and opening up the Mississippi River to American merchants. Spain had recently gone to war against Britain, and the Spanish government could not afford an Anglo-American alliance, which would have threatened all of Spanish possessions in the Americas. See Bailey, *Diplomatic History*, 115–23.

155. John Askin Jr.'s Report to Colonel England on His Mission to Greenville, August 19, 1795, in Quaife, *John Askin Papers*, 1:564. Although John Askin Jr., a mixed-blood Ottawa, was technically not yet on the Indian Department's payroll, his father, a prominent Detroit merchant, worked closely with the Indian Department, meeting many of its logistical needs. Moreover, the younger Askin was secretly functioning in the capacity of a British Indian agent at the Greenville peace proceedings. After intercepting the young man's mail, Anthony Wayne believed—perhaps correctly—that Askin was a spy. See *Historical Collections*, 15:693–94, n48; see also Tanner and Wheeler-Voegelin, *Indians of Ohio and Indiana*, 2:704–8. Askin Jr. officially procured a commission in the Indian Department in 1807, serving as interpreter and storekeeper at Fort St. Joseph, northern Lake Huron. Significant in the king's cause during the War of 1812, he was promoted to captain in the Indian Department in 1814, before serving as superintendent of Indian Affairs at Amherstburg from 1816 until his death in 1820. Allen, *British Indian Department*, 106.

156. Dowd, *Spirited Resistance*, 113; Weld, *Travels*, 2:211–13; Sword, *Washington's Indian War*, 306.

157. Nelson, *Jonathan Alder*, 116–17.

158. Cayton, "'Noble Actors,'" 266. The treaty proceedings at Greenville, replete with Native speeches, are found in *American State Papers*, 1:564–83.

159. Weld, *Travels*, 2:216.

160. Many of the Delawares and a few Shawnee bands such as Tecumseh's ultimately moved into central and southern Indiana. Other Shawnees from Ohio joined the Shawnee community at Cape Girardeau, along the eastern bank of the Mississippi River in the latter 1790s. Tanner, *Atlas*, 93, 98–99; Callendar, "Shawnee," 632.

2. A New Diplomacy at Amherstburg

1. Regarding the location of British posts ceded to the United States as a result of Jay's Treaty, see Bailey, *Diplomatic History*, 42. Though not shown in Bailey's sketch, the treaty also included Britain's cession of Fort Miami (present-day Toledo, Ohio) to the United States in July 1796.

2. Though officially named Fort Amherstburg, the post came to be known as Fort Malden, the latter being the township in which the post stood. Today the local village is Amherstburg and the historic park and visitor center, Fort Malden. The post was situated on the Canadian (east) side of the Detroit River, near the river's mouth at the northwest end of Lake Erie, approximately eighteen miles south of Detroit.

3. After the conflicts of the 1790s, George Girty probably moved west into central Illinois with a Delaware band; his descendants were thought to still be among them by the 1830s. Tanner, *Atlas*, 140–41. Records indicate that George Girty, like his brothers, initially owned property near Amherstburg after the American Revolution, but unlike his siblings, he was not even listed among the "superannuated" pensioners of Upper Canada's Indian Department by the end of the War of 1812. See Calloway, "Simon Girty," 51, 55.

4. Sugden, *Blue Jacket*, 195–96; Speech of the Mekoche Shawnees, May 1795, Claus Papers, 7:124, mg 19 g 1, lac; Howard, *Shawnee!* 24–30.

5. Sugden, *Tecumseh*, 94–97. Another Kishpoko Shawnee of future significance, Tecumseh's younger brother, Tenskwatawa, probably dwelled with Tecumseh's band at this time.

6. Edmunds, *Potawatomis*, 153–55, 159.

7. Rafert, *Miami Indians*, 62–63. Wells, a captive youth among the Miamis, had fought against the American armies of Josiah Harmar and Arthur St. Clair in 1790 and 1791, respectively, but he inexplicably switched to the American side in 1792, thenceforth scouting for Anthony Wayne's U.S. Legion. Wells, who was married to Little Turtle's daughter, quickly reconciled with his father-in-law, and the two remained close for the duration of their lives. Wells temporarily served as U.S. Indian agent at Fort Wayne prior to the War of 1812.

Only weeks after the death of Little Turtle in July 1812, Wells tragically lost his life in the infamous Fort Dearborn massacre on the morning of August 15, while bravely assisting with the evacuation of the hapless American garrison and their families.

While moving along the sandy dunes near the southwestern shore of Lake Michigan (the site of present-day downtown Chicago), Wells and the small party of American soldiers and civilians were overwhelmed by hundreds of Potawatomis under Blackbird and Mad Sturgeon. After dispatching Wells, the Potawatomis removed his heart, divided it among themselves, and consumed it, a fate accorded only to the bravest and most resilient of adversaries. Edmunds, *Potawatomis*, 186–88; White, *Middle Ground*, 500–501. Though no full-length scholarly biography exists on Wells, one should consult Hutton, "William Wells," and Carter, "Frontier Tragedy."

8. The St. Joseph River mentioned here refers to the river that passes through present-day South Bend, Indiana, and empties into Lake Michigan, not to be confused with the St. Joseph River that flows into the Maumee River in present-day Fort Wayne, Indiana. Both rivers emanate from Hillsdale, Michigan, but they are not connected and flow in opposite directions.

9. Weld, *Travels*, 2:200–21, 289–91.

10. Weld, *Travels*, 2:187.

11. Weld, *Travels*, 2:200. Weld also asserted that the Natives in Canada had the utmost "predilection . . . for the French" settlers living there. *Travels*, 2:200.

12. Alexander McKee's Address to Indians at Chenail Ecarte, August 30, 1796, RG 10, Indian Affairs, Vol. 9, 9170, LAC.

13. Dorchester to the Duke of Portland, June 18, 1796, in *Historical Collections*, 25:126.

14. Sugden, *Blue Jacket*, 212.

15. McKee's Speech at Chenail Ecarte, August 30, 1796, RG 10, Indian Affairs, Vol. 9, 9167, 9170–71, LAC.

16. McKee to Johnson, January 20, 1797, in Cruikshank and Hunter, *Correspondence of the Honourable Peter Russell* (hereafter cited as *Russell Correspondence*), 1:130–31.

17. Johnson to McKee, December 30, 1796, in *Russell Correspondence*, 1:104.

18. Talk between Captain William Mayne and Indian Chiefs, Amherstburg, June 30, 1797, File 3, 151–52, John Marsh Papers, Fort Malden Historical Archives; *Historical Collections*, 20:519–20; RG 8, Military C Series, Vol. 250-1, 233–38, LAC.

19. McKee to Elliott, October 13, 1797, in *Historical Collections*, 25:158.

20. Capt. Hector McLean to Capt. James Green, Military Secretary, August 10, 1797, RG 8, Military C Series, Vol. 250-1, 128, LAC. For Dorchester's instructions, see "Instructions for the good Government of the Indian Department," Dorchester to Sir John Johnson, March 27, 1787, RG 10, Indian Affairs, Vol. 789, 6759–65, LAC. Although Dorchester instructed the Indian Department to distribute gifts to the Indians in the presence of the post's commandant and junior officers, the governor-general also instructed "the Commanding Officer . . . not under pretence of this regulation to interfere with the Agent in the management of the Indian Department." Under these ambiguous orders, it remained unclear as to who actually possessed the greater authority. War years tended to favor the Indian Department, peacetime the military leaders.

21. McLean to Green, September 14, 1797, in *Historical Collections*, 20:538; RG 8, Military C Series, Vol. 250-1, 150–51, LAC.

22. McLean to Green, September 23, 1797, in *Historical Collections*, 20:548.

23. For the various returns for provisions requested at Chenail Ecarte, see *Historical Collections*, 20:556, 25:157. Also, Lieutenant Thomas Fraser's census at Chenail Ecarte, taken October 26, 1797, is found in RG 8, Military C Series, Vol. 250-2, 339, LAC.

24. Prescott to Russell, December 15, 1797, in *Historical Collections*, 20:585; *Russell Correspondence*, 2:43. See also Russell's letter to Elliott, relaying Prescott's order, February 6, 1798, in *Historical Collections*, 25:165–66.

25. For further reading on the McLean-Elliott controversy, see Horsman, *Matthew Elliott*, chapter 6; and Allen, *British Indian Department*, 60–63.

26. McKee had also approved Elliott's inflated order for the Indians at Chenail Ecarte, and the deputy superintendent general could have also been fired for submitting this supposedly fabricated report.

27. The mere 160 Ojibwas present at Chenail Ecarte were very likely from the immediate vicinity and certainly do not represent the numbers that British agents expected, particularly when it was thought that more than fifteen thousand Ojibwas were interspersed throughout Canada and the Northwest at the time. For population estimates (circa 1768), see Tanner, *Atlas*, 66.

28. McLean to James Green, Military Secretary, August 27, 1799, RG 8, Military C Series, Vol. 252, 234, LAC.

29. Russell to Prescott, February 1, 1799, L18, Peter Russell Papers, Letterbook, Correspondence with Governor-General Robert Prescott, 1796–99, Toronto Public Library; *Russell Correspondence*, 3:82–83.

30. McLean to Military Secretary James Green, September 14, 1797, in *Historical Collections*, 20:536; RG 8, Military C Series, Vol. 250-1, 146–47, LAC; File 3, 178–79, John Marsh Papers, Fort Malden Historical Archives.

31. Prescott to Russell, September 28, 1797, RG 10, Indian Affairs, Vol. 1, 91, LAC.

32. Prescott to Russell, September 28, 1797, RG 10, Indian Affairs, Vol. 1, 93, LAC.

33. McLean to Military Secretary James Green, September 14, 1797, in *Historical Collections*, 20:536–37; RG 8, Military C Series, Vol. 250-1, 147, 149, LAC; File 3, 179–80, John Marsh Papers, Fort Malden Historical Archives.

34. Prescott to Russell, September 16, 1798, RG 10, Indian Affairs, Vol. 1, 228, LAC.

35. "Memorandum Respecting the Public Matters in the Province of Quebec submitted for the consideration of the Right Honourable Lord Sydney by General Haldimand," March 16, 1785, Colonial Office, MG 11, CO 42, Vol. 48, 251, LAC; "Means Suggested as the Most Probable to Retain the Six Nations and Western Indians in the King's Interest," circa 1784, in Johnston, *Valley of the Six Nations*, 53.

36. Previously, the French had also developed familial relationships with the same groups through elaborate gift-giving. White, *Middle Ground*, 179–83.

37. Jacobs, *Dispossessing the American Indian*, 75–82; Dowd, *War Under Heaven*, 70–75; Steele, *Warpaths*, 236.

38. McLean to Captain James Green, Military Secretary, August 18, 1797, File 3, 155–56, John Marsh Papers, Fort Malden Historical Archives; RG 8, Military C Series, Vol. 250-1, 126, LAC.

39. Portland to Russell, November 5, 1798, Colonial Office, Record 42, Vol. 322, 143.5–144, National Archives of the United Kingdom, Kew Gardens (hereafter cited as NAUK).

40. Hunter to Portland, March 8, 1800, Colonial Office, MG 11, CO 42, Vol. 325, 110, LAC.

41. Russell to Lieutenant General Count Joseph de Puisaye, June 11, 1799, Colonial Office, Record 42, Vol. 324, 169.5, NAUK; *Russell Correspondence*, 3:211.

42. Russell to Colonel McKee, Capt. Claus, Thos. McKee, Esq., Jas. Givens, Esq., June 15, 1798, L18, Peter Russell Papers, Letterbook, Indian Affairs, 1798–99, Toronto Public Library. See also Portland to Russell, November 4, 1797, in *Russell Correspondence*, 2:3.

43. McLean to Capt. James Green, Military Secretary, September 14, 1797, in *Historical Collections*, 20:536; RG 8, Military C Series, Vol. 250-1, 146–47 LAC; File 3, 178–79, John Marsh Papers, Fort Malden Historical Archives.

44. McLean to Major James Green, Military Secretary, July 18, 1798, in *Historical Collections*, 20:613; RG 10, Indian Affairs, Series A, Vol. 1, 230, LAC.

45. McLean to Thomas McKee, June 17, 1799, RG 10, Indian Affairs, Vol. 26, 15269, LAC; Prescott to Russell, September 16, 1798, RG 10, Indian Affairs, Vol. 1, 228, LAC.

46. McLean to Thomas McKee, June 17, 1799, RG 10, Indian Affairs, Vol. 26, 15269, LAC.

47. Thomas McKee to Claus, June 5, 1799, File 6, 291, John Marsh Papers, Fort Malden Historical Archives; *Historical Collections*, 20:573; RG 8, Military C Series, Vol. 252, 163, LAC; *Russell Correspondence*, 3:220–21.

48. Johnson to Prescott, June 3, 1799, in *Russell Correspondence*, 3:219.

49. Indians Served at Amherstburg, 1798–1803, RG 10, Indian Affairs, Vol. 10, 9369, LAC.

50. For returns of numbers of Indians settled at Chenail Ecarte in 1798 and 1799, see *Historical Collections*, 20:617–18, 641–42; RG 8, Military C Series, Vol. 251, 148, and Vol. 252, 145, LAC.

51. Some Christian Delawares, primarily near the Fairfield Mission (Moravian Town) along the Thames River, did live in Upper Canada, but probably none of them participated in the late war against the Americans, nor did they typically have dealings with the Indian agency at Amherstburg.

52. According to one scholar, the Miamis even moved farther southward from where they had previously lived when they returned to the Wabash River valley after their defeat at Fallen Timbers and the Treaty of Greenville. The new village sites not only placed them farther from Amherstburg, but the American agency at Fort Wayne now sat squarely between them and the British. See Rafert, *Miami Indians*, 63.

53. Goods Recommended to be Given to the Indians, Fort Malden, September 20, 1797, File 3, 188–90, John Marsh Papers, Fort Malden Historical Archives; *Historical Collections*, 20:545–47. According to Elliott's report, none of the bands visiting Amherstburg came from villages farther south than the Elkhart River, a tributary to the St. Joseph River and Lake Michigan in present-day northern Indiana. The communities that still sought ties with the British at Amherstburg also included some of the villages situated along the Sandusky, Thames, and Huron rivers, Brownstown being at the mouth of the Huron River.

54. Joseph Jackson, the informant Alexander McKee sent westward only days before McKee died, reported in May 1799 that "the Delaware . . . I met on the White River informed me they were all going this Spring to join the Shawnees on the west side of the Mississippi." See Report of Joseph Jackson sent as a Messenger to the Mississippi by order of the late Deputy Superintendant [*sic*] General, May 5, 1799, Claus Papers, 8:91, mg 19 g 1, lac. Although some Delawares may have moved West, the journals of the Moravian mission on the White River indicate that some Delawares continued to live there at least through 1806, and probably longer. For these journals, see Gipson, *Moravian Indian Mission*.

55. Indians served at Amherstburg, 1798–1803, rg 10, Indian Affairs, Vol. 10, 9369, lac. The Munsee people, originally from the southern Hudson Valley and northern New Jersey during the colonial period, survived a string of defeats at the hands of the Mohawks and Dutch in the seventeenth century and eventually migrated to the regions of Pennsylvania and Ohio during the eighteenth century. As with other Delawares, a number of Munsees developed close ties to Moravian missionaries, and by the beginning of the nineteenth century a Munsee community existed on the Thames River, Upper Canada, near the Moravian mission of Fairfield. The presence of this community in southern Upper Canada probably accounts for the Munsees receiving provisions at Fort Amherstburg in the early 1800s. Dowd, "Indians and Overseas Empires," 56–57; Goddard, "Delaware," 236–37; Tanner, *Atlas*, 88, 96, 99, 107; White, *Middle Ground*, 498 (see also n50).

56. McLean to Sir John Johnson, May 24, 1799, in *Historical Collections*, 20:634; File 5, 290, John Marsh Papers, Fort Malden Historical Archives.

57. McLean to Thomas McKee, 10 May 1799, in *Russell Correspondence*, 3:193–94.

58. William Dunn to William Windham, Secretary at War, June 6, 1807, Colonial Office, mg 11, co 42, Vol. 132, 286, lac.

59. Remarks Submitted to the Commander in Chief, by Hector McLean, November 10, 1797, File 4, 221, John Marsh Papers, Fort Malden Historical Archives; *Historical Collections*, 20:573.

60. Thomas McKee to Claus, June 5, 1799, in *Russell Correspondence*, 3:219–20; *Historical Collections*, 20:637; File 6, 291–92, John Marsh Papers, Fort Malden Historical Archives; rg 8, Military C Series, 252, 163, lac.

61. Claus to Russell, June 6, 1799, in *Russell Correspondence*, 3:221.

62. Russell to McLean, June 19, 1799, L18, Peter Russell Papers, Letterbook, Indian Affairs, 1798–99, Toronto Public Library; RG 8, Military C Series, Vol. 252, 165, LAC.

63. Russell served on the ill-fated expedition with General Braddock in 1755, and he assisted Sir Henry Clinton with his history of the American Revolution, but this work remained unpublished until 1954. See Firth, "Administration of Peter Russell," 163.

64. Minutes of the Executive Council, York, June 17, 1799, in *Russell Correspondence*, 3:236.

65. Prescott to Russell, July 18, 1799, in *Russell Correspondence*, 3:277.

66. In fact, the Indian budgets continued their downward trend, and late in 1802, when John Chew, the Indian Department's storekeeper general, submitted his budget request for 1803, Lieutenant Governor Peter Hunter slashed Chew's request by more than 20 percent before approving the budget. Remarkably, Hunter's stiff reductions came after the war in Europe had temporarily ceased, albeit briefly, with the short-lived Peace of Amiens. James Green, Military Secretary to John Chew, December 17, 1802, RG 8, Military C Series, Vol. 1210, 240–41, LAC.

67. For the Indians wintering near the fort, see Johnson to Prescott, June 3, 1799, in *Russell Correspondence*, 3:219. Although Johnson's letter did not specifically indicate the permanent dwelling sites of these groups wintering at Amherstburg, the Ottawas mentioned possibly lived on the American side of the border during the summer and other seasons of the year, since a number of Ottawas were known to have returned to the Maumee Valley after the Treaty of Greenville. Tanner, *Atlas*, 99.

68. Johnson to Prescott, June 3, 1799, in *Russell Correspondence*, 3:219.

69. Johnson to Prescott, June 3, 1799, in *Russell Correspondence*, 3:219.

70. Kellogg, *British Regime*, 163–69.

71. Prideaux Selby to Russell, forwarding the instructions of the late Alexander McKee, January 23, 1799, in *Russell Correspondence*, 3:61; *Historical Collections*, 25:186.

72. Report of Joseph Jackson, May 5, 1799, in *Russell Correspondence*, 3:188; Claus Papers, 8:90, MG 19 G 1, LAC. Jackson's report corroborated that of another informant, James Day, who had previously traveled to the lower Mississippi Valley in 1797. According to Day, the Shawnees and Delawares living there professed loyalty to Britain and claimed that they could "never forget the friendship of Col. McKee and Capt. Elliott and that they will always keep it in their minds in whatever situation they may be." Information of James Day, October 10, 1797, Claus Papers, 8:35–37, MG 19 G 1, LAC; *Russell Correspondence*, 1:300–301.

73. Brant to Russell, January 27, 1799, in *Russell Correspondence*, 3:69–70; *Historical Collections*, 25:188.

74. Russell to Prideaux Selby, February 2, 1799, in *Russell Correspondence*, 3:90.

75. For the memorials of Matthew of Elliott, see *Historical Collections*, 25:178–82, 210–12.

76. McLean to James Green, Military Secretary, March 21, 1799, RG 8, Military C Series, Vol. 252, 63, LAC.

77. McLean to James Green, Military Secretary, August 8, 1799, in *Historical Collections*, 20:656; McLean to Commodore Grant, August 23, 1799, RG 10, Indian Affairs, Vol. 26, 15291, LAC.

78. Firth, "Administration of Peter Russell," 163, 167–68.

79. McLean to Green, March 21, 1799, RG 8, Military C Series, Vol. 252, 63, LAC.

80. McLean to Commodore Grant, August 23, 1799, RG 10, Indian Affairs, Vol. 26, 15289, LAC; McLean to Major James Green, Military Secretary, September 7, 1799, in *Historical Collections*, 20:659.

81. Extract from the minutes of a Council held the 11th July 1799 at Amherstburg with several Chiefs of the Saakies and Foxes, RG 10, Indian Affairs, Vol. 26, 15271, LAC.

82. Thomas McKee to Claus, July 28, 1799, RG 10, Indian Affairs, Vol. 26, 15278, LAC.

83. Extract from the minutes of a Council held the 11th July 1799 at Amherstburg with several Chiefs of the Saakies and Foxes, RG 10, Indian Affairs, Vol. 26, 15271–72, LAC.

84. One of the elder McKee's primary deathbed concerns was to determine the disposition of these very peoples who lived on or near the Wisconsin and Fox rivers and to secure their continued friendship and fidelity at all costs. Alexander McKee to Prideaux Selby, January 10, 1799, and Selby to Russell, January 23, 1799, both in *Russell Correspondence*, 3:49, 60–62.

85. Thomas McKee to Claus, July 28, 1799, RG 10, Indian Affairs, Vol. 26, 15278, LAC.

86. At a council held at Amherstburg, August 10, 1799, with the chiefs of the Wyandots, RG 10, Indian Affairs, Vol. 26, 15283, LAC.

87. At a council held at Amherstburg, August 10, 1799, with the chiefs of the Wyandots, RG 10, Indian Affairs, Vol. 26, 15284, LAC.

88. At a council held at Amherstburg, August 10, 1799, with the chiefs of the Wyandots, RG 10, Indian Affairs, Vol. 26, 15285, LAC.

89. Thomas McKee to Claus, August 15, 1800, Claus Papers, 8:117–18, MG 19 G 1, LAC; *Historical Collections*, 15:24–25.

90. Thomas McKee to Claus, August 15, 1800, Claus Papers, 8:117–18, MG 19 G 1, LAC; *Historical Collections*, 15:24–25; Sugden, *Blue Jacket*, 194–95, 223–24.

91. Thomas McKee to Claus, August 15, 1800, Claus Papers, 8:117, MG 19 G 1, LAC; *Historical Collections*, 15:24.

92. Some circumstances and Remarks relating to the Indian Department to be submitted to the consideration of the Commander in Chief [by Captain Hector McLean], November 10, 1797, in *Historical Collections*, 20:573; File 4, 221, John Marsh Papers, Fort Malden Historical Archives.

93. John H. James' Notes on Conversations with General Simon Kenton, February 13, 1832, Simon Kenton Papers, *Draper Mss.*, Vol. 5BB118 (microfilm), State Historical

Society of Wisconsin, Madison (hereafter cited as SHSW). Regarding the British officers who participated in the ceremony, apparently neither Girty nor Simon Kenton's informant, Solomon McCulloch, told Kenton these men's identities (with the exception of Thomas McKee, of course). The officers who danced were most likely Indian agents, or formerly so, and in addition to the younger McKee, they probably included the Girty brothers, Elliott, George Ironside, and William Caldwell, all of whom lived and served in the vicinity of Amherstburg. After all that had passed between McLean and the Indian Department, one suspects that the commandant and his staff of regular army officers did not participate in the ceremony, but all would have attended the late agent's official funeral held several months earlier.

3. British-Indian Relations in the North

1. Four of the five primary portages separating the great water systems of the Great Lakes and St. Lawrence Seaway and the Mississippi River and Gulf of Mexico entailed travel through Lake Michigan and the Mackinac Straits. The fifth portage, which did not require travel through Lake Michigan or past Mackinac, had a route from Lake Erie, up the Maumee River, then a seven-mile portage from Fort Wayne to a tributary of the Wabash, and from the Wabash on down to the Ohio and Mississippi rivers. See Winsor, *Critical History of America*, 4:200, 224.

2. Chequamegon collectively refers to the Island of La Pointe and the nearby peninsula along the northern Wisconsin coastline.

3. Kellogg, *British Regime*, 237–44, 255–64; Danziger, *Chippewas of Lake Superior*, 60–65; Beck, *Siege and Survival*, 77–82. See also Gates, *Five Fur Traders*.

4. Originally chartered and granted a monopoly by King Charles II in 1670, the Hudson's Bay Company is the only such colonial enterprise to flourish to the present day. At first active throughout "Rupert's Land," the region of northern lakes and rivers that empty into the Hudson Bay, the company expanded throughout Canada and has grown into a modern chain of department stores spanning the nation. In 1821, after nearly forty years of bitter rivalry with the North West Company, the two merged, but the Hudson Bay group controlled the merger by drafting its terms. Moreover, the Hudson Bay officers retained their company's name and infrastructure, and they emerged from the union with confirmed legal recognition of their possession of Rupert's Land. Soon the new company enjoyed virtually complete control of trade north and west across the continent, and even southwest into the American Rocky Mountains. See Rich, *Hudson Bay Company*; Innis, *Fur Trade in Canada*; Woodcock, *Hudson's Bay Company*; and Gray, *Lord Selkirk*. Gray's biography of Lord Selkirk is especially good for its coverage of the latter years of struggle between the Hudson's Bay Company and the North West Company prior to the their merger.

5. Prevost to Bathurst, July 10, 1814, Andrew Bulger Papers, MG 19 E 5, Vol. 1, File 1, 15, LAC.

6. Wright, *Britain and the American Frontier*, 66–76, 82–85.

7. Johnston, *Ojibway Heritage*, 13–17; Danziger, *Chippewas of Lake Superior*, 7, 20–22. During his travels through the northern Lakes country in the 1760s, English trader Alexander Henry alluded to Nanabush and commented that the people whom he encountered on the north shores of Lake Superior also referred to this supernatural being as "The Great Hare." See Henry, *Travels and Adventures*, 205; and Clifton, *Prairie People*, 35.

8. Blackbird, *History*, 21, 22. Blackbird claimed that for a time these spirit beings continued to dwell near Pine Lake in Charlevoix County, northern Michigan, but departed when too many whites settled in the area. Blackbird, *History*, 22–23. For a good analysis of the Ojibwa myth of creation and its aftermath, see Vecsey, *Ojibwa Religion*, 84–99.

9. Although Blackbird regards Mackinac Island as a sacred point of origin, historical evidence places the Ottawa peoples on Manitoulin Island in northern Lake Huron at the time of the initial French entry into the upper country in the 1630s and also seemingly prior to the tribe's presence at Mackinac. See Feest and Feest, "Ottawa," 772–73. As for the Ojibwas, they were far more dispersed throughout the northern Lakes at the time of French contact, and they might very well have fanned out from Mackinac prior to a European presence, as Blackbird claimed. Rogers, "Southeastern Ojibwa," 760–61; Ritzenthaler, "Southwestern Chippewa," 743.

10. Warren, *History of the Ojibway People*, 81–82; Vecsey, *Ojibwa Religion*, 12–13; Danziger, *Chippewas of Lake Superior*, 7–8.

11. Warren, *History of the Ojibway People*, 83, 96.

12. In spite of this rapid westward expansion, the Ojibwas permanently retained their presence at the important site of Sault Ste. Marie, north of Mackinac.

13. Hickerson, *Chippewa and Their Neighbors*, 52–54. Scholars differ on the origins and antiquity of the Midewiwin. While Warren dates its origin prior to European contact, the Jesuits made no mention of this religious society in their published *Relations* between 1664 and 1700. Ritzenthaler, "Southwestern Chippewa," 755. Thus it seems that the movement might have arisen at a time coinciding with the Ojibwa expansion into western Lake Superior.

14. Schoolcraft, *Indian Tribes of the United States*, 5:420.

15. For more on the Midewiwin, see Hickerson, *Chippewa and Their Neighbors*, 54–63; Landes, *Ojibwa Religion*, 89–188; and Vecsey, *Ojibwa Religion*, 174–90.

16. Quimby, *Indian Life*, 122. Robert Ritzenthaler and Pat Ritzenthaler claim that at the time of Columbus, fifty thousand Ojibwas, four thousand Ottawas, and eight thousand Potawatomis dwelled in the Great Lakes region. See Ritzenthaler and Ritzenthaler, *Woodland Indians*, 13. Regardless of the degree of accuracy of these figures, the authors' implication is well taken that Ojibwas were numerous and potentially dominant when united, and that their population exceeded the combined numbers of other peoples living in the Great Lakes region. Tanner more modestly numbers the

eighteenth-century figures for Ojibwas throughout the Great Lakes at roughly sixteen thousand, circa 1768. Tanner, *Atlas*, 66.

17. Vecsey, *Ojibwa Religion*, 184–85; Hickerson, *Chippewa and Their Neighbors*, 55–57; Warren, *History of the Ojibway People*, 77–80.

18. Schoolcraft, *Indian Tribes of the United States*, 5:416. An ethnographic field study conducted and carried out by American officials in 1824 still found the Ojibwa tribe to be "[r]epublican in all its features." Taken from "Col. Boyd's Account," Chippewa Manuscripts, MS/14c, Trowbridge Papers, Burton Historical Collection.

19. Warren, *History of the Ojibway People*, 99.

20. All three sites served as both trading posts and military forts under the French regime. Later, however, the British, while retaining trading posts at each of the three locales, only maintained a military presence at Michilimackinac.

21. Henry, *Travels and Adventures*, 188–89.

22. Warren, *History of the Ojibway People*, 217–20.

23. Burt, *United States*, 146.

24. Calloway, *Crown and Calumet*, 136–47.

25. The North West Company assumed financial responsibility for its traders' wives and families, and by 1806 the burden had become so great that the company's proprietors attempted to prevent further marriages and/or mingling between its employees and Native women. See Wallace, *Documents Relating to the North West Company*, 210–11. For more on interpersonal relations between Native peoples and the men of the North West Company, see Brown, *Strangers in Blood*, 81–110, 153–76; and Peterson, "Many Roads to Red River." For fur trade families associated with the Hudson's Bay Company, see Van Kirk, *"Many Tender Ties."*

26. Barnouw, "Acculturation and Personality," 44–48.

27. For more on the XY Company, see Davidson, *North West Company*, 69–91. Existing from 1798 through 1804, the XY Company temporarily became a more formidable threat to the North West Company when Sir Alexander MacKenzie, formerly a key shareholder with the North West Company, took charge of the XY enterprise. Davidson, *North West Company*, 76–77.

28. Vecsey, *Ojibwa Religion*, 15; Danziger, *Chippewas of Lake Superior*, 57, 60, 62–63. In addition to enjoying the benefit of bartering for cheaper supplies from competing traders, the Indians freely received goods of equal quality from Indian agents (albeit in decreasing quantities during peacetime), and if the northerners were willing to travel, they could also cheaply trade for U.S. government goods sold by U.S. agents under the newly formed factory system, another institution that tended to keep the traders' prices in check. Danziger, *Chippewas of Lake Superior*, 63–64; Stevens, *Northwest Fur Trade*, 158–61. John Tanner, a thirty-year white captive in the North, also recalled the advantage to the Indians when dealing with rival trading companies. Tanner, *Falcon*, 172–73.

29. Tanner, *Falcon*, 173.

30. Tanner, *Falcon*, 16, 18–19.

31. Vecsey, *Ojibwa Religion*, 135–36; Barnouw, "Acculturation and Personality," 42–48, 53–60.

32. Vecsey, *Ojibwa Religion*, 136; Barnouw, "Acculturation and Personality," 58–59.

33. Henry, *Travels and Adventures*, 146.

34. Jones, *History*, 207.

35. Entries for August 10, 1797, May 23, 1798, June 13 and 27, 1799, Duggan Journal, gabla.

36. Tanner, *Falcon*, 16.

37. Calloway, *Crown and Calumet*, 137. For the meaning of gifts to Indians, the protocol of gift-giving, and a comparison of the British and French Indian diplomacy, see Jacobs, *Wilderness Politics and Indian Gifts*, chapters 1 and 2.

38. Dorchester's Instructions, March 27, 1787, rg 8, Military C Series, Vol. 789, 6759, lac.

39. Dorchester's Instructions, March 27, 1787, rg 8, Military C Series, Vol. 789, 6759, lac. Recall from chapter 1 that Dorchester, in keeping with Whitehall's orders, wished to cut costs while simultaneously striving to continue Native dependence upon the British.

40. Sugden, *Blue Jacket*, 212–13, 229–31; White, *Middle Ground*, 511–12.

41. Burt, *United States*, 82–85; Stevens, *Northwest Fur Trade*, 159–61.

42. Peter Drummond to James Green, Military Secretary, October 28, 1799, in *Historical Collections*, 20:668.

43. Kellogg, *British Regime*, 201–2; Vincent, *Fort St. Joseph*, 53.

44. *Historical Collections*, 11:489–96, 501–6, 514–620; State Historical Society of Wisconsin, *Collections of the State Historical Society of Wisconsin* (hereafter cited as *cshsw*), 31 vols. (Madison, 1854–1931), 12:83–91.

45. Dease's family link to the Johnsons probably did not hurt in helping him gain his acquittal. Furthermore, Dease at least received the dignity of a trial. A decade later, Matthew Elliott would be refused both a hearing and any type of formal inquiry. Elliott hounded his superiors for eleven years, asking for a reinstatement, but Dease passively accepted his own dismissal.

46. Dorchester's Instructions for the good Government of the Indian Department, to Sir John Johnson, Baronet, Superintendant [sic] General and Inspector General of Indian Affairs, March 27, 1787, rg 8, Military C Series, Vol. 789, 6761, lac.

47. For Gauthier, see Captain William Doyle to Colonel Richard England, February 2, 1793, rg 8, Military C Series, Vol. 247, 10, lac.

48. Lieutenant Robert Cowell to James Green, Military Secretary, February 10, 1802, rg 8, Military C Series, Vol. 254, 3–4, lac; Cowell to Green, October 29, 1801, rg 8, Military C Series, Vol. 253, 341–42, lac. Apparently, Duggan also drank heavily, further complicating his difficulties and abuses. Cowell brought formal charges against

Duggan in a special council called for that purpose, January 25, 1802, RG 8, Military C Series, Vol. 254, 7–9, LAC. See also Vincent, *Fort St. Joseph*, 106–7.

49. Entry for October 5, 1796, Duggan Journal.

50. For the annuity disbursements sanctioned by the Treaty of Greenville, see Treaty of Greenville, *American State Papers*, 1:563; *Historical Collections*, 20:413.

51. Examination of a Patawatime Warrior [Prisoner], July 23, 1794, Shawnee File, July–December 1794, GABLA; Cruikshank, "Diary," 641; Alexander McKee to Joseph Chew, July 7, 1794, in *Simcoe Correspondence*, 2:310; Diary of an Officer in the Indian Country, in *Simcoe Correspondence*, 5:94; Alexander McKee to R. G. England, July 10, 1794, in *Simcoe Correspondence*, 2:315; Sword, *Washington's Indian War*, 278; Sugden, *Blue Jacket*, 167–68; Nelson, *Man of Distinction*, 169.

52. Stevens, "Fur Trading Companies," 286.

53. Amable's Speech, June 27, 1796, Duggan Journal.

54. Russell to Prescott, August 29, 1796, in *Historical Collections*, 25:130; Colonial Office, MG 11, CO 42, Vol. 320, 675–76, LAC.

55. Thomas Duggan to Prideaux Selby, June 20, 1796, Claus Papers, 7:230, MG 19 G I, LAC.

56. Ogaw's Speech at St. Joseph's, October 26, 1796, Duggan Journal.

57. Mitaminance's Speech and the British response, March 12 and 13, 1797, Duggan Journal.

58. Drummond to James Green, Military Secretary, June 29, 1797, in *Historical Collections*, 20:518.

59. Kellogg, *British Regime*, 233–34; Russell to the Duke of Portland, September 28, 1796, in *Historical Collections*, 25:132.

60. Duggan to Chew, July 9, 1797, RG 8, Military C Series, Vol. 250-1, 256, LAC; *Historical Collections*, 20:522.

61. Barnouw, "Acculturation and Personality," 46.

62. Clifton argues that the Potawatomis, also a member of the Three Fires' triumvirate (with the Ojibwas and Ottawas), never had chiefs until their contact with the French brought about the evolution of this role late in the seventeenth century. See Clifton, *Prairie People*, 55. Dowd argues that virtually no formal criteria existed that would determine an Ottawa leader, nor was the tribe defined by any clan or divisional structure. Instead, Ottawa headmen and spokesmen frequently held ad hoc, temporary appointments, and the most influential were often those who rose to prominence through trade with Europeans, enabling a leader to distribute more goods among his followers. Dowd, *War Under Heaven*, 9–11; White, *Middle Ground*, 37.

63. Entry for May 19, 1798, Duggan Journal.

64. Entry for June 14, 1798, Duggan Journal. Duggan was here alluding to Charles Langlade Jr., the mixed-blood (three-quarters Ottawa) son of the more famous Charles Langlade, who faithfully served the French from Mackinac during the French and Indian War (1754–63), and later the British there during the American

Revolution (1775–83). The elder Langlade is also remembered for leading the famous raid in 1752 against the British trading post and their Miami allies and trade partners at the village of Pickawillany on the upper Great Miami River (near present-day Piqua, Ohio). He then went on to fight in most of the major engagements against the British during the ensuing French and Indian War; after the French defeat, he accepted a commission in the British Indian Department at Mackinac. Though the elder Langlade died in 1800, Charles Jr. continued to serve the British Indian Department and was active in the War of 1812, including a role in the British capture of Fort Mackinac from the Americans at the war's outset.

The Langlades founded the first permanent settlement at Green Bay in the 1740s, and according to family tradition, the French and British regimes in Wisconsin both recognized the family's title to the area; in the early 1780s British lieutenant governor Patrick Sinclair at Mackinac confirmed this with a written grant. The Grignon family of early Wisconsin had intermarried with the Langlades and shared in this claim, but the U.S. government ultimately did not recognize any claims stemming from the original Langlade grant. Augustin Grignon, grandson of Charles Langlade Sr. and nephew to Charles Jr., provided this information in his "Recollections," in CSHSW, 3:195–295. See also Kellogg, *British Regime*, 227, 329, and 256, which features Augustin Grignon's portrait.

65. Drummond to Major James Green, Military Secretary, June 24, 1799, in *Historical Collections*, 20:640–41.

66. Entry for June 14, 1798, Duggan Journal. In seeking remuneration over retribution, the officers' resolution coincided well with Ottawa custom, but the victim's relatives would have still ultimately possessed the right to demand the perpetrator's life. Feest and Feest, "Ottawa," 783.

67. Dowd, *War Under Heaven*, 11; White, *Middle Ground*, 33–40.

68. Entry for May 9, 1796, Duggan Journal; RG 8, Military C Series, Vol. 249, 213, LAC.

69. Entry for July 4, 1796, Duggan Journal.

70. Aupaumut, "A Narrative of an Embassy to the Western Indians," 103; see also White, *Middle Ground*, 455.

71. As the virtual protégé of Sir William Johnson, Brant was exceptional among Native leaders. Blue Jacket stood as another notable exception, having received a commission from Sir John Johnson. But even then, Blue Jacket was already an established war chief among the Shawnees, and did not derive his authority from the British. Sugden, *Blue Jacket*, 27, 68. Furthermore, some rival Shawnee chiefs from the Mekoche tribal division made "a great noise about Blue Jacket's Commission," and "blame[d] the English very much for having made any chiefs among them especially the younger Brothers [referring to Blue Jacket's Piqua division], if any were made, they say it ought to have been some of them." See George Ironside to Alexander McKee, February 6, 1795, in *Simcoe Correspondence*, 3:288–89; and Calloway, *Crown and*

Calumet, 43. The Mekoche division of the Shawnees provided hereditary peace chiefs who presided over affairs involving the entire nation. Blue Jacket, a war chief from a different division, had no permanent or hereditary authority. Sugden, *Blue Jacket*, 9–10, 27; Howard, *Shawnee!* 27, 38–39; Trowbridge, *Shawnese Traditions*, 8.

72. Alexander McKee to Joseph Chew, June 19, 1796, RG 8, Military C Series, Vol. 249, 216, LAC.

73. Joseph Chew to Captain James Green, Military Secretary, July 14, 1796, RG 8, Military C Series, Vol. 249, 218, LAC.

74. Alexander McKee to Joseph Chew, June 19, 1796, RG 8, Military C Series, Vol. 249, 216, LAC.

75. Vincent, *Fort St. Joseph*, 105. In truth, Thomas McKee assumed Elliott's position at Amherstburg upon the latter's dismissal, thereby holding the assignment of deputy superintendent for both posts simultaneously between 1797 and 1808. It therefore made sense for him to reside at Amherstburg during that period. Nonetheless, McKee chose not to reside at his assigned post, both prior to Elliott's dismissal and after the latter's restoration. Although from a distance, McKee held the position as St. Joseph's deputy superintendent until the War of 1812.

76. Vincent, *Fort St. Joseph*, 106.

77. Vincent, *Fort St. Joseph*, 106–7; Lieutenant Robert Cowell to Major James Green, Military Secretary, August 29, 1801, RG 8, Military C Series, Vol. 253, 341–43, LAC; Lieutenant Robert Cowell to Major James Green, February 10, 1802, RG 8, Military C Series, Vol. 254, 3–6, LAC.

78. Vincent, *Fort St. Joseph*, 107. Cowell ordinarily had to translate instructions into French for Chaboillez. After Cowell was eventually transferred to a different assignment, Chaboillez informed his superiors, "I have the greatest difficulty with respect to the instructions I receive and hope there is no impropriety in my requesting that in future they may be Sent in both English and French, or the latter alone, when I can have not doubts respecting their meaning." Charles Chaboillez, Storekeeper and Clerk to Prideaux Selby, May 31, 1803, RG 10, Indian Affairs, Vol. 26, 15481, LAC.

79. Entry for July 3, 1797, Duggan Journal.

80. Tanner, *Atlas*, 58, 62, 132.

81. Entry for May 23, 1798, Duggan Journal.

82. Entry for May 23, 1798, Duggan Journal.

83. Drummond to James Green, March 21, 1799, in *Historical Collections*, 20:630.

84. Kellogg, *British Regime*, 237–38, 242.

85. Tohill, "Robert Dickson," 8.

86. Though the North West Company was dominant in the region of Lake Superior and areas farther northwest, the company could not completely shut out its competition. The Indian groups of the upper Mississippi Valley also had the option to trade with competing Spanish—and after 1803, American—fur trade interests from St. Louis, while Natives farther north had the opportunity to also engage Hudson's Bay traders.

87. Drummond to Major James Green, Military Secretary, March 21, 1799, RG 8, Military C Series, Vol. 252, 51–52, LAC; *Historical Collections*, 20:630.

88. Kellogg, *British Regime*, 241; Tohill, "Robert Dickson," 12–14.

89. Tohill, "Robert Dickson," 14.

90. Anderson, *Kinsmen of Another Kind*, 76.

91. Sir John Johnson to Major James Green, Military Secretary, December 3, 1798, RG 10, Indian Affairs, Series A, Vol. 1, 251, LAC; Johnson to ?, July 7, 1797, Claus Papers, 8:11, MG 19 G 1, LAC.

92. Johnson to ?, July 7, 1797, Claus Papers, 8:12, MG 19 G 1, LAC.

93. Johnson to Green, Military Secretary, December 3, 1798, RG 10, Indian Affairs, Series A, Vol. 1, 252–53, LAC.

94. Hickerson, *Chippewa and Their Neighbors*, 83; Danziger, *Chippewas of Lake Superior*, 61–62. Years later, Lieutenant Zebulon Montgomery Pike, American emissary to the Upper Mississippi, commented on why the British had failed to quell the Indian wars there: "[T]he British government . . . often brought the chiefs of the two nations together, at Michilimackinac; made them presents, &c. but the Sioux, still haughty and overbearing, spurned the proferred [*sic*] *calumet*; and returned to renew the scenes of slaughter and barbarity . . . .the British government, it is true, requested, recommended, and made presents; but all this at a distance; and when the chiefs returned to their bands, their thirst of blood soon obliterated from their recollection the lectures of humanity, which they had heard in the councils of Michilimackinac." Jackson, *Journals of Zebulon Montgomery Pike*, 1:216–17; Danziger, *Chippewas of Lake Superior*, 64–65.

95. Kellogg, *British Regime*, 258.

96. See "The Narrative of Peter Pond," in Gates, *Five Fur Traders*, 47. On the eve of the American Revolution, Pond and the other traders had solicited the intervention of Mackinac's commandant, Arent de Peyster, to negotiate a peace between the Sioux and Ojibwas, but the colonel "told them it was O[u]t of his Power to Bring the Government Into Eney Expens in Sending to thise But Desird that we would fall on wase and Means among Ourselves and he would Indaver to youse his Enfluans as CumMandin[g] Ooffiser." Even at that early date, British leaders knew that they did not hold the authority necessary to impose a peace, and they expected the traders to influence the Indians for the benefit of British diplomacy.

97. In 1806 the Sioux killed Michael Curot, a trader of the North West Company, for having supplied weapons to the Ojibwas. See Gates, *Five Fur Traders*, 240. More than a dozen years earlier, the Sioux had killed David Monin, a clerk of the North West Company, and his companion. See "The Diary of John MacDonell," in Gates, *Five Fur Traders*, 112.

98. John Tanner's description of the raid that the Nor'westers fomented against the Hudson Bay outpost on the Red River near Lake Winnipeg stands as a rare exception. In that incident, the traders of the North West Company had little to fear

in the way of reprisals, but one of them was sentenced to death in a court of law. See Tanner, *Falcon*, 209–10.

99. Council at St. Joseph's with Ottawa delegation from Arbre Croche, October 1797, Duggan Journal. Captain Drummond recorded the delegations' official statement at this council, and he took the signatures of all the chiefs present, five village chiefs and five war chiefs. These are listed in Captain Peter Drummond to the Chiefs and their Reply, October 19, 1797, in *Historical Collections*, 20:561; RG 8, Military C Series, Vol. 250-2, 317–18, LAC.

100. Entry for June 7, 1798, Duggan Journal.

101. Entry for June 12, 1797, Duggan Journal.

102. Drummond to Green, June 24, 1799, in *Historical Collections*, 20:640. Though he was writing from his post at St. Joseph Island, Drummond's letter indicates that Mackinac remained an important center of trade after coming under American control in 1796.

103. Duggan to Prideaux Selby, Military Secretary, July 6, 1801, Claus Papers, 8:15, MG 19 G 1, LAC.

104. See letter from the Duke of Portland to Lieutenant Governor Peter Hunter, October 4, 1799, RG 8, Military C Series, Vol. 252, 270–71, LAC.

4. A New Society on the Grand River

1. For the purposes of this study and specifically for the context of this chapter, the term "sovereignty" is used to describe the extent to which the Natives, specifically the Six Nations' community at the Grand River, could conduct themselves as an independent nation, govern themselves by their own laws, practice their own customs, enter into agreements with foreign peoples and other indigenous tribes, and conduct land transactions and distribute reserve property, all without the consent of the British government.

2. Specifically, the Seven Nations included the Onondagas and Cayugas of Akwesasne (St. Regis), the Mohawks and Algonquins at Kanesatake, the Mohawks of Caughnawaga, the Abenakis at Odanak (St. Francis), and the Hurons at Lorette. Thus only four of these seven groups were Iroquois. Surtees, "Iroquois in Canada," 67–70; Calloway, *American Revolution*, 35, n34. Calloway's second chapter features "Odanak" (65–84). Kanesatake (or Oka), the Algonquin and Mohawk village at the confluence of the Ottawa and St. Lawrence rivers, was previously known as the Lake of the Two Mountains; a number of Nipissings dwelled there as well. Day, "Nipissing," 787; Day and Trigger, "Algonquin," 795; Snow, *Iroquois*, 140; Tanner, *Atlas*, 59, 99.

3. The Mohawk division between the supporters of Brant and those of Deserontyon might have originated prior to the American Revolution, when those parties still dwelled in the Mohawk Valley. Brant and his family were from Canajoharie, while Deserontyon's people lived farther downstream along the Mohawk River, mainly at

the Mohawk village and mission situated adjacent to Fort Hunter. Graymont, *Iroquois in the American Revolution*, 284; Kelsay, *Joseph Brant*, 42–44, 370. See also John Deserontyon to Sir John Johnson, February 15, 1785, Claus Papers, 4:69, MG 19 G 1, LAC. For more information on Deserontyon's career and the formation of his Mohawk settlement at the Bay of Quinte, see Herrington, "Captain John Deserontyou."

4. These listed tribes and their population figures are found in "A Census of the Six Nations on the Grand River, 1785," in Johnston, *Valley of the Six Nations*, 52. The Oghguagas were an independent band of Oneidas who chose not to remain in the United States with their brothers and sisters who supported the American cause in the Revolution. They were so named for their original village of "Oquaga," situated along a stream of this name, a tributary to the upper Susquehanna River in southern New York (present-day Windsor, Broome County). Colin Calloway devotes a chapter of his *American Revolution in Indian Country* to this community and its demise. Joseph Brant met his first wife, Peggie (also referred to as Margaret in some accounts), at Oquaga, but American forces destroyed the village in 1778. At the time of its destruction, at least seventeen of Oquaga's inhabitants favored the American cause and moved to the pro-U.S. community at Oneida; the rest became Loyalist refugees, explaining the presence of those listed in the Grand River census. Before the Revolution, several missionaries lived in Oquaga, and though predominantly Oneida peoples, the village consisted of a high percentage of mixed-bloods and was also home to a few Mohawks and Tuscaroras. Kelsay, *Joseph Brant*, 24, 99–100, 185–86, 188–89, 228, 669 n6, n7; Jennings, Fenton, Druke, and Miller, *Iroquois Diplomacy*, 222. In his journal, John Norton referred to the village; although he used inconsistent spellings—"Oghkwaga," "Oghkwague," and "Oghguaga"—each of these references seem to identify the same village. Klinck and Talman, *Journal of Major John Norton*, 101, 270–71, 284. Calloway also noted dozens of variations in the term's spelling. Calloway, *American Revolution in Indian Country*, 108.

5. For Brant's origins and position within Mohawk society, see Kelsay, *Joseph Brant*, 39–41; for the chief's final visit to London, see Kelsay, *Joseph Brant*, 380–91.

6. Graymont, *Iroquois in the American Revolution*, 293–94; Brant's Address to William Claus, November 24, 1796, in Johnston, *Valley of the Six Nations*, 82; Six Nations' Address to William Claus, September 3, 1806, in Johnston, *Valley of the Six Nations*, 275.

7. Kelsay, *Joseph Brant*, 554–55, 561–62; Benn, *Iroquois in the War of 1812*, 25; Snow, *Iroquois*, 164.

8. Speech by John Deseronto (Deserontyon) at Council at the Bay of Quinte (recalling events of September 1788), September 2–10, 1800, in Johnston, *Valley of the Six Nations*, 54.

9. Statement by Sir John Johnson in Dorchester's Name to Aaron and Isaac Hill, Montreal, September 20, 1788, in Johnston, *Valley of the Six Nations*, 72.

10. "Haldimand Grant," in Graymont, *Iroquois in the American Revolution*, 299; Kelsay, *Joseph Brant*, 363.

11. Excerpt from Joseph Brant's speech at Niagara, late 1780s, Marquis, *Builders of Canada*, 202–3.

12. Wright, *Britain and the American Frontier*, 38–39; Gregory Dowd, *War Under Heaven*, 3, 185.

13. A good example of an eighteenth-century perspective on the relationship between the colony of New York and the Iroquois is Colden, *History of the Five Indian Nations*; see also Jennings, *Iroquois Empire*, 11–17; and White, *Middle Ground*, 351–54.

14. Clark, *Native Liberty*, 19–20; Harring, "Indian Law," 453–55; Dowd, *War Under Heaven*, 178–79.

15. When Brant first dined at the Simcoe residence late in 1792, Mrs. Simcoe hinted at this mistrust, describing the Mohawk leader as possessing "a countenance of art or cunning." Entry for December 9, 1792, in Innis, *Mrs. Simcoe's Diary*, 82–83.

16. Simcoe to Dorchester, December 6, 1793, in *Simcoe Correspondence*, 2:114.

17. Simcoe's Patent of the Grand River Lands to the Six Nations, January 14, 1793, in Johnston, *Valley of the Six Nations*, 74. See also Noon, *Law and Government*, 86–87.

18. Simcoe's Patent, January 14, 1793, in Johnston, *Valley of the Six Nations*, 73.

19. Noon, *Law and Government*, 86; Cork, *"Worst of the Bargain,"* 90–91, 94–97.

20. Brant to McKee, February 25, 1793, in Johnston, *Valley of the Six Nations*, 75.

21. Simcoe to Dorchester, December 6, 1793, in Johnston, *Valley of the Six Nations*, 76.

22. Simcoe to Henry Dundas, September 20, 1793, in *Simcoe Correspondence*, 5:59.

23. Simcoe to Dorchester, December 6, 1793, in Johnston, *Valley of the Six Nations*, 76.

24. Simcoe to Henry Dundas, September 20, 1793, in *Simcoe Correspondence*, 5:59.

25. Simcoe to Dorchester, December 6, 1793, in Johnston, *Valley of the Six Nations*, 75.

26. Simcoe and Dorchester partially based Simcoe's argument on the rationale of the Proclamation of 1763, which prohibited British subjects in North America from purchasing or settling on Indian lands.

27. In this same speech, Brant complained that Simcoe had informed the Grand River nations that, as "only Allies," the Six Nations "cannot possibly have the King[']s Subjects to be . . . Tennants [*sic*]." Speech of Joseph Brant at an Indian Council, Newark, Upper Canada, November 24, 1796, in *Russell Correspondence*, 1:93; Johnston, *Valley of the Six Nations*, 82.

28. Simcoe to Dorchester, March 3, 1794, in *Simcoe Correspondence*, 2:174.

29. Simcoe to Dorchester, October 9, 1795, in *Simcoe Correspondence*, 4:101–2; Kelsay, *Joseph Brant*, 523, 540; Klinck and Talman, *Journal of Major John Norton*, 285; Taylor, *Divided Ground*, 357.

30. Simcoe to Brant, March 2, 1796, in *Simcoe Correspondence*, 4:206.

31. Brant to Joseph Chew, May 17, 1796, in *Simcoe Correspondence*, 4:268.

32. At the time of Simcoe's departure in the summer of 1796, he left the province on the basis of a temporary leave, due to ill health. Therefore he did not immediately resign his position, and his successor, former receiver general of Upper Canada, Peter Russell, held the official title "President of the Executive Council and Administrator of Upper Canada." Though Russell would have ordinarily been addressed as "president," I have opted to use "lieutenant governor" as Russell's title, since he acted in this capacity and was the ranking British leader of the province, 1796–99. When Simcoe officially resigned late in 1798, Russell hoped to become his permanent replacement, but Peter Hunter was named the next lieutenant governor. After Simcoe's departure, Simcoe spent some time in England before taking a temporary command in the West Indies. He died in England (Exeter) in 1806, at the age of fifty-four.

33. Russell to Brant, October 23, 1796, in *Russell Correspondence*, 1:75–76. All prospective purchasers of Grand River tracts had to first undergo a process of verification in order to confirm their status as loyal British subjects.

34. Brant to Russell, October 24, 1796, in *Russell Correspondence*, 1:76.

35. Russell to the Duke of Portland, November 14, 1796, in *Russell Correspondence*, 1:84.

36. Brant's speech at Newark, November 24, 1796, in *Russell Correspondence*, 1:93–94; Johnston, *Valley of the Six Nations*, 82–83.

37. Brant's speech at Newark, November 24, 1796, in *Russell Correspondence*, 1:94–95.

38. Brant to Russell, June 11, 1799, in *Russell Correspondence*, 3:228.

39. John White to Russell, September 26, 1796, L18, Peter Russell Papers, Letterbook, Indian Affairs, 1798–99, 16, Toronto Public Library; *Russell Correspondence*, 1:46.

40. William Claus, "Remarks and Observations upon Indn. Politics as to their Political Maxims in Time of War between White People," undated but presumably about 1804, Claus Papers, 11:65–66, MG 19 G 1, LAC.

41. Russell to Portland, January 28, 1797, in *Russell Correspondence*, 1:131, 133. This letter is also found in L18, Peter Russell Papers, 36–42, Toronto Public Library; and Colonial Office, Record 42, Vol. 321, 91–104, NAUK.

42. Russell to Portland, January 28, 1797, in *Russell Correspondence*, 1:133.

43. Portland to Russell, March 10, 1797, in *Russell Correspondence*, 1:155–56. This letter is also found in L18, Box 2, Peter Russell Papers, Toronto Public Library; Peter Russell's Letterbook, Indian Affairs, MG 23 H 12, 5–11, LAC; and Colonial Office, Record 42, Vol. 321, 80–84, NAUK.

44. Portland to Russell, March 10, 1797, in *Russell Correspondence*, 1:156.

45. Liston to Prescott, April 8, 1797, L18, Russell Letterbook, 93–94; *Russell Correspondence*, 1:160. The italics are from Cruikshank and Hunter's edited version; the phrase is underlined in the original letter.

46. Brant to D. W. Smith, June 18, 1797, in *Russell Correspondence*, 1:189.

47. Brant to Russell, June 19, 1797, in *Russell Correspondence*, 1:190; Colonial Office, Record 42, Vol. 321, 234, NAUK.

48. Johnston, "Joseph Brant," 275.

49. Johnston, "Joseph Brant," 280–81.

50. Portland to Russell, March 10, 1797, in *Russell Correspondence*, 1:155–56.

51. Russell to Brant, July 3, 1797, in *Russell Correspondence*, 1:204.

52. Portland to Russell, November 4, 1797, in *Russell Correspondence*, 2:3; Colonial Office, Record 42, Vol. 321, 345–49, NAUK.

53. Brant to Russell, July 10, 1797, in *Russell Correspondence*, 1:211. Cruikshank and Hunter's italics in the first portion of this quote indicate emphasis in the original letter.

54. Russell to Portland, July 21, 1797, in *Russell Correspondence*, 1:219–21.

55. Russell to Portland, July 21, 1797, in *Russell Correspondence*, 1:221.

56. Russell to Portland, July 21, 1797, in *Russell Correspondence*, 1:222.

57. Russell to Portland, July 21, 1797, in *Russell Correspondence*, 1:222.

58. Russell to Portland, July 29, 1797, in *Russell Correspondence*, 1:228.

59. Russell to Portland, July 29, 1797, in *Russell Correspondence*, 1:228.

60. Anthropologist William Fenton makes an important point in explaining that Iroquois people "distinguished 'talk in the bushes' when an issue might be explored or an agenda formulated from more formal meetings or conferences preliminary to a treaty." This sheds light on Brant's apparent inconsistencies during these public and private talks at York in the summer of 1797. See Fenton, "Structure, Continuity, and Change," 27.

61. Portland to Russell, November 4, 1797, in *Russell Correspondence*, 2:3; Colonial Office, Record 42, Vol. 321, 345–49, NAUK.

62. Russell to Prescott, July 17, 1797, L18, Peter Russell Papers, Letterbook, Correspondence with Governor-General Robert Prescott, 1796–99, Toronto Public Library.

63. Brant to Russell, June 11, 1799, in *Russell Correspondence*, 3:228; Colonial Office, MG 11, CO 42, Vol. 324, 166, LAC; Calloway, *Crown and Calumet*, 61–63, 233–34. Former governor-general of Quebec, Sir Frederick Haldimand, believed that "some Presents and marks of Friendship are . . . due to Their past Services," according to his report, "Means Suggested as the Most Probable to Retain the Six Nations and Western Indians in the King's Interest," circa 1784, in Johnston, *Valley of the Six Nations*, 53. See also "Memorandum Respecting the Public Matter in the Province of Quebec submitted for the consideration of the Right Honourable Lord Sydney by General Haldimand," March 16, 1785, Colonial Office, MG 11, CO 42, Vol. 48, 251, LAC. Thus Portland's views and mandates indicate how much British Indian policy had shifted since the 1780s. In 1800 Lieutenant Governor Peter Hunter clearly informed Brant of the new policy. Hunter to Portland, 8 March 1800, Colonial Office, MG 11, CO 42, Vol. 325, 110, LAC.

For the Six Nations' self-perceived sovereign status, see Brant to James Green, December 10, 1797, in *Russell Correspondence*, 2:39; Brant to Russell, June 19, 1797, and Brant to Russell, June 27, 1797, in *Russell Correspondence*, 1:190, 196; Brant's address to William Claus in council, November 24, 1796, in Johnston, *Valley of the Six Nations*, 81–84.

64. Portland to Russell, November 4, 1797, in *Russell Correspondence*, 2:3.

65. Kelsay, *Joseph Brant*, 546–47. For Brant's initial request, see Brant to Johnson, December 15, 1797, in Johnston, *Valley of the Six Nations*, 238–39.

66. Lydekker, *Faithful Mohawks*, 186–87.

67. Bishop of Quebec to Russell, January 11, 1798, in *Russell Correspondence*, 2:63.

68. Russell to Bishop of Quebec, confidential, February 22, 1798, in *Russell Correspondence*, 2:99.

69. Russell to Bishop of Quebec, confidential, February 22, 1798, in *Russell Correspondence*, 2:99.

70. Portland to Russell, January 24, 1799, Colonial Office, Record 42, Vol. 324, 3–4, NAUK.

71. For a background of this schism, see Graymont, *Iroquois in the American Revolution*, 42–47; Nester, *Frontier War*, 69, 72–73; and Taylor, *Divided Ground*, 65–68, 74–76.

72. Bishop of Quebec to Russell, Private, June 12, 1798, in *Russell Correspondence*, 2:180.

73. Brant to Russell, May 8, 1798, in *Russell Correspondence*, 2:148; Colonial Office, Record 42, Vol. 322, 155, NAUK.

74. Instead, the bishop of Quebec petitioned the Society for the Propagation of the Gospel (SPG) for an augmentation of Rev. Robert Addison's salary, and the bishop directed him to make frequent itinerant visits to the Grand River. Addison served a parish in Newark, near Niagara, and after he accepted the additional ministry, he managed to travel to the Grand River four times per year. In essence, this arrangement hardly differed from what the Six Nations at the Grand River had experienced for more than a decade, and it did not meet the demand for a resident clergyman. See Bishop of Quebec to Russell, June 12, 1798, in *Russell Correspondence*, 2:180–81; and Reverend John Stuart's Report to the S.P.G., October 11, 1798, in Johnston, *Valley of the Six Nations*, 241.

The Grand River finally received a resident clergyman when the New England Company, an Anglican missionary society in existence since 1649, sent Rev. Robert Lugger there in 1827. See "History of the New England Company on the Grand River," in Johnston, *Valley of the Six Nations*, 256, n23, n24; Weaver, "Six Nations," 526.

75. Reverend Robert Addison's Report to the S.P.G., December 29, 1799, in Johnston, *Valley of the Six Nations*, 241–42.

76. Liston to Lord Grenville, April 4, 1798, in *Russell Correspondence*, 2:168.

77. Portland to Russell, most secret, June 7, 1798, in *Russell Correspondence*, 2:167; Colonial Office, Record 42, Vol. 322, 100–102, NAUK.

78. Portland to Russell, most secret, June 7, 1798, in *Russell Correspondence*, 2:167; Colonial Office, Record 42, Vol. 322, 100–102, NAUK.

79. Portland to Russell, November 4, 1797, in *Russell Correspondence*, 2:3. In a letter two months earlier, Portland had already given Russell virtually the same instructions. See Portland to Russell, September 11, 1797, in *Russell Correspondence*, 1:277–78; Colonial Office, Record 42, Vol. 321, 193–95, NAUK.

80. Russell to Portland, March 21, 1798, in *Russell Correspondence*, 2:122. The Mississaugas are actually a branch of Chippewas (or Ojibwas) who lived in the southern portion Upper Canada, mostly along the northern shore of Lake Ontario. When Russell used the expression "Chippewas," he was most likely using this interchangeably with "Mississaugas," because later in the letter the president referred to them as "the Chippewas who come from the Vicinage of Lake Simcoe," who were actually Mississaugas. Moreover, Russell also used the expression "Mississaugas" at another place in the document. British leaders in Canada also used the names interchangeably on other occasions. See Smith, "Who Are the Mississauga?," 211, 221–22. Despite the small Mississauga population, the British respected the tribe's capacity for war, knowing that the Mississauga would probably manage to procure the assistance of their more numerous Ojibwa cousins to the North and West. See Schmalz, *Ojibwa of Southern Ontario*, 104.

81. For Givens's appointment, see Russell to Givens, June 25, 1797, in *Russell Correspondence*, 1:231–32.

82. Russell to Portland, March 21, 1798, in *Russell Correspondence*, 2:122. The old city of York was later renamed Toronto.

83. The location of the new Mississauga council fire is the site of the present-day city of Mississauga, Ontario, situated on the northwest end of Lake Ontario.

84. Rogers, "Southeastern Ojibwa," 760–64.

85. Sir John Johnson, Return of the Mississaugas, September 23, 1787, RG 10, Indian Affairs, Vol. 15, 197, LAC; Schmalz, *Ojibwa of Southern Ontario*, 104–5.

86. Snow, *Iroquois*, 141–57; Weaver, "Six Nations," 525–27; Tooker, "League of the Iroquois," 432–37.

87. For British-Mississauga relations and the land cessions during this period, see Schmalz, *Ojibwa of Southern Ontario*, 102–10, 120–30; Surtees, *Indian Land Surrenders*, 13–60.

88. Russell to Portland, March 21, 1798, in *Russell Correspondence*, 2:122.

89. Kelsay, *Joseph Brant*, 568–69. A group of Mississaugas issued a deposition regarding the event to officers near Fort George, September 11, 1796, RG 8, Military C Series, Vol. 249, 369–70, LAC.

90. Speech of the Mississauga Chiefs at the Mohawk Village on the Grand River, April 13, 1798, in *Russell Correspondence*, 2:186.

91. Russell to Prescott, Secret and Confidential, June 15, 1798, in *Russell Correspondence*, 2:186.

92. Brant to Russell, November 5, 1798, in *Russell Correspondence*, 2:307.

93. Council between the Mississaugas and Claus at the head of Lake Ontario, November 3, 1798, in *Russell Correspondence*, 2:306.

94. Council between the Mississaugas and Claus at the head of Lake Ontario, November 3, 1798, in *Russell Correspondence*, 2:306.

95. Council between the Mississaugas and Claus at the head of Lake Ontario, November 3, 1798, in *Russell Correspondence*, 2:305–6.

96. Brant to Claus, June 4, 1798, RG 8, Military C Series, Vol. 251, 113, LAC.

97. Brant to Claus, June 4, 1798, RG 8, Military C Series, Vol. 251, 113–14, LAC.

98. Brant to Claus, June 4, 1798, RG 8, Military C Series, Vol. 251, 114–15, LAC.

99. Prescott to Russell, August 2, 1798, in *Russell Correspondence*, 2:227. See also Prescott to Portland, August 22, 1798, in *Russell Correspondence*, 2:247.

100. Portland to Russell, November 5, 1798, in *Russell Correspondence*, 2:300; Colonial Office, Record 42, Vol. 322, 143, NAUK.

101. Brant to Russell, April 10, 1799, in *Russell Correspondence*, 3:168.

102. Brant to Johnson, May 10, 1799, in *Russell Correspondence*, 3:195. Halifax currency, a medium of exchange in Canada between the 1750s and 1871, was valued slightly less than British pounds sterling, at an approximate exchange rate of 111.11 pounds Halifax currency for 100 pounds sterling, or roughly 90 percent. Yet the price that the Mississaugas originally demanded in Halifax currency still easily exceeded anything that they had ever previously received for land payments. A single pound of Halifax currency was worth four Spanish dollars, also a popular medium of exchange in Canada and the United States at the time. For an excellent study on Canadian currency in this period, see McCullough, *Money and Exchange*, 20–21, 74–75, 92–93; the exact month-to-month exchange rates for Halifax currency and the British pound sterling (between 1758 and 1871) are found listed beginning on page 274. See also Chalmers, *History of Currency*, 179, 183.

103. Russell to Brant, April 25, 1799, in *Russell Correspondence*, 3:183.

104. Russell to Prescott, May 26, 1799, in *Russell Correspondence*, 3:209. See also Russell to Portland, May 26, 1799, in *Russell Correspondence*, 3:205–6. According to Brant's best biographer, Isabel Thompson Kelsay, the Mississaugas further exacerbated matters with Canadian leaders by later increasing their demands to three shillings fourpence sterling per acre, a value three times higher than their original demands in Halifax currency. See Kelsay, *Joseph Brant*, 590.

105. Russell to Count de Puisaye, May 26, 1799, and June 11, 1799, both in *Russell Correspondence*, 3:211.

106. Russell to Brant, June 10, 1799, in *Russell Correspondence*, 3:226; italicized in Cruikshank and Hunter's edition.

107. Russell to Prescott, June 22, 1799, L18, Peter Russell Papers, Letterbook, Correspondence with Governor-General Robert Prescott, 1796–99, Toronto Public Library.

108. Prescott to Russell, July 18, 1799, in *Russell Correspondence*, 3:278.

109. Brant to Thomas Morris, December 26, 1800, quoted in Stone, *Joseph Brant*, 2:405. Kelsay argues that the chief had no intention of moving from the Grand River, but that he merely wanted to turn a profit from this American land scheme. Yet Kelsay does not offer any better explanation indicating why Brant would not have been sincere in stating his desire to move. Kelsay, *Joseph Brant*, 620–21. In fact, the thought of moving to the United States had occurred to Brant at least once before, as seen nearly five years earlier in a letter Brant sent to Israel Chapin, U.S. Superintendent of Indian Affairs, New York State, January 19, 1796, in Johnston, *Valley of the Six Nations*, 78. In *Divided Ground*, Alan Taylor argues that Brant was even conspiring with American officials, contemplating an armed rebellion in Upper Canada (352–57). By late 1800 Brant had simply come to the end of his patience with the British, and his subsequent speech to the western Indians at Detroit in the summer of 1801 demonstrated his sincerity.

110. Though the manuscript source of Brant's speech (RG 8, Military C Series, Vol. 254, 18–20, LAC) does not specifically indicate which bands of Ojibwas, Ottawas, and Potawatomis comprised his audience, the Ottawas to whom Brant spoke were probably from the Maumee River valley in the northwestern Ohio Territory, and the Ojibwas most likely lived in the area of Lake St. Clair, north of Detroit. The Potawatomis were scattered throughout southeastern Michigan and northern Indiana.

111. Brant's speech at Detroit, Summer 1801, RG 8, Military C Series, Vol. 254, 18–20, LAC.

112. Brant's speech at Detroit, Summer 1801, RG 8, Military C Series, Vol. 254, 18–20, LAC.

113. Brant's speech at Detroit, Summer 1801, RG 8, Military C Series, Vol. 254, 19–20, LAC.

114. At Camperdown, the Royal Navy defeated a Dutch fleet; at Cape St. Vincent, a Spanish fleet. Both enemy fleets were allied to revolutionary France. John Sugden, who has done much to inspire this study with his seminal works on Tecumseh and Blue Jacket, is also an authority on the history of the Royal Navy, including the period under study here. See Sugden, *Nelson*, especially the rich section on the famed victory by Nelson and Admiral Sir John Jervis at Cape St. Vincent (686–706).

115. Portland to Prescott, December 6, 1798, in *Russell Correspondence*, 3:23; Liston to Russell, December 1, 1798, in *Russell Correspondence*, 3:1.

116. Hunter to Portland, March 8, 1800, Colonial Office, MG 11, CO 42, Vol. 325, 111, LAC.

117. Johnson to Brant, September 1, 1801, quoted in Stone, *Joseph Brant*, 2:406. See also Kelsay, *Joseph Brant*, 625.

118. Brant to Johnson, November 1801, quoted in Stone, *Joseph Brant*, 2:407–9.

119. Taylor, *Divided Ground*, 353.

5. John Norton and the Continuing Struggle

1. Kelsay, *Joseph Brant*, 619, 624–26.

2. To date, the best biographical study of Norton is Carl F. Klinck, "Biographical Introduction," in Klinck and Talman, *Journal of Major John Norton* (xiii–xcvii). Other biographical essays on Norton include Klinck, "New Light on John Norton," 167–77; and Murray, "John Norton," 7–16.

3. John Norton's Speech to the Five Nations at Onondaga, Grand River, February 12, 1807, Norton Letterbook, Ayer Ms, 654, 119, Newberry Library, Chicago; Klinck and Talman, *Journal of Major John Norton*, xxxiv–xxxv; Murray, "John Norton," 9; Klinck, "New Light on John Norton," 173.

4. Thomas Scott to his brother, Sir Walter Scott, ca. 1815, John Norton Papers, Weldon Library, University of Western Ontario, London ON; Klinck and Talman, *Journal of Major John Norton*, xx.

5. A reform-minded evangelical Christian fellowship during the early nineteenth century, the Clapham Sect met regularly in Clapham, a village just south of London. In addition to Wilberforce, the group also included renowned reformer Hannah More and Thomas B. Macaulay's father, Zachary.

6. In his retirement, Norton also later translated the gospel of St. Matthew. Benn, *Iroquois in the War of 1812*, 186.

7. In 1816 Norton gave and dedicated his transcribed version of this volume, along with a journal of his travels to Cherokee country (1809–10), to his friend Hugh Percy, second Duke of Northumberland, but due to the duke's untimely death the following year, the manuscript remained unpublished in the Percy family library at Alnwick Castle until its publication in 1970.

8. Kelsay, *Joseph Brant*, 538; Joseph Chew to James Green, Military Secretary, September 19, 1796, RG 8, Military C Series, Vol. 249, 340, LAC.

9. Klinck and Talman, *Journal of Major John Norton*, xxxvii; Kelsay, *Joseph Brant*, 552. As deputy for the Six Nations, Norton represented their interests publicly on at least two occasions when Brant sent him to meet with the governors of New York, (John Jay and George Clinton) in 1799 and 1802.

10. Norton's Speech at Onondaga, Grand River, February 12, 1807, Norton Letterbook, Ayer Ms, 119–20.

11. Klinck and Talman, *Journal of Major John Norton*, xxxvii–xxxix, xl–xli.

12. Snow, *Iroquois*, 64–65.

13. See Norton's address at Trinity College, Cambridge, March 12, 1805, quoted in Klinck and Talman, *Journal of Major John Norton*, xxxviii.

14. Kelsay, *Joseph Brant*, 38–45, 109. Despite never having formally been selected a civil chief, Brant apparently had become considered a de facto civil chief at the Grand River by the time of his death. His widow, Catherine, leading matron of the Mohawk Turtle clan, took the initiative to appoint her son (and Joseph's) as his successor. See Lydekker, *Faithful Mohawks*, 188–89; Stone, *Joseph Brant*, 2:500.

15. Address of the Six Nations to William Claus, September 3, 1806, York, Norton Letterbook, Ayer Ms, 62–63; Johnston, *Valley of the Six Nations*, 273–74.

16. Kelsay, *Joseph Brant*, 650.

17. The western Indians, though allies, had not shared this view of Iroquois hegemony.

18. Prucha, *Great Father*, 48–57; Wallace, *Jefferson and the Indians*, chapters 6 and 7.

19. Norton to John Owen, August 12, 1806, Norton Letterbook, Ayer Ms, 30–31.

20. See Martin, *Sacred Revolt*, chapter 4; McLoughlin, *Cherokee Renascence*, chapters 2 and 3; Edmunds, "'Watchful Safeguard,'" 162–99; Wallace, *Death and Rebirth*, 217–36, 272–77; Wallace, *Jefferson and the Indians*, 180–205.

21. Norton to Owen, August 12, 1806, Norton Letterbook, Ayer Ms, 29.

22. The rapid transformation of Cherokee culture during the eighteenth and early nineteenth centuries is well documented in McLoughlin, *Cherokee Renascence*, 37–91; and Hatley, "Three Lives of Keowee."

23. Klinck and Talman, *Journal of Major John Norton*, 59.

24. Norton to Robert Barclay, Esq., June 16, 1810, Norton Letterbook, Ayer Ms., 130–31.

25. Klinck and Talman, *Journal of Major John Norton*, 60.

26. Norton to an unknown recipient (probably Owen), January 1807, Norton Letterbook, Ayer Ms., 142–43. For Norton's speech to the Cherokee council at Willstown, see Klinck and Talman, *Journal of Major John Norton*, 72–73.

27. Klinck and Talman, *Journal of Major John Norton*, 68.

28. Norton to Owen, August 12, 1806, Norton Letterbook, Ayer Ms, 36.

29. The State of Missions amongst the Iroquois about 1810, taken from a survey completed by John Norton, in Johnston, *Valley of the Six Nations*, 244.

30. Norton to Owen, August 12, 1806, Norton Letterbook, Ayer Ms, 36–37; State of Missions amongst the Iroquois about 1810, in Johnston, *Valley of the Six Nations*, 244.

31. The Rev. Clark Kendrick's Opinion of the Six Nations, 1809, in Johnston, *Valley of the Six Nations*, 243–44. For additional assessments regarding the state of Christian missions among the Indians of Upper Canada at this time, see Report to Lord Castlereagh, enclosure in Gore to Castlereagh, September 4, 1809, Colonial Office, Record 42, Vol. 349, 94–95, NAUK. Rev. John Strachan, rector at York, Upper Canada, during this period, also made a very similar report corroborating Gore's findings. See Strachan's undated report on the Indians of Upper Canada, G983, Vol. 9, Ms 35, Reel 9, John Strachan Papers, Ontario Historical Archives, Toronto.

32. The Rev. Samuel Kirkland's Account of Religious Practices on the Grand River, February 26, 1800, in Johnston, *Valley of the Six Nations*, 242 (italicized in Johnston).

33. The Rev. Samuel Kirkland's Account of Religious Practices on the Grand River, February 26, 1800, in Johnston, *Valley of the Six Nations*, 242.

34. Wallace, *Death and Rebirth*, 315–17.

35. Wallace, *Death and Rebirth*, 239–54, 278–85; Snow, *Iroquois*, 158–62.

36. Wallace, *Death and Rebirth*, 280–81.

37. Wallace, *Death and Rebirth*, 282–85; Snow, *Iroquois*, 161; Benn, *Iroquois in the War of 1812*, 24–25.

38. Though it would seem that Handsome Lake's religion, with its strict moral code, was to a degree syncretic, combining elements of Christianity and the Seneca tradition, it in fact rejected the core elements of Christian doctrine. Handsome Lake never considered Christ's deity and sacrificial death as essential for the Indians' salvation, and Handsome Lake regarded himself as Jesus's equivalent counterpart among the Senecas. Consequently, the Iroquois peoples experienced a permanent split early in the nineteenth century between Christians and Longhouse devotees. Wallace, *Death and Rebirth*, 266, 279–80, 301–2; Reaman, *Iroquois Indians*, 83; Dowd, *Spirited Resistance*, 124, 129, 141–42; Snow, *Iroquois*, 165. The religious perspectives of contemporary Seneca leaders Cornplanter and Red Jacket are also found in Wallace, *Death and Rebirth*, 202–8.

39. Norton to an unknown correspondent, August 10, 1808, in Johnston, *Valley of the Six Nations*, 278; Colonial Office, Record 42, Vol. 140, 176–77, NAUK.

40. Norton to William Wilberforce, September 1, 1808, Colonial Office, Record 42, Vol. 140, 180, NAUK; Johnston, *Valley of the Six Nations*, 278; RG 10, Indian Affairs, Vol. 27, 15823, LAC.

41. Klinck and Talman, *Journal of Major John Norton*, 48 (editors' emphasis); Norton to Wilberforce, September 1, 1808, Colonial Office, Record 42, Vol. 140, 180–81, NAUK; Johnston, *Valley of the Six Nations*, 278–79; RG 10, Indian Affairs, Vol. 27, 15825, LAC.

42. Norton to an unknown correspondent, August 10, 1808, Colonial Office, Record 42, Vol. 140, 175–76, NAUK; Johnston, *Valley of the Six Nations*, 277.

43. Norton to Owen, August 12, 1806, Norton Letterbook, Ayer Ms, 34.

44. Norton to Owen, August 12, 1806, Norton Letterbook, Ayer Ms, 33–35.

45. Norton to an unknown correspondent, August 10, 1808, Colonial Office, Record 42, Vol. 140, 175–76, NAUK; Johnston, *Valley of the Six Nations*, 277.

46. Norton to ?, August 10, 1808, Colonial Office, Record 42, Vol. 140, 177, NAUK.

47. In a council held at York in early September 1806, William Claus raised the concern that the Six Nations intended to destroy the Indian Department. Though a legitimate allegation, Brant denied it. See "A Six Nations' Address to William Claus," September 3, 1806, in Johnston, *Valley of the Six Nations*, 274; Norton Letterbook, Ayer Ms, 66.

48. Norton to Lord Castlereagh, July 23, 1805, Colonial Office, MG 11, CO 42, Vol. 340, 123, LAC. In the case alluded to, recall that Whitehall's attempt to divide the tribes was primarily an effort to prevent Brant from gaining a position of ascendancy over a combination of tribes in Upper Canada.

49. White, *Lord Selkirk's Diary*, 245. The best biography on Lord Selkirk is Gray, *Lord Selkirk of Red River*.

50. Norton to Castlereagh, July 23, 1805, Colonial Office, MG 11, CO 42, Vol. 340, 123–

24, LAC; Six Nations' Address to Claus, September 3, 1806, York, Norton Letterbook, Ayer Ms, 66; Norton to Owen, January 28, 1807, Norton Letterbook, Ayer Ms, 82.

51. Norton to Barclay, October 20, 1806, Norton Letterbook, Ayer Ms, 77.

52. Norton to Barclay, June 16, 1810, Norton Letterbook, Ayer Ms, 130.

53. Norton to Owen, August 12, 1806, Norton Letterbook, Ayer Ms, 26–27, 30.

54. Norton to Owen, August 12, 1806, Norton Letterbook, Ayer Ms, 27.

55. Norton to Owen, August 12, 1806, Norton Letterbook, Ayer Ms, 28, 32.

56. Claus was appointed deputy superintendent general in 1800. Johnston, "William Claus," 103. Though informative, Johnston's essay is a less favorable assessment of Norton.

57. Thomas Scott to Sir Walter Scott, ca. 1815, John Norton Papers, University of Western Ontario; Klinck and Talman, *Journal of Major John Norton*, xx.

58. Sir John Johnson and Daniel Claus, respectively.

59. Claus's speech at Fort George, August 17, 1803, in Johnston, *Valley of the Six Nations*, 136; Kelsay, *Joseph Brant*, 631–32.

60. For more on Claus's manipulative activities against Brant, see Taylor, *Divided Ground*, 350–52.

61. Lord Castlereagh to Sir James Craig, April 8, 1809, in Johnston, *Valley of the Six Nations*, 280; Norton's speech at Onondaga, Grand River, February 12, 1807, Norton Letterbook, Ayer Ms, 106. According to Norton, most Grand River chiefs never succumbed to supporting Claus's scheme to discredit him or his mission.

62. Kelsay, *Joseph Brant*, 636–37; Klinck and Talman, *Journal of Major John Norton*, cviii–cix.

63. Certificate of Captain Leonard and others, October 20, 1805, Stone, *Joseph Brant*, 2:xxxiv. See also Brant's letter to the Duke of Northumberland, circa 1805, explaining the events surrounding Claus's council, Stone, *Joseph Brant*, 2:417.

64. Kelsay, *Joseph Brant*, 636; Klinck and Talman, *Journal of Major John Norton*, cviii–cix.

65. Norton to Earl Camden, July 20, 1805, Colonial Office, MG 11, CO 42, Vol. 340, 122, LAC.

66. Kelsay, *Joseph Brant*, 635.

67. Speech of Teyoninhokarawen the Mohawk Chief to the Bath and West of England Agricultural Society on his being elected an Honorary Member on the 24th December 1804, Norton Letterbook, Ayer Ms, 141; Klinck and Talman, *Journal of Major John Norton*, li; Calloway, *Crown and Calumet*, 114.

68. Taylor, *Divided Ground*, 360–62.

69. Norton to Camden, July 20, 1805, Colonial Office, MG 11, CO 42, Vol. 340, 121–22.5, LAC; Norton to Castlereagh, July 23, 1805, Colonial Office, MG 11, CO 42, Vol. 340, 123–24.5, LAC.

70. It seems odd that the British government could not produce a copy of such an important document, and one would tend to believe that the government officials

could have found a copy had they really wanted to do so. Furthermore, Simcoe and Dorchester both lived in England at the time of Norton's visit, and both men possibly had copies of the original Grand River grant, but no evidence indicates that either of the retired administrators was ever specifically petitioned for the document.

71. Kelsay, *Joseph Brant*, 639; Brant's complaints against Claus in council at Fort George, July 28, 1806, in Johnston, *Valley of the Six Nations*, 106–8.

72. Six Nations' speech to Claus at York, September 3, 1806, Norton Letterbook, Ayer Ms, 63; Johnston, *Valley of the Six Nations*, 274.

73. Speech of Benjamin Okoghsenniyonte, July 28, 1806, Fort George, Norton Letterbook, Ayer Ms, 51.

74. Norton's speech at Onondaga, Grand River, February 12, 1807, Norton Letterbook, Ayer Ms, 98–123.

75. Norton's speech at Onondaga, Grand River, February 12, 1807, Norton Letterbook, Ayer Ms, 106, 116.

76. Claus to Gore, April 2, 1807, RG 10, Indian Affairs, Vol. 2, Series A, 562–63, LAC.

77. Norton's speech, Grand River, April 14, 1807, RG 10, Indian Affairs, Vol. 27, 15699, LAC.

78. Brant to the Duke of Northumberland, January 24, 1806, Stone, *Joseph Brant*, 2:425.

79. Norton to John Owen, August 10, 1808, Norton Letterbook, Ayer Ms, 128–29.

80. Klinck and Talman, *Journal of Major John Norton*, lviii–lix.

81. Castlereagh to Craig, April 8, 1809, in Johnston, *Valley of the Six Nations*, 279–80.

82. Castlereagh to Craig, April 8, 1809, in Johnston, *Valley of the Six Nations*, 280.

83. Gore to Castlereagh, September 4, 1809, Colonial Office, Record 42, Vol. 349, 90–91, NAUK. This important letter, Gore's response to Castlereagh, is also found in Colonial Office, MG 11, CO 42, Vol. 349, 88–92, LAC; and in G440, Ms 94, John Norton Papers, Ontario Historical Archives. Johnston's *Valley of the Six Nations* contains a fragment of it on 112–13.

84. Gore to Castlereagh, September 4, 1809, Colonial Office, MG 11, CO 42, Vol. 349, 89, LAC.

85. In the final sentence of his letter to Castlereagh, Gore indicated that much of his information had come from Claus. Gore to Castlereagh, September 4, 1809, Colonial Office, MG 11, CO 42, Vol. 349, 92, LAC.

86. Gore to Castlereagh, September 4, 1809, Colonial Office, MG 11, CO 42, Vol. 349, 89–91, LAC.

87. Kelsay, *Joseph Brant*, 631–32. Like Claus, Brant was also bewildered as to where the Six Nations' land revenue actually went, and during a council held in July 1806, he publicly blamed the agent for having appropriated $38,000 of the Six Nations' supposedly missing funds. Brant's unfounded allegations against Claus did more to re-

veal the sachem's ignorance and lack of accounting skills than it did his perfidy. Upon hearing Brant's accusation, Claus abruptly left the council. Brant's speech in council at Fort George, July 28, 1806, Norton Letterbook, Ayer Ms, 45; Johnston, *Valley of the Six Nations*, 108; Klinck and Talman, *Journal of Major John Norton*, cx.

88. John Askin to Thomas Smith, January 5, 1793, and Smith to Askin, March 3, 1793, both in Quaife, *John Askin Papers*, 1:457, 466–67; Klinck and Talman, *Journal of Major John Norton*, xxxiv, lxxxvi–lxxxvii; Kelsay, *Joseph Brant*, 637; Murray, "John Norton," 15.

89. Klinck and Talman, *Journal of Major John Norton*, xcv–xcvii.

90. Gore to Castlereagh, September 4, 1809, Colonial Office, Record 42, Vol. 349, 91, NAUK.

91. Gore to Edward Cooke, Esq., ca. 1810, Colonial Office, Record 42, Vol. 349, 186, NAUK.

92. Gore to Castlereagh, September 4, 1809, Colonial Office, Record 42, Vol. 349, 92, NAUK. Gore also confessed that "at present there is not a Blanket for every Seventh Person, which is the occasion of a good deal of remark and observation, on our breach of faith towards them in this respect." Points to which Lord Castlereagh desires to be informed, September 4, 1809, Colonial Office, Record 42, Vol. 349, 94, NAUK.

93. For good discussions on these events, see Hickey, *War of 1812*, 17–24; and Bailey, *Diplomatic History*, 115–23.

94. Distribution of the Forces in Upper Canada serving under Lieutenant General Peter Hunter, December 1, 1801, RG 8, Military C Series, Vol. 1209, 108a, LAC. See also Allen, *British Indian Department*, 67; and Allen, *His Majesty's Indian Allies*, 119.

95. Craig to Gore, December 6, 1807, Colonial Office, Record 42, Vol. 136, 153–54 NAUK; Castlereagh to Craig, September 1, 1807, Colonial Office, Record 43, Vol. 22, 110, NAUK.

96. Craig to Gore, December 6, 1807, Colonial Office, Record 42, Vol. 136, 155, NAUK; Castlereagh to Craig, April 8, 1809, Colonial Office, Record 43, Vol. 22, 135, NAUK.

97. Claus Journal at Fort Malden, June 13 and 14, 1808, Claus Papers, 9:206, MG 19 G 1, LAC; *Historical Collections*, 23:53. According to his journal, Claus spoke with Tecumseh for three hours during this first meeting.

98. Allen, *British Indian Department*, 68. For records and speeches in this council, see RG 10, Indian Affairs, Vol. 11, 9884–904, LAC. After Gore's meeting, Native visits to the post continued to increase dramatically, and nearly five thousand Indians arrived at Amherstburg that autumn. Claus to Prideaux Selby, January 18, 1809, RG 8, Military C Series, Vol. 256, 5, LAC; *Historical Collections*, 23:66–67.

99. Gore to Castlereagh, September 4, 1809, Colonial Office, Record 42, Vol. 349, 92, NAUK.

100. Calloway, *Crown and Calumet*, 230. Craig not only proclaimed British neutrality to the Americans, but early in 1811 he attempted to make his claims even more

convincing by warning the American government of imminent Indian attacks along the country's frontiers. This crafty attempt to absolve Britain of responsibility for an Indian war failed to convince American leaders, as seen in President Madison's reasons for asking Congress for a declaration of war against Great Britain in June 1812. See Turner, *War of 1812*, 33.

101. Klinck and Talman, *Journal of Major John Norton*, 286.

102. Klinck and Talman, *Journal of Major John Norton*, 287.

103. Klinck and Talman, *Journal of Major John Norton*, 287.

104. Klinck and Talman, *Journal of Major John Norton*, 288.

105. Klinck and Talman, *Journal of Major John Norton*, 288, 293, 295–96.

106. Klinck and Talman, *Journal of Major John Norton*, 289; Benn, *Iroquois in the War of 1812*, 40.

107. Klinck and Talman, *Journal of Major John Norton*, 290. A few lines of a speech by one Captain Strong, also a pro-U.S. Seneca leader and participant of this council, are found in Snyder, *New York Frontier*, 47–48. Captain Strong mirrored Little Billy's views.

108. Klinck and Talman, *Journal of Major John Norton*, 290–92.

109. Klinck and Talman, *Journal of Major John Norton*, 291.

110. Klinck and Talman, *Journal of Major John Norton*, 293.

111. Benn, *Iroquois in the War of 1812*, 48; entry for August 5, 1812, Sabathy-Judd, *Moravians in Upper Canada*, 483–84.

The Moravian Christian denomination, also known as the Unitas Fratrum (United Brethren), officially began as an evangelical sect in 1722 in Saxony, where the group founded the town of Herrnhut on the properties of Count Nikolaus Ludwig von Zinzendorf. Himself a believer among the sect, Count Zinzendorf assumed control of the community and became its spiritual leader.

The first Moravians in North America arrived in Savannah, Georgia, in 1735. By 1741 they had established two settlements in Pennsylvania, including Bethlehem, which remains the Moravian headquarters to this day. In the ensuing decades, these German-speaking missionaries established numerous mission-settlements among the Indians, stretching from New England to the Ohio Valley. The Moravians enjoyed their greatest successes among the Delaware and Munsee peoples, specifically in the cluster of villages along the Muskingum and Tuscarawas rivers in present-day southeastern Ohio.

During the American Revolution, British leaders, suspecting (probably justly so) the Moravians of spying for the United States, forcibly removed these communities nearer to Detroit's pro-British sphere of influence. In 1792 Moravian missionary David Zeisberger oversaw the establishment of the mission village of Fairfield upon the Thames in Upper Canada, the place near where Tecumseh, on October 5, 1813, would lose his life fighting the Americans. On that day the American army, under William Henry Harrison, followed up their victory over the British and Indians by burning the village of Fairfield, denying its potential refuge to British troops and Canadian militias.

112. Benn, *Iroquois in the War of 1812*, 51.

113. Brock to Prevost, July 26, 1812, Cruikshank, *Invasion of Canada*, 91; Benn, *Iroquois in the War of 1812*, 46–47.

114. Brock to Prevost, July 26, 1812, Cruikshank, *Invasion of Canada*, 91; Benn, *Iroquois in the War of 1812*, 47.

115. In July 1812 Upper Canada's general assembly denied Brock's request to suspend habeas corpus, but once the Executive Council permitted this on August 3, Brock exercised his increased powers to dismiss the general assembly two days later. Sheppard, *Plunder, Profits, and Paroles*, 53–55; Horsman, *War of 1812*, 38.

116. Council minutes at the Government House, York, Upper Canada, August 3, 1812, Colonial Office, Record 42, Vol. 352, 109, NAUK.

117. Brock to Colonel Edward Baynes, August 4, 1812, Cruikshank, *Invasion of Canada*, 120.

118. Klinck and Talman, *Journal of Major John Norton*, 288.

119. Landon, *Western Ontario*, 28.

120. Sheppard, *Plunder, Profits, and Paroles*, 18; Brock to Prevost, July 12, 1812, Wood, *Select British Documents*, 1:352.

121. Brock to Baynes, July 29, 1812, Wood, *Select British Documents*, 1:396; Turner, *British Generals*, 71–72.

122. Though Brock certainly believed that most of the Grand River warriors had shirked their duty, he nevertheless recognized the significant roles of Indians in the captures of Detroit, Mackinac, and Dearborn. He seems to have regarded Norton and Tecumseh as friends, specifically honoring the latter after the capture of Detroit. Sugden, *Tecumseh*, 299–308. Several sketches, illustrations, and maps pertaining to Detroit at the time of its surrender in 1812 are found in Dunnigan, *Frontier Metropolis*, 132–43. Dunnigan rightly credits the contributions of Norton, Tecumseh, and their estimated six hundred warriors for providing the necessary means to capture Detroit, including the psychological edge that unnerved U.S. general William Hull and possibly others among the American garrison.

In an unpublished study, George C. Chalou lucidly demonstrates the positive ripple effect that the British-Indian capture of Detroit had on previously neutral Indians throughout much of the Old Northwest, and how this colossal turning point inspired these scattered groups to resist the Americans and join the British. Chalou, "Red Pawns," 113–45.

123. Klinck and Talman, *Journal of Major John Norton*, 293.

124. Joseph Willcocks to John MacDonnell, September 1, 1812, in Johnston, *Valley of the Six Nations*, 196–97.

125. Brock to Prevost, September 7, 1812, in Johnston, *Valley of the Six Nations*, 197; Klinck and Talman, *Journal of Major John Norton*, 302.

126. The few Moravian Indians involved most likely dwelled at the Fairfield mission on the Thames River, Upper Canada.

127. Benn, *Iroquois in the War of 1812*, 110–12.

128. Klinck and Talman, *Journal of Major John Norton*, cvi–cxx, 299–370; Benn, *Iroquois in the War of 1812*, 86–173; Stanley, "Six Nations," 218–31.

129. The famed Winfield Scott was among the nine hundred American prisoners taken at Queenston.

130. After Brock's death, the Six Nations honored him in a traditional condolence ceremony, recognizing the fallen general for "his kindness towards us," and expressing hope that Brock's successor's "heart is warmed with similar sentiments of affection and regard towards us." A General Council of Condolence held at the Council House, Fort George, November 6, 1812, War of 1812 Collection, Folder 6a, McCord Museum, Montreal.

131. Weaver, "Six Nations," 526–27; Clark, *Native Liberty*, 19; Montgomery, "Legal Status of the Six Nations," 93–103.

132. Weaver, "Six Nations," 532–33.

6. *Restoring the Chain of Friendship*

1. The Wyandot leader Roundhead was the only known signatory of the Treaty of Greenville in 1795 to later join the Native resistance movement. However, an inordinate number of those who signed the treaty died soon after the peace proceedings. White, *Middle Ground*, 494; Sugden, *Blue Jacket*, 216–17. Rumors of witchcraft and poisonings were quick to spread, associating the deaths as punishment for cooperation with the Americans, but this does not explain the postwar livelihoods of Little Turtle (Miami), Blue Jacket (Shawnee), Black Hoof (Shawnee), and Tarhe (Wyandot). For a complete list of Indian signatories to the treaty, see *Historical Collections*, 20:416–18; and Wilson, "Treaty of Greenville," 145–56. The latter source also includes the symbol of the clan totem of each signatory.

2. Kellogg, *British Regime*, 233–82; Danziger, *Chippewas of Lake Superior*, 61–65; Tanner, *Falcon*, 55–57, 172–80; Beck, *Siege and Survival*, 76–81. For the static relations between the British and the Dakotas in the upper Mississippi Valley during this period, see Anderson, *Kinsmen of Another Kind*, 65–76. Regarding the lack of northerners' dependence on American annuities, see Captain J. Dunham, American commandant at Mackinac, to William Hull, Governor of Michigan Territory, June 18, 1807, in *Historical Collections*, 40:143. Dunham claimed that the northern Ottawas and Ojibwas had not yet received any U.S. annuity distributions determined by the Treaty of Greenville twelve years earlier.

3. Tanner, *Falcon*, 147; Jackson, *Black Hawk*, 58; Blackbird, *History*, 29–30; White, *Middle Ground*, 512–13; Clifton, *Prairie People*, 193–94; Danziger, *Chippewas of Lake Superior*, 66; Ourada, *Menominee Indians*, 55–56.

4. Indians Served at Amherstburg, 1798–1803, RG 10, Indian Affairs, Vol. 10, 9369, LAC.

5. Indians Served at Amherstburg, 1798–1803, RG 10, Indian Affairs, Vol. 10, 9369, LAC.

6. The American government made large annuity distributions from Detroit, where the British had formerly distributed gifts, weapons, and supplies. By replacing the British in this capacity at Detroit, the U.S. government hoped to further undermine the connection between Britain and its former Native allies. In 1802 Miami leader Little Turtle and Five Medals, a Potawatomi, convinced President Jefferson and Secretary of War Henry Dearborn also to begin making annuity payments at Fort Wayne. See Edmunds, *Potawatomis*, 160–61. For a short sketch of Five Medals' career, see Edmunds, "Redefining Red Patriotism." Five Medals' village sat near present-day New Paris, Indiana, and was situated along the Elkhart River, approximately fourteen miles southeast of the river's confluence with the larger St. Joseph River. The village was roughly sixty miles west-northwest of Fort Wayne and a little more than thirty miles southeast of South Bend. Tanner, *Atlas*, 98, 106, 109, 116. For a description of the village's surrounding countryside at the time, see William Johnston's account, 1809, in McCord, *Travel Accounts*, 53–57.

7. See Edmunds, "'Watchful Safeguard.'"

8. The Wyandot leader Tarhe, "the Crane," whose village was situated on the lower Sandusky River, seems to have not only welcomed a peaceful transition and accommodation with whites after the Greenville Treaty, but he had a reputation for kindness and fair treatment of civilian whites prior to the peace. See Charles Johnston's account, "Three Came Back," in Drimmer, *Captured by the Indians*, 212. Tarhe would later oppose the prophetic movement of Tenskwatawa and Tecumseh.

9. Thomas McKee to Lt. Colonel John Vincent, September 9, 1803, RG 8, Military C Series, Vol. 254, 143–44, LAC.

10. Adam Brown's statement relayed to Thomas McKee, December 3, 1807, RG 8, Military C Series, Vol. 255, 139–40, LAC; *Historical Collections*, 23:42.

11. Ironside to Claus, June 11, 1801, and Ironside to Claus, June 12, 1801, both in RG 10, Indian Affairs, Vol. 26, 15368–73, LAC; Ironside to Selby, June 15, 1801, Claus Papers, 8:150, MG 19 G I, LAC; White, *Middle Ground*, 510–11; Sugden, *Blue Jacket*, 221–25.

12. Goods Recommended to be Given to the Indians, Fort Malden [Amherstburg], September 20, 1797, File 3, 188–90, John Marsh Papers, Fort Malden Historical Archives; *Historical Collections*, 20:545–47.

13. Speech of Potawatomi chief Wawickasa at Amherstburg, June 1, 1801, in Ironside to Claus, June 11, 1801, RG 10, Indian Affairs, Vol. 26, 15369, LAC.

14. A meeting with the Saakies, Foxes, Northern Ottawas, Poutawatomis held at Amherstburg on the 8th June 1805, RG 10, Indian Affairs, Vol. 10, 9601–2, LAC.

15. A meeting with the Saakies, Foxes, Northern Ottawas, Poutawatomis held at Amherstburg on the 8th June 1805, RG 10, Indian Affairs, Vol. 10, 9602–4, LAC. See also Claus to Major James Green, July 24, 1805, RG 10, Indian Affairs, Vol. 10, 9616, LAC; and White, *Middle Ground*, 512.

16. A meeting with the Saakies, Foxes, Northern Ottawas, Poutawatomis held at Amherstburg on the 8th June, RG 10, Indian Affairs, Vol. 10, 9605, LAC.

17. Robert Forsyth to Capt. McKee, May 19, 1805, RG 10, Indian Affairs, Vol. 10, 9598, LAC. For more on the increasing frequency of Kickapoo depredations at this time, see Gibson, *Kickapoos*, 52–57.

18. Speech of the Saakies and Potawatomies at Amherstburg, June 28, 1806, RG 10, Indian Affairs, Vol. 1, series A, 417, LAC.

19. Answer to the Chiefs of the Saakies and Potawatomies, June 28, 1806, RG 10, Indian Affairs, Vol. 1, series A, 419, LAC.

20. Claus to Prideaux Selby, February 1, 1805, Claus Papers, 9:75, MG 19 G 1, LAC.

21. Governor Harrison's Address to the Indiana General Assembly, July 29, 1805, in Esarey, *Messages and Letters*, 1:153.

22. William Wells to Harrison, June 19, 1806, E392, H3 1994, William Henry Harrison Collection, Reel 2, 572, Indiana Historical Society, Indianapolis.

23. Governor Harrison's Message to the Indiana Legislature, August 17, 1807, in Esarey, *Messages and Letters*, 1:236.

24. See Perkins, *Causes of the War of 1812*, 116–17; and Bailey, *Diplomatic History*, 129–36.

25. Harrison to Eustis, December 24, 1810, in Esarey, *Messages and Letters*, 1:497. In this statement regarding the nativist practice of viewing land as commonly held property, Governor Harrison was not indicating his dismay as much as he was expressing his concern to the secretary of war. Harrison well understood from his earlier years of frontier warfare and diplomacy that such a view was characteristic of pan-Indian resistance movements, and the greater context of this letter to the secretary of war demonstrated that the governor interpreted the nativist understanding of land possession as a direct threat to U.S. Indian policy.

26. White, *Middle Ground*, 493–517; Dowd, *Spirited Resistance*, 116–22, 130–39; Edmunds, *Potawatomis*, 153–70.

27. Edmunds, *Shawnee Prophet*, 28–29, 33–34, 197 n1. Tenskwatawa's first visions occurred near present-day Anderson, Indiana, possibly as early as April 1805. On May 21 Hendrick Aupaumut, a pro-American Stockbridge Indian, wrote to Henry Dearborn, secretary of war, complaining of the influence "of the Shawanee Impostor [*sic*]." Aupaumut to Dearborn, May 21, 1805, Shawnee File, GABLA. John Sugden believes that Tenskwatawa's first visions occurred a bit later in the year. Sugden, *Tecumseh*, 116.

28. Dowd, *Spirited Resistance*, 131–39.

29. Speech of La Maigouis, or the Trout, at Arbre Croche, May 4, 1807, Alexander McKee Papers, MG 19 G 16, 13–15, LAC. La Maigouis acted as the Shawnee Prophet's messenger in the northern country.

30. See editor Lawrence Henry Gipson's diary of the White River Mission, especially entries for December 1805 and March 1806, in Gipson, *Moravian Indian Mission*, 392–93, 407–12.

31. Dowd, *Spirited Resistance*, 137; Edmunds, *Shawnee Prophet*, 43–46; Miller, "1806 Purge," 254–62. For the Moravian missionaries' accounts of these executions, see Gipson, *Moravian Indian Mission*, 411–21, 556–65, 619–24.

32. Dowd, "Thinking and Believing," 320; Dowd, *Spirited Resistance*, 137–38.

33. There exists considerable confusion regarding a Wyandot purge in 1810. While some Wyandots were most likely killed by Tenskwatawa's followers, the execution of Leather Lips, a Wyandot leader who signed the Treaty of Greenville, is less clear. Leather Lips' pro-American sympathies have led contemporaries and some subsequent scholars to conclude that he was another of the Prophet's victims. However, the pro-American Wyandot leader Tarhe, also a signatory at Greenville, was possibly responsible for Leather Lips' execution. If so, then this particular killing had nothing to do with politics, but instead resulted from the growing internal strife and suspicion in a Wyandot society that was riddled with disease, drunkenness, and death.

In his history, Moravian missionary John Heckewelder indicated that Tarhe was responsible. Yet the ordinarily reliable Heckewelder simultaneously cast doubt upon his own account by first confusing the Shawnee Prophet with his brother, Tecumseh, and then by suggesting that Tarhe carried out the deed at Tecumseh's bidding, an impossible scenario since Tarhe was an avowed enemy to the prophetic movement and certainly never cooperated with Tecumseh. Jonathan Alder, a twenty-four-year captive among the Shawnees and an acquaintance of Leather Lips, similarly attributed the chief's death to the prophetic movement at "Tippecanoe," but specifically claimed that the nativist leader Roundhead was responsible, thus giving a more consistent assertion than that of Heckewelder and making Leather Lips a victim of the Prophet's anti-American purge after all. See Heckewelder, *History, Manner, and Customs*, 295–99; and Nelson, *History of Jonathan Alder*, 147–48. The contemporary account of Rev. James B. Finley gives details of the execution but without naming any of the perpetrators. See Finley, *Autobiography*, 218–22. This latter account is also found in Curry, "Wyandot Chief." Richard White also sees Leather Lips as a victim of the Shawnee brothers' prophetic movement, which would seem to vindicate Tarhe of the murder. See White, *Middle Ground*, 515.

However, John Sugden and R. David Edmunds argue that Tarhe was indeed behind the execution and that Leather Lips was not condemned as a witch for harboring pro-American sympathies, but the exact contrary, that Tarhe orchestrated Leather Lips' death for the latter having defected to the Prophet. Further, Sugden argues that the confusion surrounding these events originated with William Henry Harrison, Indiana's territorial governor at the time, and first emerged in Benjamin Drake's early biography of Tecumseh. Sugden, *Tecumseh*, 209, 436–37, n13; Edmunds, *Shawnee Prophet*, 85; Drake, *Life of Tecumseh*, 118.

34. Not until 1810 did Tecumseh seek a formal connection with the British.

35. Dowd, *Spirited Resistance*, 138; Edmunds, *Shawnee Prophet*, 69–70. The Potawatomi leader Five Medals accompanied Little Turtle to this meeting with the Prophet.

See also William Wells to Henry Dearborn, Secretary of War, April 2, 1808, Carter, *Territorial Papers*, 7:541.

36. Wells to Dearborn, April 23, 1808, Carter, *Territorial Papers*, 7:560.

37. Wells to Dearborn, April 22, 1808, Carter, *Territorial Papers*, 7:558.

38. Harrison to the Secretary of War, July 15, 1801, in Esarey, *Messages and Letters*, 1:29.

39. Horsman, "Indian Policy," 54.

40. Harrison's superiors also advocated this strategy. In a well-known letter, President Thomas Jefferson in 1803 instructed the governor to "push our trading houses, and be glad to see the good and influential individuals among them run in debt, because we observe that when these debts get beyond what the individuals can pay, they become willing to lop them off by a cession of lands." Jefferson to Harrison, February 27, 1803, in Esarey, *Messages and Letters*, 1:71.

41. For Harrison's Indian treaties, see Kappler, *Indian Affairs*, 2:64–68, 70–77, 80–82, 89–90, 101–7, 117–18; Prucha, *American Indian Treaties*, 116–23, 451–55, 456. In the summer of 1803, Harrison negotiated two treaties involving most tribes dwelling in Indiana, one at Fort Wayne and another at his home, "Grouseland," in Vincennes. These were followed by a treaty in 1804 at Vincennes with the Delawares and Pinkashaws; two more in 1805, including one at Grouseland with the Delawares, Miamis, Potawatomis, Eel Rivers, and Weas; and another with the Pinkashaws at Vincennes. Moreover, the governor conducted additional treaties with the Kaskaskias, a people in Illinois, and he negotiated an altogether separate treaty with the Sauks and Fox at St. Louis in November 1804. Harrison's final treaty as Indiana governor (at Fort Wayne) in September 1809—with Miamis, Delawares, Potawatomis, and Eel Rivers—proved most significant, as it involved a cession of roughly three million acres. For proceedings and Indian responses, see Esarey, *Messages and Letters*, 1:117–18, 121–23, 137–39, 358–78. See also Indiana Historical Society, E 392, H3 1994, William Henry Harrison Collection, Reels 1–3, 10.

42. The Eel River peoples, though possessing political autonomy, had common origins with the Miamis. The Eel River is a tributary to the Wabash in northern Indiana.

43. Wells to Dearborn, April 22, 1808, Carter, *Territorial Papers*, 7:558.

44. See John Johnston to Harrison, June 24, 1810, in Esarey, *Messages and Letters*, 1:430; Sugden, *Tecumseh*, 180–81; Edmunds, *Tecumseh*, 126–27; Edmunds, "Watchful Safeguard," 172–73; Klinck and Talman, *Journal of Major John Norton*, 174–75.

45. Tecumseh's speech at Vincennes, August 20 or 21, 1810, Klinck, *Tecumseh*, 71; Esarey, *Messages and Letters*, 466.

46. Tecumseh's speech at Vincennes, August 20 or 21, 1810, Klinck, *Tecumseh*, 71; Esarey, *Messages and Letters*, 465–66.

47. Sugden, *Tecumseh*, 187–89; Edmunds, *Tecumseh*, 124–25; Horsman, *American Indian Policy*, 152–53, 166–67.

48. Dowd, "Thinking and Believing," 322; Dowd, *Spirited Resistance*, 139–40.

49. Tustenuckochee to Lyman Draper, August 22, 1883, Tecumseh Papers, *Draper Mss.*, Vol. 4YY2, SHSW; John Juniper to Lyman Draper, January 11, 1882, Tecumseh Papers, *Draper Mss.*, Vol. 4YY16–16.1, SHSW; Dowd, *Spirited Resistance*, 197.

50. Narrative of Spoon Decorah, in *CSHSW*, 13:459. Generations after the famed Shawnee's death at Moraviantown (Thames River, Upper Canada) in 1813, the older Winnebagoes still spoke often of Tecumseh, recounting his miraculous feats. Although Tecumseh's violent death might have seemingly undermined the notion of his omnipotence, his followers did not view this as Tecumseh's loss of power; but rather, they interpreted the event as the Great Spirit's wrath against them for having compromised their nativist ways. The famed Sauk leader Black Hawk, who allegedly saw Tecumseh die, later recalled, "As soon as the Indians discovered that he was killed, a sudden fear came over them, and thinking the Great Spirit was angry, they fought no longer, and were quickly put to flight." See "The Death of Tecumseh: Black Hawk's Account," in Klinck, *Tecumseh*, 209; Drake, *Life of Tecumseh*, 202. Today the Shawnee people remember Tecumseh as one of their greatest prophets. Howard, *Shawnee!* 211.

51. Draper's notes, 1882, taken from Thomas Forsyth's notes, Tecumseh Papers, *Draper Mss.*, Vol. 8YY54.2, SHSW.

52. Edmunds, "Main Poc," 21–22; Edmunds, *Potawatomis*, 20.

53. Wells to Secretary of War Henry Dearborn, April 20, 1808, Carter, *Territorial Papers*, 7:556; Wells to Dearborn, January 7, 1808, Potawatomi File, GABLA.

54. Owsley, "Prophet of War," 277; Martin, *Sacred Revolt*, 126, 134; Dowd, *Spirited Resistance*, 169–70.

55. Matson, *Memories of Shaubena*, 19; Dowd, *Built Like a Bear*, 24. Though Ottawa by birth, Shabonee became a Potawatomi leader after marrying into their tribe and dwelling among them for some time in Illinois.

56. Sugden, *Tecumseh*, 4, 132–33; Edmunds, *Tecumseh*, 96. For Roundhead's signature, see the Treaty of Greenville, in *Historical Collections*, 20:416. He is listed as "Staye-tah" under the Wyandot section of signatures. For Roundhead's support of the nativists in 1807, see his speech against Black Hoof's faction, June 6, 1807, Tecumseh Papers, *Draper Mss*, 3YY72–73, SHSW.

57. Major Muir's Official Report of the Expedition to Fort Wayne, September 30, 1812, Appendix I, Casselman, *Richardson's War*, 298–99; Edmunds, "Main Poc," 29.

58. James, *Military Occurrences of the Late War*, 1:291–92; Klinck, *Tecumseh*, 158–59; Edmunds, *Tecumseh*, 180; Sugden, *Tecumseh*, 308, 447.

59. Dowd, *Spirited Resistance*, 21, 183.

60. For the dwindling Indian population in Ohio at this time, see Tanner, *Atlas*, 96–104. Further information on the Indian presence in northwestern Ohio near the turn of the nineteenth century is available in the publication of the joint report for the Indian Claims Commission by Erminie Wheeler-Voegelin and Helen Hornbeck Tanner, *Indians of Northern Ohio and Southeastern Michigan*, particularly 265–87 and 358–69.

61. Claus to Sir John Johnson, Superintendent General, November 2, 1807, Claus Papers, 9:161–62, MG 19 G 1, LAC; Edmunds, *Shawnee Prophet*, 63.

62. By May 1808 Governor-General Sir James Craig also viewed the French as a significant threat. See Craig to Lieutenant Governor Francis Gore, May 11, 1808, in *Historical Collections*, 25:245–46; Colonial Office, Record 42, Vol. 136, 163–64, NAUK.

63. Harrison's Speech to the Indiana Legislature, August 17, 1807, in Esarey, *Messages and Letters*, 1:235–36.

64. Claus to Lieutenant Governor Francis Gore, February 27, 1808, in *Historical Collections*, 15:44; Claus Papers, 9:177–79, MG 19 G 1, LAC; File 10, 405, John Marsh Papers, Fort Malden Historical Archives.

65. Claus to Prideaux Selby, Military Secretary, May 3, 1808, in *Historical Collections*, 15:49; File 10, 415, John Marsh Papers, Fort Malden Historical Archives; Claus Papers, 9:193, MG 19 G 1, LAC; Edmunds, *Shawnee Prophet*, 70–71; Edmunds, *Tecumseh*, 113–14.

66. Diary of William Claus at Amherstburg, May 16, 1808, in *Historical Collections*, 23:50. The original diary is in Claus Papers, 9:195–215, MG 19 G 1, LAC.

67. Diary of William Claus at Amherstburg, entries for June 13, 14, and 15, 1808, in *Historical Collections*, 23:53–54.

68. Regarding conditions at Prophetstown, see John Conner's Statement before William Wells at Fort Wayne, June 18, 1808, Shawnee File, GABLA; Harrison to Henry Dearborn, February 14, 1809, in Esarey, *Messages and Letters*, 1:355; Carter, *Territorial Papers*, 7:640, 356; Wells to Dearborn, April 23, 1808, Carter, *Territorial Papers*, 7:560; White, *Middle Ground*, 509; Edmunds, *Shawnee Prophet*, 72, 75–76. For the Prophet's relationship with the Shakers, see MacLean, "Shaker Mission," 215–29.

69. However, Tecumseh had previously met with white leaders, including an occasion when he made a public speech in the courthouse at Chillicothe in September 1807, calming the citizens by refuting allegations that Indians had committed a recent murder in western Ohio. See Sugden, *Tecumseh*, 3–8.

70. Sugden, *Tecumseh*, 92–93, 96–97, 130–31. As Shawnees of the Kishpoko division, Tecumseh and Tenskwatawa held less institutional authority than Black Hoof of the preeminent Mekoche division, and war leaders were expected to defer to the prerogative of village chiefs in formal council settings. Howard, *Shawnee!* 26–27, 108–9. For Tecumseh's rivalry with Black Hoof and the Wapakoneta council, see Sugden, *Tecumseh*, 97, 131; Gilbert, *God Gave Us This Country*, 192.

71. Tecumseh's Kishpoko followers, like their leader, would not have felt much devotion to the Mekoche Shawnee headmen at Wapakoneta, perhaps also resenting Black Hoof's control of the annuity that the U.S. government paid to the Shawnees.

72. Claus to Prideaux Selby, Military Secretary, January 18, 1809, RG 8, Military C Series, Vol. 256, 5, LAC.

73. Harrison and his officers claimed to have found British muskets and supplies scattered on the battlefield at Tippecanoe, November 7, 1811. See Allen, *His Majesty's Indian Allies*, 117.

74. Craig to Francis Gore, Lieutenant Governor, December 6, 1807, Colonial Office, Record 42, Vol. 136, 155, NAUK.

75. Craig to Gore, December 28, 1807, in *Historical Collections*, 25:232–33; Colonial Office, Record 42, Vol. 136, 158, NAUK.

76. Most of Britain's Indian allies heeded this advice, but Main Poc ignored it, choosing instead to prematurely begin raiding white settlements in southern Illinois in 1810 and 1811. Edmunds, *Potawatomis*, 173–77.

77. Craig to Gore, May 11, 1808, in *Historical Collections*, 25:245–46; Colonial Office, Record 42, Vol. 136, 163–64, NAUK; Gore to Craig, January 5, 1808, in *Historical Collections*, 25:169–70; Horsman, *Matthew Elliott*, 163–71.

78. The best study on this topic is Horsman, "British Indian Policy."

79. Lieutenant Governor Gore's Speech to the Western Confederacy, July 11, 1808, RG 10, Indian Affairs, Vol. 11, 9886, LAC.

80. Recall that in 1793, the former confederacy, at the urging of Alexander McKee, unsuccessfully demanded that the U.S. government recognize the Ohio River as the permanent boundary.

81. Speech of the different Indian Nations, July 13, 1808, RG 10, Indian Affairs, Vol. 11, 9891, LAC.

82. Gore to Craig, July 27, 1808, RG 10, Indian Affairs, Vol. 11, 9902, LAC.

83. Gore to Craig, July 27, 1808, RG 10, Indian Affairs, Vol. 11, 9902, LAC.

84. Sugden, *Tecumseh*, 435, n3.

85. Gore to Craig, July 27, 1808, RG 10, Indian Affairs, Vol. 11, 9902, LAC. The Indians bitterly complained about this incident regularly. See also Isaac Brock to Sir George Prevost, December 2, 1811, Wood, *British Documents*, 1:273; Klinck, *Tecumseh*, 117.

86. Tecumseh's Speech at Vincennes, August 20, 1810, in Esarey, *Messages and Letters*, 1:464, 466–67.

87. For U.S. Indian policy during the Jefferson administration, see Wallace, *Jefferson and the Indians*, 220–26.

88. Tecumseh's Speech at Vincennes, August 20, 1810, in Esarey, *Messages and Letters*, 1:467–68.

89. Tecumseh's Speech at Vincennes, August 20, 1810, in Esarey, *Messages and Letters*, 1:468–69.

90. Certain other leaders, such as Main Poc, for example, would not have acquiesced to Tecumseh's claims.

91. Sugden, *Tecumseh*, 174–75.

92. Matthew Elliott to Major Halton, May 19, 1809, RG 10, Indian Affairs, Vol. 3, 990, LAC; White, *Middle Ground*, 514.

93. Harrison to Eustis, June 14, 1810, in Esarey, *Messages and Letters*, 1:423–24. This gesture by the Brownstown council, however, did not necessarily mean that Wyandots intended to become the Prophet's religious converts.

94. Harrison to Eustis, June 14, 1810, in Esarey, *Messages and Letters*, 1:423.

95. For contemporary descriptions of Brownstown, see Jacob Visgar to William Hull, October 12, 1807, in *Historical Collections*, 40:239–40; and Hopkins, *Mission to the Indians*, 102–3.

96. Kappler, *Indian Affairs*, 2:92–95; Prucha, *American Indian Treaties*, 125–26.

97. Speech of [Wyandot] Indian Chiefs to Governor Hull, September 30, 1809, in *Historical Collections*, 40:304–7.

98. Proceedings of a Private Meeting with the Shawenoes, March 25, 1808, in *Historical Collections*, 25:242.

99. Quaife, *War on the Detroit*, 79, 101.

100. Klinck and Talman, *Journal of Major John Norton*, 300.

101. Lossing, *Pictorial Field-Book*, 344, n2. For Governor Hull, the loss of the Wyandots to the British was a crushing blow, since he believed even after the war began that they would remain neutral. See Hull to Eustis, July 14, 1812, in *Historical Collections*, 40:413–15; Hull to Eustis, July 19, 1812, in *Historical Collections*, 40:418; Cruikshank, *Invasion of Canada*, 53.

According to Edmunds, Walk in the Water and the Wyandots of the Detroit region later wavered in their support of the British. See Edmunds, "Tecumseh's Native Allies," 65–66. In *Tecumseh*, Sugden articulately argues that the Detroit/Brownstown Wyandots under Walk in the Water had sought official neutrality for as long as possible, but once the American military efforts faltered in the war's opening weeks, Wyandot sentiment shifted more heavily toward Tecumseh and the British. When the fortunes of war later turned in favor of the Americans the following year, these Wyandots again claimed neutrality, arguing that they had been physically compelled to evacuate to Canada by Tecumseh and pro-British elements in the summer of 1812. Sugden demonstrates that in spite of their vacillation, the Detroit-area Wyandots were in fact sympathetic and supportive of Tecumseh, the nativist allies, and the British. Sugden, *Tecumseh*, 290–91.

102. Elliott to Claus, November 18, 1810, Colonial Office, MG 11, CO 42, Vol. 351, 40, LAC.

103. The Shawnees most likely received this belt from Sir William Johnson at Detroit in the summer of 1761 during the first general council held with the western nations after Britain's occupation of the former French posts throughout the Great Lakes.

104. Speech of Tukumthai, Brother of the Shawanoe Prophet, Fort Malden, November 15, 1810, Colonial Office, MG 11, CO 42, Vol. 351, 42, LAC; Klinck, *Tecumseh*, 79–81.

105. Allen, *His Majesty's Indian Allies*, 116; Allen, *British Indian Department*, 69–70.

106. For the St. Louis Treaty of 1804, see Kappler, *Indian Affairs*, 2:74–77; Prucha, *American Indian Treaties*, 120; and Wallace, *Jefferson and the Indians*, 248–51.

107. Although the Treaty of Greenville entitled both the Ojibwa and Ottawa na-

tions to annuities amounting to $1,000 per tribe, the United States made these payments at Detroit, and thus to those Ojibwas and Ottawas living in that region. By the summer of 1807, the northern Ojibwas and Ottawas had not yet received any annuity distributions stemming from the Treaty of Greenville. Captain J. Dunham to William Hull, June 18, 1807, in *Historical Collections*, 40:143.

108. Davidson, *North West Company*, 171–72; Kellogg, *British Regime*, 238–41, 256.

109. Henry, *Travels and Adventures*, 188; Calloway, *Crown and Calumet*, 134; Anderson, *Kinsmen of Another Kind*, 66–67.

110. Calloway, *Crown and Calumet*, 137.

111. Pike's journal entries for January 3, February 6, and February 10, 1806, Jackson, *Journals of Zebulon Montgomery Pike*, 1:76, 92–93. Previously on this expedition Pike met Black Hawk, who refused to lower his village's British flags at Pike's request. See Jackson, *Black Hawk*, 52.

112. McGillis to Pike, February 15, 1806, Jackson, *Journals of Zebulon Montgomery Pike*, 1:260.

113. Pike's journal entry for January 27, 1806, Jackson, *Journals of Zebulon Montgomery Pike*, 1:84.

114. Anderson, *Kinsmen of Another Kind*, 88.

115. Pike's Observations on the North West Company, Jackson, *Journals of Zebulon Montgomery Pike*, 1:180.

116. Tanner, *Falcon*, 209–10.

117. Jackson, *Black Hawk*, 58, 60, 62–64.

118. Kellogg, *British Regime*, 292–300; Calloway, *Crown and Calumet*, 56, 134; Anderson, *Kinsmen of Another Kind*, 67–68, 87–88; Anderson, "American Agents," 17–18.

119. Tohill, "Robert Dickson," 85–86, 96. For Dickson's qualifications, see Captain J. B. Glegg to Colonel Edward Baynes, November 11, 1812, in *Historical Collections*, 15:180–82. For letters and documents pertaining to Dickson's appointment and Prevost's instructions, see *Historical Collections*, 15:218–23.

120. The Prophet's principal tenets are listed in Thomas Forsyth to William Clark, January 15, 1827, Forsyth Papers, *Draper Mss.*, Vol. 9T52–53, SHSW. Those items in the list most directed against Indian participation in the fur trade are numbers 7, 9, 11, and 12.

121. Zeisberger's entry for May 26, 1787, Bliss, *Diary of David Zeisberger*, 1:346; Hulbert and Schwarze, *David Zeisberger's History*, 9:14; Stevens, "Fur Trading Companies," 286; Dowd, *Spirited Resistance*, 120.

122. Stevens, *Northwest Fur Trade*, 104; Thomas Jefferson to William Henry Harrison, February 27, 1803, in Esarey, *Messages and Letters*, 1:71.

123. The records of Fort Wayne's Indian Agency provide a glimpse of the declining fur trade. Between 1804 and 1811, the agency took in an average of 1,071 deerskins per year, with the number of deerskins gradually decreasing. The bumper year of 1807 stands as an exception, when the agency recorded the receipt of 2,052 deerskins. Nev-

ertheless, with prices at a mere \$.44 per deerskin, the resulting per capita profits to the Indians did not stretch very far. See Griswold, *Fort Wayne*, 433–35, 453–54, 480–82, 504–7, 563–64, 580–81, 661–63; Dowd, *Spirited Resistance*, 120.

124. Calloway, "Foundations of Sand," 155, 157–58, 163; Calloway, *Crown and Calumet*, 160.

125. Thomas Forsyth to William Clark, January 15, 1827, Forsyth Papers, *Draper Mss.*, Vol. 9T52–53, Tenet no. 9, SHSW; Dowd, *Spirited Resistance*, 130–31.

126. Speech of La Maigouis, May 4, 1807, Alexander McKee Papers, MG 19 G 16, 13, LAC. This speech is also found in *Historical Collections*, 40:127–33.

127. Duncan McGillivray to William McGillivray, June 18, 1807, G 983, Reel Ms. 35, RI, John Strachan Papers, Ontario Historical Archives. For brief biographical sketches on these McGillivray brothers, see Wallace, *Documents Relating to the North West Company*, 469, 471–72.

128. Captain Dunham's Speech at Arbre Croche, May 20, 1807, G 983, Reel Ms. 35, RI, John Strachan Papers, Ontario Historical Archives.

129. Dunham to Hull, May 20, 1807, in *Historical Collections*, 40:125–26.

130. Wells to Harrison, August 20, 1807, in Esarey, *Messages and Letters*, 1:239.

131. Charles Jouett to Secretary of War, August 22 and December 1, 1807, both in Carter, *Territorial Papers*, 7:472, 496–97; Charles Reaume, Justice of the Peace at Green Bay, to Captain J. Dunham, June 1807, Winnebago File, GABLA; Hagan, *Sac and Fox Indians*, 39.

132. "Manners, Customs, and International Laws of the Win-nee-baa-goa nation" (1823), Winnebago Manuscripts, MS/14ME, Trowbridge Papers, Burton Historical Collection; Radin, *Winnebago Tribe*, 115, 159.

133. Keesing, *Menomini Indians*, 69, 78; Danziger, *Chippewas of Lake Superior*, 10–11.

134. "Col. Boyd's Account," Chippewa Manuscripts, MS/14C, Trowbridge Papers, Burton Historical Collection.

135. "Traditions, Manners, and Customs of the Mun-noa-min-nee nation," Menominee Manuscripts; and "Manners, Customs, and International Laws of the Win-nee-baa-goa nation" (1823), Winnebago Manuscripts, both in MS/14ME, Trowbridge Papers, Burton Historical Collection.

136. Beck, *Siege and Survival*, 76–81; Kellogg, *British Regime*, 237–42, 292–300.

137. Charles Reaume, Justice of the Peace, Green Bay, to Captain J. Dunham, June 12, 1807, Winnebago File, GABLA; Keesing, *Menomini Indians*, 91. See also Tomah's speech to Tecumseh, 1810, in *CSHSW*, 1:53–54.

138. Radin, *Winnebago Tribe*, 239, 391–92; Howard, *Shawnee!* 175–76, 206. Similarly, the Winnebagoes also believed that the secondary deities occupied the world just below the Great Spirit's dwelling place.

139. Edmunds, *Shawnee Prophet*, 34.

140. Radin, *Winnebago Tribe*, 21–22.

141. Jouett to the Secretary of War, May 2, 1808, Carter, *Territorial Papers*, 7:564–65.

142. Jackson, *Black Hawk*, 58; Tanner, *Falcon*, 147.

143. Edmunds, *Shawnee Prophet*, 59–60, 66, 70, 76; Warren, *History of the Ojibway People*, 323.

144 Tanner, *Falcon*, 146–47.

145. Blackbird, *History*, 29–30. For a similar episode among the Ojibwas, see Warren, *History of the Ojibway People*, 323.

146. Tanner, *Falcon*, 145.

147. Warren, *History of the Ojibway People*, 323; Barnouw, "Acculturation and Personality," 67; Danziger, *Chippewas of Lake Superior*, 66.

148. Edmunds, *Shawnee Prophet*, 76; White, *Middle Ground*, 513; Sugden, *Tecumseh*, 174; Matthew Elliott to Major Halton, May 19, 1809, RG 10, Indian Affairs, Vol. 3, 990, LAC; William Wells to Henry Dearborn, March 31, 1809, Shawnee File, GABLA; John Johnston to the Prophet, May 3, 1809, Thornbrough, *Letter Book*, 49–50.

149. Edmunds, *Shawnee Prophet*, 82; Harrison to the Secretary of War, April 26, 1809, in Esarey, *Messages and Letters*, 1:342; Harrison to the Secretary of War, June 26, 1810, in Esarey, *Messages and Letters*, 1:433–34.

150. Hull to Eustis, June 16, 1809, Potawatomi File, GABLA. See also Hull to Eustis, August 2, 1809, and Hull to Eustis, July 20, 1810, both in Potawatomi File, GABLA.

151. Harrison to Eustis, August 28, 1810, in Esarey, *Messages and Letters*, 1:471.

152. The North West Company maintained several trading posts along the northern Great Lakes, including one at Fort St. Joseph and another at nearby Sault Ste. Marie. Tanner, *Atlas*, 98–99. These tended to offset any budding influence of American trade at Mackinac between 1796 and 1812.

153. Council minutes at St. Joseph's, May 20 and 21, June 8 and 19, 1807, RG 10, Indian Affairs, Vol. 2, 689–702, LAC.

154. Indian Council held at St. Joseph's, May 20, 1807, RG 10, Indian Affairs, Vol. 2, 699, LAC.

155. Claus to Lieutenant Governor Gore, February 27, 1808, in *Historical Collections*, 40:44–45.

156. Claus to Lieutenant Governor Gore, February 27, 1808, in *Historical Collections*, 40:44–45.

157. Claus to Lieutenant Governor Gore, February 27, 1808, in *Historical Collections*, 40:44–45.

158. Matthew Elliott to Major Halton, May 19, 1809, RG 10, Indian Affairs, Vol. 3, 990, LAC.

159. John Askin Jr., the half-Ottawa son of John Askin (prominent trader and close liaison with the British Indian Department at Detroit in the 1790s), was the individual who fell afoul of Anthony Wayne during the Greenville peace negotiations during the summer of 1795. Wayne regarded Askin Jr. as a spy at the time and temporarily incarcerated him at Fort Jefferson.

160. John Askin Jr. to William Claus, December 26, 1815, Claus Papers, 10:207, MG 19 G 1, LAC. Askin regarded his combined service as agent, storekeeper, and interpreter between 1807 and 1812 as his most important accomplishment. The Indian Department did not employ a regular deputy superintendent at St Joseph's at that time, forcing Askin to hold several positions simultaneously, without extra pay.

161. Neither Gregory Dowd's *Spirited Resistance* nor Richard White's *Middle Ground* fully addresses the northern sector of Indian-white relations. Both authors allude to the prophecy of the Ottawa La Maigouis in 1807, briefly treating it as significant, but neither follows this up with a discussion on the ensuing years in the North and why the Indians there ultimately rejected revitalization. Consequently, their readers are left with the impression that the nativist ideals held firm in the North. Moreover, neither author discusses the significance of the northern fur trade, although the fur trade's participants resisted both nativism and the notion of a common cultural middle ground with the tribes of the southern Great Lakes (White's discussion of the trade in his final chapter is in a different context, one in which the author is attempting to play down the extent of growing Native dependency). Nor does R. David Edmunds (in *Shawnee Prophet*) discuss the failure of revitalization in the North, and like Dowd and White, Edmunds does not attempt to cover the northern and western regions (that is, Wisconsin and northern Michigan) after the Prophet's brief outburst of popularity there in 1807.

162. Harrison to Secretary of War, July 25, 1810, in Esarey, *Messages and Letters*, 1:449; Jackson, *Black Hawk*, 58; Gilbert, *God Gave Us This Country*, 271–72; McAfee, *History of the Late War*, 34. Other firsthand accounts of the action on November 7, 1811, are found in McCollough, *Battle of Tippecanoe*. However, one excerpt in this publication, "Shabonee's Account," must be disregarded, as it originated in a nineteenth-century historical novel. See also John Tipton's "Tippecanoe Journal" of the entire expedition, in Robertson and Riker, *John Tipton Papers*, 1:62–88.

163. Some scholars have argued that the degree of the Shawnee Prophet's loss of power and influence in the wake of Tippecanoe has been exaggerated. Most recently, Alfred A. Cave makes this point in his fine study *Prophets of the Great Spirit*, 115–31. Previously, Gregory Dowd insightfully made this case in an important article, "Thinking and Believing," 327; and H. C. W. Goltz Jr., the first scholar in modern historiography to seriously consider the role of the Prophet, also emphasizes the Shawnee holy man's continued influence based on primary quotes and reports, and the Indians' continued will to fight after their loss at Tippecanoe. Goltz, "Tecumseh," 300–306. While these arguments may hold a kernel of truth and consequently deserve further consideration, the Prophet's subsequent career after Tippecanoe simply did not compare with the earlier phase of his spiritual leadership, and few took him seriously as he harmlessly remained under British protection throughout the War of 1812 and its aftermath. As for the firsthand observers who argued that the Prophet preserved his influence based on continued Native hostilities, they linked too closely

the Native will to fight to the Prophet's personal vicissitudes. The frontier war that followed proved that Indians would ultimately resist American expansion, with or without the Prophet. While these authors' sagacious scholarship provides a necessary contribution to this area of study by correctly uniting Native sacred and secular worlds, Edmunds's *Shawnee Prophet* best illustrates the realities of Tenskwatawa's life after Tippecanoe (113–64). See also White, *Middle Ground*, 516–23.

Epilogue

1. Lieutenant Edward Dewar to Colonel Procter, August 28, 1812, and Major P. L. Chambers to Procter, August 24, 1812, Cruikshank, *Invasion of Canada*, 173–76; entry for August 20, 1812, Journal of Charles Askin, Wood, *Select British Documents*, 1:541.

2. Harrison, *Aborigines of the Ohio Valley*, 37.

3. Harrison, *Aborigines of the Ohio Valley*, 38.

4. The best biography on Harrison, particularly for his later years, is Goebel, *William Henry Harrison*. More recently, Horsman provides a good biographical sketch in "William Henry Harrison."

5. For a biography of Cass that focuses heavily on his years as a soldier and governor in Michigan, see McLaughlin, *Lewis Cass*.

6. Cass, "Service of Indians," 370. For more of Cass's writings regarding Indians, see Cass, "Indians of North America." Also, an earlier unpublished report by Cass, dated 1815, can be found in the Newberry Library's Ayer Manuscripts, record 601, under the title "Report on the Formation of a System of the Regulation of Indian Affairs."

7. Cass, "Service of Indians," 375.

8. Cass continued to suspect British intrigue at work among the Indians well into the 1820s. More concerning his views during this period can be found in his records of personal correspondence in the Lewis Cass Papers at the Clements Historical Library and the Lewis Cass Papers at the Bentley Historical Library, Ann Arbor MI. Though bearing the same title, these collections actually contain different sets of correspondence; both research facilities are located at the University of Michigan, Ann Arbor.

9. Cass, "Service of Indians," 369.

10. For Cass on Indian removal, see Cass, "Removal of the Indians" (reprinted as *Considerations on the Present State of the Indians, and Their Removal to the West of the Mississippi* [New York: Arno Press, 1975]). See also McLaughlin, *Lewis Cass*, 159–61; Prucha, *Lewis Cass*; Prucha, *American Indian Policy*, 246–47, 256–57.

11. Perkins, *Prologue to War*, 283–84; Speech of John A. Harper, New Hampshire, January 4, 1812, 12th Congress, 1st session, 657, in Gales, *Annals of Congress*.

12. Iroquois leaders and headmen among groups situated in the eastern Great Lakes were more likely to publicly use the expression "Chain of Friendship," or similar rhetoric related to the metaphor. Joseph Brant and the Grand River peoples spoke of the Chain on occasion, and Red Jacket also used the "Chain of Friendship" in

multiple public speeches, including once at the Glaize in October 1792, then again at Buffalo Creek the following month. *Simcoe Correspondence*, 1:221, 257. As for western peoples, an unnamed Ojibwa leader from Michilimackinac spoke of "the Great Covenant Chain" at Niagara in 1764 (*Johnson Papers*, 11:309–11; see the introduction of this study), and the Shawnee leader Painted Pole remembered to use the "Chain of Friendship" at the Glaize twenty-eight years later. *Simcoe Correspondence*, 1:223. Finally, Tecumseh and an intertribal delegation of hundreds of warriors met with British officials at Fort Malden in the summer of 1808, claiming to support the newly "brightened . . . Chain of Friendship." See Indian speech at Amherstburg, July 13, 1808, RG 10, Indian Affairs, Vol. 11, 9891, LAC.

13. Painted Pole's speech at the Glaize epitomized this position, October 7, 1792, in *Simcoe Correspondence*, 1:227.

14. Sugden, *Blue Jacket*, 192–98.

15. Thomas Smith to Alexander McKee, October 11, 1794, in *Simcoe Correspondence*, 5:113.

16. Although evidence suggests that Tecumseh might have opposed the witch hunts and purges that the Prophet and some of his followers carried out against a handful of pro-U.S., Christian Indians, Tecumseh did threaten to kill the chiefs who made any land cessions to the Americans. See Tecumseh's speech at Vincennes, August 20, 1810, in Esarey, *Messages and Letters of William Henry Harrison*, 1:466; Klinck, *Tecumseh*, 71–72. Regarding the witch hunts, see Edmunds, *Shawnee Prophet*, 42–47; Edmunds, "Thin Red Line," 7–8; Edmunds, "Tecumseh," 268–69; and Miller, "1806 Purge," 245–66. For Tecumseh's reaction to the Prophet's witch hunts, see Sugden, *Tecumseh*, 154, 209; and Edmunds, *Tecumseh*, 85.

17. Speech of La Maigouis, the Ottawa Prophet, May 4, 1807, Alexander McKee Papers, MG 19 G 16, 13, LAC; *Historical Collections*, 40:127–33. American and British assessments of the northern phase of revitalization are found in Duncan McGillivray to William McGillivray, June 18, 1807, G 983, Reel Ms. 35, RI, John Strachan Papers, Ontario Historical Archives; and Captain Dunham's Speech at Arbre Croche, May 20, 1807, G 983, Reel Ms. 35, RI, John Strachan Papers, Ontario Historical Archives. See also Dunham to William Hull, May 20, 1807, in *Historical Collections*, 40:125–26.

18. See Speech of Tukumthai, Brother of the Shawanoe Prophet, Fort Malden, November 15, 1810, Colonial Office, MG 11, CO 42, Vol. 351, 42, LAC; and Klinck, *Tecumseh*, 79–81. Regarding Tecumseh's distrust of the British, see Lieutenant Governor Francis Gore to Sir James Craig, Governor General, July 27, 1808, RG 10, Indian Affairs, Vol. 11, 9902, LAC; and Thomas Forsyth to General William Clark, January 15, 1827, Thomas Forsyth Papers, *Draper Mss.*, 9T54, SHSW.

19. Jackson, *Journals of Zebulon Montgomery Pike*, 1:216–17. Pike was certainly mistaken; American authorities also would find it impossible to broker a lasting peace between these groups.

20. Noon, *Law and Government*, 86–88; Weaver, "Six Nations," 525.

21. Prucha, *Lewis Cass*, 14–17. The Cherokees had developed a centralized national government, based on a constitution that not only proclaimed the Cherokee government as sovereign over tribal lands but also claimed that the Cherokee nation did not exist apart from the land. Perdue and Green, *Cherokee Removal*, 13–14.

22. The Grand River, Chenail Ecarte, and the Bay of Quinte.

23. In the incident known as the *Chesapeake* Affair, the HMS *Leopard* fired three broadsides into the USS *Chesapeake*, killing or wounding several of its crew, before the *Leopard*'s royal marines forcibly boarded the crippled American vessel and removed suspected British deserters.

24. John Strachan to Thomas Jefferson, January 30, 1815, Coffin, *1812*, 282; Antal, *Wampum Denied*, 201–2; Nelson, *Men of Patriotism*, 77; Casselman, *Richardson's War*, 153–54; Klinck and Talman, *Journal of Major John Norton*, 321–22. John Norton ascribed the massacre of Dudley's men to "[a] Worthless Chippawa [Ojibwa] of Detroit having with him a number of wretches like himself." Robert McAfee, American veteran of the War of 1812 and early historian of that epoch, attributed this atrocity to the Potawatomis, while claiming that the Miamis and Wyandots "were on the side of humanity" and attempted to grant mercy to the defenseless Americans. McAfee, *History of the Late War*, 272. These incidents are also found in Gilpin, *War of 1812*, 127–28, 137, 170, 187.

25. This surviving contingent of retreating Indians continued in the region of Burlington Bay at Lake Ontario's western end for the remainder of the war. Sugden, *Tecumseh's Last Stand*, 193; Horsman, *Matthew Elliott*, 214–18. George C. Chalou illustrates the immense logistical burden that plagued British leaders in Canada as they attempted to feed and maintain these refugee allies and their families for the duration of the war. Chalou, "Red Pawns," 306–15.

26. Cook, *Six Months among Indians*, 15–18. The accounts included here were those given by the former Ottawa war leaders dwelling in present-day Allegan County, southwestern Michigan—Saginaw, Noonday, and Gosa. The Saginaw in Darius Cook's memoir might be the same individual listed in Tanner's *Atlas* (134) as "Sagimaw," a Potawatomi village-chief, circa 1830, near today's Three Rivers, Michigan. However, in his account, Cook spent the winter of 1839–40 at least forty miles north of this location—most likely among Ottawas—and the author never spelled Saginaw's name with an "m." According to Cook, Saginaw showed him a pipe that allegedly once belonged to Tecumseh, a gift from the British. Cook, *Six Months among Indians*, 12–15. For the activities along the Niagara frontier in December 1813, see Horsman, *Matthew Elliott*, 215–18; and Lossing, *Pictorial Field-Book*, 633–37.

27. Procter to Prevost, August 9, 1813, Wood, *Select British Documents*, 2:46; Procter to Prevost, July 11, 1813, Wood, *Select British Documents*, 2:253–54. Procter's superior, Sir George Prevost, did not understand the peril of the situation, and he scorned the general for "having allowed the clamour of the Indian Warriors to induce you to commit a part of your valuable force." Prevost to Procter, August 22, 1813, Wood, *Select British Documents*, 2:48.

28. Testimony of Lt. Colonel Augustus Warburton, December 9, 1814, Procter Court-Martial, War Office, Record 71/243, 11, NAUK. These records are also available in War Office, MG 13, WO 71/243, LAC. Gentleman volunteer John Richardson also believed that these Indians would not hesitate to kill their allies in certain circumstances. See Casselman, *Richardson's War of 1812*, 30.

29. Depositions of Warburton, Lieutenant Colonel William Evans, Captain Peter Chambers, Captain Thomas Coleman, Francis Baby, Captain William Caldwell (legitimate son of father of same name), Billy Caldwell (Col. Caldwell's illegitimate son), Colonel William Caldwell, and William Jones. These depositions are located in War Office, Record 71/243, 11, 50, 83, 109, 151, 156–57, 160, 176, 178, NAUK. For more on Procter's court-martial, see Antal, *Wampum Denied*, 371–77, 392–93; and Sugden, *Tecumseh's Last Stand*, 183–86. Also, in his retreat through the woods after the battle of the Thames, Private Shadrach Byfield of the Forty-first Regiment of Foot was harassed and intimidated by his former Indian allies, and according to him, they deliberated for a time on "how I was to be disposed of." Shadrach Byfield, "A Narrative of a Light Company Soldier's Service in the 41st Regiment of Foot, 1807–1814," 22–23, National Army Museum, Chelsea District, London. Anthropologist James Clifton has written two excellent biographical essays on Billy Caldwell: "Personal and Ethnic Identity," and "Merchant, Soldier, Broker, Chief."

30. This refers to the incident when the British garrison under Major William Campbell closed the gates of the fort, denying refuge to the Indians fleeing from the American army led by Anthony Wayne at Fallen Timbers, August 20, 1794. Gaff, *Bayonets*, 325–27, 364–65.

31. Colonel William Caldwell's deposition, January 11, 1815, Procter Court-Martial, War Office, Record 71/243, 176, NAUK.

32. Wabasha's speech, circa June 1812, addendum to Dickson's Report to Indian agency at Fort George, June 18, 1812, in Wood, *Select British Documents*, 1:425.

33. Dickson's commission and specific instructions from Prevost, January 14, 1813, are found in *Historical Collections*, 15:218–21.

34. Tohill, "Robert Dickson," 14; Anderson, *Kinsmen of Another Kind*, 67. The Native peoples with whom Dickson dealt affectionately dubbed him "Red Head" due to his blazing red hair and beard.

35. Lake Traverse is situated a short distance north of Big Stone Lake along the present border of Minnesota and South Dakota. For a time, Dickson made his home and headquarters at Big Stone Lake. Tanner, *Atlas*, 98, 100. For a contemporary, panoramic view of the region, see Tanner, *Atlas*, 149.

36. Biographical sketches of Dickson, McKay, and Anderson (along with several other agents discussed in this study) are found in *Dictionary of Canadian Biography*. For Dickson, McKay, and Anderson, see *Dictionary of Canadian Biography*, 6:209–11, 6:464–66, 10:11–13.

37. In honor of William McKay, ranking militia commander of the expedition.

38. William McKay's Report to Lt. Col. Robert McDouall on the capture of Prairie du Chien, July 29, 1814, Supplement, RG 8, Military C Series, Vol. 685, 4, LAC; Wood, *Select British Documents*, 3:264; Allen, *His Majesty's Indian Allies*, 160.

39. Hagan, *Sac and Fox Indians*, 68–72; Allen, *His Majesty's Indian Allies*, 159–61.

40. For Tomah's spurning of Tecumseh, see his speech to the latter, 1810, in *CSHSW*, 1:53–54.

41. Beck, *Siege and Survival*, 80–81.

42. "Captain T. G. Anderson's Journal, 21 September 1814," in *CSHSW*, 9:235–36. Captain Anderson's journal is also found in the Library and Archives Canada, Ottawa, MG 24 G 19. However, Anderson's militia muster rolls of Canadian volunteers are better organized (by militia and rank) in the journal's printed version in *CSHSW* 9; this latter version also contains Anderson's reminiscences in the "Personal Narrative of Captain Thomas G. Anderson," in *CSHSW* 9:134–206.

43. McDouall to Anderson, August 21, 1814, Anderson Journal, in *CSHSW*, 9:230.

44 Procter to Prevost, August 9, 1813, Wood, *Select British Documents*, 2:44.

45. Casselman, *Richardson's War of 1812*, 102.

46. Casselman, *Richardson's War of 1812*, 157–58.

47. Casselman, *Richardson's War of 1812*, 27–31. Much of this vengeance on the part of the Indians from south of the Great Lakes was specifically directed against Kentuckians, with whom these tribes were locked in a bitter feud spanning nearly forty years. The American forces in 1812 and 1813, whether regulars or militia, were comprised largely of Kentuckians; according to contemporary accounts, their appearance and fighting methods were similar to that of their Indian adversaries. See John Richardson's description in Klinck, *Tecumseh*, 199, and that of Colonel Allan H. McLean in Coffin, *1812*, 226.

A large portion of Harrison's victorious army that defeated Tecumseh and Major General Henry Procter at the Thames, Upper Canada, October 5, 1813, were Kentuckians seeking revenge for the loss of their brethren in the dismal American defeats earlier in the year at the River Raisin and in Dudley's Defeat, along the lower Maumee. "Remember the Raisin" became the Kentuckians' rallying cry. John Sugden illuminates these emotions in the events surrounding Tecumseh's death, lucidly depicting the temperament of the Kentuckians before, during, and after the battle of the Thames. Sugden demonstrated the sentiments of sixty-year-long Indian fighter William Whitley, the special role of Richard Mentor Johnson's volunteers as shock troops, and the Kentuckians' behavior after the battle in desecrating Tecumseh's remains, or at least a corpse they thought to be Tecumseh's. (Although popular myth suggests that surviving Indians spirited away Tecumseh's body, Sugden argues that the Kentucky troops made no mistake of identity and indeed mutilated the fallen Shawnee's remains. In a more recent study, Guy St-Denis concurs with Sugden, arguing that Tecumseh's remains are yet buried near the site where he fell. See St-Denis, *Tecumseh's Bones*, 138–42.) Speculation that Johnson had slain the celebrated Shawnee gave the Kentucky officer enough political clout to ascend to the vice-presidency under Martin Van Buren, 1837–41. Sugden, *Tecumseh's Last Stand*, 101, 125–35, 166–81; Hickey, *War of 1812*, 137–39. See also Stone, *Brittle Sword*, 44–50.

48. Jackson, *Black Hawk*, 66 (statement italicized by autobiography's editor).

49. Tecumseh is the Native leader best remembered for saving American lives in this affair, but Black Hawk's claims are also plausible, since so many American prisoners were in need of saving that day. John Richardson's allusion to separate acts of Indian mercy on the Ohio campaign support the possibility, including the incident mentioned in the text in which Metoss spared an American prisoner. Casselman, *Richardson's War of 1812*, 157.

50. Jackson, *Black Hawk*, 66–67. The one near exception to these findings is an account by Matthew Elliott, who blamed "Indians . . . who came in with [Robert] Dickson, . . . [for ruining] the country, by killing the cattle and robbing the inhabitants." Elliott to William Claus, August 29, 1813, RG 10, Indian Affairs, Vol. 28, 16528, LAC. Yet the statement is uncorroborated by evidence from other officers, agents, and militia, such as John Richardson's account. Moreover, Elliott, who had been most closely tied to Shawnees and Wyandots throughout his career, possibly held a bias against other Indians under the control of a rival agent. Furthermore, the alleged plunder of the local inhabitants took place as the Sauks prepared to return home. After an unsuccessful expedition against American forts in Ohio, the western warriors would certainly have expected to be compensated for their troubles before making the long trek home without enemy plunder, perhaps leading to some isolated incidents. Finally, such rare behavior by the Sauks—if it did occur—was a far cry from actually turning on their allies and killing British soldiers as the Detroit-region Native allies had done—and threatened to do—on multiple occasions.

51. Calloway, *Crown and Calumet*, 204; Anderson, *Kinsmen of Another Kind*, 88–91.

52. Benn, *Iroquois in the War of 1812*, 36–53.

53. Benn, *Iroquois in the War of 1812*, 142–43, 156–57; Klinck and Talman, *Journal of Major John Norton*, lxxviii; Noah Freer, Military Secretary to Lieutenant General Gordon Drummond, March 1, 1814, in Johnston, *Valley of the Six Nations*, 219–20, and in RG 10, Indian Affairs, Vol. 3, 1299–1301, LAC. See also Freer to Captain Loring, July 9, 1814, RG 10, Indian Affairs, Vol. 3, 1463–64, LAC.

54. Benn, *Iroquois in the War of 1812*, 184–87.

55. Key leaders supporting Norton at this time included Earl Bathurst, secretary for war and the colonies; Bathurst's undersecretary, Henry Goulburn; and Hugh Percy, second Duke of Northumberland.

56. It appears that the commissary general's office (through which the Indian Department was financed in 1816) ultimately covered the expense of the gift rifles. London gun craftsman Henry Tatham provided three different designs specifically intended as Indian presentation rifles within Norton's gift set. Bailey, *British Military Flintlock Rifles*, chapter 16, especially 180–87. I am grateful to my friend Grif Cook of

Sumnerville, Michigan—and to his expertise on historical armor and weaponry—for bringing this publication to my attention.

57. Henry R. Schoolcraft, "Movements of the North Western Indians During the Late War," Discourse Delivered Before the Historical Society of Michigan, Detroit, 1834, Shawnee File, 1803–1804, Winnebago File, 1797–1806, GABLA. There were also two other documents written by Americans during the war that acknowledged regional groupings and differences between the Indians, yet without applying this to the British alliance. These are Thomas Forsyth to John Gibson, July 26, 1812, Thomas Forsyth Collection, Box 134, Chicago Historical Society; and Duncan McArthur, "Report on the Indian tribes East of the Mississippi River with Whom the United States are Connected by Treaty," March 22, 1814, Duncan McArthur Papers, Vol. 1, 122–32, Burton Historical Collection.

58. McDouall to Major General Robinson, September 22, 1815, in *Historical Collections*, 16:284.

59. McDouall to Major General Robinson, October 4, 1815, in *Historical Collections*, 16:310. See also Robert McDouall Orderly Book, 1815, Burton Historical Collection.

60. Speech of McDouall to the Indians at Michillimackinac, June 5, 1814, Colonial Office, MG 11, CO 42, Vol. 157, 15–18, LAC.

61. "Instructions to Mr. Guillory Interpreter for the Saulk [*sic*] Nation," A. Bulger, April 8, 1815; "Instructions to Lieutenant Renville Interpreter for the Scoux [*sic*] Nation," A. Bulger, April 8, 1815, Andrew Bulger Papers, MG 19 E 5, File 6, 505, 510, LAC.

62. McDouall to Bulger, May 2, 1815, Andrew Bulger Papers, MG 19 E 5, File 6, 573, LAC.

63. Allen, *His Majesty's Indian Allies*, 175. At a council held at Amherstburg on June 10, 1816, a delegation of "Principal Chiefs" of several of the refugees residing near the Western District claimed that the British had promised them that they "would get back again the old French lines," likely meaning the Allegheny watershed. Proceedings of a Council held at Amherstburg, June 10, 1816, RG 10, Indian Affairs, Vol. 27, 16106, LAC. This, of course, was impossible by 1812, and the statement may have been an effort on the part of the Indians to extract more gifts from the British. More realistically, British officers and agents may have given the Indians hope of restoring all of their country lost since the Treaty of Greenville in 1795.

64. Speech of Karamanke, Winnebago leader, June 11, 1816, William McKay Papers, File 5, McCord Museum. A year previous to Karamanke's visit, another Winnebago leader, Sausamaunee, addressed McDouall and McKay at Mackinac, exclaiming, "It would be better that you had us killed at once, rather than expose us to a lingering death." Speech of Sausamaunee, June 3, 1815, "The Papers of Captain T. G. Anderson," in *CSHSW*, 10:143.

65. Speeches at Drummond Island, August 3, 1817, William McKay Papers, MG 19 G 29, LAC; also in G983, Vol. 1, John Strachan Papers, Ontario Historical Archives.

66. For Main Poc's death, see Thomas Forsyth to William Clark, January 15, 1827, Thomas Forsyth Papers, *Draper Mss.*, 9T53, SHSW.

67. After the war, the United States quickly erected posts at Green Bay (Fort Howard) and Prairie du Chien (Fort Crawford), beginning to extend the nation's sphere of influence into the region that the tiny Canadian militias and their northwestern allies so successfully held throughout the contest.

68. Speech of Sir George Prevost to Indian delegation at Quebec, March 15, 1814, RG 10, Indian Affairs, Vol. 12, 10308–12, LAC. Tecumseh's sister, still very distraught, openly wept on this occasion. John Norton and his wife were also present.

69. The discussion of an Indian buffer state at Ghent was actually the revival of an old idea that had occasionally emerged in councils of diplomacy since the mid-eighteenth century. But these discussions among the Ghent commissioners in 1814 were the first such talks of an Indian barrier since Britain's ministers and John Graves Simcoe, former lieutenant governor of Upper Canada, had sought a neutral buffer state prior to Jay's Treaty two decades earlier. See Smith, "North American Neutral Indian Zone," 46, 52–59.

70. Substance of Conference on August 9, 1814, enclosure in Henry Goulburn to Earl Bathurst, August 9, 1814, Earl Bathurst Papers, MG 24 A 8, 192, LAC.

71. Entry for September 1, 1814, Adams, *Memoirs*, 3:28.

72. Goulburn to Bathurst, August 23, 1814, Earl Bathurst Papers, MG 24 A 8, 200, LAC.

73. Hickey, *War of 1812*, 292.

74. Entry for September 1, 1814, Adams, *Memoirs*, 3:28.

75. Goulburn to Bathurst, September 16, 1814, LAC, Earl Bathurst Papers, MG 24 A 8, 213, LAC.

76. Goulburn to Bathurst, November 25, 1814, Earl Bathurst Papers, MG 24 A 8, 239, LAC.

77. Bailey, *Diplomatic History*, 149; Hickey, *War of 1812*, 291.

78. Wellington to Lord Liverpool, November 9, 1814, quoted in Hickey, *War of 1812*, 295. Wellington's concerns were well founded; the naval struggle on the Great Lakes would have made it difficult for either side to gain supremacy. By war's end, the naval race on Lake Ontario alone entailed the construction of the world's largest sailing vessels at the time. For an excellent essay on this struggle, see Stacey, "Naval Power," 54–57. See also Malcomson, *Warships of the Great Lakes*, 111–18, 134–39.

79. Langley, "Quest for Peace," 73.

80. Jones, "British View of the War of 1812," 486.

81. Kellogg, *British Regime*, 326.

82. American troops occupied this region after defeating the British and Indian forces under Henry Procter and Tecumseh at the Thames River, October 5, 1813. John Sugden plays down the significance of the British loss of the Western District, arguing that the Americans' hold on the region was feeble at best, and that the Indians there were ready to rise in support should another British army return to capture Detroit and Malden, as Lieutenant General Sir Gordon Drummond intended to do. It was not to be. Sugden, *Tecumseh's Last Stand*, 187–90, 202–4.

From this position in the Western District, the deepest subsequent American foray into Upper Canada came under the command of Duncan McArthur in November 1814; McArthur's army met heavy resistance at the Grand River, compelling them to retreat. Lossing, *Pictorial Field-Book*, 852–53; McAfee, *History of the Late War*, 446–50; Gilpin, *War of 1812*, 256–57. In *Wampum Denied*, Antal believes that McArthur's raid was significant in thwarting Drummond's hopes of recovering the Western District and Detroit for the British (381). However, John Norton, who participated in the defense of Upper Canada on this occasion, viewed McArthur's endeavors as insignificant, claiming that the Americans merely destroyed four mills, all of which were soon rebuilt. Klinck and Talman, *Journal of Major John Norton*, 369–70.

83. Hickey, *War of 1812*, 298–99, 308–9.

84. Cass to John Calhoun, Secretary of War, August 4, 1819, and Cass to John Calhoun, October 8, 1819, Lewis Cass Papers, Vol. 3, 99–102, 122–25, Bentley Historical Library.

85. Allen, *His Majesty's Indian Allies*, 184.

86. Jackson, *Black Hawk*, 60. Black Hawk's italics.

87. See *Dictionary of Canadian Biography*, 8:112–13.

88. British authorities in Upper Canada continued to officially distribute gifts to Indians who lived within the United States until 1843, when "American" Indians received their final portions of "His Majesty's bounty" on Manitoulin Island. Catherine Sims has written a fine unpublished study on British Indian policy and gift distribution in Upper Canada during the postwar period, 1815–43. See Sims, "Algonkian-British Relations," particularly 378–419, covering the final years.

89. Givens had previously served as agent to the Mississaugas during Joseph Brant's time, beginning in the 1790s.

90. In "Fur Traders in Northern Indiana," Anson reveals how a specific region was transformed as the fur trade declined. The manuscript is available on microfilm at the Newberry Library.

91. "Personal Narrative of Captain Thomas G. Anderson," in *CSHSW*, 9:198.

92. "Personal Narrative of Captain Thomas G. Anderson," in *CSHSW*, 9:197.

93. "Personal Narrative of Captain Thomas G. Anderson," in *CSHSW*, 9:198.

Bibliography

Archival Sources

Bentley Historical Library, Ann Arbor, Michigan
  Lewis Cass Papers
Burton Historical Collection, Detroit Public Library
  C. C. Trowbridge Papers
    Chippewa Manuscripts
    Delaware Manuscripts
    Menominee Manuscripts
    Winnebago Manuscripts
  Duncan McArthur Papers
  Robert McDouall Orderly Book, 1815
Chicago Historical Society
  Thomas Forsyth Collection
William L. Clements Library, Ann Arbor, Michigan
  Lewis Cass Papers
  Native American Collection
  Northwest Territory Papers
Fort Malden Historical Archives, Amherstburg, Ontario
  John Marsh Papers
Glenn A. Black Laboratory of Archaeology, Indiana University, Bloomington
  Potawatomi File
  Shawnee File
  Thomas Duggan Journal
  Winnebago File
Indiana Historical Society, Indianapolis
  William Henry Harrison Collection

Library and Archives Canada, Ottawa
(formerly the National Archives of Canada)
  MANUSCRIPT GROUPS
   Alexander McKee Papers
   Andrew Bulger Papers
   Claus Family Papers
   Colonial Office
   Earl Bathurst Papers
   Frederick Haldimand Papers
   Peter Russell's Letterbook, Indian Affairs
   Thomas G. Anderson's Journal, 1814
   War Office
  RECORD GROUPS
   Indian Affairs
   Military C Series
McCord Museum, Montreal
   War of 1812 Collection
   William McKay Papers
National Archives of the United Kingdom, Kew Gardens
(formerly the Public Record Office)
   Colonial Office
   War Office
National Army Museum, Chelsea District, London
   Shadrach Byfield Manuscript
Newberry Library, Chicago
  AYER MANUSCRIPTS
   John Norton Letterbook
   Lewis Cass, "Report on the ... Regulation of Indian Affairs"
Ontario Historical Archives, Toronto
   John Norton Papers
   John Strachan Papers
State Historical Society of Wisconsin, Madison
  DRAPER MANUSCRIPTS
   Simon Kenton Papers
   Tecumseh Papers
   Thomas Forsyth Papers
Toronto Public Library
  PETER RUSSELL PAPERS
   Letterbook, Correspondence with Governor-General
   Robert Prescott, 1796–99
   Letterbook, Indian Affairs, 1798–99

Weldon Library, University of Western Ontario, London, Ontario
John Norton Papers

Published Sources

Adams, Charles Francis, ed. *Memoirs of John Quincy Adams, Comprising Portions of His Diary from 1795 to 1848*. 12 vols. Philadelphia: J. B. Lippincott, 1874–77.

Allen, Robert S. *The British Indian Department and the Frontier in North America, 1755–1830*. Canadian Historic Sites Occasional Papers in Archaeology and History, 14. Ottawa: Department of Indian and Northern Affairs Canada, 1975.

——— . *His Majesty's Indian Allies: British Indian Policy in the Defence of Canada, 1774–1815*. Toronto: Dundurn Press, 1993.

American State Papers: Documents Legislative and Executive, of the Congress of the United States—Indian Affairs. 2 vols. Washington DC: Gales and Seaton, 1832.

Anderson, Gary [Clayton]. "American Agents vs. British Traders: Prelude to the War of 1812 in the Far West." In *The American West: Essays in Honor of W. Eugene Hollon*, edited by Ronald Lora, 3–24. Toledo OH: University of Toledo Press, 1980.

——— . *Kinsmen of Another Kind: Dakota-White Relations in the Upper Mississippi Valley, 1650–1862*. Lincoln: University of Nebraska Press, 1984.

Anson, Bert. "Fur Traders in Northern Indiana, 1800–1850." PhD diss., Indiana University, 1953.

——— . *The Miami Indians*. Norman: University of Oklahoma Press, 1970.

Antal, Sandy. *A Wampum Denied: Procter's War of 1812*. Ottawa: Carleton University Press, 1997.

Aupaumut, Hendrick. "A Narrative of an Embassy to the Western Indians from the Original Manuscript of Hendrick Aupaumut." *Memoirs of the Historical Society of Pennsylvania* 2 (1827): 61–131.

Bailey, De Witt. *British Military Flintlock Rifles, 1740–1840*. Lincoln RI: Andrew Mowbray, 2002.

Bailey, Thomas A. *A Diplomatic History of the American People*. 3rd ed. New York: F. S. Crofts, 1946.

Barnouw, Victor. "Acculturation and Personality among the Wisconsin Chippewa." American Anthropologist Association Memoir 72. *American Anthropologist* 52, no. 4, part 2 (October 1950).

Beck, David R. M. *Siege and Survival: History of the Menominee Indians, 1634–1856*. Lincoln: University of Nebraska Press, 2002.

Bemis, Samuel F. *The Diplomacy of the American Revolution*. 3rd ed. Bloomington: Indiana University Press, 1957.

——— . *Jay's Treaty: A Study in Commerce and Diplomacy*. 1923. N.p.: Knights of Columbus, 1923. Rev. ed., New Haven CT: Yale University Press, 1965.

Benn, Carl. *The Iroquois in the War of 1812*. Toronto: University of Toronto Press, 1998.

Blackbird, Andrew J. *History of the Ottawa and Chippewa Indians of Michigan: A Grammar of Their Language, Personal and Family History of the Author.* Ypsilanti MI: Ypsilantian Job Printing House, 1887.

Blair, Emma Helen, ed. *Indian Tribes of the Upper Mississippi Valley and Region of the Great Lakes.* 2 vols. Cleveland: Arthur H. Clarke, 1912.

Bliss, Eugene F., trans. and ed. *Diary of David Zeisberger, A Moravian Missionary among the Indians of Ohio.* 2 vols. Cincinnati: Robert Clarke, 1885. Reprint, St. Clair Shores MI: Scholarly Press, 1972.

Brown, Jennifer S. H. *Strangers in Blood: Fur Trade Company Families in Indian Country.* Vancouver: University of British Columbia Press, 1980.

Burt, A. L. *The United States, Great Britain, and British North America: From the Revolution to the Establishment of Peace after the War of 1812.* New Haven CT: Yale University Press, 1940.

Callendar, Charles. "Shawnee." In *Northeast*, edited by Bruce Trigger, 622–35. Vol. 15 of *Handbook of North American Indians*, edited by W. C. Sturtevant. Washington DC: Smithsonian Institution, 1978.

Calloway, Colin G. *The American Revolution in Indian Country: Crisis and Diversity in Native American Communities.* Cambridge: Cambridge University Press, 1995.

———. *Crown and Calumet: British-Indian Relations, 1783–1815.* Norman: University of Oklahoma Press, 1987.

———. "Foundations of Sand: The Fur Trade and British-Indian Relations, 1783–1815." In *Le Castor Fait Tout: Selected Papers of the Fifth North American Fur Trade Conference, 1985*, edited by Bruce G. Trigger, Toby Morantz, and Louise Dechene, 144–63. Montreal: St. Louis Historical Society, 1987.

———. *One Vast Winter Count: The Native American West before Lewis and Clark.* Lincoln: University of Nebraska Press, 2003.

———. *The Scratch of a Pen: 1763 and the Transformation of America.* Oxford: Oxford University Press, 2006.

———. "Simon Girty: Interpreter and Intermediary." In *Being and Becoming Indian: Biographical Studies of North American Frontiers*, edited by James A. Clifton, 38–58. Chicago: Dorsey Press, 1989.

———. "Suspicion and Self-Interest: The British-Indian Alliance and the Peace of Paris." *Historian* 48, no. 1 (November 1985): 41–60.

Carter, Clarence E., ed. *Territorial Papers of the United States.* 26 vols. Washington DC: Government Printing Office, 1934–62.

Carter, Harvey Lewis. "A Frontier Tragedy: Little Turtle and William Wells." *Old Northwest* 6 (1980): 3–18.

———. *The Life and Times of Little Turtle: First Sagamore of the Wabash.* Urbana: University of Illinois Press, 1987.

Cass, Lewis. "Indians of North America." *North American Review* 22 (January 1826): 53–119.

————. "Removal of the Indians." *North American Review* 30 (January 1830): 62–121.

————. "Service of Indians in Civilized Warfare." *North American Review* 24 (April 1827): 365–442.

Casselman, Alexander C., ed. *Richardson's War of 1812*. Toronto: Historical Publishing, 1902.

Cave, Alfred A. *Prophets of the Great Spirit: Native American Revitalization Movements in Eastern North America*. Lincoln: University of Nebraska Press, 2006.

Cayton, Andrew R. L. "Noble Actors' upon 'the Theatre of Honour': Power and Civility in the Treaty of Greenville." In *Contact Points: American Frontiers from the Mohawk Valley to the Mississippi, 1750–1830*, edited by Andrew R. L. Cayton and Fredrika J. Teute, 235–69. Chapel Hill: University of North Carolina Press, 1998.

Cayton, Andrew R. L., and Fredrika J. Teute, eds. *Contact Points: American Frontiers from the Mohawk Valley to the Mississippi, 1750–1830*. Chapel Hill: University of North Carolina Press, 1998.

Chalmers, Sir Robert. *A History of Currency in the British Colonies*. London: Printed for Her Majesty's Stationery Office, by Eyre and Spottiswoode, 1893.

Chalou, George C. "The Red Pawns Go to War: British-American Indian Relations, 1810–1815." PhD diss., Indiana University, 1971.

Clark, Bruce. *Native Liberty, Crown Sovereignty: The Existing Aboriginal Right of Self-Government in Canada*. Montreal: McGill-Queen's University Press, 1990.

Clifton, James A., ed. *Being and Becoming Indian: Biographical Studies of North American Frontiers*. Chicago: Dorsey Press, 1989.

————. "Merchant, Soldier, Broker, Chief: A Corrected Obituary of Captain Billy Caldwell." *Journal of Illinois State Historical Society* 71, no. 3 (August 1978): 185–210.

————. "Personal and Ethnic Identity on the Great Lakes Frontier: The Case of Billy Caldwell, Anglo-Canadian." *Ethnohistory* 25, no. 1 (Winter 1978): 69–94.

————. *The Prairie People: Continuity and Change in Potawatomi Indian Culture, 1665–1965*. Lawrence: Regents Press of Kansas, 1977.

Coffin, William F. *1812: The War and Its Moral: A Canadian Chronicle*. Montreal: J. Lovell, 1864.

Colden, Cadwallader. *History of the Five Indian Nations of Canada which are Dependent upon the Province of New York*. 2 vols. New York, 1727–47. Reprint, New York: Williams-Barker, 1904.

Colley, Linda. *Britons: Forging the Nation, 1707–1837*. New Haven CT: Yale University Press, 1992.

Cook, Darius B. *Six Months among Indians, Wolves and Other Wild Animals, in the Forests of Allegan County, Mich., in the Winter of 1839 and 1840*. Niles MI: Niles Mirror Office, 1889. Reprint, Berrien Springs MI: Hardscrabble Books, 1974.

Cork, Ella. *"The Worst of the Bargain," Concerning the Dilemmas Inherited from the Forefathers Along with Their Lands by the Iroquois Nation of the Canadian Grand River Reserve*. San Jacinto CA: Foundation for Social Research, 1962.

Cruikshank, E. A. *Butler's Rangers: The Revolutionary Period.* Welland ON: 1893. Reprint, Niagara Falls ON: Renown Printing, 1988.

———, ed. *The Correspondence of Lieut. Governor John Graves Simcoe, with Allied Documents Relating to His Administration of the Government of Upper Canada.* 5 vols. Toronto: Ontario Historical Society, 1923–31.

———, ed. "The Diary of an Officer in the Indian Country in 1794." *American Historical Magazine* 3 (1908): 639–43.

———, ed. *The Invasion of Canada and the Surrender of Detroit, 1812.* Ottawa: Government Printing Bureau, 1912.

Cruikshank, E. A., and A. F. Hunter, eds. *The Correspondence of the Honourable Peter Russell.* 3 vols. Toronto: Ontario Historical Society, 1932–36.

Curry, Wm. L. "The Wyandot Chief, Leather Lips: His Trial and Execution." *Ohio Archaeological and Historical Quarterly* 12 (1903): 30–36.

Danziger, Edmund Jefferson, Jr. *The Chippewas of Lake Superior.* Norman: University of Oklahoma Press, 1978.

Davidson, Charles Gordon. *The North West Company.* New York: Russell and Russell, 1967.

Day, Gordon M. "Nipissing." In *Northeast*, edited by Bruce Trigger, 787–91. Vol. 15 of *Handbook of North American Indians*, edited by W. C. Sturtevant. Washington DC: Smithsonian Institution, 1978.

Day, Gordon M., and Bruce G. Trigger. "Algonquin." In *Northeast*, edited by Bruce Trigger, 792–97. Vol. 15 of *Handbook of North American Indians*, edited by W. C. Sturtevant. Washington DC: Smithsonian Institution, 1978.

Deloria, Philip J., and Neal Salisbury, eds. *A Companion to American Indian History.* Malden MA: Blackwell, 2002.

Densmore, Christopher. *Red Jacket: Iroquois Diplomat and Orator.* Syracuse NY: Syracuse University Press, 1999.

The Dictionary of Canadian Biography. 14 vols. Toronto: University of Toronto Press, 1966–98.

Dowd, Gregory Evans. "Indians and Overseas Empires, 1650–1776." In *A Companion to American Indian History*, edited by Philip J. Deloria and Neal Salisbury, 46–67. Malden MA: Blackwell, 2002.

———. *A Spirited Resistance: The North American Indian Struggle for Unity.* Baltimore: Johns Hopkins University Press, 1992.

———. "Thinking and Believing: Nativism and Unity in the Ages of Pontiac and Tecumseh." *American Indian Quarterly* 16, no. 3 (Summer 1992): 309–35.

———. *War Under Heaven: Pontiac, the Indian Nations, and the British Empire.* Baltimore: Johns Hopkins University Press. 2002.

Dowd, James Patrick. *Built Like a Bear.* Fairfield WA: Ye Galleon Press, 1979.

Drake, Benjamin. *Life of Tecumseh, and of His Brother the Prophet; With a Historical Sketch of the Shawanoe Indians.* Cincinnati: E. Morgan, 1841. Reprint, New York: Arno Press, 1969.

Drimmer, Frederick, ed. *Captured by the Indians: 15 Firsthand Accounts, 1750–1870.* Mineola NY: Dover, 1985.

Dull, Jonathan R. "Foreign Relations, after 1783." In *The Blackwell Encyclopedia of the American Revolution,* edited by Jack P. Greene and J. R. Pole, 374–78. Malden MA: Blackwell, 1994.

Dunnigan, Brian Leigh. *Frontier Metropolis: Picturing Early Detroit, 1701–1838.* Detroit: Wayne State University Press, 2001.

Edgar, Matilda, ed. *Ten Years of Upper Canada in Peace and War, 1805–1815; Being the Ridout Letters with Annotations.* Toronto: William Briggs, 1890.

Edmunds, R. David. "Main Poc: Potawatomi Wabeno." In *American Indian Prophets: Religious Leaders and Revitalization Movements,* edited by Clifford E. Trafzer, 21–34. Sacramento CA: Sierra Oaks, 1986.

————. *The Potawatomis: The Keepers of the Fire.* Norman: University of Oklahoma Press, 1978.

————. "Redefining Red Patriotism: Five Medals of the Potawatomis." *Red River Valley Historical Review* 5, no. 2 (Spring 1980): 13–24.

————. *The Shawnee Prophet.* Lincoln: University of Nebraska Press, 1983.

————. "Tecumseh, the Shawnee Prophet, and American History: A Reassessment." *Western Historical Quarterly* 14, no. 3, (1983): 261–76.

————. *Tecumseh and the Quest for Indian Leadership.* New York: Harper Collins, 1984.

————. "Tecumseh's Native Allies: Warriors Who Fought for the Crown." In *War on the Great Lakes: Essays Commemorating the 175th Anniversary of the Battle of Lake Erie,* edited by William Jeffrey Welsh and David Curtis Skaggs, 56–67. Kent OH: Kent State University Press, 1991.

————. "The Thin Red Line: Tecumseh, the Prophet, and Shawnee Resistance." *Timeline* 4, no. 6 (December 1987–January 1988): 2–19.

————. "'A Watchful Safeguard to Our Habitations': Black Hoof and the Loyal Shawnees." In *Native Americans and the Early Republic,* edited by Frederick E. Hoxie, Ronald Hoffman, and Peter J. Albert, 162–99. Charlottesville: University Press of Virginia, 1999.

Esarey, Logan, ed. *Messages and Letters of William Henry Harrison.* 2 vols. Indianapolis: Indiana Historical Commission, 1922.

Faragher, John Mack. *Daniel Boone: The Life and Legend of an American Pioneer.* New York: Henry Holt, 1992.

Feest, Johanna, and Christian Feest. "Ottawa." In *Northeast,* edited by Bruce Trigger, 772–86. Vol. 15 of *Handbook of North American Indians,* edited by W. C. Sturtevant. Washington DC: Smithsonian Institution, 1978.

Fenton, William N. *The Great Law and the Longhouse: A Political History of the Iroquois Confederacy.* Norman: University of Oklahoma Press, 1998.

————. "Structure, Continuity, and Change in the Process of Iroquois Treaty Making." In *The History and Culture of Iroquois Diplomacy*, edited by Francis Jennings et al., 3–36. Syracuse NY: Syracuse University Press, 1985.

Fenton, William N., and J. N. B. Hewitt. "The Requickening Address of the Iroquois Condolence Council." *Journal of the Washington Academy of Sciences* 34, no. 3 (March 15, 1944): 65–85.

Finley, Rev. James B. *Autobiography of Reverend James B. Finley, or Pioneer Life in the West*. Ed. W. P. Strickland. Cincinnati: Methodist Book Concern, 1853.

Firth, Edith G. "The Administration of Peter Russell, 1796–1799." *Ontario History* 48, no. 4 (1956): 163–81.

Fixico, Donald L. "The Alliance of the Three Fires in Trade and War." *Michigan Historical Review* 20, no. 2 (Fall 1994): 1–23.

Fryer, Mary Beacock, and Christopher Dracott. *John Graves Simcoe, 1752–1806: A Biography*. Toronto: Dundurn Press, 1998.

Gaff, Alan D. *Bayonets in the Wilderness: Anthony Wayne's Legion in the Old Northwest*. Norman: University of Oklahoma Press, 2004.

Gales, Joseph, ed. *Annals of Congress, 1789–1824*. 42 vols. Washington DC: Gales and Seaton, 1834–56.

Gates, Charles M., ed. *Five Fur Traders in the Northwest*. Intro. by Grace Lee Nute. St. Paul: Minnesota Historical Society, 1965.

Gibson, Arrell M. *The Kickapoos: Lords of the Middle Border*. Norman: University of Oklahoma Press, 1963.

Gilbert, Bil. *God Gave Us This Country: Tekamthi and the First American Civil War*. New York: Atheneum, 1989.

Gilpin, Alec R. *The War of 1812 in the Old Northwest*. East Lansing: Michigan State University Press, 1958.

Gipson, Lawrence Henry, ed. *The Moravian Indian Mission on the White River: Diaries and Letters, May 5, 1799 to November 12, 1806*. Indianapolis: Indiana Historical Bureau, 1938.

Goddard, Ives. "Delaware." In *Northeast*, edited by Bruce Trigger, 213–39. Vol. 15 of *Handbook of North American Indians*, edited by W. C. Sturtevant. Washington DC: Smithsonian Institution, 1978.

Goebel, Dorothy Burne. *William Henry Harrison: A Political Biography*. Indianapolis: Historical Bureau of the Indiana Library and Historical Department, 1926.

Goltz, Herbert Charles Walter, Jr. "Tecumseh, the Prophet and the Rise of the Northwest Indian Confederation." PhD diss., University of Western Ontario, 1973.

Gray, John Morgan. *Lord Selkirk of Red River*. Toronto: MacMillan, 1964.

Graymont, Barbara. *The Iroquois in the American Revolution*. Syracuse NY: Syracuse University Press, 1972.

Greene, Jack P., and J. R. Pole, eds. *The Blackwell Encyclopedia of the American Revolution*. Malden MA: Blackwell, 1994.

Griswold, Bert J., ed. *Fort Wayne, Gateway of the West, 1802–1813; Garrison Orderly*

Books, *Indian Agency Account Book*. Indiana Historical Collections 15. Indianapolis: Historical Bureau of the Indiana Library and Historical Department, 1927. Reprint, New York: AMS Press, 1973.

Hagan, William T. *The Sac and Fox Indians*. Norman: University of Oklahoma Press, 1958.

Harring, Sidney L. "Indian Law, Sovereignty, and State Law." In *A Companion to American Indian History*, edited by Philip J. Deloria and Neal Salisbury, 441–59. Malden MA: Blackwell, 2002.

Harrison, William Henry. *A Discourse on the Aborigines of the Ohio Valley*. Chicago: Fergus, 1838.

Hatley, M. Thomas. "The Three Lives of Keowee: Loss and Recovery in the Eighteenth-Century Cherokee Villages." In *Powhatan's Mantle: Indians in the Colonial Southeast*, edited by Peter H. Wood, Gregory A. Waselkov, and M. Thomas Hatley, 223–48. Lincoln: University of Nebraska Press, 1989.

Heckewelder, John. *History, Manners, and Customs of the Indians Who once Inhabited Pennsylvania and the Neighboring States*. Philadelphia: Pennsylvania Historical Society, 1876.

———. *A Narrative of the Mission of the United Brethren among the Delaware and Mohegan Indians, From Its Commencement in the Year 1740, to the Close of the Year 1808*. Philadelphia: McCarty and Davis, 1820.

Helderman, Leonard. "Danger on the Wabash, Vincennes Letters of 1786–87." *Indiana Magazine of History* 34, no. 4 (December 1938): 455–67.

Henry, Alexander. *Travels and Adventures in Canada and the Indian Territories, between the Years 1760 and 1776*. Edited and with a foreword by James Bain. New York: I. Riley, 1809. Reprint, New York: Burt Franklin, 1969.

Herrington, M. Eleanor. "Captain John Deserontyou and the Mohawk Settlement at Deseronto." *Queen's Quarterly* 29, no. 2 (October 1921): 165–80.

Hickerson, Harold. *The Chippewa and Their Neighbors: A Study in Ethnohistory*. Rev. ed. Prospect Heights IL: Waveland Press, 1987.

Hickey, Donald R. *The War of 1812: A Forgotten Conflict*. Urbana: University of Illinois Press, 1989.

Hopkins, Gerard T. *A Mission to the Indians from the Indian Committee of Baltimore Yearly Meeting, to Fort Wayne, in 1804*. Philadelphia: T. Ellwood Zell, 1862.

Horsman, Reginald. "The British Indian Department and the Abortive Treaty of Lower Sandusky, 1793." *Ohio Historical Quarterly* 70, no. 3 (July 1961): 189–213.

———. "The British Indian Department and the Resistance to General Anthony Wayne, 1793–1795." *Mississippi Valley Historical Review* 49, no. 2 (1962): 269–90.

———. "British Indian Policy in the Northwest, 1807–1812." *Mississippi Valley Historical Review* 45, no. 1 (June 1958): 51–66.

———. *Expansion and American Indian Policy, 1783–1812*. East Lansing: Michigan State University Press, 1967.

―――. "The Indian Policy of an 'Empire for Liberty.'" In *Native Americans and the Early Republic*, edited by Frederick E. Hoxie, Ronald Hoffman, and Peter J. Albert, 37–61. Charlottesville: University Press of Virginia, 1999.

―――. *Matthew Elliott, British Indian Agent*. Detroit: Wayne State University Press, 1964.

―――. *The War of 1812*. New York: Alfred A. Knopf, 1969.

―――. "William Henry Harrison: Virginia Gentleman in the Old Northwest." *Indiana Magazine of History* 96 (June 2000): 125–49.

Howard, James H. *Shawnee!: The Ceremonialism of a Native American Tribe and Its Cultural Background*. Athens: Ohio University Press, 1981.

Hoxie, Frederick E., Ronald Hoffman, and Peter J. Albert, eds. *Native Americans and the Early Republic*. Charlottesville: University Press of Virginia, 1999.

Hulbert, Archer Butler, and William N. Schwarze, eds. *David Zeisberger's History of the North American Indians*. Vol. 19. Columbus: Ohio Archaeological and Historical Society, 1910.

Hutton, Paul. "William Wells: Frontier Scout and Indian Agent." *Indiana Magazine of History* 74, no. 3 (September 1978): 183–222.

Innis, Harold A. *The Fur Trade in Canada*. New Haven ct: Yale University Press, 1930.

Innis, Mary Quayle, ed. *Mrs. Simcoe's Diary*. Toronto and New York: MacMillan of Canada and St. Martin's Press, 1965.

Jackson, Donald E., ed. *Black Hawk: An Autobiography*. Urbana: University of Illinois Press, 1955.

―――, ed. *The Journals of Zebulon Montgomery Pike, with Letters and Related Documents*. 2 vols. Norman: University of Oklahoma Press, 1966.

Jacobs, Wilbur R. *Dispossessing the American Indian: Indians and Whites on the Colonial Frontier*. Norman: University of Oklahoma Press, 1972.

―――. *Wilderness Politics and Indian Gifts: The Northern Colonial Frontier, 1748–1763*. Lincoln: University of Nebraska Press, 1950.

James, William. *A Full and Correct Account of the Military Occurrences of the Late War Between Great Britain and the United States of America*. 2 vols. London: printed for the author, 1818.

Jennings, Francis. *The Ambiguous Iroquois Empire: The Covenant Chain Confederation of Indian Tribes with English Colonies from Its Beginnings to the Lancaster Treaty of 1744*. New York: W. W. Norton, 1984.

―――. "The Constitutional Evolution of the Covenant Chain." *Proceedings of the American Philosophical Society* 115, no. 2 (April 1971): 88–96.

―――. "Iroquois Alliances in American History." In *The History and Culture of Iroquois Diplomacy*, edited by Francis Jennings et al., 37–65. Syracuse ny: Syracuse University Press, 1985.

Jennings, Francis, William N. Fenton, Mary A. Druke, and David R. Miller, eds. *The*

History and Culture of Iroquois Diplomacy. Syracuse NY: Syracuse University Press, 1985.

Johnston, Basil. *Ojibway Heritage*. New York: Columbia University Press, 1976.

Johnston, Charles M. "Joseph Brant, the Grand River Lands and the Northwest Crisis." *Ontario History* 55, no. 4 (December 1963): 267–82.

——, ed. *The Valley of the Six Nations: A Collection of Documents on the Indian Lands of the Grand River*. Toronto: Champlain Society, for the Government of Ontario, University of Toronto Press, 1964.

——. "William Claus and John Norton: A Struggle for Power in Old Ontario." *Ontario History* 57, no. 2 (1965): 101–8.

Jones, Peter. *History of the Ojebway Indians*. London: A. W. Bennett, 1861.

Jones, Wilbur Devereaux, ed. "A British View of the War of 1812 and the Peace Negotiations." *Mississippi Valley Historical Review* 45 (1958–59): 481–87.

Kappler, Charles J., ed. *Indian Affairs: Laws and Treaties*. 2 vols. Washington DC: Government Printing Office, 1904.

Keesing, Felix. *The Menomini Indians of Wisconsin*. Memoirs of the American Philosophical Society 10. Philadelphia: American Philosophical Society, 1939. Reprint, New York: Johnson Reprint, 1971.

Kellogg, Louise Phelps. *The British Regime in Wisconsin and the Northwest*. Madison: State Historical Society of Wisconsin, 1935. Reprint, New York: De Capo Press, 1971.

Kelsay, Isabel Thompson. *Joseph Brant, 1743–1807: Man of Two Worlds*. Syracuse NY: Syracuse University Press, 1984.

Klinck, Carl F. "New Light on John Norton." *Transactions of the Royal Society of Canada* 4, no. 4 (June 1966): 167–77.

——, ed. *Tecumseh: Fact and Fiction in Early Records*. Englewood Cliffs NJ: Prentice-Hall, 1961.

Klinck, Carl F., and James J. Talman, eds. *The Journal of Major John Norton, 1816*. Toronto: Champlain Society, 1970.

Landes, Ruth. *Ojibwa Religion and the Midewiwin*. Madison: University of Wisconsin Press, 1968.

Landon, Fred. *Western Ontario and the American Frontier*. Toronto and New Haven CT: Ryerson Press and Yale University Press, 1941. Reprint, Toronto: McClelland and Stewart, 1967.

Langley, Harold D. "The Quest for Peace." In *War on the Great Lakes: Essays Commemorating the 175th Anniversary of the Battle of Lake Erie*, edited by William Jeffrey Welsh and David Curtis Skaggs, 68–77. Kent OH: Kent State University Press, 1991.

Lossing, Benson J. *The Pictorial Field-Book of the War of 1812*. New York: Harper and Brothers, 1869.

Lydekker, John Wolfe. *The Faithful Mohawks*. New York and Cambridge: MacMillan and Cambridge University Press, 1938.

MacLean, J. P. "Shaker Mission to the Shawnee Indians." *Ohio Archaeological and Historical Society Publications* 2 (June 1903): 215–29.

Malcomson, Robert. *Warships of the Great Lakes, 1754–1834.* Annapolis MD: Naval Institute Press, 2001.

Marquis, T. G., ed. *Builders of Canada from Cartier to Laurier.* Toronto: John C. Winston, 1903.

Martin, Joel. *Sacred Revolt: The Muskogees' Struggle for a New World.* Boston: Beacon Press, 1991.

Mason, Philip P., ed. *After Tippecanoe: Some Aspects of the War of 1812.* East Lansing and Toronto: Michigan State University Press and Ryerson Press, 1963.

Matson, Nehemiah. *Memories of Shaubena.* 2nd ed. Chicago: Donnelley, Gassette, and Loyd, Printers, 1880.

McAfee, Robert Breckinridge. *History of the Late War in the Western Country.* Lexington KY: Worsley and Smith, 1816. Reprint, Ann Arbor MI: University Microfilms, 1966.

McCollough, Alameda, ed. *Battle of Tippecanoe: Conflict of Cultures.* Lafayette IN: Tippecanoe County Historical Association, 1973.

McCord, Shirley S., ed. *Travel Accounts of Indiana, 1679–1961.* Indianapolis: Indiana Historical Bureau, 1970.

McCullough, A. B. *Money and Exchange in Canada to 1900.* Toronto and Charlottetown: Dundurn Press and Parks Canada, 1984.

McLaughlin, Andrew C. *Lewis Cass.* Boston: Houghton Mifflin, 1899. Reprint, New York: Chelsea House, 1980.

McLoughlin, William G. *Cherokee Renascence in the New Republic.* Princeton NJ: Princeton University Press, 1986.

Michigan Pioneer and Historical Society. *Historical Collections of the Michigan Pioneer and Historical Society.* 40 vols. Lansing MI: Darius D. Thorp, State Printer and Binder, 1874–1929.

Miller, Jay. "The 1806 Purge among the Indiana Delaware." *Ethnohistory* 41, no. 2 (Spring 1994): 245–66.

Montgomery, Malcolm. "The Legal Status of the Six Nations in Canada." *Ontario History* 55, no. 2 (June 1963): 93–105.

Murray, J. McE. "John Norton." *Ontario Historical Society Papers and Records* 37 (1945): 7–16.

Nelson, Larry L., ed. *A History of Jonathan Alder: His Captivity and Life with the Indians.* Akron OH: University of Akron Press, 2002.

———. *A Man of Distinction among Them: Alexander McKee and British-Indian Affairs along the Ohio Country Frontier, 1754–1799.* Kent OH: Kent State University Press, 1999.

———. *Men of Patriotism, Courage, and Enterprise!: Fort Meigs in the War of 1812.* Canton OH: Daring Books, 1985.

Nelson, Paul David. *Anthony Wayne: Soldier of the Early Republic.* Bloomington: Indiana University Press, 1985.

———. *General Sir Guy Carleton, Lord Dorchester: Soldier-Statesman of Early British Canada.* Madison NJ and London: Fairleigh Dickinson University Press and Associated University Presses, 2000.

Nester, William R. *The Frontier War for American Independence.* Mechanicsburg PA: Stackpole Books, 2004.

Noon, John A. *Law and Government of the Grand River Iroquois.* New York: Viking Fund, 1949.

Ourada, Patricia. *The Menominee Indians: A History.* Norman: University of Oklahoma Press, 1979.

Owsley, Frank L., Jr. "Prophet of War: Josiah Francis and the Creek War." *American Indian Quarterly* 9, no. 3 (Summer 1985): 273–93.

Parker, Arthur C. *Parker on the Iroquois: Book Two.* Edited and with intro. by William N. Fenton. Syracuse NY: Syracuse University Press, 1968.

Perdue, Theda, and Michael D. Green, eds. *Cherokee Removal: A Brief History with Documents.* Boston: Bedford Books of St. Martin's Press, 1995.

Perkins, Bradford, ed. *The Causes of the War of 1812: National Honor or National Interest?* New York: Holt, Rhinehart, and Winston, 1963.

———. *Prologue to War: England and the United States, 1805–1812.* Berkeley: University of California Press, 1961.

Peterson, Jacqueline. "Many Roads to Red River: Métis Genesis in the Great Lakes Region, 1680–1815." In *The New Peoples: Being and Becoming Métis in North America,* edited by Jacqueline Peterson and Jennifer S. H. Brown, 37–71. Lincoln: University of Nebraska Press, 1985.

Peterson, Jacqueline, and Jennifer S. H. Brown, eds. *The New Peoples: Being and Becoming Métis in North America.* Lincoln: University of Nebraska Press, 1985.

Poinsatte, Charles. *Outpost in the Wilderness: Fort Wayne, 1706–1828.* Fort Wayne IN: Allen County Historical Society, 1976.

Potter, William L. "Redcoats on the Frontier: The King's Regiment in the Revolutionary War." In *Selected Papers from the First and Second George Rogers Clark Trans-Appalachian Frontier History Conferences,* edited by Robert J. Holden, 41–60. Vincennes IN: Vincennes University Press, 1985.

Prucha, Francis Paul. *American Indian Policy in the Formative Years: The Indian Trade and Intercourse Acts, 1790–1834.* Cambridge MA: Harvard University Press, 1962.

———. *American Indian Treaties: The History of a Political Anomaly.* Berkeley: University of California Press, 1994.

———. *The Great Father: The United States Government and the American Indians.* Abr. ed. Lincoln: University of Nebraska Press, 1984, 1986.

———. *Lewis Cass and American Indian Policy.* Detroit: Wayne State University Press, 1967.

Quaife, Milo M., ed. *The Indian Captivity of O. M. Spencer*. New York: Citadel Press, 1968.

———, ed. *The John Askin Papers*. 2 vols. Detroit: Detroit Library Commission, 1928.

———, ed. "A Narrative of Life on the Old Frontier; Henry Hay's Journal from Detroit to the Miami River." In *Proceedings of the Wisconsin Historical Society* (1915): 208–61.

———, ed. *War on the Detroit: The Chronicles of Thomas Vercheres de Boucherville and the Capitulation by an Ohio Volunteer*. Chicago: Lakeside Press, R. R. Donnelley and Sons, 1940.

Quimby, George I. *Indian Life in the Upper Great Lakes, 11,000 B.C. to A.D. 1800*. Chicago: University of Chicago Press, 1960.

Radin, Paul. *The Winnebago Tribe*. Thirty-seventh Annual Report of the Bureau of American Ethnology. Washington DC: Smithsonian Institution, 1923. Reprint, Lincoln: University of Nebraska Press, 1970.

Rafert, Stewart. *The Miami Indians of Indiana: A Persistent People, 1654–1994*. Indianapolis: Indiana Historical Society, 1996.

Reaman, G. Elmore. *The Trail of the Iroquois Indians: How the Iroquois Saved Canada for the British Empire*. New York: Barnes and Noble, 1967.

Rich, E. E. *History of the Hudson Bay Company*. 2 vols. London: Hudson's Bay Record Society, 1958–59.

Ritcheson, Charles R. *Aftermath of Revolution: British Policy Toward the United States, 1783–1795*. Dallas: Southern Methodist University Press, 1969. Reprint, New York: W. W. Norton, 1971.

Ritzenthaler, Robert E. "Southwestern Chippewa." In *Northeast*, edited by Bruce Trigger, 743–59. Vol. 15 of *Handbook of North American Indians*, edited by W. C. Sturtevant. Washington DC: Smithsonian Institution, 1978.

Ritzenthaler, Robert, and Pat Ritzenthaler. *The Woodland Indians of the Western Great Lakes*. Milwaukee: Milwaukee Museum, 1983.

Robertson, Nellie Armstrong, and Dorothy Riker, eds. *The John Tipton Papers*. Intro. by Paul Wallace Gates. 3 vols. Indianapolis: Indiana Historical Bureau, 1942.

Rogers, E. S. "Southeastern Ojibwa." In *Northeast*, edited by Bruce Trigger, 760–71. Vol. 15 of *Handbook of North American Indians*, edited by W. C. Sturtevant. Washington DC: Smithsonian Institution, 1978.

Sabathy-Judd, Linda, ed. *Moravians in Upper Canada: The Diary of the Indian Mission of Fairfield on the Thames, 1792–1813*. Toronto: Champlain Society, 1999.

Schmalz, Peter S. *The Ojibwa of Southern Ontario*. Toronto: University of Toronto Press, 1991.

Schoolcraft, Henry Rowe. *Information Respecting the History, Condition and Prospects of the Indian Tribes of the United States*. 6 vols. Philadelphia: J. Lippincott, 1851–57.

Sheppard, George. *Plunder, Profit, and Paroles: A Social History of the War of 1812 in Upper Canada*. Montreal: McGill-Queen's University Press, 1994.

Sims, Catherine. "Algonkian-British Relations in the Great Lakes Region: Gathering to Give and Receive Presents, 1815–1843." PhD diss., University of Western Ontario, 1992.

Smith, Donald B. "Who Are the Mississauga?" *Ontario History* 47, no. 4 (December 1975): 211–22.

Smith, Dwight L. "A North American Neutral Indian Zone: Persistence of a British Idea." *Northwest Ohio Quarterly* 61, nos. 2–4 (Autumn 1989): 46–63.

Snow, Dean R. *The Iroquois*. Malden MA: Blackwell, 1994.

Snyder, Charles M., ed. *Red and White on the New York Frontier: A Struggle for Survival; Insights from the Papers of Erastus Granger, Indian Agent, 1807–1819*. Harrison NY: Harbor Hills Books, 1978.

Stacey, C. P. "Naval Power on the Lakes, 1812–1814." In *After Tippecanoe: Some Aspects of the War of 1812*, edited by Philip P. Mason, 49–59. East Lansing and Toronto: Michigan State University Press and Ryerson Press, 1963.

Stanley, G. F. G. "The Significance of the Six Nations Participation in the War of 1812." *Ontario History* 55, no. 4 (December 1975): 215–31.

State Historical Society of Wisconsin. *Collections of the State Historical Society of Wisconsin*. 31 vols. Madison, 1854–1931.

St-Denis, Guy. *Tecumseh's Bones*. Montreal: McGill-Queen's University Press, 2005.

Steele, Ian K. *Warpaths: Invasions of North America*. Oxford: Oxford University Press, 1994.

Stevens, Wayne E. "Fur Trading Companies of the Northwest." *Proceedings of the Mississippi Valley Historical Association* 9 (October 1918): 283–91.

———. *The Northwest Fur Trade, 1763–1800*. Urbana: University of Illinois Press, 1928.

Stone, Richard G. *A Brittle Sword: The Kentucky Militia, 1776–1912*. Lexington: University Press of Kentucky, 1977.

Stone, William L. *Life of Joseph Brant—Thayendanegea*. 2 vols. New York: Alexander V. Blake, 1838. Reprint, Harrison NY: Harbor Hill Books, 1969.

Sugden, John. *Blue Jacket: Warrior of the Shawnees*. Lincoln: University of Nebraska Press, 2000.

———. *Nelson: A Dream of Glory, 1758–1797*. New York: Henry Holt, 2004.

———. *Tecumseh: A Life*. New York: Henry Holt, 1997.

———. *Tecumseh's Last Stand*. Norman: University of Oklahoma Press, 1985.

Sullivan, James, Alexander C. Flick, and Milton W. Hamilton, eds. *The Papers of Sir William Johnson*. 14 vols. Albany: New York Historical Society, 1921–1965.

Surtees, Robert J. *Indian Land Surrenders in Ontario, 1763–1867*. Ottawa: Department of Indian Affairs and Northern Development, Canada, 1984.

———. "The Iroquois in Canada." In *The History and Culture of Iroquois Diplomacy*, edited by Francis Jennings et al., 67–83. Syracuse NY: Syracuse University Press, 1985.

Sword, Wiley. *President Washington's Indian War: The Struggle for the Old Northwest, 1790–1795.* Norman: University of Oklahoma Press, 1985.

Tanner, Helen Hornbeck, ed. *Atlas of Great Lakes Indian History.* Norman: University of Oklahoma Press, 1987.

———. "Coocoochee: Mohawk Medicine Woman." *American Indian Culture and Research Journal* 3, no. 3 (1979): 23–41.

———. "The Glaize in 1792: A Composite Indian Community." *Ethnohistory* 25, no. 1 (Winter 1978): 15–39.

Tanner, Helen Hornbeck, and Erminie Wheeler-Voegelin. *Indians of Ohio and Indiana Prior to 1795: The Greenville Treaty, 1795 and Ethnohistory of Indian Use and Occupancy of Ohio and Indiana Prior to 1795.* 2 vols. New York: Garland, 1974.

Tanner, John. *The Falcon: A Narrative of the Captivity and Adventures of John Tanner during Thirty Years Residence among the Indians in the Interior of North America.* 1830. Intro. by Louise Erdrich. New York: Penguin Books, 1994.

Taylor, Alan. *The Divided Ground: Indians, Settlers, and the Northern Borderland of the American Revolution.* New York: Alfred A. Knopf, 2006.

———. *William Cooper's Town: Power and Persuasion on the Frontier of the Early American Republic.* New York: Alfred A. Knopf, 1995.

Thomas, Earle. *Sir John Johnson, Loyalist Baronet.* Toronto: Dundurn Press, 1986.

Thornbrough, Gayle, ed. *Letter Book of the Indian Agency at Fort Wayne, 1809–1815.* Indianapolis: Indiana Historical Society, 1961.

———, ed. *Outpost on the Wabash, 1787–1791.* Indianapolis: Indiana Historical Society, 1957.

Tohill, Louis Arthur. "Robert Dickson, British Fur Trader on the Upper Mississippi." *North Dakota Historical Quarterly* 3, no. 1 (October 1928): 5–49; 3, no. 2 (January 1929): 83–128; 3, no. 3 (April 1929): 182–203.

Tooker, Elisabeth. "The League of the Iroquois: Its History, Politics, and Ritual." In *Northeast,* edited by Bruce Trigger, 418–41. Vol. 15 of *Handbook of North American Indians,* edited by W. C. Sturtevant. Washington DC: Smithsonian Institution, 1978.

———. "Wyandot." In *Northeast,* edited by Bruce Trigger, 398–406. Vol. 15 of *Handbook of North American Indians,* edited by W. C. Sturtevant. Washington DC: Smithsonian Institution, 1978.

Trafzer, Clifford, ed. *American Indian Prophets: Religious Leaders and Revitalization Movements.* Sacramento CA: Sierra Oaks, 1986.

Trigger, Bruce G., ed. *Northeast.* Vol. 15, *Handbook of North American Indians,* edited by W. C. Sturtevant. Washington DC: Smithsonian Institution, 1978.

Trowbridge, C. C. *Meearmeear Traditions.* Occasional Contributions from the Museum of Anthropology of the University of Michigan 7. Ann Arbor: University of Michigan Press, 1938.

———. *Shawnese Traditions.* Occasional Contributions from the Museum of Anthropology of the University of Michigan 9. Ann Arbor: University of Michigan Press, 1939.

Turner, Wesley B. *British Generals in the War of 1812: High Command in the Canadas.* Montreal: McGill-Queen's University Press, 1999.

——. *The War of 1812: The War That Both Sides Won.* Toronto: Dundurn Press, 1990.

Van Kirk, Sylvia. *"Many Tender Ties": Women in Fur-Trade Society in Western Canada, 1670–1870.* Winnipeg: Watson and Dwyer, 1981.

Vecsey, Christopher. *Traditional Ojibwa Religion and Its Historical Changes.* Philadelphia: American Philosophical Society, 1983.

Vincent, Elizabeth. *Fort St. Joseph: A History.* Parks Canada Manuscript Report Series 335. Ottawa: Department of Environment Canada, 1978.

Walker, Charles I. "The Northwest during the Revolution." *Historical Collections of the Michigan Pioneer and Historical Society* 3 (1881): 12–36.

Wallace, Anthony F. C. *The Death and Rebirth of the Seneca.* New York: Alfred A. Knopf, 1970.

——. *Jefferson and the Indians: The Tragic Fate of the First Americans.* Cambridge MA: Belknap Press of Harvard University Press, 1999.

Wallace, Paul A. W., ed. *Thirty Thousand Miles with John Heckewelder.* Pittsburgh: University of Pittsburgh Press, 1958.

Wallace, W. Stewart, ed. *Documents Relating to the North West Company.* Toronto: Champlain Society, 1934.

Waller, George M. *The American Revolution in the West.* Chicago: Nelson-Hall, 1976.

Warren, William W. *History of the Ojibway People.* Foreword by W. Roger Buffaloehead. St. Paul: Minnesota Historical Society Press, 1984.

Weaver, Sally M. "Six Nations of the Grand River, Ontario." In *Northeast*, edited by Bruce Trigger, 525–36. Vol. 15 of *Handbook of North American Indians*, edited by W. C. Sturtevant. Washington DC: Smithsonian Institution, 1978.

Weld, Isaac, Jr. *Travels through the States of North America and the Provinces of Upper and Lower Canada, during the Years 1795, 1796, and 1797.* 2 vols. 4th ed. London: John Stockdale, 1807. Reprint, New York: Augustus M. Kelley, 1970.

Welsh, William Jeffrey, and David Curtis Skaggs, eds. *War on the Great Lakes: Essays Commemorating the 175th Anniversary of the Battle of Lake Erie.* Kent OH: Kent State University Press, 1991.

Wharton, Francis, ed. *The Revolutionary Diplomatic Correspondence of the United States.* 6 vols. Washington DC: Government Printing Office, 1889.

Wheeler-Voegelin, Erminie. *Mortuary Customs of the Shawnee and Other Eastern Tribes.* Prehistory Research Series 2, no. 4. Indianapolis: Indiana Historical Society, 1944.

Wheeler-Voegelin, Erminie, and Helen Hornbeck Tanner. *Indians of Northern Ohio and Southeastern Michigan.* New York: Garland, 1974.

White, Patrick C. T., ed. *Lord Selkirk's Diary, 1803–1804.* Toronto: Champlain Society, 1958.

White, Richard. *The Middle Ground: Indians, Empires, and Republics in the Great Lakes Region, 1650–1815.* Cambridge: Cambridge University Press, 1991.

Wilson, Frazer E. "The Treaty of Greenville." *Ohio Archaeological and Historical Quarterly* 12 (1903): 128–59.

Winsor, Justin, ed. *A Narrative and Critical History of America.* 8 vols. Boston: Houghton, Mifflin, 1884.

Wood, Peter H., Gregory A. Waselkov, and M. Thomas Hatley, eds. *Powhatan's Mantle: Indians in the Colonial Southeast.* Lincoln: University of Nebraska Press, 1989.

Wood, William, ed. *Select British Documents of the Canadian War of 1812.* 3 vols. Toronto: Champlain Society, 1920–1928.

Woodcock, George. *The Hudson's Bay Company: From Trading Post to Emporium, a Tricentennial History of Canada's Pioneering Fur Traders.* Toronto: Crowell-Collier Press, 1970.

Wright, J. Leitch, Jr. *Britain and the American Frontier, 1783–1815.* Athens: University of Georgia Press, 1975.

Index

Page numbers in italics refer to illustrations.

acculturation: American attempts at, 245–46; American policy of, 206; and British government, 251; degree of, 197; of Natives, 6, 29, 169, 260; prevention of, by Indian Department, 170

Adams, John Quincy, 265, 266

agriculture, 168–69, 206

Akwesasne (St. Regis), 124, 300n2

alcohol, 98

alcoholism, 29, 206

Alder, Jonathan, 56, 57, 279n53, 320n33

Algonquin Indians, 300n2

Allen, Robert S.: *His Majesty's Indian Allies*, 7

alliances: between France and the United States, 87; between sovereign powers, 247; with Natives, 219; in the West, 199–205

Amable (Ottawa), 106, 119, 120, 121

American expansion, 209, 266; effect of, on Natives, 186, 225, 268; and Indian buffer, 39, 266; and military posts, 281n99; Native resistance to, 197, 202, 245–46, 329n163; and Upper

Canada, 281n95; as violation of Treaty of Fort Stanwix, 220

American Fur Company, 227

American Revolution, 1, 254

Amherst, Jeffrey, 4

Amherstburg, 59, 199, 215, 268, 269; capture of, 337n82; councils at, 86, 87, 186, 203, 336n63; diminished rations from, 66; diplomacy at, 59–89; Indian agency at, 6, 75, 200; Indian Department at, 237; Little King at, 239; Native visits to, 78, 86, 203, 219, 314n98; regulations at, 104, 105; Tecumseh at, 330n12; William Claus at, 216

Anderson, Thomas G. "Tige," 256, 257, 262, 333n36; as Indian agent, 262, 269–70; journal of, 334n42; as liaison to Indians, 255; retirement of, 271

Anishnabeg Indians, 94

annuity payments, 60, 88, 102, 105, 141, 200, 217, 317n2, 318n6; control of, 323n71; inadequacy of, 206; lack of, 63, 226; Native reliance on, 92, supplementary, 139; from Treaty of Greenville, 325n107. *See also* gifts

anti-American confederacy, 208

anti-American sentiment, 203, 204

of, 140; and use of "Chain of
Friendship," 330n12; as war chief, 164
Britain, 1–2, 252, 273n2; allies of, 257;
attitudes of, 70–71; betrayals by, 56,
261; distribution of medals by, 115;
and gift-giving, 61–75; influence
of, 19; and Iroquois interests, 128,
260; logistical difficulties of, 257,
332n25; maritime policy of, 5, 184,
268; Native dependence on, 38, 82;
and Native discontent, 246; naval
supremacy of, 158, 308n114; and
policy making, 8. *See also* British-
Indian relations
British and Foreign Bible Society, 163,
172
British-Indian relations, 5, 12, 22,
38, 119, 122, 187, 243, 249, 251–52;
American views of, 244–45; delicacy
of, 85; and military, 113–14, 195;
motives for, 244; in the North, 92–
105, 248–49; postwar, 14–16; regional
differences in, 241; turning point in,
207; and Upper Canada, 73, 124, 237
British Right Division, 253
Brock, Isaac, 187–89, 190; death of, 193;
as governor of Upper Canada, 250;
and John Norton, 191; and Robert
Dickson, 229; and Tecumseh, 214;
views of, of Indians, 191–92
Brown, Adam, 19, 23, 200–201, 223,
277n28
Brownstown, 28, 61, 87, 197, 224, 255;
coalition formed at, 23, 112, 200–201;
council at, 18, 19, 215, 222, 223, 247,
277n25, 324n93; neutrality of, 201
Buchanan, James, 245
Buckongahelas (Delaware), 41, 48, 77;
authority of, 206; at the Glaize, 34;
and relations with Americans, 200;
as war leader, 19, 38

Buffalo (town), 252
Buffalo Creek, 125, 134, 175, 330n12
Buffaloe (Shawnee), 66
Bulger, Andrew, 262, *263*; and Chain of
Friendship, 267–68; at Fort Douglas,
269–70
Butler, John, 282n122
Butler's Rangers, 254
Byfield, Shadrach, 333n29

Cadotte, Michael, 235
Caldwell, Billy, 254, 333n29
Caldwell, Captain William, 333n29
Caldwell, Colonel William, 254,
291n93, 333n29; marriage of, 22,
254–55
Caldwell, John, *20*
Calloway, Colin, 274n3, 301n4; *Crown
and Calumet*, 7
Camden, Earl of, 163, 176, 183
Campbell, William, 56, 237–38, 239,
240, 333n30
Canning, George, 163
Canterbury, archbishop of, 44
Cape Girardeau, 285n160
Cape St. Vincent, 158, 308n114
Captain Johnny (Shawnee): and
British, 61, 64; at Foot of the Rapids
council, 50–51; at the Glaize, 34; as
informant to Isaac Weld, 62; and
Muskingum compromise, 48; as
war leader, 23, 27, 38; and William
Mayne, 66, 67
Captain Pipe (Delaware), 24, 25,
278n38
Carleton, Guy. *See* Dorchester, Lord
Carter, Harvey Lewis, 279n70
Cass, Lewis, 24, 269, 330n5, 330n8;
assessments of, 249; and Cherokees,
251; criticism of British by, 244–45,
247, 248, 250

Cruikshank, E. A., 277n28
Curot, Michael, 120, 299n97

Dakota-Ojibwa wars, 250
Dakota Sioux Indians, 93, 117, 118,
    205; and British, 91, 122, 249, 258;
    and defeat of Americans, 256;
    dissatisfaction of, 262; loyalty of, to
    traders, 254; and Ojibwas, 95, 109,
    117–18, 249; and Robert Dickson, 255;
    sovereignty of, 225
Day, James, 290n72
Dearborn, Henry, 318n6, 319n27
Dease, John, 103, 118, 119, 183
Delaware Indians, 23, 81; and
    Americans, 77, 247, 276n20;
    and annuities, 200; and British,
    197, 290n72; and Brownstown
    confederacy, 18; and C. C.
    Trowbridge, 24; as Christians,
    288n51; clan and kinship system of,
    24–25; and councils, 14, 112; defeat
    of, at Fallen Timbers, 101; at the
    Glaize, 34; at Grand River, 125; and
    land cessions, 210; and Maumee
    confederacy, 53; and Miamis, 26,
    86; missions among, 165; and
    Moravians, 315n111; as refugee tribes,
    123; religious beliefs of, 25; and
    succession of chiefs, 24; and William
    Johnson, 3; and witches, 207
de Puisaye, Joseph, 153, 154
Deserontyon, John, 125, 134, 300n3
Detroit. See Fort Detroit
Detroit River, 200
Dickson, Robert, 118, 229, 258, 261,
    333n34, 333n36; arrival of, at Fort
    Detroit, 257; at Big Stone Lake,
    333n35; and Chain of Friendship,
    267–68; as Indian agent, 254; and
    Indians, 256, 269–70; influence of,
    255

Discourse on the Aborigines of the Ohio
    Valley (Harrison), 244
disease, 29, 206, 235, 240
The Divided Ground (Taylor), 7–8
Dorchester, Lord, 21, 34, 312n70; and
    British-Indian relations, 17–18, 22,
    28–29, 30, 58, 64, 102; and Chenail
    Ecarte, 63; and gift-giving, 71; and
    Grand River, 128; instructions of, 68,
    101, 108, 286n20; and Joseph Brant,
    130–31; and land, 126–27; speech by,
    52, 283n132; and trade, 103
Douglas, Thomas, 171, 292n4
Dowd, Gregory, 212, 329n161, 329n163
Doyle, William, 106, 107, 114, 237; and
    commissions to chiefs, 111, 113
Dragging Canoe (Chickamauga), 19
Drummond, Gordon, 337n82
Drummond, Peter, 102, 110, 117, 118, 121,
    122; and council at Fort St. Joseph,
    120, 300n99
Drummond Island, 262, 270
Dudley's Defeat, 252, 253, 258, 334n47
Duggan, Thomas, 100, 103, 104,
    107; drinking by, 114, 295n48; and
    Ottawas, 121
Dunham, J., 231, 238, 317n2
Dunn, William, 78–79

Earl Bathurst. See Bathurst, Henry
Edmunds, R. David, 320n33, 329n161
Eel River nations, 210, 321n42
Eethsaguam (Ottawa), 109
Egushwa (Ottawa), 47–48
Elliott, Matthew, 37, 54, 55, 104, 222, 253,
    295, 335n50; dismissal of, 68–69, 76,
    78, 83, 113, 200; and embezzlement of
    goods, 183; and French-led invasion,
    83; friendship of, with Indians,
    290n72; as Indian agent, 111–12; and
    Indian Department, 60; lifestyle

intertribal factionalism, 60
intertribal relations, 6, 260
Iowa River, 255
Ironside, George, 27, 28, 36–37, 291n93;
    and Brownstown council, 201;
    and Indian Department, 60, 66;
    marriage of, 22, 255
Iroquois Indians, 15, 165, 190, 259. *See
    also* Six Nations
Iroquois League, 3, 15–16, 276n15; and
    Americans, 43; and John Norton,
    163; leadership of, 17; at Lower
    Sandusky council, 14

Jackson, Andrew, 204, 245, 251, 268
Jackson, Joseph, 82–83, 289n54, 290n72
Jay, John, 55, 56
Jay's Treaty, 55, 56, 57, 58, 104, 284n154;
    as British betrayal, 69; and
    evacuation of posts, 247–48; terms
    of, 59, 91, 108; third article of, 97
Jefferson, Thomas, 184, 204, 321n40
Jennings, Francis, 276n16
Johnson, John, 13, 103, 275n6, 279n59,
    312n58, 325n103; and Amable, 120;
    and British-Indian relations, 75,
    81–82, 119, 121; as grandfather of
    William Claus, 173; and Iroquois, 16,
    17; and Joseph Brant, 145–46, 159, 162;
    and land negotiations, 15, 153–55; and
    Lord Dorchester, 126; and Samuel
    Kirkland, 147
Johnson, John Smoke, 270
Johnson, Richard Mentor, 334n47
Johnson, William, 13; and British-
    Indian relations, 4, 17, 19, 97;
    and Joseph Brant, 43, 125,
    297n71; marriage of, 254–55; as
    superintendent of British-Indian
    affairs, 3, 16, 40, 247
Johnson Hall, 255, 275n6

Jones, Peter, 99–100
Jouett, Charles, 231, 233

Kanesatake (Oka), 124, 300n2
Karamanke (Winnebago), 336n64
Keekwitamigishcam (Ojibwa), 111
Keeminichaugan (Ottawa), 116, 117, 121
Kekionga, 60, 81, 255, 277n33; and
    British trade relations, 30; burning
    of, 32; intertribal villages at, 247; as
    principal Miami village, 23; refugees
    from, 34, 35; and Shawnees, 27
Kellogg, Louise Phelps, 268
Kelsay, Isabel Thompson, 307n104
Kendrick, Clark, 167, 310n31
Kenton, Simon, 277n22, 291n93
Kickapoo Indians: and American
    expansion, 197, 203; and defeat of
    Americans, 256; support of, for
    British, 205, 257; support of, for
    revitalization, 241; and William
    Johnson, 3
Kinzie, John, 27
Kirkland, Samuel, 7, 146–47, 167
Kishpoko Shawnee Indians, 218,
    323nn70–71
Kitche Manitou. *See* Great Spirit
Knox, Henry, 44, 279n72

La Baye (Green Bay), 92, 96
La Guthrie, Edward, 229
Lake Indians. *See* Three Fires, alliance
    of
Lake Ontario, 337n78
Lake Traverse, 255, 333n35
Lake Winnipeg, 91
La Maigouis (Ottawa), 230–31, 235,
    329n161, 331n17
land: acquisition of, 134, 209, 246; as
    gift, 87; Indians' sovereignty over, 152,
    169, 250; loss of, by Six Nations,

of, 50; and Joseph Brant, 130, 132,
150, 155, 163; and Little Turtle, 55;
marriage of, 37, 254–55; and military
influence, 113–14; and Muskingum
compromise, 48; and Ohio River, 54,
282n121, 324n80; and Shawnees, 49;
speech by, 13, 64–65; as translator, 33;
and William Doyle, 113

McKee, Thomas, 88, 202, 291n93; and
Blue Jacket, 87; at council, 86; as
deputy superintendent at Fort St.
Joseph, 114; and gift-giving, 78, 85;
and Hector McLean, 74, 79; and
Indian Department, 60, 66, 82; and
provision distribution, 74, 200–201;
as replacement for Matthew Elliott,
68, 298n75

McLean, Hector: attitude of, toward
Indians, 70–71, 79, 82, 85, 88; as
commander at Fort Amherstburg,
104, 199–200; at council, 86; and
gift-giving, 73–74, 78, 215; and Indian
Department, 66, 80, 84, 113, 286n20;
and Matthew Elliott, 68–69

Meatoosikee (Ojibwa), 104

Mekoche Shawnee Indians, 218,
323nn70–71

Menominee Indians: and British, 91,
199, 236, 249, 258; clan system of, 232;
and Fort Mackinac, 256, 257; loyalty
of, to traders, 233; and Ojibwas, 118,
249; and Robert Dickson, 255; and
Shawnee Prophet, 233; sovereignty
of, 225; visit to Fort St. Joseph by,
93

Miami Indians, 22, 23, 36, 170, 332n24;
and Americans, 61, 77, 247, 276n20,
318n6; and annuities, 200; and
British, 197; and C. C. Trowbridge,
24; clan and kinship system of,
24–25; at councils, 112; defeat of, at

Fallen Timbers, 101; and Delawares,
26, 86; at the Glaize, 34; and land
cessions, 210; as part of Brownstown
confederacy, 18; as part of Maumee
confederacy, 53; religious beliefs of,
25; and Shawnees, 27; and succession
of chiefs, 24; and William Johnson, 3

Miami Rapids, 45–51. *See also* Foot of
the Rapids

Miamitown (Le Gris), 23

Michilimackinac, 94, 96, 193, 299n94,
316n122

Michilimackinac Company, 227

Midewiwin. *See* Ojibwa Grand
Medicine Society

Milwaukee, 92

Mingo Indians, 14, 18, 280n81

Mishinemackinawgo Indians, 94

missions, 165, 207

Mississauga Indians, 73; as a branch of
Chippewas, 306n80; council fire of,
151; at Grand River, 194; as hunters
and gatherers, 149; and Iroquois, 144;
and loss of leader, 149; neutrality of,
191; and Six Nations, 148–49, 151

Mississinewa River, 208

Mississippi River, 60, 201, 206

Mohawk Indians: as first Nation, 16;
loyalty of, 123; at Oquaga, 301n4;
as part of Iroquois League, 3; as
part of Seven Nations, 300n2; at
Tyendinaga, 125

Moira, Earl of, 163, 176

Monin, David, 299n97

Montour Indians, 125

Moravian Indians, 194, 317n126

Moravians, 165, 315n111, 322n50

More, Hannah, 309n5

Morris, Thomas, 156

Mountain, Jacob, 146–47

Brownstown confederacy, 18; as part of Maumee confederacy, 53; political organization of, 117; and Prophetstown, 236; and revitalization movement, 231; and Robert Dickson, 255; and Shawnee Prophet, 234; sovereignty of, 225; and Tecumseh, 222; and trade, 98; and traders, 104, 235; and whites, 269; and William Johnson, 3; and Wyandots, 87

Okoghsenniyonte, Benjamin, 177

Oneida Indians, 3, 17, 146, 301n4

Onondaga, 17, 147

Onondaga Indians, 3, 123, 300n2

Oquaga, 301n4

Ottawa Indians, 22, 47, 95, 204, 293n9, 293n16; and Americans, 105, 197, 276n20; and Amherstburg, 81, 202; and annuities, 325n107; and Arbre Croche, 116; atrocities committed by, 54; and British, 61, 91, 93, 97, 106, 112, 115, 199, 236–37, 249, 258; clan system of, 232; and defeat at Fallen Timbers, 101; defection of, 54; and epidemic, 235; and gift-giving, 76, 102; and Indian agents, 239; influence of military on, 109; infrastructure of, 232; and John Norton, 170; and John Tanner, 228; and Joseph Brant, 156–57, 174; and La Maigouis, 230; at Lower Sandusky council, 14; loyalty of, 98, 121, *227*; and lunar eclipse, 32; and Mackinac, 94; and nativists, 240; and Ojibwas, 280n74; as part of Brownstown confederacy, 18; as part of Maumee confederacy, 53; political organization of, 117; and Prophetstown, 236; and revitalization movement, 231; and Robert Dickson, 255; and Shawnee

Prophet, 234–35; and Sioux-Ojibwa wars, 120; sovereignty of, 225; and Tecumseh, 222; and William Johnson, 3; and Wyandots, 87

Owen, John, 163, 165, 170, 172, 176

Pacanne (Miami), 23, 77

Painted Pole (Shawnee), 40–45, 330n12, 331n13

Parkman, Francis, 273n6

Peace of Amiens, 204

Peace of Paris. *See* Treaty of Paris (1783)

Penetanguishene, 270

Percy, Hugh. *See* Northumberland, Duke of

Peyster, Arent de, 299n96

Phelps, Davenport, 146

Pigeon Roost Massacre, 252

Pike, Zebulon Montgomery, 228, 249–50, 299n94, 331n17

Pinckney's Treaty. *See* Treaty of San Lorenzo

Pitt, William, 73

Pond, Peter, 299n96

Pontiac's Conspiracy, 4, 273n6

Pontiac's War, 74, 75, 79, 96

portages, 92, 292n1

Portland, Duke of, 73, 136, 146; and Joseph Brant, 145, 148, 150, 158; and land, 138–39, 152, 155; and Peter Russell, 140–41, 143–44; and William Claus, 171

Potawatomi Indians, 47, 94, 95, 204, 205, 280n74, 293n16; and Americans, 197, 200, 276n20, 318n6; and Amherstburg, 202–3; and British, 61; and Brownstown council, 201; and gift-giving, 76; and John Norton, 170; and Joseph Brant, 156–57, 174; and land cessions, 210; at Lower

as Thunderbird, 233; and Tomah,
256; as usurper, 218
Thames River, 214, 334n47, 337n82
Three Fires, alliance of, 280n74
Thunderbirds, 233
Thunder clan, 232
timber, excessive cutting of, 87
Tippecanoe, 255
Tippecanoe River, 210, 214, 329n163
Tomah (Menominee), 256–57
traders, 39, 97, 120
trading houses, 229
Trafalgar, 216
Treaty of Detroit, 224
Treaty of Fort Stanwix, 280n81
Treaty of Fort Wayne, 209–10, 212,
222
Treaty of Ghent, 258, 261–62, *263*,
267–69
Treaty of Greenville, 5, 11, 61, 75, 265,
336n63; acculturation after, 206,
218; and annuities, 325n107; and
Anthony Wayne, 58; cessions made
at, 220; effects of, 92, 239, 246;
Indian view of, 104, 209; signing
of, by Blue Jacket, 87; signing of, by
pro-U.S. chiefs, 101; signing of, by
Roundhead, 317n1
Treaty of Hopewell, 166
Treaty of Paris (1763), 274n3
Treaty of Paris (1783), 11, 12, 52, 265,
273n1, 275n11
Treaty of San Lorenzo, 284n154
Trout. *See* La Maigouis (Ottawa)
Trowbridge, C. C., 24, 25, 32, 278n38
Turtle Creek, 217
Tuscarora Indians, 17, 123, 146, 301n4
Tutelo Indians, 125
Tutlee, John, *270*
Tyendinaga, 125

Unitas Fratrum (United Brethren). *See*
Moravians
United Empire Loyalists, 127
United States: European sympathy
for, 267; expansionist policy of, 5, 11,
39, 41; independence of, 1; Indian
policy of, 17, 166; and Joseph Brant,
144; military failure of, 268; peace
proposals of, 42, 44; as threat to
Natives, 26
Upper Canada, 12, 274n10; and
American expansion, 281n95;
creation of, 129; and Indians, 58, 74,
105, 181; Native reserves in, 6, 251;
and possibility of war, 185; protection
of, 39, 41, 94; Western District of,
59–60
"upper country," 12, 38, 274n1
U.S. Legion, 7, 56, 222, 244, 285n7

Van Buren, Martin, 334n47
Vergennes, Count de, 12
Vincennes, 222

Wabakenin (Mississauga), 149
Wabash, 208, 248
Wabasha (Dakota), 254, 262
Wabash River, 23, 60, 77, 201, 210
Walk in the Water (Wyandot), 223,
224, 243, 264, 325n101
wampum, 225, 237–38
Wapakoneta, 200, 207, 218, 224, 323n71
Warburton, Augustus, 333nn28–29
Warner, Jacob, *270*
War of 1812, 161, 243, *263*; Native
resistance during, 214; and northern
tribes, 250, 263; and southern Great
Lakes region, 244
Warren, William, 95, 235
Washington, George, 44

CPSIA information can be obtained at www.ICGtesting.com
Printed in the USA
BVOW07s0627020714

357927BV00002B/2/P